CREATIO EX NIHILO

CREATIO EX NIHILO

The Doctrine of 'Creation out of Nothing' in Early Christian Thought

Gerhard May

Translated by
A. S. Worrall

T&T CLARK
EDINBURGH

T&T CLARK LTD
59 GEORGE STREET
EDINBURGH EH2 2LQ
SCOTLAND

Copyright © T&T Clark Ltd, 1994

Authorised English translation of *Schöpfung aus dem Nichts*
Copyright © Walter de Gruyter & Co, Berlin 30

The publishers gratefully acknowledge the support of Inter Nationes,
Bonn, in the preparation of the English translation

All rights reserved. No part of this publication may be reproduced, stored in a retrieval system, or transmitted, in any form or by any means, electronic, mechanical, photocopying, recording or otherwise, without the prior permission of T&T Clark Ltd.

First published 1994

ISBN 0 567 09695 5

British Library Cataloguing-in-Publication Data
A catalogue record for this book is available from the British Library

Typeset by Trinity Typesetting, Edinburgh
Printed and bound in Great Britain by Bookcraft, Avon

Contents

Preface to English Edition	vii
Foreword	xi
Some English Translations of Foreign Books Cited in the Notes	xv

1. **The Problem of the Creation of the World in Hellenistic Judaism and Early Christianity before the Gnostic Crisis in the Second Century**   1
   - The starting-point   1
   - I. World-creation in Hellenistic Judaism   6
     - Philo   9
     - Factors tending to the doctrine of *creatio ex nihilo* in Judaism   21
     - Limits of Jewish statements about creation   22
   - II. World-creation in early Christianity   26
     - Beginnings of anti-heretical polemic   31
     - The state of the question in the first half of the second century   35

2. **The Question of the Origin of the World in Christian Gnosticism**   39
   - I. The gnostic approach to the problem   39
   - II. Marcion   53

3. **The Creation of the World in Basilides and the Valentinians**   62
   - I. Basilides   62
   - II. Valentinus   85
     - The myth of the Valentinian school   91

4. **Christian and Platonist Cosmology**   118
   - Christianity as the true philosophy   118
   - Aristides   118
   - Justin   120
   - The treatise 'On the Resurrection'   133
   - Athenagoras   137
   - Hermogenes   140

5.	**The Church Doctrine of *Creatio Ex Nihilo***	148
	Conflict on two fronts against gnosis and philosophy	148
I.	Tatian	148
	Academic debates at Rome	154
II.	Theophilus of Antioch	156
III.	Irenaeus	164

Recapitulation 179

Editions of Ancient Texts 181

Index of Biblical References 185

Index of Ancient Authors and Sources 187

Index of Modern Authors 191

Index of Subjects 196

Preface to English Edition

The German original of this book appeared in 1978 with the title *Schöpfung aus dem Nichts. Die Entstehung der Lehre von der creatio ex nihilo*. After more than thirteen years, during which research has been intensively pursued in most of the fields affected, the question arises whether the book should be extended or revised. As I see no reason to alter my position on the subject, I have after long hesitation also given up the idea of working the new material into the notes: in this way further expansion of the already comprehensive notes is avoided, and the reader retains a clear view of the grounds on which the book's conclusions are based. The English and German editions are thus substantially the same. In order not to pass over the new discussion in complete silence, I detail below a series of publications which have appeared since the printing of the book. In addition to this I have limited myself to correcting a small number of errors and to checking some of the source quotations. The translator of the book, Dr A. S. Worrall, has taken the trouble to give the English translations of the secondary literature in foreign languages.

G. C. Stead draws attention in his review of my book[1] and in a later article[2] to the philosophical precursors and parallels to the Christian doctrine of *creatio ex nihilo* and asks whether a philosophical influence on the development of the Christian theory is to be discerned. He advances the idea that as early as the first century BC a doctrine of *creatio ex nihilo* arose from the linking of the idea held by neo-pythagorean thinkers that God is the cause of everything, including matter, with a literal interpretation of the creation myth of Plato's *Timaeus*; and further that this was accepted 'as a minority view in Greek philosophical circles' and could have influenced the peculiar creation doctrine of the gnostic Basilides. Scanty as the tradition is,

---

[1] JThS n.s. 30 (1979), pp. 547f.
[2] 'Die Aufnahme des philosophischen Gottesbegriffes in der frühchristlichen Theologie: W. Pannenbergs These neu bedacht', *Theologische Rundschau* 51 (1986, pp. 349–371), pp. 358–360.

viii   *Creatio Ex Nihilo*

the approaches to an elimination of the contradiction between God and matter in the Platonism of the early Empire are not to be ignored, and Basilides was a man who from his level of education can be credited with familiarity with the contemporary interpretations of the *Timaeus*. Up to this point I agree with Stead. But Basilides was an outsider, and those theologians who represent the orthodox line of clarification leading to the doctrine of *creatio ex nihilo* do not reveal in their statements any acquaintance with philosophical theories about the creation of the world out of nothing. They conceive the formation of the world from eternal matter according to the cosmological model of the Platonists, whether adopting it like Justin Martyr or contesting it like Theophilus of Antioch and Irenaeus. The driving motive which underlies the Christian doctrine of *creatio ex nihilo* is the attempt to do justice to the absolute sovereignty and unlimited freedom of the biblical God acting in history. This interest is lacking in the philosophical discussion of principles of being and world-formation. One may assume a certain convergence between the tendencies in philosophy to understand God as the sole cause of reality and the Christian doctrine of creation by God out of nothing. Perhaps one may also speak of a common intellectual climate. I nevertheless consider an influence from the pythagorean-neoplatonic quarter, through Basilides as intermediary, upon the orthodox Christian theology of creation in the second half of the second century to be well-nigh impossible. Christian theology has developed its doctrine of *creatio ex nihilo* from its own presuppositions, albeit, as I have shown in detail, within the ambit of the philosophical teaching of world-formation. Incidentally, a close scrutiny of philosophical teachings on the origin of the world in the three centuries before Plotinus constitutes in my view a much needed task for research.

The present state of research on the philosophy of the era of the principate is documented in four volumes (II 36, 1–4) of the work *Aufstieg und Niedergang der antiken Welt* (1987–1990). The monumental work of H. Dörrie, which has appeared posthumously, opens up the tradition of Platonism.[3] On Middle Platonism in particular I would refer to the general depiction by J. Dillon.[4] The debate on whether Philo of Alexandria already

---

[3] *Der Platonismus in der Antike*, begun by H. Dörrie, continued by M. Baltes with F. Mann, I (Stuttgart and Bad Canstatt 1987), II (1990). The majority of Dörrie's individual studies on Platonism are now available in the collection *Platonica Minora* (Munich, 1976).

[4] *The Middle Platonists* (London, 1977). The view put forward for some time by M. Giusta and J. Whittaker, that the 'Diadaskalikos', generally attributed to Albinus, is the work of Alcinous, who is mentioned in the manuscripts, is gradually gaining acceptance; the picture of Middle Platonism is thus becoming more complicated. Cf. Whittaker, 'Platonic

taught creation out of nothing seems to continue unabated. Affirmative responses to this question are given categorically by G. Reale[5] and cautiously by R. Sorabji.[6] D. T. Runia, on the other hand, doubts that Philo developed a rigorous theory of *creatio ex nihilo*.[7] His view roughly coincides with mine. F. Siegert makes a similar judgment in his commentary on the Philo fragment *De Deo*, which has come down to us through Armenian channels.[8] The lack of clarity in Philo's position appears to be reflected in the differences of opinion among researchers.

For the present state of research on Marcion I refer to my essay 'Marcion in Contemporary Views: Results and Open Questions', *The Second Century* 6 (1987/88), pp. 129–152, and to H. J. W. Drijvers, 'Marcionism in Syria: Principles, Problems, Polemics', *op. cit.*, pp. 153–172. E. Mühlenberg's article 'Basilides' in *Theologische Realenzyklopädie* 5 (1980), 296–301 provides not only a summary of previous research but also an original interpretation. Important contributions on Valentinianism are brought together in the collection *The Rediscovery of Gnosticism I. The School of Valentinus*, ed. B. Layton (Leiden, 1980). That by G. C. Stead, 'In Search of Valentinus' (pp. 75–102), is outstanding; it is an attempt at a systematic interpretation of the few authentic Valentinus fragments on the basis of Platonic Ideas.

A noteworthy contribution to the discussion on Justin's attitude to philosophy has been made by C. J. de Vogel, 'Problems concerning Justin Martyr: Did Justin find a Certain Continuity between Greek Philosophy and Christian Faith?', *Mnemosyne* 31 (1978), pp. 360–388. Justin's and Irenaeus's understanding of heresy and the structures of their anti-heretical polemic are examined by A. Le Boulluec in the first volume of his comprehensive work *La notion d'hérésie dans la littérature grecque (IIe–IIIe siècles)* (Paris, 1985). In the commentary on Genesis by Didymus of Alexandria (from the Tura papyrus) P. Nautin sees correspondences with Tertullian's writing *Adversus Hermogenem*. He suspects in the passages

Philosophy in the Early Centuries of the Empire', ANRW II 36, 1 (1987) 81–123. Meanwhile the long awaited critical edition of the *Diadaskalikos* by Whittaker has appeared in a French translation by P. Louis, *Enseignement des doctrines de Platon* (Paris, 1990).

[5] 'Filone di Alessandria e la prima elaborazione filosofica della dottrina della creazione', in *Paradoxos politeia. Studi patristici in onore di Giuseppe Lazzati* (Milan, 1979), pp. 247–287.

[6] *Time, Creation and the Continuum: Theories in Antiquity and the Early Middle Ages* (London, 1983), pp. 203–209.

[7] 'Philo of Alexandria and the Timaeus of Plato' (Thesis, Amsterdam, 1983), I 376–381.

[8] Philo of Alexandria, *Über die Gottesbezeichnung 'wohltätig verzehrendes Feuer' (De Deo)* (Tübingen, 1988), pp. 57–59, 112f., 115, 117.

concerned, by way of Origen's lost commentary on Genesis, an echo of the likewise lost writing of Theophilus of Antioch against Hermogenes.[9] Unfortunately we do not learn anything new from Didymus about the teaching of Hermogenes. Finally mention must be made of A. Orbe's penetrating analysis of the statements of Irenaeus on the creation of matter, 'San Ireneo y la creación de la materia', *Gregorianum* 59 (1978), pp. 71–127.

I should like to thank the publishers for the care devoted to this book. I am particularly grateful to Dr A. S. Worrall for undertaking the laborious task of translation.

Gerhard May
Mainz

Publishers' Note

Dr Worrall died in November 1991 and was unable to finalise the work. Final checks were made by Dr John Dunstan, for the translation from the German, and by Professor Frances Young, Dr Worrall's daughter, for the scholarly content.

---

[9] Thus Nautin in the introduction to the edition by himself and L. Doutreleau, *Didyme l'Aveugle, Sur la Genèse* I (SC 233, Paris, 1976), pp. 24–26.

Foreword

The doctrine of *creatio ex nihilo* proclaims in the most pointed manner the absolutely unconditioned nature of the creation and specifies God's omnipotence as its sole ground. Together with the corresponding idea of the unconditioned freedom and contingence of God's creative work, it possesses constructive meaning for the Christian understanding of creation. When did the doctrine of *creatio ex nihilo* arise? To be sure, it corresponds factually with the Old Testament proclamation about creation, but as a theory it is not yet present in the Old Testament. According to a widespread view, its formulation is the achievement of hellenistic-Jewish theology, and 2 Maccabees 7:28 is adduced as the oldest classical evidence for this. This would mean that primitive Christianity had found the doctrine ready-made in the Jewish tradition. One would be able to presuppose it for the New Testament, and the emergence among second-century Christian theologians of the Platonising doctrine of the eternity of matter and its mere shaping into the cosmos would be a more or less conscious reinterpretation of the authentic Christian doctrine of creation. The question of the origin of the doctrine of *creatio ex nihilo* would simply not be posed by historians of early Christian theology.

The view thus summarised of the origin of the doctrine of *creatio ex nihilo* can today no longer be sustained. Earlier research had already cast doubt on the idea that hellenistic-Jewish theology had taught *creatio ex nihilo* in the strict sense, and more recent work, especially the contributions of H.-F. Weiss and G. Schmuttermayr, has, it seems to me, finally demonstrated that this was not the case.[1] It is true that hellenistic Jews could talk of a creation by God 'out of nothing', but the formula was demonstrably not meant in an ontological sense and in no way excluded the acceptance of an eternal material for the world. Thus the proposition of the creation of the world

---

[1] H. F. Weiss, *Untersuchungen zur Kosmologie des hellenistischen und palästinischen Judentums* (1966); G. Schmuttermayr, '"Schöpfung aus dem Nichts" in 2 Macc. 7:28?', BZ N. F. 17 (1973), pp. 203–228.

'out of nothing' does not have from the beginning the meaning that we quite naturally associate with it. If we look into the early Christian sources, it becomes apparent that the thesis of *creatio ex nihilo* in its full and proper sense, as an ontological statement, only appeared when it was intended, in opposition to the idea of world-formation from unoriginate matter, to give expression to the omnipotence, freedom and uniqueness of God. The concept of *creatio ex nihilo* presupposes a conceivable alternative and in the intellectual situation of early Christianity this means that it is formulated as an antithesis to the Greek model of world-formation. The opposite of the philosophical cosmology must of course be seen dialectically: the doctrine of *creatio ex nihilo* indeed breaks through principles of philosophical metaphysics, but it can only be articulated within the latter's frame of reference and by using its terms.

These facts determine the starting-point and direction of our enquiry: the origin of the doctrine of *creatio ex nihilo* must be understood and explained as part of the controversy of early Christianity with philosophy. As the proposition of creation 'out of nothing' is, in itself, ambiguous, enquiry must be made into the understanding of creation of which it forms part. Only from the general intellectual position of an author or a source can we find out whether he presents the doctrine of *creatio ex nihilo* in unambiguous form. It is quite possible that in a text there is formal talk of *creatio ex nihilo*, without that being, in its strict sense, the underlying idea; it is equally possible that the idea of *creatio ex nihilo* is in fact unambiguously expressed, but without use of the corresponding formula. Of course, it must always be kept in mind that a line runs from the Old Testament formulations of the idea of creation to the developed doctrine of *creatio ex nihilo*. So far the older unsophisticated statements of the Old Testament-Jewish and the Christian tradition express more than is explicitly stated, and most importantly the formula 'out of nothing' develops a dynamic (even when used in a quite imprecise way) which presses on towards the *creatio ex nihilo* in the strict and particular sense. Yet the historical interpretation of the sources must distinguish between what they contain implicitly and what they directly say and intend. It is only when one tries to put oneself back into problems as posed by the sources, paying attention to their level of reflection, the relegation of old and the emergence of new problems, that one can grasp and follow through the historical process in which the doctrine of *creatio ex nihilo* originated.

The intellectual pre-conditions for the formulation of the doctrine of *creatio ex nihilo* were achieved by Christian theology in the second century. It is a question in itself, and one which will still concern us, why Philo of Alexandria, possessing as he did the necessary philosophical education, had not already at an earlier date characterised the biblical ideas of creation as *creatio ex nihilo*. The Christian gnostics bring into play the question about the origin of the cosmos. In their expositions of cosmogony they can just as readily revert to the platonist model of world-formation as specifically develop the idea of *creatio ex nihilo*. At the same time 'orthodox' theology, as it is retrospectively judged to be, begins with increasing intensity to debate with the philosophical tradition. In doing so the leading theologians in that field at first understand creation in Platonist fashion as world-formation. Only in the second half of the second century does the theology of the Church develop, in opposition to philosophical cosmology and to Platonising gnosis, the doctrine of *creatio ex nihilo* in the strict sense, which in the Catholic Church very quickly attains an almost unquestioned validity. Of course, the thesis that the doctrine of *creatio ex nihilo* arose from the debates of the second century is not new.[2] But, so far as I can see, the history of its origin has never yet been presented in all its stages, least of all in its relationship with gnostic theology. Such a reconstruction of the process by which the doctrine of *creatio ex nihilo* came to be is the purpose of this book. For me this is not just a matter of solving a special problem in the history of theology, I wanted at the same time to make a contribution to the more general question how, in the decisive early times, Christian doctrine came into being.

The way the problem is stated determines the construction of the book and the choice of material: in the first chapter it is not intended to give an anywhere near complete summary of the understanding of creation in hellenistic Judaism and primitive Christianity. It will be shown in passing that until the turn of the first and second centuries and in part later than that there was no reflection on the nature of the creation process, and the problems which dominated the discussion in the second century had not yet arisen. Only against this background do the newer questions asked in the second century emerge with full clarity. In describing the most important gnostic systems I have gone rather further (chapters 2 and 3). It was my objective not only to show how at this point the question of the origin of the cosmos took on a pressing topicality and what answers were found to it, but also to make visible the connection between the cosmology of the gnostics in the narrower sense and their general understanding of the world. In describing the development from Justin to Irenaeus (chapters 4 and 5) I have again confined myself more severely to the problem of creation,

---

[2] See H. Schwabl, art. 'Weltschöpfung' in PW suppl. IX (1962), 1573ff.; Weiss, pp. 146ff.

otherwise I should have had to write a history of theology in the second century. I have purposely gone no further than Irenaeus. With him the doctrine of *creatio ex nihilo* took a settled form and a specific conclusion was reached. The thinking of Tertullian and Hippolytus offers no decisive new aspects to our theme, while an adequate treatment of the creation doctrine of the Alexandrians, Clement and Origen, would have gone beyond the scope of this work.

In the matter of abbreviations, I have not followed a unified system. For the better-known periodicals and reference works I use the current abbreviations; they can be elucidated with the help of S. Schwertner, *International Index of Abbreviations used in Theology and Kindred Subjects* (1974). I have shortened the titles of less well-known periodicals and series so that they can be identified without a key.

The stimulus to concern myself with early Christian creation doctrine came to me from H. Chadwick under whom I studied in Oxford in 1965. In the years 1966 to 1969, during my time as an Assistant with H. von Campenhausen in Heidelberg, the present work took its first form. To both these teachers my thanks are due. A grant from the Deutsche Forschungsgemeinschaft made possible the completion of the work, which was accepted as a 'Habilitationsschrift' by the Protestant Faculty of Theology in the University of Munich in Autumn 1971. My examiners were G. Kretschmar, J. Bauer, P. Stockmeier (all of Munich), and the late W. C. van Unnik (Utrecht). I am grateful to them all for their advice and critical queries. The work was then left for some time before I got round to revising it for the press. I kept in touch with new literature on the subject until the spring of 1977.

It only remains to thank all the colleagues and friends who either read the first draft of this work or discussed my theses orally. I also thank the audience at the lectures I gave in the winter semester of 1975–76 on 'The origin of the Christian doctrine of creation'. I also thank the publishers of 'Arbeiten zur Kirchengeschichte' for accepting the book for inclusion in that series. In particular, C. Andresen helped me by encouraging me to bring the revision of the book to completion. To the Deutsche Forschungsgemeinschaft I owe thanks for double support. They not only made available a two-year research grant but also made it possible for the book to appear through a publication grant. Finally I thank Miss Lilly Kühnert for the preparation of the typescript and the publishers for their careful typesetting and good collaboration.

Munich, March 1978   Gerhard May

Some English Translations of Foreign Books Cited in the Notes

Where Professor May gives a page reference to a foreign book, the book is cited in the notes by its foreign title and the reference reproduced, so that the original can be consulted. If the letters ET follow, an English translation of the work will be found in this list. Where it has been possible to check the page reference in the English translation, this will be found in the note, following the letters ET. The bibliographical details will be found once in this list, and not repeatedly in the notes.

Bauer	*Rechtgläubigkeit und Ketzerei im altesten Christentum; Orthodoxy and Heresy in Earliest Christianity* (London: SCM, 1972).
Baur	*Das Christentum und die christliche Kirche der drei ersten Jahrhunderte; The Church History of the First Three Centuries* (London: Williams and Norgate, 1878).
Bultmann	*Das Evangelium des Johannes; The Gospel of John. A Commentary* (Oxford: Blackwell, 1971).
Bultmann	*Das Christentum im Rahmen der antiken Religionen; Primitive Christianity in its Contemporary Setting* (London: Thames and Hudson, 1956).
Campenhausen	*Die Entstehung der christlichen Bibel; The Origin of the Christian Bible* (London: Black, 1972).
Campenhausen	*Kirchliches Amt und geistliche Vollmacht; Ecclesiastical Authority and Spiritual Power* (London: Black, 1969).
Conzelmann	*I Korinther; I Corinthians* (Philadelphia: Fortress Press, 1975).
Conzelmann	*Apostelgeschichte; Acts* (Philadelphia: Fortress Press, 1987).
Daniélou	*Message évangélique et culture hellénistique; Gospel Message and Hellenistic Culture* (London: Darton, Longman and Todd, 1972; and Philadelphia: Westminster Press, 1973).

Daniélou	*Théologie de Judéo-Christianisme; The Theology of Jewish Christianity* (London: Darton, Longman and Todd, 1964).
Duhem	*Le système du monde; Medieval Cosmology* (Chicago: University of Chicago Press, 1985).
Festugière	*L'idéal religieux des grecs et l'Evangile; Personal Religion among the Greeks* (Berkeley, CA: University of California Press, 1954).
Frank	*Philosophische Erkenntnis und religiöse Wahrheit; Philosophical Understanding and Religious Truth* (Oxford and New York: Oxford University Press, 1945).
Goppelt	*Christentum und Judentum im ersten und zweiten Jahrhundert;* first half in *Jesus, Paul and Judaism* (London: Nelson, 1964).
Harnack	*Lehrbuch der Dogmengeschichte; History of Dogma* (London: Williams and Norgate, 1894–99).
Harnack	*Mission und Ausbreitungde Christentums; The Mission and Expansion of Christianity in the First Three Centuries* (London: Williams and Norgate; and New York: G. P. Putnam, ²1908).
Lietzmann	*Geschichte der alten Kirche; A History of the Early Church* (London: Lutterworth, 1981).
Lohse	*Die Briefe an die Kolosser und an Philemon; Colossians and Philemon* (Philadelphia: Fortress Press, 1971).
Rordorf	*Der Sonntag; Sunday. The History of the Day of Rest and Worship in the Earliest Centuries of the Christian Church* (London: SCM, 1968).
Scheffczyk	*Schöpfung und Vorsehung; Creation and Providence* (London and New York: Herder, 1970).
Schelkle	*Theologie des Neuen Testaments; Theology of the New Testament* (Collegeville, MN: Liturgical Press, 1980).

Special note on
Jonas   *Gnosis und spätantiker Geist*

After moving to America Professor Jonas himself wrote a book in English, entitled *The Gnostic Religion* (Boston, MA: Beacon Press, 1958), which he describes in his preface as 'retaining the point of view of the larger work and restating many of its arguments'. No ET of the German work exists and it is not possible to refer readers to passages in the new work that represent the quotations listed in the notes.

1

The Problem of the Creation of the World in Hellenistic Judaism and Early Christianity before the Gnostic Crisis in the Second Century

The starting-point
Belief in creation belongs to Christianity's inheritance from Judaism. The proposition that God created the world and everything in it was for early Christian thinking a presupposition which possessed axiomatic validity and was not called in question before the end of the first century. Only after the turn of the century did creation begin, in gnostic circles, to be a theological problem.

The first attempts to formulate in philosophical concepts the belief in One God who had created heaven and earth were undertaken in the context of the hellenistic-Christian mission preaching.[1] People were, indeed, by no means equally aware of the difficulties for Greek thought which were contained in the Old Testament views of God and creation. The appropriation by Christian theology of the philosophical tradition and its way of looking at problems took place at first only slowly. Not before the middle of the second century was the debate with philosophy recognised as the central task of Christian thinking and tackled as such. Now Christians began to take seriously the lofty claim to be systematically knowing and teaching the one universal God, of whom the classical philosophers of the

---

[1] For primitive Christian missionary preaching and its themes cf. A. von Harnack, *Die Mission und Ausbreitung des Christentums in den ersten drei Jahrhunderten* I (⁴1924), pp. 114ff. (ET pp. 86ff.); G. Bornkamm, 'Glaube und Vernunft bei Paulus', in *Studien zu Antike und Urchristentum* (Collected Essays II, ³1970) pp. 119–137, 122–124; and pp. 28ff. below.

past had known scarcely anything. This happened not only because of the needs of outwardly directed apologetics. Christians with a philosophical education wanted to understand and thoroughly penetrate the message to which they were committed. For them Christianity was the true philosophy. How to reconcile the idea of the God who creates freely and unconditionally with the concepts of Greek metaphysics now becomes a central theme of Christian theology. This group of questions forms, alongside the gnostic problem, the second focal point of the controversy over ideas of creation which took place in the second century.[2] It was within the scope of the questions thus raised that the doctrine of *creatio ex nihilo* was developed.

In the philosophy of the first and second centuries the Stoa occupied the dominating position and determined, far beyond the formal philosophising of the schools, the general intellectual climate, but alongside it Platonism was now gaining in importance. Since the first century BC it had undergone a profound renewal, and when the Stoa in the first half of the third century was with surprising speed extinguished as an independent school, Platonism as the only still living and productive philosophical movement, became without question the philosophy of late antiquity.[3] As intellectual rivals of early Christianity only the Stoa and Platonism played a decisive role. The epicurean teaching was rejected by the Christians, using the same arguments as their philosophical critics, as godless,[4] and the peripatetic philosophising was too much limited to specialist learned circles to have much

---

[2] Along with the theological-metaphysical problems of the idea of creation, the second central theme of the controversy between Christian thought and the Greek cosmology is the comparison between the biblical and Greek conceptions of the world. This was of particular concern to the scholarly exegesis of Genesis; cf. on the first direction taken F. E. Robbins, *The Hexaemeral Literature* (Chicago, 1912). The exposition of the cosmology of the Church Fathers to be found in P. Duhem, *Le système du monde, Histoire des doctrines cosmologiques de Platon à Copernic* II (Paris, 1914), pp. 393–501 (ET is insufficient); cf. also the statement by Ilona Opelt, art. 'Erde', RAC V (1962) 1113–1179, 1167ff., which however overemphasises the hostility to scholarship in the theology of the early Church. On the attempt by Cosmas Indicopleustes to develop a coherent biblical cosmology, cf. Wanda Wolska, *La topographie chrétienne de Cosmas Indicopleustes. Théologie et science au VIe siècle* (Paris, 1962). A general sketch of the history of early church creation theology is given by L. Scheffczyk, 'Schöpfung und Vorsehung' (*Handbuch der Dogmengeschichte*, ed. M. Schmaus and A. Grillmeier, IIa, 1963), pp. 1ff., a general review of the problem by A. Hamman, 'L'enseignement sur la création dans l'Antiquité chrétienne' in *Rev. Sc. Rel.* 42 (1968), pp. 1–23, 97–122. The by and large unsuperseded work of E. W. Möller, *Geschichte des Kosmologie in der Griechischen Kirche bis auf Origenes* (1860) and R. A. Norris, *God and World in Early Christian Theology* (London, 1966), are limited to the first three centuries.

[3] Cf. M. Pohlenz, *Die Stoa* ([4]1970), pp. 277ff.

[4] Cf. W. Schmid, art. 'Epicurus', RAC V (1962) 681–819, 774ff.

The Problem of the Creation of the World in Hellenistic Judaism 3

effect on Christians of the first century, save for a very small group. The doctrine of the eternity of the world and the view attributed to Aristotle, that the effect of Providence only reached down to the sphere of the moon and not into the sublunary world, were strongly opposed by Christian theology, nor did the world-affirming peripatetic ethics have any attraction for the Christendom of later times.[5] The Stoa had an effect on Christianity especially through its ethics, but also its teleological proof of God and its anthropocentric teaching about providence were quickly taken up by Christian creation theology, producing an effect which lasted until the Enlightenment.[6] And so the emphatic declarations of the Stoa about God as the creator and disposer of the world entered Christian theological language, the Stoic statements being thereby quite naturally reshaped in a theistic sense.[7] At the same time, however, the Christians severely criticised Stoic pantheism and materialism and their teaching of the periodical renewal of the world.[8]

Most important, however, for the completion of the Christian doctrine of creation was the controversy with Platonism. Middle Platonism, whose period runs from the second half of the first century BC until the first half of the third century AD, had realised its tendency towards theology which gave it an affinity with Christian thinking.[9] The central metaphysical theme

---

[5] Cf. J. H. Waszink and W. Heffening, art. 'Aristoteles' RAC I (1950), 657–667.

[6] On this see Pohlenz, *Die Stoa* I, pp. 400ff.; M. Spanneut, *Le Stoicisme des pères de l'Eglise de Clément de Rome à Clément d'Alexandrie* (Paris, 1957, 2nd ed. no date). Origen with great skill deployed the Stoic doctrine of providence against the Platonist theory of Celsus: H. Chadwick, 'Origen, Celsus and the Stoa' in JThS 48 (1947), pp. 34–49.

[7] Cf. H. Hommel, *Schöpfer und Erhalter. Studien zum Problem Christentum und Antike* (1956). Ilona Opelt, *Jahrbuch Ant. und Christ.* 4 (1961), pp. 163f., reproaches Hommel for having misunderstood theistically the immanent cosmos-god of the Stoics; but the corresponding modification of Stoic theological statements was easily possible to hellenistic-Jewish and Christian thought; cf. Pohlenz, 'Paulus und die Stoa', ZNW 42 (1949), pp. 69–104 (89f.). For the connection between the themes of creation, sustaining and salvation in hellenistic-Jewish and early Christian literature see W. Nauck, 'Die Tradition und Komposition der Areopagrede', ZThK 53 (1956), pp. 11–52, pp. 24ff.

[8] Evidence in Pohlenz, *Die Stoa* I, p. 409; II (⁴1972), p. 198, Spanneut, pp. 88–94.

[9] A good general description of Middle Platonism is still to be found in K. Praechter, 'Die Philosophie des Altertums' in F. Uberwegs *Grundriss der Geschichte der Philosophie* I (¹²1926), pp. 524–536; cf. further C. Andresen, *Logos und Nomos. Die Polemik des Kelsos wider das Christentum* (1955), pp. 239ff.; P. Merlan in A. H. Armstrong, *The Cambridge History of Later Greek and Early Mediaeval Philosophy* (Cambridge, 1967), pp. 53–83; and the researches of D. Dörrie, especially 'Die Frage nach dem Transzendenten im Mittelplatonismus' in *Entretiens sur l'antiquité classique* V: *Les sources de Plotin* (Vandoeuvres-Geneva 1960), pp. 191–223. Somewhat different ways of interpretation are followed by H. J. Kraemer, *Der Ursprung der Geistesmetaphysik* (Amsterdam, ²1967), pp. 92ff.

is no longer, as it was for the historical Plato, the doctrine of the Ideas, but God.[10] The Demiurge of the *Timaeus*, the basic Platonic dialogue for Middle Platonism, is equated with the supreme God, who is thought of as Nous and the sum of the Ideas.[11] And the cosmogony of the *Timaeus* is systematised into the characteristic 'Three principles' doctrine: the three first ontological principles, thought to be equal in rank, God, Ideas and Matter, constitute the world.[12] The eternity of matter, the stuff from which the world is made, is generally accepted, but on the other hand the question is debated whether the ordered cosmos had an origin in time. Cicero and Philo of Alexandria testify that in their day the *Timaeus* was understood literally and that it was accepted that the world had been created at a specific point in time. Plutarch likewise held this view, and still in the second century, when the doctrine of the eternity of the world had become practically general among the Platonists, Atticus came forward with the creation of the world in time.[13] These views taken from the *Timaeus* represented for Christian theology of the second and third centuries the cosmology of Plato and it was partly to express opposition to them that the doctrine of *creatio ex nihilo* was developed.

But Middle Platonist thinking is looking for a single, universal Ground of Being and therefore presses on towards the suppression of the three first principles scheme. On the one hand the Ideas are understood as the thoughts of God and relegated to the divine Nous,[14] on the other hand various attempts are made to set up the highest God above the Nous-God.[15] Numenius clearly distinguishes between the first, the highest God and the Demiurge, the actual creator of the world.[16]

---

[10] Cf. Dörrie, 'Die Frage nach dem Transzendenten', pp. 202f. For Plutarch, de E. ap Delph. 19, 20 (392Eff.) the ὄντως ὄν is God – for Plato it was the Ideas: Phaedr. 247E; polit. X 597D; Tim. 27D=28A; cf. W. Theiler, *Die Vorbereitung des Neuplatonismus* (²1964), pp. 12–17.
[11] The theology of Middle Platonism is tersely summarised in Albinus, did. 10.
[12] Cf. Dörrie, 'Die Frage nach dem Transzendenten', pp. 205ff.
[13] Cf. Dörrie, 'Le renouveau du platonisme à l'époque de Cicéron', in *Revue de Théologie et de Philosophie* 24 (1974), pp. 13–29, pp. 20f; M. Baltes, *Die Weltentstehung des platonischem Timaeos nach den antiken Interpreten* I (Leiden, 1976), pp. 28ff.
[14] Cf. A. H. Armstrong, 'The background of the Doctrine "that the Intelligibles are not Outside the Intellect"', in *Les sources de Plotin*, pp. 391–425.
[15] Thus in Albinus, did. 10 (pp. 164, 6ff. Hermann); in addition Dörrie, 'Zum Ursprung der neuplatonischen Hypostasenlehre', *Hermes* 82 (1954), pp. 331–342, pp. 339f; also Kraemar, *Ursprung*, pp. 381f. For the same problem in Celsus see Dörrie, 'Die platonische Theologie des Kelsos in ihrer Auseinandersetzung mit der christlichen Theologie', NAG 1967/2, pp. 43–55.
[16] Cf. Theiler, art. 'Demiurgos', RAC III (1957), 694–711, 701f; M. Baltes, 'Numenios von Apamea und der platonische Timaeos', *Vig. Chr.* 29 (1975) pp. 241–270, pp. 257ff.

The Problem of the Creation of the World in Hellenistic Judaism 5

The search for an ultimate principle beyond the Nous is finally accomplished through the teaching of Plotinus about the One. It excludes setting alongside each other a plurality of equal principles. The One is the original ground of all Being, and thereby Plotinus explains that not only the hypostases of Nous and soul, but also matter, have come into being. As the last emanation of the One, it forms the transition into non-being and can only be thought of as pure privation.[17] By deriving matter from the One and surrendering its character as a principle, Plotinus breaks through a philosophical dogma and achieves at this point a consensus with Christian thinking.[18] Above all, Porphyry then rebutted the conjecture that matter must necessarily have been provided for the Demiurge with arguments that came very near the Christian train of thought.[19] Nevertheless the Neo-Platonist cosmology is distinguished fundamentally in more than one aspect from Christian doctrine: matter does not originate by an act of creation in time but exists, like the whole cosmos, eternally; so its 'having become' means only an ontological relationship, an eternal causality.[20] But above all it is the thought, decisive for Christianity, of the freedom and contingency of the divine creation which is unacceptable to New Platonism. Being necessarily proceeds from the One.[21] Only after the fifth century does there come about, especially in Alexandria, a rapprochement of Neo-Platonism and Christianity, which leads to attempts to bind together philosophical metaphysics and the Christian doctrine of creation.[22]

---

[17] Cf. Plotinus, Enn. IV, 8.6; I, 8.7ff; IV, 3.9.12ff; II, 4.13ff.

[18] This convergence is strongly emphasised by Krämer, *Ursprung*, p. 336, n. 531. He rightly sees the specific feature of Christian creation doctrine which distinguishes it from Neo-platonist metaphysics in the single, once for all, creative act 'which as the will and free choice of God among endless possibilities (Augustine) is the consequence of conceiving God *personally*'.

[19] See the evidence in Theiler, 'Porphyrios und Augustin', in *Forschungen zum Neuplatonismus* (1966), pp. 160–251, pp. 176–180; R. Beutler, art. 'Porphyrios', PW 22/1 (1953), pp. 275–313, 303f; see pp. 124f. below.

[20] Cf. W. Beierwaltes, *Proklos. Grundzüge seiner Metaphysik* (1965), pp. 136–143; M. Wacht, *Aeneas von Gaza als Apologet* (1969), pp. 64f, 71–73.

[21] On this Beierwaltes, pp. 143ff; similarly Wacht, pp. 75ff. against G. Kraemer, 'Das Warum der Schopfung: "quia bonus" vel/et "quia voluit"? Ein Beitrag zum Verständnis von Neuplatonismus und Christentum an hand des Prinzips "bonum est diffusivum sui"', in *Parusia. Studien zur philosophie Platons und zur Problemgeschichte des Platonismus* Festschrift for J. Hirschberger (1965), pp. 241–264; but cf. also the remarks of A. H. Armstrong in JThS n.s. 10 (1959), p. 176.

[22] Hierokles of Alexandria in the fifth century, who accepts that God creates eternally (in Photius, bibl. 251 [461 Aff.]) but at the same time holds creation out of nothing (bibl. 214 [172A]; 251 [460B–461B], is probably influenced by Christianity; Praechter, 'Christlich-

I. World-creation in Hellenistic Judaism

The theology of hellenistic Judaism has adopted in broad terms philosophical ideas and teaching, but has not engaged in a fundamental debate with philosophical ontology and cosmology. From the apologetic point of view the unity of God, his role as creator, and the effectiveness of his providence were declared;[23] but the doctrine of the fashioning of the world out of an eternal matter could be accepted without embarrassment. And where statements about the sovereignty and omnipotence of the creator seemed to demand the formulation of the *creatio ex nihilo* or to approach that doctrine, the theoretical consequence was not drawn. Thus the Wisdom of Solomon speaks of the almighty hand of God, which created the cosmos out of formless matter, obviously without seeing in this statement a diminishing of God's omnipotence.[24] Yet we find alongside this a few texts which seem to assert a creation out of nothing. The best known, constantly brought forward as the earliest evidence of the conceptual formulation of the doctrine of *creatio ex nihilo*, is 2 Maccabees 7:28.[25] The need for caution in evaluating this is apparent from the context in which there is talk of creation 'out of nothing'. There is here no theoretical disquisition on the nature of the creation process, but a paraenetic reference to God's creative power: the mother of the seven martyrs calls her youngest son to steadfastness by

---

neuplatonische Beziehungen', *Byz. Zeitschrift* 21 (1912), pp. 1–27; cf. now Baltes, *Weltentstehung* I, pp. 187–190. The most comprehensive attempt at a philosophical basis for Christian creation doctrine was made in the time of Justinian by the Christian neoplatonist John Philoponus, in controversy with Proclus and Simplicius; cf. H.-D. Saffrey, 'Le chrétien Jean Philoponos et la survivance de l'école d'Alexandrie au VIe sicle', REG 67 (1954), pp. 396–410; W. Wieland, 'Die Ewigkeit der Welt (Der Streit zwischen Joannes Philoponus und Simplicius)' in *Die Gegenwart der Griechen im neueren Denken* Festschrift for H. G. Gadamer (1960), pp. 291–316.

[23] Cf. Ep. Arist. 132ff; Philo, opif. 170–172.

[24] Wisdom 11:17: ἡ παντοδύναμός σου χεὶρ καὶ κτίσασα τὸν κόσμον ἐξ ἀμόρφου ὕλης. That the Septuagint with the translation of Genesis 1:2a ἡ δὲ γῆ ἦν ἀόρατος καὶ ἀκατασκεύαστος is thinking of matter, has often been suggested; cf. J. Bernays, 'Über die unter Philon's Werken stehende Schrift über die Unzerstörbarkeit des Weltalls', AAB 1882–83 (1883) p. 32; J. B. Schaller 'Genesis 1.2 im antiken Judentum (Untersuchungen über Verwendung und Deutung der Schöpfungsaussagen von Gen. 1.2 im antiken Judentum)' (Thesis, Göttingen 1961), pp. 8–11, and already Clement of Alexandria, strom. V 90.1.

[25] Ἀξιῶ σε, τέκνον, ἀναβλέψαντα εἰς τὸν οὐρανὸν καὶ τὴν γῆν καὶ τὰ ἐν αὐτοῖς πάντα ἰδόντα γνῶναι ὅτι οὐκ ἐξ ὄντων ἐποίησεν αὐτὰ ὁ θεός, καὶ τὸ τῶν ἀνθρώπων γένος οὕτω γίνεται. On this now see G. Schmuttermayr, '"Schöpfung aus dem Nichts" in 2 Macc 7:28?', BZ N.F. 17 (1973), pp. 203–228.

The Problem of the Creation of the World in Hellenistic Judaism 7

holding before his eyes that God, who has shown his might by creating the world and mankind 'out of non-being', will, 'in the time of mercy' awaken the righteous from death.[26] A position on the problem of matter is clearly not to be expected in this context. The text implies no more than the conception that the world came into existence through the sovereign creative act of God, and that it previously was not there.[27] In this way the omnipotence of God is expressed, which guarantees the future awakening of the dead; but a critical move away from the doctrine of world-formation out of eternal matter is quite outside the scope of this text.[28] The first speech of the Jewish mother, preceding this one, which offers a parallel to our point, is not intended to give scientific information about the origin of mankind and the rest of the creation, but is exclusively concerned with the idea of basing the hope of resurrection on the omnipotence of God.[29] One might naturally suppose that the statement about the world being created 'out of non-being' was the formal summary of a thorough-going theory of creation, drawn from a firm tradition. But for such an interpretation all the factors that would support it are lacking: a corresponding older creation theory is not to be directly traced in Judaism, and it will appear that the hellenistic Jewish theology says nothing in a principled anti-Greek sense about creation 'out of nothing', so that arguing back from the formal turn of phrase to an underlying theological tradition is ruled out.

That the formulation found in the second book of Maccabees in no way necessitates the thought of the absolute unconditionality of the creation, is

---

[26] Schmuttermayr, p. 206, speaks of the 'prayer-style' of the text and declares its paraenetic character. The thesis which Arn. Ehrhardt put forward in 'Creatio ex nihilo', in *The Framework of the New Testament Stories* (Manchester, 1964), pp. 200–233, 214f., is fanciful: that the speech is related to Eleatic ways of thought about non-being and is a criticism of the hellenistic ruler-ideology which regarded the earthly ruler as the image of the divine monarch Zeus, protector of the eternal order of the cosmos.

[27] The form of words οὐκ ἐξ ὄντων is, according to F. Blass, A. Debrunner and F. Rehkopf, *Grammatik des neutestamentlichen Griechisch* ([14]1976), §433.3 (p. 361), good classical usage, meaning the same as ἐξ οὐκ ὄντων. The combination οὐκ ἐξ ὄντων also appears in Ps. Aristotle, De Melisso Xenophane Gorgia 1.15 (ed. Diels, AAB 1900, pp. 18, 16); Hippolytus, ref. VIII, 17.1; X, 28; cf. also Plotinus, Enn. III, 6.6.25, in Theiler's reconstruction of the text. Schmuttermayr, pp. 218ff., adopts a different meaning and translates οὐκ ἐξ ὄντων in 2 Macc. 7:28 by 'not out of things being, i.e. already existent individual things' (p. 224). For the fundamental understanding of the text the question whether the form of words gives expression to a particular nuance of meaning is not essential.

[28] Cf. Schmuttermayr; similarly H. F. Weiss, *Untersuchungen zur Kosmologie des hellenistischen und palästinischen Judentums* (1966), pp. 73f.

[29] 7:23: ὁ τοῦ κόσμου κτίστης ὁ πλάσας ἀνθρώπου γένεσιν καὶ πάντων ἐξευρὼν γένεσιν καὶ τὸ πνεῦμα καὶ τὴν ζωὴν ὑμῖν πάλιν ἀποδίδωσιν μετ' ἐλέους, ὡς νῦν ὑπεροράτε ἑαυτοὺς διὰ τοὺς αὐτοῦ νόμους. Compare Schuttermayr, p. 205.

also clear from an informative parallel in Xenophon. He says in one place in his *Memorabilia* that parents 'bring forth their children out of non-being'. Naturally that does not mean that the children come to be out of nothing, and it will occur to no one to understand the statement in terms of a *creatio ex nihilo*.[30] For the philosophical thought of the Greeks the axiom was valid from Parmenides onwards that 'ex nihilo nihil fit'. Clearly what we have in Xenophon is an unphilosophical everyday turn of phrase, which tells us that something new, something that was not there before, comes into being; whether this something new comes through a change in something that was already there, or whether it is something absolutely new, is beside the question. The statements of hellenistic-Jewish theology about God creating 'out of non-being' are also to be understood in the sense of this usage.

We must hold fast to the methodological principle that enquiry must not be limited to the connotation as such of the formula 'to create out of non-being'; this need not have the sense of an ontological principle. Only when the formula is seen from the train of thought to be an intentional antithesis of the idea of world-formation, is it to be taken as a testimony to the doctrine of unconditional creation.

Another text which plays a part in the discussion whether hellenistic Judaism developed a doctrine of *creatio ex nihilo* is the Letter of Aristeas. When it is explained here that men, who on account of their inventions were raised to be gods, had merely brought together things discovered in creation without themselves bringing them into existence, this seems to entail the consequence that the true God creates everything that has being. But the thought is not pursued, and the question of the origin of matter is not posed. The idea of *creatio ex nihilo* can only be found in this passage if it is already presupposed.[31]

---

[30] Mem. II, 2.3: τίνας οὖν, ἔφη, ὑπὸ τίνων εὕροιμεν ἂν μείζω εὐηργετημένους ἢ παῖδας ὑπὸ γονέων; οὓς οἱ γονεῖς ἐκ μὲν οὐκ ὄντων ἐποίησαν εἶναι. (The reference to this passage I owe to a lecture by Paul Henry; Schmuttermayr p. 297, n. 19 also cites it.) Similar formulations are to be found in Philo: decal. 111; spec. leg. II. 2.225, 229; virt. 130. Cf. also Plato, Symposium, 205B: 'For whenever anything from non-being comes into being (ἐκ τοῦ μὴ ὄντος εἰς τὸ ὂν ἰόντι), every time the cause is a making (ποίησις).'

[31] Epist. Arist. 136: τῶν γὰρ ἐν τῇ κτίσει λαβόντες τινὰ συνέθηκαν καὶ προσυπέδειξαν εὔχρηστα, τὴν κατασκευὴν αὐτῶν οὐ ποιήσαντες αὐτοί, cf. 139. On this H. A. Wolfson, *Foundations of Religious philosophy in Judaism, Christianity and Islam* I (Cambridge, Mass. 1968), p. 303. Weiss (pp. 72f.) finds, incorrectly, in Aristeas a polemic against the platonist demiurge. Pohlenz, *Die Stoa* I p. 368; II p. 180 finds creation out of nothing expressed in Aristobulus (Eusebius, Praep. ev. VIII 10.10f.; XIII 12.11), and W. Foerster, art. κτίζω, ThW III (1938), p. 1016 brings in Sibylline Oracles III, 20f. as evidence

Philo

It is Philo who has given the most comprehensive account of the philosophical cosmology. His statements about the being, construction and origin of the cosmos show a connection, characteristic of the philosophical situation of his time, between Platonic and Stoic conceptions. Even Philo did not advocate *creatio ex nihilo* in the later Christian sense and seems to have found no contradiction between the philosophical model of world-formation and the biblical conception of creation. He saw no problem at this point. Therefore his statements about the creation of the world seem remarkably vague, if the question is asked whether they imply *creatio ex nihilo* or not. Philo's creation doctrine has so often been treated from the point of view of *creatio ex nihilo*[32] that we shall not attempt an exhaustive

for its presence in hellenistic Judaism. But none of these passages are unambiguously about *creatio ex nihilo*; cf. also Schmuttermayr, pp. 211–217. Josephus also has not thought through the problem of matter: A. Schlatter, *Die Theologie des Judentums nach dem bericht des Josefus* (1932), pp. 12f.; cf. Antiquities I, 27f.; III, 183f.

[32] I refer to J. Drummond, *Philo Judaeus: or the Jewish Alexandrian Philosophy in its Development and Completion* I (London and Edinburgh 1888), pp. 299–307; cf. Bäumker, *Das Problem der Materie in der griechischen Philosophie* (1890), pp. 380–388; E. Zeller, *Die Philosophie der Griechen* III/2 (⁵1923), pp. 436–438; E. Bréhier, *Les idées philosophiques et religieuses de Philon d'Alexandrie* (Paris ³1950), pp. 80–82 and above all to Weiss, pp. 18–72. They all deny to Philo the doctrine of *creatio ex nihilo*. On the other hand Wolfson I, pp. 300–310 tries to maintain that Philo accepted the creation of matter by God. But methodologically his argument is highly questionable: he equates the 'void', the idea of which God according to opif. 29 creates on the first day of creation (= ἄβυσσος, Gen. 1:2), with the primary matter of Timaeus 48E-52E, the χώρα. Out of this material God subsequently created the elements. But according to his statements about matter elsewhere Philo, no more than the Middle Platonists, understood matter as empty space; cf. Bäumker, p. 383, and on the problem of the Platonist Chora H. Happ, *Hyle, Studien zum aristotelischen Materie-Begriff* (1971), pp. 90ff. In conf. ling. 136 it says, to be sure, that God begot the space that bodies occupy as well as the bodies themselves; here, however, the problem of matter does not arise, but in an exposition of Gen. 1:5 the anthropomorphic idea that God is corporeal and moves in space is to be rejected. (Similarly in connection with Exod. 19:17–20 Aristobulus in Clement of Alexandria, Strom. VI, 33.1 = Eusebius, praep. ev. VII, 10.15. Also in leg. all. I 44 matter is not meant by the void; cf. Bäumker, p. 382, n.1.) Besides, in opif. 26–29 any clear reference to the passage from the Timaeus adduced by Wolfson is lacking. Philo is here explaining Gen. 1:1–3 and simply reads the creation of the seven ideas of Heaven, Earth, Air, (=σκότος), Void, Water, Spirit and Light from the biblical text. W. Pannenberg correctly opposes Wolfson's interpretation in 'Die Aufnahme des philosophischen Gottesbegriffs als dogmatisches Problem der frühchristlichen Theologie', in *Grundfragen systematischer Theologie* (Ges. Aufs. 1967), pp. 296–346, 316, n. 70. To this criticism it may be added that in leg. all. III 7, where Pannenberg also finds the idea of *creatio ex nihilo* potentially expressed, we have perhaps the Stoic idea that there is only one active cause of being; the passive material is then necessarily conceived as its correlate (see n. 60 below).

exposition here and shall be content to look at some disputed texts and to bring out the theological and philosophical motifs which determine his statements about the creation of the world.

That Philo postulates a pre-existent matter alongside God is apparent from the very beginning of the work *De opificio mundi*. Philo starts from the Stoic proposition that there must be an active and a passive principle of being. The former is the perfect Nous – God – the latter is no doubt the formless matter, although the concept does not occur; the passive principle is in itself without soul or motion, but it is moved, formed and ensouled by the Nous, and turned into the visible cosmos.[33] The idea that the acceptance of a passive principle could diminish the omnipotence of God and therefore that matter also must be thought of as created, does not arise. And the question why everything was created is answered by Philo with an allusion to the famous Platonic saying (*Timaeus* 29E): it was the ungrudging goodness of God which caused him to order and form the stuff that had no beauty or order of its own.[34] It is scarcely conceivable that Philo should have attributed to God matter understood in so negative a way. The point of his statement consists precisely in the thesis that God's creative goodness is expressed in the forming of the stuff, while the question of the origin of the matter in its original unformed condition is not the subject of reflection.[35] In the recapitulatory remarks at the end of his writing, Philo says, again alluding to the *Timaeus*, that God used up all the material for his work of creation, by which he means to point out the existence of one single world, but where the primaeval material came from is again not discussed; it is obviously presupposed.[36] That Philo in the *De opificio mundi* does not treat the question of where the matter came from is also apparent from his exposition of Genesis 1:2: He does not relate this verse to the unformed matter, as the rest of the hellenistic Jews and their Christian successors

[33] Opif. 8f.
[34] Opif. 21f: εἰ γάρ τις ἐθελήσειε τὴν αἰτίαν ἧς ἕνεκα τόδε τὸ πᾶν ἐδημιουργεῖτο διερευνᾶσθαι, δοκεῖ μοι μὴ διαμαρτεῖν σκοποῦ ψάμενος, ὅπερ καὶ τῶν ἀρχαίων εἶπέ τις, ἀγαθὸν εἶναι τὸν πατέρα καὶ ποιητήν, οὗ χάριν τῆς ἀρίστης αὑτοῦ φύσεως οὐκ ἐφθόνησεν οὐσίᾳ μηδὲν ἐξ αὑτῆς ἐχούσῃ καλόν, δυναμένῃ δὲ πάντα γίνεσθαι. ἦν μὲν γὰρ ἐξ αὑτῆς ἄτακτος ἄποιος ἄψυχος (ἀνόμοιος), ἑτεροιότητος ἀναρμοστίας ἀσυμφωνίας μεστή· τροπὴν δὲ καὶ μεταβολὴν ἐδέχετο τὴν εἰς τἀναντία καὶ τὰ βέλτιστα, τάξιν ποιότητα ἐμψυχίαν ὁμοιότητα ταὐτότητα, τὸ εὐάρμοστον, τὸ σύμφωνον, πᾶν ὅσον τῆς κρείττονος ἰδέας. *Ousia* is the Stoic term for matter, which Philo uses just as Plutarch does; cf. Bäumker, p. 383.
[35] How self-evident the idea of world-formation is to Philo is shown by another statement: that the heaven, as the best of created things, is made from the purest part of matter (opif. 27).
[36] Opif. 171; cf. Plato, Timaeus 32C; Aristotle, de Caelo I 9 (278a 27): Albinus, did. 12 (p. 167, 11f); Timaios Locros, de univ. nat. 8.

The Problem of the Creation of the World in Hellenistic Judaism 11

prefer to do, but he finds described in Genesis 1:1-5, the creation of the world of Ideas.[37] The origin of matter is not treated at all. But Philo also knows the interpretation of Genesis 1:2, which relates the passage to the pre-existent unformed matter, and he is able to set the doctrine of Moses and that of Plato in the *Timaeus* in parallel.[38]

In the work *Quis rerum divinarum heres sit*, Philo sketches the creation of the world in a series of diahireses. He lets the creation process begin with God dividing matter into the heavy and the light, and through further divisions he reaches the origin of the cosmos and the different forms of life.[39] Philo does not go into the question of the origin of matter here either. Likewise Philo describes the creation process in various other passages as obviously the forming of a given material.[40] And the supposition that Philo tacitly presupposed in all these statements that God had also created the formless matter beforehand, is seen to be untenable when he explains that God did not himself form the formless material, since it is unthinkable that he should touch the endless confused matter, but that he used for this purpose his incorporeal energies, the Ideas.[41] A similar negative conception of matter is apparent from an exposition of Genesis 1:31: Philo declares that God was not praising the lifeless, transitory matter, but only the works of his creation,[42] and occasionally Philo can even expressly describe matter as bad and as one of the causes of evil.[43] Such statements make it appear

---

[37] Opif. 26–37. On the Jewish exegesis of Gen. 1 cf. Chalcidius in Tim. 278.

[38] Prov. 1:22; another stoicising exegesis of Gen. 1:2 is extant in gig. 22.

[39] Heres 133–140; cf. 146ff. On this Ursula Früchtel, *Die kosmologischen Vorstellungen bei Philo von Alexandrien* (Leiden, 1968), pp. 41–52.

[40] Spec. leg. III 180; IV 187; plant. 3.5; fuga 8–12; somn. I, 241; leg. all. II, 19; quaest Gen. I, 64.

[41] Spec. leg. I, 329: οὐ γὰρ ἦν θέμις ἀπείρου καὶ πεφυρμένης ὕλης ψαύειν τὸν εὐδαίμονα καὶ μακάριον. Cf. spec.leg. I, 47f. Behind these stands Tim. 30B.

[42] Heres 160: ἐπῄνεσε δὲ ὁ θεὸς οὐ τὴν δημιουργηθεῖσαν ὕλην, τὴν ἄψυχον καὶ πλημμελῆ καὶ διαλυτήν, ἔτι δὲ φθαρτὴν ἐξ ἑαυτῆς ἀνώμαλόν τε καὶ ἄνισον, ἀλλὰ τὰ ἑαυτοῦ τεχνικὰ ἔργα. The δημιουργηθεῖσα ὕλη is, of course, the 'formed', not the 'created' matter; cf. Marguerite Harl in her edition of 'Quis rerum divinarum heres sit' (Paris, 1966), pp. 63–65. If Philo calls matter transitory (cf. leg. all. I 88; ebr. 132; somn. II, 253; post. 115, 165; congr. 112), he is obviously not distinguishing between matter as the original material and the corporeal: Drummond I pp. 301f; Bäumker p. 384, n. 5. The becoming and the passing of the visible and corporeal is a basic platonist idea: Tim. 27D–28C; Plutarch, def. or 29 (426B); Ep. ap Delph. 21 (393F). According to stoic teaching the whole, including the elements, is periodically dissolved in the world conflagration and to that extent counts as transitory; cf. Philo, aet. 8f; prov. I, 16–19; SVF II 596ff; 1049ff.

[43] Spec. leg. IV, 187 (χείρων οὐσία); prov. II, 82; fuga 198.

unthinkable that Philo could have reckoned with the creation of matter by God. Philo took over the Greek teaching about pre-existent matter, without thinking it through independently, and in particular he did not reflect on the problem how the omnipotence of the biblical God could be united with the view of a mere formation of the world. This shows how deeply Philo was rooted in the traditions of Greek thought.[44]

In the writing *De somniis* Philo seems to compare, for once, the idea of the creator in the biblical sense with the thought of a world-former: in connection with Genesis 1:4, he explains that God not only made everything visible, as the rising sun makes things visible, but that he created what was not there before; he is not merely the demiurge, but also κτίστης.[45] But he does not enquire into the question whether matter also belongs to what is created and only on that point might the Platonic ontology have been refuted at the theoretical level. Philo wants to say that God is not only the master builder carrying out the creation, but also its founder and planner, and so really its 'creator'.[46] This does not, of course, mean that God must have created the world, in the strict sense, 'out of nothing'. Philo's other statements show that he saw in the acceptance of a matter that had not originated in time no limitation of God's creative omnipotence. Perhaps one can go on to interpret the formulation in *De somniis* that God was to be thought of not only as the demiurge, who – in accordance with the Middle Platonist scheme of three principles – created the world on the pattern already contained in the Ideas, but was also the 'creator' of the Ideas. Philo would then have in view here the picture broadly offered in *De opificio mundi*, 16–24, of the cosmic founder of a city, who first creates the idea of the cosmos in his mind, and then carries out the creation according to that plan.[47] So it might only be a matter of modification of the Middle Platonist view that the Ideas are the thoughts of God, while the problem of matter does not arise.

There are in any case some texts in which Philo seems to assert the creation of matter or at least clearly to presuppose it. But these texts are, with

[44] Also the repeated declaration of the basic proposition 'nihil de nihilo' (aet. 5; prov. II, 109; spec. leg. I, 266) shows how Philo's thought starts from the presupposition of Greek ontology.

[45] Somn. I, 76. E. Frank, *Philosophical Understanding and Religious Truth* (London and New York, 1945), p. 75, n. 10, says that this passage is the only one 'in which Philo shows a clear understanding of the difference between the Jewish and the Platonist conception of creation'; cf. also R. Walzer, *Galen on Jews and Christians* (London, 1949), p. 30.

[46] For the use of the term κτίστης to describe the creator in hellenistic Judaism the meaning 'city-founder' was determinant: Foerster, pp. 1024–1027.

[47] Cf. Drummond I, p. 304; Weiss, pp. 55–58. On opif. 16ff. cf. Früchtel, pp. 7ff.

one exception, only to be found in an Armenian translation, so that their evaluation encounters special difficulties.[48] In the fragment *De Deo* Philo notes of the biblical text 'The Lord your God is a consuming fire' (Deut. 4:24) that God does not 'consume' the stuff by annihilating it; rather he brings it out of nothing into being.[49] But according to the context it is not the creation of the original stuff that is thought of here, but the forming of it into the four elements.[50]

Right at the beginning of *De Providentia* I Philo contests the view that God creates the world eternally, because he is never without activity (I. 6–8). In Aucher's translation Philo seems in this context to be critically opposed to the assumption that matter is uncreated and co-exists with God as an eternal principle. But this is by no means so clear in the Armenian text.[51] Philo merely asserts the creation of the world in time and apparently

[48] Only for prov. II, 50 is the Greek text available, in Eusebius, praep. ev. VII, 24.1–4.
[49] De deo 7f.: Quando dicimus zoographum consumpsisse (sive impendisse) tinturas omnes in picturam perficiendam, aut a statuario consumptum fuisse aeneam in statuam, aut a fabro ligna et saxa in domum vel generatim ab artifice materiam in opus artificiosum, num corrumpere eum dicimus? Minime. Quoniam manet color in tabula et aes in statua et saxa lignaque in aedificiis atque ceterae materiae in singulis rebus peractis; manent autem in meliore quadam habitudine, receptis in se figura, ordine et qualitate. Simili modo et deus secundum Mosen omnesque secundum illum physiologos factos consumet materias non ad nihilem vertens, sed ex adverso de nihilo in exsistentiam ducens conservandam, estque in cunctis salutis causa. Eam que crassior ac densior et gravior inter materias est, consumpsit in terrae substantiam; subtiliorem autem et leviorem in ignis generationem; in aquae subtiliorem, terrae crassiorem, ignis et aquae magis aeream – nihil enim extra haec manet – atque quattuor illas, omnium principia, materias in cunctis consumpsit, ut dixi, non volens corruptionem sed salutem.
[50] M. Harl, 'Cosmologie grêcque et représentations juives dans l'oeuvre de Philon d'Alexandrie', in *Philon d'Alexandrie* (Colloques nationaux du Centre national de recherche scientifique, Paris, 1967), pp. 189–205, p. 195 n. 2 points out, on De Deo 7, that Philo can describe the formation of matter in another way, as a calling-into-being of non-being (cf. especially spec. leg. IV, 187). In De Deo 6 it says, obviously referring to the angels: natura, qua creatur, formaturque materia. In spite of the 'creatur' – the Greek equivalent of which is, however, uncertain – it can only refer in this context to the forming of matter.
[51] I, 7 (Aucher): Superest itaque ut dicant materiam ornatu ac forma et figura carentem qualitate ac forma ab eo donatum fuisse et quae non erant in ea figuras deinde sumpsisse: non enim unquam Deus illam creare juxta eos coepit. Quodsi sapiens illa creatio per Deum facta speciosam mundi formam condidit ex ipsa materia atque inde materia pulchram valde speciem sortita est, num hoc unumne aiunt Deum fecisse cum mundum creare coepit et quae antea sine ordine et lege atque errabunde movere solita erat materia tunc speciosum ordinem cum ornamento adepta est? Num materia ipsa fuit Deo principii loco (cum mundum conderet)? at creator iugiter istam intelligendo adornavit. This is differently translated by C. Hannick in Baltes, *Weltentstehung*, I p. 89: 'it stands on the contrary, for nothing remains (?): they said the material was without adornment, form or shape and

reckons here also with the eternity of matter.[52] In the second book of the work Philo makes the point that the non-origination in time of matter does not exclude origin in time of the cosmos: God can have made the latter out of eternal matter, just as an artist makes his work out of material he did not produce.[53] One might assume from Philo's exposition that according to his own conviction the matter was also created by God — that is how Eusebius understood the text when he used an excerpt from it to support his doctrine of the creation of matter in his *Praeparatio evangelica* — but this interpretation is scarcely sustainable.[54] Philo's reflections point in another direction: he wants to say that God by manipulating all the material available had created a world perfect in every respect, thereby doing better than any human artist, who may in measuring the material for his work fall into error.[55] It is also highly evident from *De providentia* II that Philo contra-

receives its formation from him (God), and the form which was not in it, it took on; for in their opinion God did not begin to create. But if reasonable creation comes from him and has made the beautiful form of the world and matter has taken on its most beautiful form, how then did God begin to create the world, if matter was in disorderly and haphazard movement, without proper sequentiality, but the world now received beauty and adornment and the beginning became matter (?)?' P. Wendland, *Philos Schrift über die Vorsehung* (1892), pp. 4–7, finds in this a polemic against the doctrine of the pre-existence of matter. W. Bousset disagrees in *Jüdisch-christlicher Schulbetrieb in Alexandria und Rom* (1915), pp. 143–146; also Pohlenz, 'Philon von Alexandrien', NAG 1942/45, pp. 409–487, 417f; H. Chadwick, 'St Paul and Philo of Alexandria', *Bulletin of the John Rylands Library* 48 (1965–66), pp. 286–307, p. 292, n. 6 suspects that 1–7 have been reworked by Christians. The doctrine of continuous creation of the world, to which Philo refers, was probably entertained by Platonists influenced by Aristotle: Baltes I, pp. 90–93.

[52] I, 9–23; cf. especially I, 22: Haec Plato a Deo facta fuisse novit; et materiam per se ornatu carentem in mundo cum ornatu ipso prodiisse; hae enim erant primae causae, unde et mundus fuit. Quoniam et Judaeorum legislator Moyses aquam, tenebras et chaos dixit ante mundum fuisse. On this Bousset, *Schulbetrieb*, pp. 143–146; Baltes, *Weltenstehung* I, pp. 35–37.

[53] Prov. II, 45–51 (50f. = Eusebius, praep. ev. VII, 21.1–4); cf. Wendland, pp. 62f.

[54] Prov. II, 50 = Eusebius, praep. ev. VII, 21.1: περὶ δὲ τοῦ ποσοῦ τῆς οὐσίας, εἰ δὴ γέγονεν ὄντως, ἐκεῖνο λεκτέον. ἐστοχάσατο πρὸς τὴν τοῦ κόσμου γένεσιν ὁ θεὸς αὐταρκεστάτης ὕλης, ὡς μήτ' ἐνδέοι μηδ' ὑπερβάλλοι. Καὶ γὰρ ἄτοπον ἦν τοὺς μὲν κατὰ μέρος τεχνίτας, ὁπότε τι δημιουργοῖεν καὶ μάλιστα τῶν πολυτελῶν, τὸ ἐν ὕλαις αὔταρκες σταθμήσασθαι, τὸν δ' ἀριθμοὺς καὶ μέτρα καὶ τὰς ἐν τούτοις ἰσότητας ἀνευρηκότα μὴ φροντίσαι τοῦ ἱκανοῦ. The words εἰ δὴ γέγονεν ὄντως perhaps take up the sense of II 48: 'Age, interim ponamus inter nos universum ingenitum et sempiternum' and should then be applied to the cosmos: Bréhier, p. 81, n. 2; Mireille Hadas-Lebel in her edition of De Providentia (Paris, 1973), p. 279 n. 1. But if matter should be meant, then that is a hypothetical assumption which need by no means correspond with Philo's own conception.

[55] Philo develops the same view in opif. 171; det. pot. 154; plant. 6; de deo 8; the source is Timaeus 32C; see n. 36 above.

The Problem of the Creation of the World in Hellenistic Judaism   15

dicted the thought that matter could have been created, and that was already surprising enough. For in the first book Philo can assert on the contrary that Moses and Plato were in agreement in accepting a pre-existent material.[56] In any case he nowhere brings forward as his own idea the claim that matter came into being. And above all he lacks the decisive basis of the doctrine of *creatio ex nihilo*, that the biblical conception of God demands that matter also be created.

Philo's cosmology is dependent on the philosophy of his time.[57] But it is now essential also to see that Philo is concerned, within the framework of his Platonist ontology to validate the omnipotence and the sovereignty of the biblical God. This theological interest guides him as he works out his Platonist thoughts and determines his position on controversial questions, so that his statements about creation derive from this their inner unity and decisiveness.

Even when Philo postulates the pre-existence of matter, he in no way envisages it as an ontologically equal principle alongside God. There is no question with him of a specific dualism. Philo can, as we have seen, suggest a connection between matter and evil.[58] But he all the more strongly declares its total passivity, its lack of quality or form.[59] God alone is αἴτιον: in this statement Philo sides with the Stoic usage, according to which only the active principle counts as *causa*.[60] It is apparent, therefore, that picturing the creation as a forming of the unformed matter is for Philo no more than a conventional thought-form, which clarifies the process of creation, but from which he draws no theological conclusions.

Philo is familiar with the discussion over the question, whether the myth of the creation of the world in the *Timaeus* is to be taken literally, meaning that Plato taught that God created the world at a specific point in time, or whether it is merely a figurative presentation of a timeless causal relationship.[61] Philo supports, as might be expected, the literal understanding of the *Timaeus* and the temporal creation of the world. He explains that Plato taught, in consensus with Moses, that the world had come into being but

---

[56] I 22.
[57] U. Früchtel in particular has brought out the relations with Middle Platonism.
[58] See n. 43 above.
[59] Cf. the contribution in Bäumker, p. 381, n. 5.
[60] Leg. all. III, 7; cherub. 127; fuga 8, 11ff; cf. J. Pépin, *Théologie cosmique et théologie chrétienne* (Ambroise, Exam. I, 1, 1–4) (Paris, 1964), pp. 358f.
[61] Aet. 14; heres 246 on the controversy over the interpretation of the Timaeus, cf. Baltes, *Weltentstehung* I.

that it was protected by the will of God from going out of being.[62] This conception is in agreement with the position of Plutarch, Atticus and other Platonists, who also understood the forming of the unformed matter into the cosmos as a once-for-all real act and, following *Timaeus* 41 AB, saw the will of God as the guarantee of the world's performance.[63] The thesis that the world must have been made, because otherwise a providential concern for it on God's part would be unthinkable, is found again in Atticus and is probably also held by Plutarch.[64] Philo thus looks very like a precursor of the 'religious Platonism' of Atticus and Plutarch.

Many times Philo speaks of God as creating 'out of non-being' or creating 'non-being' (i.e. creating what previously was not).[65] To understand these expressions we must consider what has already been said about 2 Maccabees 7:28: they mean that the world has not existed eternally but was created by means of a single act in time. Such statements could only be interpreted in the specific sense of the *creatio ex nihilo* if it were inescapable from the context in which they stand that Philo also accepted a creation of matter out of nothing. But that is nowhere the case, and the texts in which Philo sets out the eternal constitution of matter show convincingly the impossibility of this interpretation.[66] That the phrase about creation of the non-existent in no way carries the meaning of *creatio ex nihilo* is evident, in that Atticus also in his defence of the creation-in-time arrives at formulations which coincide almost word for word with Philo's: that God created the cosmos which was not there before, and if a terrestrial worker is in a position to bring something not being into being, this must be even more true of God.[67]

---

[62] Opif. 12; decal. 58; aet. 13–16; prov. I 20–22; cf. Bernays, pp. 24–28; Baltes, *Weltentstehung* I, pp. 32–38.

[63] Plutarch, de an. procr. 4–10 (1013E–1017C); Atticus in Eusebius, praep. ev. XV 6; cf. Proclus in Timaeus 116B (I 381, 26ff. Diehl); 84F–85A (I 276.31ff).

[64] Opif. 9–11; praem. 42; cf. Atticus in Eusebius, praep. ev. XV 6.2. Calvinus Taurus only wants to call the world 'originate' so as not to endanger providence; in strict philosophical language the cosmos is 'unoriginate': John Philoponus, de aet. mundi VI, 21 (pp. 186f. Rabe); cf. Andresen, *Logos und Nomos*, pp. 281f.; Baltes, *Weltentstehung*, I, pp. 50–53.

[65] Ἐκ τοῦ μὴ ὄντος: Mos. II 267; de Deo 7 (de nihilo); cf. deus imm. 119; ἐκ μὴ ὄντων: leg. all. III, 10; τὰ μὴ ὄντα: opif. 81; Mos. II, 100; spec. leg. IV, 187; mut. 46; heres 36; migr. Abr. 183.

[66] Philo places the creation of the cosmos 'out of non-being' and the transformation of the elements in the manna miracle (Ex. 16) in parallel to Mos. II 267; cf. also Weiss, pp. 60ff.

[67] In Eusebius, praep. ev. XV, 6.7: οὐκ ὄντα πρότερον ἐποίησε τὸν κόσμον (sc. ὁ τοῦ κόσμου ποιητής) cf. XV, 6.12. Similarly Philo, somn, I 76: ἃ πρότερον οὐκ ἦν

The Problem of the Creation of the World in Hellenistic Judaism 17

People have even ventured the opposite possibility, that Philo by 'non-being' meant pre-existent matter.[68] Aristotle had asserted that Plato had described matter as 'not being' and an utterance by Plato's disciple Hermodor, preserved by Simplicius, confirms this.[69] Most of all Plotinus then conceived matter as μὴ ὄν.[70] But it seems to me ruled out that Philo speaks of 'non-being' in this Platonist sense. When he says that God created 'the non-being', he always uses the plural τὰ μὴ ὄντα and clearly means individual things: through the act of creation they move from non-being into being. In the places where it says that God creates 'out of non-being', the expressions ἐκ μὴ ὄντος and ἐκ μὴ ὄντων are interchangeable, without visible change of meaning. This oscillation between singular and plural decisively counts against the view that Philo is here talking about unformed matter, for, as the indefinite and unlimited something, which is potentially everything, matter can only be described as μὴ ὄν.[71] Also the fact that Philo always forms the expression 'non-being' with the negative μή, is no sure indication that he looks upon matter as only relatively 'non-being'.[72] In philosophical texts μὴ ὄν generally stands as the term for absolute 'non-being'.[73] Furthermore in the Greek of imperial times μή is in general use,

ἐποίησεν. Philo and Atticus are both dependent on Plato, Soph. 256BC; cf. also Plutarch, de E. ap. Delph. 21 (393EF). On the problem of time in Atticus cf. E. P. Meijering, 'ΗΝ ΠΟΤΕ ΟΤΕ ΟΥΚ ΗΝ Ο ΥΙΟΣ. A discussion on Time and Eternity' in *God Being History. Studies in Patristic Philosophy* (Amsterdam, 1975), pp. 81–88.

[68] This is how Chadwick expresses himself, *Early Christian Thought and the Classical Tradition* (Oxford, 1966), pp. 46f.; similarly Zeller, III/2, pp. 435ff.

[69] Aristotle, Phys. I 9 (192a 6–8); on this cf. Bäumker, pp. 210ff; Happ, p. 294. Hermodor in Simplicius, in phys. I 9 (248, 13f. Diels = 256, 35f.); cf. Happ, pp. 137–140. Also Clement of Alexandria is aware of these platonist thoughts: strom. V 89.6; cf. S. Lilla, *Clement of Alexandria. A study in Christian Platonism and Gnosticism* (Oxford, 1971), pp. 195f.

[70] Cf. Plotinus, Enn. II 5.4f; III 6.7; I 8.3; on this Bäumker, pp. 405ff.

[71] Cf. the reflections of Plotinus, Enn. II 4.8ff; III 6.16–18. Bäumker, p. 382, n. 1 points out that in Philo too the use of term *ousia* for matter scarcely permits the view that he regarded it as 'non-being'.

[72] Otherwise Chadwick (n. 68 above).

[73] As examples may be cited Plutarch, quaest. conv. VIII 9.2 (731D); Plato, quaest. 4 (1003A); de an. procr. 5 (1014B); adv. Col 8 (1111A); 12 (1113C); Marcus Aurelius V 13.1; Porphyry in Proclus, on Timaeus 86 BC (I 281, 5ff. Diehl); 92A (I 300.10) Sallustius, De diis et mundo 17 uses the expressions ἐκ μὴ ὄντος and ἐκ μὴ ὄντων as equivalents, with the meaning 'out of (absolute) nothing'. Cf. also Aristotle, phys. I 8f. and Pseudo Aristotle, De Mel. Xen. Gorg. I (pp. 15ff. Diels) How fluid the usage was is shown by the fact that, on the other hand, Hermodor (n. 69 above) describes matter as οὐκ ὄν; similarly Porphyry in Proclus, on Timaeus 71D (I 233, 4 Diehl); cf. P. Hadot, *Porphyre et Victorinus* I (Paris, 1968), p. 148. Also Beierwaltes, p. 137 n. 37 declares that nothing is to be concluded from

being considered more elegant than οὐ, and is specifically preferred with the participle.[74] We are therefore left to decide according to the train of thought whether ἐκ μὴ ὄντος means 'out of matter' or 'out of nothing'. Philo's statements, however, nowhere approach the Platonising understanding.[75] When Philo speaks of a creation by God 'out of non-being', this is not to be interpreted either as *creatio ex nihilo* or as formation of the 'non-being' matter. This alternative does not present itself to him. He will simply say that the world, which hitherto did not exist, came into being through God's creative act, which the Platonists could also teach, and he seems to take for granted the eternity of matter.

Philo also took over the doctrine of the Ideas and combined this with his Logos doctrine. The theory developed from Middle Platonism, that the Ideas are the thoughts of God, formed the basis of this synthesis and immediately accommodated Philo's interest in setting forth the 'monarchy' of God as resolutely as was possible with Platonist means of thought.[76] The Ideas, which are located in the Logos, are fully subordinate to God and have lost their character as principles. Even the Logos himself possesses over against God no self-determination. Philo understands him as the sum of the Ideas and as the tool by means of which God creates.[77] H. Dörrie has shown that Philo so modified the Platonist series of prepositions, to which W. Theiler drew attention – ὑφ' οὗ, ἐξ οὗ, πρὸς ὅ, expressing the relationship of the three principles, God, matter and ideas – that absolute causality is attributed to God and the Logos can be understood simply as the 'organon' of the creation, not as its second principle.[78] The ὑφ' οὗ, δι οὗ refers to

the use of the negations μή and οὐ as to whether an absolute or a relative non-being is meant. Philo himself speaks of the μὴ 'όν as absolute nothing, spec. leg. I 266; aet. 5 f.; prov. II, 109 (Eusebius, praep. ev. VIII 14.66).

[74] E. Schwyzer, *Griechische Grammatik* II (³1966), pp. 594f.; Blass–Debrunner–Rehkopf §430 (pp. 358f.). On the change from μή to οὐ cf. also R. Knopf, *Die Apostolischen Väter* I (HNT, Supplementary Volume, 1920), pp. 155f. (on 2 Clement I.8).

[75] Weiss, pp. 65ff. considers in the cases of Mos. II 267 and deus imm. 119 (where there is however no talk of world-creation) that the reference to matter is probable, but can produce no thorough-going proof of this.

[76] Cf. Chadwick in Armstrong, *The Cambridge History of Later Greek and Early Mediaeval Philosophy*, p. 142; Pohlenz, *Philon*, p. 437f.

[77] On the Logos as organon cf. Weiss, pp. 267–272.

[78] Dörrie, 'Präpositionen und Metaphysik. Wechselwirkung zweier Prinzipienreihen', *Mus. Helv.* 26 (1969), pp. 217–228, pp. 223–225. Dorrie emphasises the difference between Philo's doctrine of the creation of world and that of Plutarch and Atticus: for Atticus the Ideas are still παραίτια (Eusebius, praep. ev. XV, 13.5), for Philo on the other hand the Logos is not a principle separate from God. According to Theiler, 'Philo von Alexandrien und der kaiserzeitliche Platonismus', in *Parusia. Studien zur Philosophie Platons und zur*

God, δι οὗ means the 'organon', ἐξ οὗ the elements, and δι' ὅ the ground of the creation, which Philo attributes to the goodness of the creator.[79] God alone is the active originator of the creation.

In connection with the well-known passage from the *Timaeus*, Philo teaches that God creates out of ungrudging goodness.[80] God never rests, creating is as essential to him as burning is to fire, and cold to snow;[81] he never leaves off perfecting the most beautiful, for God does not change.[82] It can, however, just as well be said of the unchanging God, who knows no weariness nor weakness, that he is in constant rest.[83] Further, God's creative action has no extension in time; the distinction of the days of creation in the biblical creation story represents an order, not a succession in time. The creation of the world is achieved once for all and is not amenable to temporal categories.[84] Frankly such statements cannot hide the problems which arise for the concept of God from the acceptance of a beginning of the world: The creative act in time implies that God is not eternal creator; and so through the creation we come to a change in God.[85] Philo tries to master this difficulty when he says God is always sufficient unto himself, the creation of the world involves no alteration in his being and is not necessary for him.[86] Philo already knows the solution: that God eternally creates the

---

Problemgeschichte des Platonismus Festschrift for J. Hirschberger (1965), pp. 199–218, pp. 215f., Philo took the organon-concept from an anti-platonist tract going back to Areios Didymos; otherwise, the same author, *Die Vorbereitung des Neuplatonismus*, pp. 18ff.

[79] Cherub. 127; cf. the context, pp. 124–128, where Philo on the basis of Genesis 4:1 and 40:8 refuses to apply the word διά to God, for that would reduce him to a mere organon; of him one must always say ὑπό; the same series of principles prov. I 23; quaest. Gen. I, 58. Philo brings up another distinction in leg. all. I 41: whatever originates originates partly ὑπό and διά θεοῦ and partly only ὑπό θεοῦ. Ὑπὸ θεοῦ and διὰ θεοῦ are valid for the human nous, but the unreasoning part of the Soul on the other hand has arisen only ὑπὸ θεοῦ, for it receives life directly from the human nous. Dörrie, *Präpositionen*, p. 224 says 'not δι' αὐτοῦ' means 'not through the law and not corresponding to the law'; but this interpretation certainly does not work. With the help of his scheme of prepositions Philo is here formulating his doctrine that God only created directly the nous of man but created the other parts through subordinate powers: cf. fuga 68–72; opif. 74f; mut. nom. 29–31.

[80] Opif. 21; cherub. 127; cf. Timaeus 29E.

[81] Leg. all. I 5.6.

[82] Cherub. 87; plant. 89.91.

[83] Cherub. 90 (cf. Exod. 20:11); also from Gen. 2:3 it is not to be concluded that God really rests, for even after the completion of the creation of the cosmos and of man, God remains creatively active: leg. all. I 518; cf. prov. I 6, 7; cf. Aristobulus in Eusebius, praep. ev. XIII, 12, 11f.

[84] Opif. 13. 18; leg. all. I, 2.3.20.

[85] On this problem in Platonism cf. Dörrie in *Gnomon* 29 (1957), p. 192; Wacht, pp. 64f.

[86] Mut. nom. 46; cf. plant. 89–91.

spiritual world, while the visible cosmos has a specific beginning.[87] These answers do not amount to much philosophically, but they do show that Philo understands the creation as contingent and not as a necessary expression of God's goodness. In the same way later the Platonist Atticus echoes Philo with the problem of creation and time, without succeeding in finding any clear solution.[88] Not before the stupendous reflections of Augustine will decisive progress be made on this question.

Even when Philo declares the omnipotence of God, who is free to bring about good and evil, but only does good,[89] biblical and philosophical conceptions intermingle in his thought. For in Stoic convictions, too, God is almighty and no limits can be imposed from without on his will.[90] But in Philo's statements about the creation of the world, the saying that nothing is impossible to God plays no part.[91] And only in discussions of the guiding activity of God can Philo express the conviction that God could also destroy his creation as an act of penal justice.[92]

Philo's level of philosophical education was first attained in Christian circles by Clement of Alexandria, the first Christian theologian whom we can be sure had read Philo. But for the Christian debate with philosophical

---

[87] Prov. I, 21; on this Baltes, *Weltentstehung* I, pp. 36f. on the question of eternal creation in the theology of the early Church cf. Wacht, pp. 85ff.

[88] In opif. 26; leg. all. I 2; II 3 Philo puts forward the idea that time originated with the cosmos. On the other hand in Decal. 58 it says of the cosmos: ἦν ποτε χρόνος, ὅτε οὐκ ἦν. On Atticus cf. Meijering (n. 67 above); Baltes, *Weltentstehung* I, pp. 44–47.

[89] Opif. 46; Quaest. Gen. III 56; spec. leg. I 282; IV 127; Abr. 112.268; plant. 89; virt. 26; Mos. I 173f.

[90] Walzer, pp. 28–30, draws attention to Cicero, de nat. deorum III 92: Vos enim ipsi (sc. Stoici) dicere soletis nihil esse quod deus efficere non possit, et quidem sine labore ullo; ut enim hominum membra nulla contentione mente ipsa ac voluntate moveantur, sic numine deorum omnia fingi, moveri, mutarique posse, Neque id dicitis superstitiose atque aniliter sed physica constantique ratione; materiam enim rerum, ex qua et in qua omnia sint, totam esse flexibilem et commutabilem, ut nihil sit quod non ex ea quamvis subito fingi convertique possit, eius autem universae fictricem et moderatricem divinam esse providentiam; haec igitur quocumque se moveat efficere possit quicquid velit: de divin. II 86: Nihil est, inquiunt, quod deus efficere non possit; cf. Pohlenz, *Die Stoa* I 95; II 54; R. M. Grant, *Miracle and Natural Law in Graeco-Roman and Early Christian Thought* (Amsterdam, 1952), pp. 128f.

[91] Cf. Walzer, p. 30; at most one could point to a statement like that in heres 301: God guides heaven and earth in a free, self-directing royal rulership; but this idea is also conventional; cf. E. Peterson, 'der Monotheismus als politisches Problem' in *Theologische Traktate* (1951), pp. 45–147, 54ff.

[92] Quaest. Gen. II 13; prov. I 23.34–36 (cf. Wendland, pp. 11f., who considers I 34 to be a Christian interpolation); Abr. 121ff.; spec. leg. I 307; quaest. Ex. II 62, 65, 66, 68; mut. nom. 19ff; Mos. II 99; cf. Pohlenz, *Philon*, pp. 422f.

cosmology Philo's thought could have no importance in pointing the way. Philo went much further in acceptance of the philosophical tradition than Christian theologians, even Clement, were willing to go. The relation between Jewish and philosophical thought in Philo cannot be reduced to a simple formula. Philo will not give up his Jewish faith at any price, but he is convinced that the Pentateuch is to be read and interpreted as a philosophical book. Neither does he let his thinking operate one-sidedly as pure apologetics, although he gives much space to apologetics in his writings, nor can one say that his theology is thoroughly hellenised and has betrayed his Jewish heritage. But to speak of a conscious synthesis in his work between biblical and philosophical thought would be unhistorical, for Philo did not reflect critically enough on his intellectual conceptions. Jewish and Greek elements are not disentangled from each other in Philo. H. Chadwick has made no bones about this: 'Philosophy, especially Platonism, genuinely mattered to him and he could not have expressed his faith adequately without it'.[93]

Factors tending to the doctrine of creatio ex nihilo *in Judaism*
Hellenistic-Jewish theology expressly declared the omnipotence of God and his role as creator, but it did not engage in a fundamental debate with the Platonic and Stoic doctrine of principles. And so it could not develop a doctrine of *creatio ex nihilo*. The statements about creation of non-being or from non-being, which seem to come near to an interpretation in that sense, are not to be understood as antitheses to an eternal matter and to the principle 'ex nihilo nihil fit', but to be considered as an unreflective, everyday way of saying that through the act of creation something arose which did not previously exist. As soon as it was freely recognised that creation by the biblical God was more than the forming of matter, that he brought forth the world in sovereign freedom and without any external conditions, the expression 'Creation out of nothing' offered itself as a formula pregnant to describe the particular character of the biblical concept of creation. The formula preceded the thought.

An early stage in making precise the concept of creation is to be seen in one of the original Jewish prayers preserved in the seventh book of the Apostolic Constitutions.[94] Here it says, in the setting of a paraphrase of the

---

[93] *St Paul and Philo of Alexandria*, p. 306. The judgment of K. Reinhardt, *Poseidonius über Ursprung und Entargung* (1928), p. 14, was quite different: 'Philo's ecstasy has as little in common with the Greek Dionysos as his ideas have with the Ideas of Plato. The formulae are Greek but the sense is oriental.'

[94] Cf. W. Boussett, 'Eine jüdische Gebetssammlung im siebenten Buch der apostolischen Konstitutionen', NGG 1915, pp. 435–489.

creation story, that God created the soul of mankind from nothing, but his body from the 'four bodies', i.e. the four elements.[95] We have here an echo of Genesis 2:7: the breathing in of the breath of life is understood as the creation of the soul 'out of nothing' and, with the omission of the making of the body from the four elements, this creative act assumes the unambiguous meaning of a *creatio ex nihilo*.[96] To the creation of the world such a pointed conception of the act of creation was not applied. Such approaches to a clarification of the idea of creation do not seem to have been followed through coherently in the theology of hellenistic Judaism. Only with Christian theologians of the second century did the traditional saying, that God created the world out of nothing, take on a principled ontological sense: the expression 'out of nothing' now meant that absolutely, and excluded the idea that the creator had merely imposed form on a pre-existent material.

Limits of Jewish statements about creation
Neither did Palestinian Judaism formulate any firm doctrine of the *creatio ex nihilo*.[97] Here we need only go into the rabbinic understanding of

---

[95] Const. Apost. VII, 34.6: ἐκ μὲν τῶν τεσσάρων σωμάτων διαπλάσας αὐτῷ τὸ σῶμα, κατασκευάσας δ' αὐτῷ τὴν ψυχὴν ἐκ τοῦ μὴ ὄντος. Likewise VIII 12.17; cf. also V 7.19: μὴ ὄντα τὸν ἄνθρωπον ἐκ διαφόρων ἐποίησεν, δοὺς αὐτῷ τὴν ψυχὴν ἐκ τοῦ μὴ ὄντος. The statement that the world was created out of nothing is not to be found in Const. Apost. VII 34 (cf. 34.1). In the eucharistic Preface VIII 12.66ff. into which was interpolated a long piece of the introduction of VII 34 (cf. Bousset, pp. 451ff., 471ff.), it appears in a section that is not dependent on the Jewish source (VIII 12.7): cf. Bousset, p. 472.

[96] The formulation that the souls were made 'out of nothing', does not seem to occur elsewhere in hellenistic-Jewish literature. The traditional Greek idea that man consists of the four elements is present in Philo (opif. 145; aet. mundi 29) and is also familiar to rabbinic Judaism: R. Meyer, *Hellenistisches in der rabbinischen Anthropologie* (1937), pp. 122ff. On the exposition of Gen. 2:7 cf. Wisdom of Solomon 15:11; Philo, opif. 134–147; leg. all. I 31–42; det. pot. 80ff.; heres 55–57; spec. leg. IV 123. An exact parallel to Const. Apost. VII 34.6 (VIII 12.17) is found in Theodoret, graec. aff. cur. IV 69.

[97] Cf. the exhaustive account by Weiss, pp. 75–138. In two prayers in the Syriac Apocalypse of Baruch it says: 'Thou who hast at the beginning of the world called forth what previously was not' (21.4) and 'By a word Thou callest into life what is not there' (48.8). That corresponds to Philo's statements about the creation of the 'non-being'; cf. above pp. 16–18 and Weiss, pp. 125f. For similar phraseology in the Samaritan literature cf. Weiss, p. 132. R. Bultmann, *Das Urchristentum im Rahmen der antiken Religionen* ([3]1963) (ET: *Primitive Christianity in its Contemporary Setting*, Philadelphia, 1980), p. 17, as evidence of the gradual formation of the idea of creation out of nothing, speaks, in relation to 2 Maccabees 7:28, of the passage in Jubilees 12:4 about creation through the word; cf. Ehrhardt, p. 216.

creation. To rabbinic Judaism the problems raised by the philosophical doctrine of 'first principles' were remote and its speculations about creation turned on other themes. But in the immediate refutation of Platonising interpretations of the creation of the world the rabbinic theologians were able to formulate the idea of *creatio ex nihilo*. The most important evidence for the express rejection of the view that God created the world out of an unformed stuff is in a debate between Rabban Gamaliel II (90/110) and a philosopher, reproduced in the midrash Genesis rabba. The philosopher explains that God was indeed a great artist, but he had also found good 'colours' ready for his use, which served him as material for his creation of the world. The primitive stuffs were, in line with Genesis 1:2, defined as Tohuwabohu, darkness, water, spirit and 'deep'. Gamaliel refutes this scheme by pointing out that all the available primitive stuffs named by the philosopher are described in the Bible expressly as created by God.[98] Gamaliel thus denies that Genesis 1:2 refers to unformed matter and thereby implicitly asserts *creatio ex nihilo*.[99] But such sayings remain isolated, they arise occasionally from the needs of ongoing discussions, and a firm, unambiguously formulated doctrine of *creatio ex nihilo* is not worked out in ancient Jewry.

It seems to us that an almost obvious step leads from the Jewish belief in creation to the formulation of the idea of *creatio ex nihilo*. And Gamaliel's debating speech shows that in defence of the unlimited creative power of God this logical conclusion could actually be drawn. So the question presses, why the Jewish theology of antiquity did not bring its conception of creation to the unambiguous conceptual form of the *creatio ex nihilo*, while on the Christian side this happened after a relatively short period of debate with philosophical ontology. H.-F. Weiss is of the opinion that historically orientated Jewish thought had no interest in developing a theory of the origin of the world in the sense of the cosmological questions asked by the Greek philosophers; it was enough to take up particular cases of direct attack on the absolute creative action of God. With Philo, according to Weiss, there is the added apologetic interest that causes him

---

[98] Gen. r. I 9 (I 8.1-6 Theodor-Albeck). The biblical passages to which Gamaliel appeals are Is. 45:7; Ps. 148:4f; Amos 4:13; Prov. 8:24. Cf. G. F. Moore, *Judaism in the First Centuries of the Christian Era* I (Cambridge, Mass.[10]1966), pp. 381f.; H. L. Strack and P. Billerbeck, *Kommentar zum Neuen Testament aus Talmud und Midrash* I ([5]1969) p. 48; Schaller, pp. 130f; Weiss, pp. 89-92, 176f. According to Schaller the philosophical interlocutor could have been a hellenistic Jew.

[99] A similar exposition of Gen. 1:2 is to be found in Philo, prov. I 22; cf. also Gen. r. X 3 (pp. 75, 76ff); on this Weiss, p. 97.

to try and harmonise all contradictions between Jewish and Greek understanding of the world, so far as he was himself aware of them. Weiss also finds the unspeculative Jewish conception of the creation in primitive Christianity; it is only the collision with the radical dualism of gnosticism that brings a change: then, in order to protect the divine omnipotence, Christian theology is compelled to formulate the doctrine of *creatio ex nihilo*. It is not, in Weiss's view, a matter of a cosmological theory but of a theological affirmation that is forced to use cosmological categories.[100] But the reference to unspeculative Jewish thought seems to me problematic. The historical effectiveness of Jewish and Christian thought rests to an essential degree on the fact that it could become philosophical. The doctrine of *creatio ex nihilo* not only represents an attempt to draw a line against the philosophical doctrine of the origin of the world, but is also an interpretation of the biblical idea of creation in philosophical terms. It is of course correct that the debate with gnostic dualism, emphasised by Weiss, was important for the enunciation of the doctrine of *creatio ex nihilo*. But in the later chapters of this enquiry we shall see that the doctrine of *creatio ex nihilo* was developed not only out of contradiction of the creation notions of gnosticism, but just as much in direct debate with the philosophical model of world-formation. Among the critics of the philosophical teaching are also to be found gnostic theologians, among whom Basilides specifically asserts the *creatio ex nihilo*. The question why ancient Jewry did not achieve a clearly formulated and coherently reasoned doctrine of *creatio ex nihilo* has not, in Weiss's view, been satisfactorily answered. A differentiation must be made: Philo is certainly in the highest degree an apologist, but the philosophical concepts are for his thought much more than an agreeable form of langauge. He is so strongly dependent on the Platonist ontology that he cannot think of the creation of the world without the presupposition of a pre-existent material. He has not grasped the biblical conception of creation in its uniqueness, and therefore he cannot undertake the task of mediating it philosophically and fundamentally setting aside the Platonist doctrine of 'first principles'. To rabbinic Judaism the questions raised by Greek ontology were relatively remote. But the chief reason why it did not come to the formation of a specific doctrine of *creatio ex nihilo* is to be seen in the fact that it was not demanded by the text of the Bible. The mention of chaos in Genesis 1:1 could also support the view that an eternal material existed, which God had merely ordered in creating the world. Jewish thought is in its entire essence undogmatic; in the question of the creation

---

[100] Weiss, pp. 167–180.

of the world it did not find itself tied down by the statements in the Bible and so possessed wide room for manoeuvre for highly variant speculations on creation. It was left for the Jewish philosophers of the Middle Ages to develop in controversy with Arabic neoplatonism and Aristotelianism a specific doctrine of *creatio ex nihilo*. But even then this did not achieve sole validity, but the biblical statements about creation continued to be interpreted in various ways.[101]

Christian thought is from the beginning in a different position from Jewish. No longer the Old Testament as such, but Jesus Christ, is understood as the creative revelation of God. The Old Testament writings are applied to Christ, expounded in relation to him, and thereby Christian theology cannot remain 'biblicist' to the same extent as the Jewish. From the interpretation of the Christ-confession stems the dogma of the early Church. Thus the Easter faith forms the starting point of the formation of Christian dogma.[102] The creation faith does not stand at the centre of the history of dogma in antiquity; it was one of those themes which in later centuries, when definitive dogmatic formulations had already been found for the doctrine of the Trinity and Christology, could still be handled with a certain speculative freedom. But the creation problem was by no means without import for Christian confession and the formation of doctrine. The Christian faith set forth the Old Testament belief in God and creation as its necessary historical background. This is shown in full clarity in the struggle with gnosticism. But faith in Christ prevented a transposition into Greek philosophical ideas as extensive as Philo had provided for the Old Testament. If in Christ the whole truth of God has been made available, then one could no longer simply start from the apparent or actual convergences between what Moses said, and what the great Greek thinkers taught, about God, man and the world; but now the philosophical questions themselves must be stated anew in the light of the Christian confession. From the beginning, therefore, Christianity – in a similar missionary situation to hellenistic Judaism – had to debate with philosophy in an altogether more critical way than did the latter. In defence of the biblical creation-faith against its relativisation through gnosticism and in the contemporaneous critical debate with the Greek idea of world-formation – when philosophical cosmology was over and over again seen as the source of gnostic teachings – the insight gained ground in the Church towards the

---

[101] H. Simon, 'Weltschöpfung und Weltewigkeit in der jüdischen Tradition', *Kairos* N.F. 14 (1972), pp. 22–35; cf. also Weiss, pp. 75ff.

[102] Cf. G. Kretschmar 'Wahrheit als Dogma – die alte Kirche', in H.-R. Müller-Schwefe, *Was ist Wahrheit?* (1965), pp. 94–120.

end of the second century that the unity and absolute creativity of God were only safeguarded if his creation was understood as *creatio ex nihilo*.

II. World-creation in early Christianity

Primitive Christianity confesses God in the Old Testament sense as the free and almighty creator. The belief in creation is nowhere in the New Testament weakened or shaken. What the New Testament statements about the creation intend is quite legitimately interchangeable with the idea of *creatio ex nihilo*.[103] But at the same time it must be noted that the 'How' of the creation did not yet pose a problem for primitive Christianity; therefore nowhere in the New Testament is the doctrine of *creatio ex nihilo* explicitly developed as a cosmological theory.[104] The controversy with Greek teaching about the formation of the world, which first made it necessary for Christian theology to think through its own understanding of creation and to reach its conceptual formulation in the proposition of creation out of nothing, still lay beyond the horizon when the earliest Christians talked of creation. Until the beginning of the second century there was for Christian thought no alternative to the elementary confession that God created heaven and earth.[105] Only through

---

[103] Cf. Foerster, p. 1028.

[104] The difference between the sense of the New Testament statements, as it is disclosed to present-day theological consciousness, and the problems with which their compilers were directly confronted, is to a large extent unheeded. Thus D. E. Whiteley, *The Theology of St Paul* (Oxford, 1970), p. 18, infers from Col. 1:16 that Paul, with the statement 'All things were created by God in Christ', meant to exclude the idea of a pre-existent matter. Bultmann, *Das Evangelium des Johannes* (1968), p. 20 (ET p. 37), remarks on John 1:3: 'Thus it is emphatically said that everything without exception was created through the Logos; but reflection on the How and the When is totally lacking. The ἐγένετο is a mere expression of the idea of creation and excludes the idea of emanation as much as it does the idea of an original duality of light and darkness and that of the world originating in a tragic collision of those two powers. Also excluded is the Greek view that seeks to comprehend the world from the correlation of form and matter; the creation is not the ordering of a chaotic material but the καταβολὴ κόσμου (17.24), creatio ex nihilo.' Both interpretations are basically correct, but they consider the statements in the text from the standpoint of questions which did not yet exist in this form for Paul and John.

[105] To this extent the New Testament understanding of the creation does not differ from that of the Old Testament, in respect of which C. Westermann declares *Genesis I-11* (1974), p. 59: 'The createdness of the world and of mankind was always something pre-supposed or already given, a presupposition which stood completely beyond the possibility of any alternative between believing it or not. An understanding of existence or of the world which was not based on the createdness of the world and of mankind, was not yet conceivable.' Cf. also W. Elstester, 'Schöpfungsoffenbarung und natürliche Theologie im frühen Christentum', NTS 3 (1956/57), pp. 93–114.

The Problem of the Creation of the World in Hellenistic Judaism 27

gnosticism did belief in creation become a theological problem, and out of the encounter with philosophical metaphysics arose the necessity of formulating conceptually the freedom and the unconditioned character of God's creative activity.

The passages repeatedly quoted as New Testament witnesses for the idea of *creatio ex nihilo* are Romans 4:17, where Paul says that God 'calls into being the things that are not', and Hebrews 11:3, where it says that 'the visible came forth from the invisible'. But these formulations fit in with the statements of hellenistic Judaism – already known to us – about the creation of non-being, or out of non-being, and mean, no more than those, to give expression to creation out of nothing, in the strict sense, as a contradiction in principle of the doctrine of world-formation.[106] Also when in the next century Hermas, in turns of phrase that sound formal, says that God has created being out of nothing, he still stands in the tradition of this Jewish way of talking.[107] Only when advanced reflection had recognised the divine creation as *creatio ex nihilo*, were the sayings of Hermas also understood in that sense and taken as welcome witness to the doctrine of creation out of nothing.[108]

It is not possible, nor is it necessary, to give within the scope of this enquiry a comprehensive exposition of the primitive Christian understanding of creation. I limit myself to a few indications, the purpose of which is mainly to make clear the distinction between the statements of the primitive Christian authors and the new problems that were posed in the second century.[109] For primitive Christianity God's creation is action in history. There is neither reflection on the relation of God's creative activity to the

---

[106] Cf. the commentaries and Weiss pp. 139ff. on Rom. 4:17; also K. L. Schmidt, art. καλέω, *ThW* III (1938), p. 491; H. Schwantes, *Schöpfung der Endzeit* (1963), pp. 15–17; on Heb. 11:3 K. Haacker, 'Creatio ex auditu', *ZNW* 60 (1969), pp. 279–281 and Schmuttermayr, pp. 223f. On 1 Cor. 1:28 see n. 114 below.

[107] 1.6 (viz. I 1–6): κτίσας ἐκ τοῦ μὴ ὄντος τὰ ὄντα. 26.1 (mand. I, 1): ποιήσας ἐκ τοῦ μὴ ὄντος εἰς τὸ εἶναι τὰ πάντα. Cf. M. Dibelius, 'Der Hirt des Hermas', in *Die apostolische Väter* IV (HNT Supplementary Volume II, 1923), pp. 433f., 497f. On the creation of man out of nothing, 2 Clem. 1:8; on this Weiss p. 143.

[108] The first reference of this kind from mand. I, 1 (26.1), is found in Irenaeus, Haer. IV, 20.2. The later quotations are collected in the edition of O. von Gebhardt and Harnack: O. von Gebhardt, A. Harnack and T. Zahn, *Patrum Apostolicorum Opera* III (1877), p. 70; cf. also Chadwick, 'The New Edition of Hermas', JThS n.s. 8 (1957), pp. 274–280.

[109] From the literature mention may be made of: Foerster (n. 31 above); G. Lindeskog, *Studien zum neutestamentlichen Schöpfungsgedanken* I (Uppsala-Weisbaden, 1952); O. Cullmann, 'Die Schöpfung im Neuen Testament' in *Ex auditu verbi* Festschrift for G. C. Berkouwer (Kampen, 1965), pp. 56–72; K. H. Schelkle, *Theologie des Neuen Testaments* I (1968), pp. 13ff.; A. Vögtle, *Das neue Testament und die Zukunft des Kosmos* (1970).

ordering of 'nature' and the cosmos, nor is the creation isolated from God's work of salvation. It is the presupposition and at the same time the beginning of salvation history. For this way of looking at things, it is self-evident that mankind is seen as the goal and centre-point of the creation and that cosmology as such was never made an independent theme. The dimensions of nature and of history do not yet fall apart.

Above all it is to be seen in Paul how the salvation-event is understood as a creative act of God. The faith of Abraham, which was reckoned to him as righteousness, was directed by God, who makes the dead live and calls into being the things that are not.[110] God's creative might sustains his promises.[111] The primitive Christian apocalyptic expects a new heaven and a new earth at the end of the ages.[112] For Paul the new creation is already present. The proclamation of the Gospel, which enlightens the hearts of believers, corresponds in its effect to the creation of light on the first day of creation,[113] and the Christians who lead a new life through the Spirit are themselves 'new creation'.[114]

Faith in Christ has immediate consequences for the understanding of creation. From the ascension of Christ there follows his pre-existence and his decisive participation in the creation. It is not the question of the principle of the cosmos that forms the starting-point for the assertions of pre-existence, but these 'sprang from christological reflection which was enquiring about the ultimate origin of the Christ-event and the ascension to be divine messianic Lord contrasting most strongly with the earthly life ending in death'.[115] The thought that Christ was the pre-existent agent of creation presupposes the Jewish speculations on Wisdom and the Logos,[116] but the primitive Christian conception of the agent of creation lacks the philosophical features particularly characteristic of Philo's Logos-idea.

---

[110] Rom. 4:17.

[111] Rom. 4:17ff. I decline here to enter into controversy with the recent discussion about the relationship of justification and creation in Paul.

[112] Rev. 21:1ff.; 2 Pet. 3:12f.

[113] 2 Cor. 4:6.

[114] Gal. 6:15; 2 Cor. 5:17; cf. Col. 3:10; Eph. 2:10, 15; 4:24. It is open to question whether Paul in his statement in 1 Cor. 1:28, about the choice of things that are not was taking up the cosmological terminology and applying it to the idea of the new creation: cf. H. Conzelmann, *Der erste Brief an die Korinther* (1969), p. 67, n. 23 (ET p. 51, n. 23).

[115] Vögtle, p. 22.

[116] Cf. H. Hegermann, *Die Vorstellung vom Schöpfungsmittler im hellenistischen Judentum und Urchristentum* (1961); Weiss, pp. 305ff.; G. Schneider, 'Präexistenz Christi. Der Ursprung einer neutestamentlichen Vorstellung und das Problem ihrer Auslegung' in *Neues Testament und Kirche* Festschrift for R. Schnackenburg (1974), pp. 399–412.

The Problem of the Creation of the World in Hellenistic Judaism 29

Neither is the pre-existent Christ the bearer of the Ideas, nor is he thought of as a subordinate hypostasis whose function it is to bridge the gap between the transcendental God and the world.[117] The goal of the New Testament statements about Christ as the agent of creation is much more to show that the whole creation is dependent on Christ and subordinate to him, who himself stands wholly at God's side. Only in the later controversies with philosophical ontology did the Johannine Logos-conception emerge as a powerful connecting point for a Platonising interpretation of the New Testament message of Christ.[118]

The proclamation of the one God, who created the world and sustains it in his goodness and wisdom, held its place in the mission preaching directed to the heathen by early Christianity.[119] Over against the polytheism of the hellenistic world the monotheistic preaching of God the creator was a necessary preparation for the message of Christ. Language and imagery were adapted to the hellenistic audience, for which an example was provided by the mission preaching and apologetics of the hellenistic synagogue.[120] But the limits of the impact on the hearers are clearly visible: God is indeed proclaimed as the creator, but no attempt is made to base the belief in Creation on philosophical arguments in the style of the Apologists of the second century.[121] The bearers of the early Christian mission were, of course, aware of the difficulties which their proclamation to the heathen presented, but they still did not seek for themselves philosophical justification for their belief. The biblical presentation of the Almighty God who

---

[117] W. L. Knox, *St Paul and the Church of the Gentiles* (Cambridge, 1961), p. 159, interprets Col. 1:15–20 too platonically when he calls the pre-existent Christ, with reference to Timaeus 20C and Philo, opif. 17, 'the divine pattern of the world in which all things were potentially present before they were created in a material form'; cf. the cautious analysis by E. Lohse, *Die Briefe an die Kolosser und an Philemon*, pp. 77f. (ET pp. 41ff.).

[118] Cf. Plotinus's disciple Amelius on the Prologue to St John's Gospel in Eusebius, praep. ev. XI 19.1; the utterance of an unknown Platonist in Augustine, civ. dei X 29; and the remarks of Augustine, conf. VII 9.13f; on this Dörrie, 'Une exégése néo-platonicienne du prologue de l'Evangile de saint Jean', in *Epektasis* Festschrift for J. Daniélou (Paris, 1972), pp. 75–87.

[119] Acts 14:15ff.; 17:24ff. In the summary account of the content of the mission preaching offered by 1 Thess. 1:9 and Heb. 6:1, only belief in the true God is mentioned and the creation is not specifically brought out. On the form of the mission preaching cf. U. Wilckens, *Die Missionsreden der Apostelgeschichte* (^{3}1974), pp. 72–91.

[120] Here reference should be made above all to the copious literature on the Areopagus speech, from which I single out: M. Dibelius, 'Paulus auf dem Areopag', *Aufsätze zur Apostelgeschichte* (^{5}1968), pp. 29–70; Pohlenz, *Paulus und die Stoa*; Nauck (n. 7 above); B. Gärtner, *The Areopagus Speech and Natural Revelation* (Uppsala, 1955); H. Conzelmann, 'Theologie als Schriftauslegung' (Collected Essays, 1974), pp. 91–105.

[121] Conzelmann, *Die Apostelgeschichte* (^{2}1972), p. 104 (ET pp. 147ff.).

created the world and continued to work in history as creator, possessed for early Christianity an overwhelming self-evidence and was not perceived as a metaphysical problem. This new question first concerned the theologians of the second century, deeply rooted in philosophical thinking, and wanting consciously to understand the truth of Christianity as the truth of philosophy.

If one turns to the Christian literature of the expiring first century and the first decades of the second, there is no further development of any weight in creation doctrine to be taken into account, although we are approaching the time of the great struggle against gnosticism. The First Letter of Clement can be seen as the basis of the appeal, addressed to the Church at Corinth along with a lot of other arguments, to bring in the harmony and order of the cosmos, an appeal which is broadly sketched in half biblical and half Stoic language.[122] And the appeal to good works is underlined by the reference to God, who decked himself with the good works of the creation and rejoiced over them. This is drawn out more precisely in a stoicizing paraphrase of the biblical creation story, which is dependent very likely on hellenistic-Jewish traditions.[123] No doubt such arguing from creation in a paraenetical context, beside which the reference to Christ retreats into the background and is no longer conceived in its fundamental sense for all precepts and order in the Church, means a clear shift of theological accent as compared with the older Christian views.[124] But in Clement's discussions, in spite of their hellenistic language, there is no sign of a deeper appreciation of the philosophical problem of the creation idea. For Irenaeus the writing was a welcome help in his theological effort to demonstrate against gnosticism that the God of the Old Testament was the one almighty creator. In the context of his review of tradition he brings in the Letter as a document which is older than the teaching of the heretics and which witnesses to the unanimous tradition of the Church that the God of the Old Testament is the Father of Jesus Christ.[125] W. Bauer based on Irenaeus his attempt to show that the First Letter of Clement was a campaign document against a Christianity tainted with gnosticism, whose statements on creation possessed a current barb.[126] But

---

[122] 1 Clem. 19:2 – 20:12. On the question of stoic influence cf. Knopf pp. 76ff.; H. Fuchs, *Augustin und der antike Friedensgedanke* (1965), pp. 18–105 and – especially restrained – W. C. van Unnik, 'Is 1 Clement 20 purely Stoic?' *Vig. Chr.* 4 (1950), pp. 181–189.

[123] 1 Clem. 33; cf. Nauck, pp. 16–20.

[124] Cf. on this the Hamburg dissertation of H. U. Minke, *Die Schöpfung in der frühchristlichen Verkundigung nach dem ersten Clemensbrief und der Areopagrede* (1966).

[125] Haer. III 3.3.

[126] *Rechtgläubigkeit und Ketzerei im ältesten Christentum* (1964), pp. 106–108 (ET pp. 94–104).

The Problem of the Creation of the World in Hellenistic Judaism

the utterances of Irenaeus scarcely justify the conclusion that the Letter had such an anti-gnostic bearing. What we have here is a bringing up to date, as Irenaeus offers in a similar way for St John's Gospel, which he sees as a broadsheet against the gnostic Cerinthus and the Nicolaitans.[127] It is, of course, not to be fully ruled out that in the Corinthian controversies, with which the First Letter of Clement was intended to grapple, theological contradictions have also played a part,[128] but should that have been the case it must be immediately obvious that Clement refused to go into the particular questions at issue, and restricted himself to the protection of formal church order.

Beginnings of anti-heretical polemic

It is even more surprising that well into the second century, writings which contain direct polemic against the growing gnostic movement do not go thoroughly into the question of creation either. The sole exception is the Epistle to the Colossians, whose composition by Paul seems to me scarcely open to doubt. Here key words are taken from the cosmological speculation of his gnosticising opponents, and Paul opposes to the reverence advocated by the heretical teachers for the cosmic powers the cosmic importance of Christ as the agent of creation, thus outbidding them.[129] But the creation of the world by one God was not called in question by the Colossian heretics, nor do the angelic principalities and powers whom they reverenced seem to have been portrayed as wholly hostile forces.[130] So Paul merely needed to show that the cosmos has its existence solely from Christ and he has shown himself through his act of salvation as the Universal Redeemer and Lord, to whom principalities and powers are subject.[131]

Things are quite different in the Pastoral Epistles. If an attempt is made to determine their historical setting and the reason for their composition, there is much to support the view that they are an effort, made in the middle of the open gnostic crisis of the second century, to interpret Paul correctly

---

[127] Haer. III 11.1.

[128] But cf. the thought expressed against such an explanation of the conflict in H. von Campenhausen, *Kirchliches Amt und geistliche Vollmacht in den ersten drei Jahrhunderten* (1963), p. 94 (ET p. 87).

[129] This view, that Paul enters into the thinking of his opponents in order to beat them on their own ground is especially emphasised by Chadwick, "'All things to all men' (1 Cor. 9.22)', NTS I (1954–55), pp. 261–275, pp. 270ff.

[130] Cf. Lohse, *Die Briefe an die Kolosser und an Philemon*, p. 187 (ET p. 128). In view of the absence of a particular cosmological dualism, Hegermann, pp. 161ff., characterises the false teachers not as gnostics but as promoters of hellenistic-Jewish heretical ideas.

[131] 1:16f.; 2:8–23; 3:1–4; cf. Lohse, p. 191 (ET p. 129).

and so to save him for the Church.[132] In view of the fragmentary state of the tradition coming down from the first half of the second century, such a historical placing of the letters must remain a hypothesis, and it would also be possible to place them a few decades earlier.[133] But the further back in time one takes the Pastoral Epistles, the more unaccountable it becomes why Marcion left them out of his canon.[134] Fortunately we do not need to solve the dating problem here, but it does concern us by what manner of means the Pastoral Epistles further the controversy with heresy.[135] Characteristic is the failure to state objectively the assertions of their opponents. This is, to be sure, the deliberate style of polemic.[136] The doctrine of the opponents is rejected in advance as false and demonic.[137] They have only fruitless verbal conflicts and speculations to offer, and for them one must leave the Way.[138] Just as sweepingly is the true, 'healthy' doctrine set against heresy.[139] Thus controversy over content is deliberately avoided. We get somewhat nearer to the ascetic demands and prohibitions of the false teachers,[140] when we hear that they held that the resurrection had already taken place,[141] and that they were distinguished as teachers of the Law and in contact with Judaism.[142] But from these bald assertions one must not conclude definitely that no more highly developed gnosticism was being opposed, especially if the flat rejection of the error was shown to be a matter of style like the moral denigration of their exponents.[143]

---

[132] Bauer, *Rechtgläubigkeit*, pp. 225–230 (ET p. 226); Campenhausen, 'Polykarp von Smyrna und die Pastoralbriefe', in *Aus der Früzeit de Christentums. Studien zur Kirchengeschichte des ersten und zweiten Jahrhunderts* (1963), pp. 197–252; id., *Die Entstehung der christlichen Bibel* (1968), pp. 212f.

[133] The late dating has often been disputed; cf. the thoughtful discussion of the question of author and date in the commentary by N. Brox, *Die Pastoralbriefe* (1969), pp. 9ff., who himself puts the composition at around the year 100 (p. 38).

[134] Bauer, *Rechtgläubigkeit*, pp. 225–227 (ET p. 223); Campenhausen, 'Polykarp', pp. 204–206; cf. Brox, p. 28.

[135] On this Brox, pp. 39–42.

[136] Thus M. Dibelius and H. Conzelmann, *Die Pastoralbriefe* (⁴1966), p. 2 (ET Philadelphia 1972, p. 2).

[137] 1 Tim. 1:4–6; 4:1; 2 Tim. 2:16; 3:9; Tit. 3:9; cf. 1 Tim. 1:19f.

[138] 1 Tim. 6:4, 20f.; 2 Tim. 2:14, 23–25; Tit. 3:9.

[139] 1 Tim. 1:10; 4:6f, 16; 6:3f; 2 Tim. 4:3–5; Tit. 2:1.

[140] 1 Tim. 4:3–8; Tit. 1:14f.

[141] 2 Tim. 2:18; cf. Brox, pp. 36f.

[142] 1 Tim. 1:6f.; Tit. 1:10, 14.

[143] For the moral inadequacies of the false teachers, see 1 Tim. 6:3–5; 2 Tim. 3:1ff.; Tit. 1:10–16. Brox, pp. 31–38, comes to the conclusion that the heresy opposed in the Pastoral Epistles was an early Jewish-Christian gnosticism which was still perfectly possible in the first century, but for the interpretation of the anti-heretical statements, however, he invariably has to adduce information on the gnosticism of the second century.

The Problem of the Creation of the World in Hellenistic Judaism 33

By the repeatedly mentioned myths and genealogies which play a part in the thought of the false teachers speculation about aeons may already be meant,[144] and it is not to be ruled out that the warning about the antitheses of the false gnosis in the First Epistle to Timothy is aimed at the Marcionite catchword.[145] To be sure, the polemic of the epistle cannot be directed exclusively against Marcion, the reproaches are not sufficiently explicit for that; more generally all the forms of the gnostic heresy are meant to be attacked.[146] The charge of judaising brought against the false teachers could become, on the contrary, a polemical topic.[147] For us it is in any case decisive that the writer of the Pastoral Epistles did not enter more closely into the cosmology of his opponents and nowhere raised the problem of the creation of the world. Only the demand for asceticism in diet is backed up by express recourse to creation: God created food so that it might be enjoyed with thanksgiving; for everything that God created is good.[148]

Related in various ways to the Pastoral Epistles, the Letter of Polycarp of Smyrna to the Philippians describes the death of Ignatius of Antioch, and so must have been composed at the earliest in the twenties of the second century; but the main part of the Letter may well have originated decades later.[149] In the paraenetic writing Polycarp warns of heretical views, and indeed it looks as if he is dealing with the teaching of Marcion.[150] Polycarp

[144] 1 Tim. 1:4; 4:6f; 2 Tim. 4:3–5; Tit. 1:14; 3:9; cf. Brox, pp. 35f. Dibelius and Conzelmann, pp. 14f., are still not thinking of an articulated cosmological speculation (ET pp. 15ff, n. 136 above).

[145] 1 Tim. 6:20; cf. Campenhausen, 'Polykarp', pp. 205f; otherwise Dibelius and Conzelmann, p. 70 (ET p. 92).

[146] Campenhausen, 'Polykarp', p. 205, n. 24: 'The Pastoral Epistles are in their significant indefiniteness already a kind of ἔλεγχος of all conceivable heresies.'

[147] Cf. Bauer, Rechtgläubigkeit pp. 92ff. (ET p. 88). Also the opponents whom Ignatius confronts in the epistle to the Magnesians and the epistle to the Philadelphians seem to be labelled 'Judaists' for polemical reasons only: E. Molland, 'The heretics combatted by Ignatius of Antioch', JEH 5 (1954), pp. 1–6. L. Goppelt, Die apostolische und nachapostolische Zeit (1966), p. 70, puts the contrary view that it is precisely the Jewish tone of the errors refuted in the Pastoral Epistles that assigns them to the end of the Pauline period. Also for Brox, pp. 33f., the Jewish or Jewish-Christian features are part of the image of the heresy being opposed.

[148] 1 Tim. 4:3f.

[149] Harnack, Geschichte der altchristlichen Literatur II 1 (²1958), pp. 381–388. The hypothesis of division put forward by P. N. Harrison, Polycarp's Two Epistles to the Philippians (Cambridge, 1936), according to which chapters 13 and 14 comprise a note written in the lifetime of Ignatius, while the detailed letter covering chapters 1–12 was composed at a much later date, does not solve the dating problem completely.

[150] 6.3 – 7.2: cf. Harrison, pp.172–206; Campenhausen, 'Polykarp', p. 238; and, with an accumulation of not always convicing arguments P. Meinhold, art. 'Polykarpos von Smyrna'

turns against a radical docetic christology, by which the 'witness of the cross' is brought to nought, against the distortion of the Lord's words and the denial of resurrection and judgment. All this fits Marcion excellently. Yet in a striking way the dualism between creator-God and redeemer-God remains unmentioned; and it is precisely the blasphemy against the creator which for all later opponents of Marcion counts as his gravest heresy.[151] P. N. Harrison has therefore suggested that Polycarp was combatting an early stage of the theology of Marcion, who at first had held fast to the unity of God and only in Rome, under the influence of the gnostic Cerdo developed his doctrine of two Gods.[152] But for that kind of reconstruction of Marcion's intellectual development there is no evidence whatever. If Polycarp in his Letter is controverting Marcionite doctrine, we must conclude that he knew it in its mature form. One can only accept that systematic refutation does not matter to him: he sees faith in Christ threatened by the heresy at its central point and he counters this threat with his confessional-style affirmations. Polycarp is said to have dismissed Marcion, who – probably when still in Asia Minor – wanted to be recognised by him as the 'first-born of Satan'[153] and when he later stayed at Rome under Anicetus, he reputedly won back numerous Marcionites to the Catholic Church.[154] The main Letter may stem from the time of this conflict, but we cannot be sure of this.[155] But in any case Polycarp's silence on the creation problem shows that this was not yet, in the first half of the second century, a central theme of controversy with the false teachers.

The *Epistula apostolorum* also, which dates from about the middle of the second century, turns against gnostic teachers – Simon and Cerinthus are named as prototype exponents of the heresy[156] – but gives no more exact an

PW 21/2 (1962) 1685–1687. Finally, K. Beyschlag, *Simon Magus und die christliche Gnosis* (1974), p. 194, again argues against the antimarcionite interpretation, and assumes that Polycarp was writing 'against the radical docetism also opposed in the Johannine and Ignatian writings'.

[151] Thus already Justin, apol. I 26.5; apocryphal letter of the Corinthians to Paul 11–15.
[152] Harrison, pp. 183ff.
[153] Irenaeus, haer III 3.4 = Eusebius, H.E. IV 14.7; Polycarp also uses the expression in his letter: 7.1. Cf. from a later period Ephraem, hymn c. haer. 22.17: 'Marcion is the first thorn – the first-born of the thicket of sin – the weed that was the first to sprout'; and Pseudo Ignatius, Trall. 9.1, where Simon Magus is described as the 'first-born of Satan'.
[154] Irenaeus, haer. III 3.4 = Eusebius, H.E. IV 14.5.
[155] Harnack, *Marcion, das Evangelium vom fremden Gott* ([2]1924), p. 5*, n. 4, disputed, because the doctrine of two Gods and the rejection of the Old Testament are not mentioned, that Phil. 5f. was aimed at Marcion; but this kind of polemic, lacking in sharpness, is characteristic of the time.
[156] 1 (12); 7 (18); cf. Beyschlag, p. 73.

The Problem of the Creation of the World in Hellenistic Judaism 35

account of the views that are opposed, and enters into no serious theological debate with them.[157] The anti-gnostic emphasis is likewise clear in this writing: the penetrating description of the creative acts of God, which stands right at the beginning[158] and the use for God of the terms 'Ruler of the whole world'[159] and 'Father of all'[160] may well be directly aimed at the gnostic denigration of the creator God.[161] A topical purpose is surely also in mind in the 'Apology of Paul', which the writing contains.[162] The apocryphal letter of the apostle shows how the conflict with the fully developed gnostic movement from now on compelled the protection of all the essential content of the church tradition.

The state of the question in the first half of the second century
The statements on the creation of the world which we still possess from the time before Justin Martyr by authors who are not declared gnostics, only serve to make it clear that the question of the origin of the cosmos had not yet become a problem. A few examples may illustrate this. According to a communication by Anastasius Sinaites in his Hexaemeron commentary, Papias held – as did also the Alexandrians Pantaenus, Clement and

---

[157] 7 (18) says, in the Coptic version, of the false teachers 'For they trade in the words and the deed, i.e. Jesus Christ' (cf. Pol. Phil. 7.1); to this corresponds in the Ethiopic version: '... who in reality cause those to turn away who believe in the true word and in the deed i.e. Jesus Christ'. 29 (40) shows a threat put in the mouth of Christ against those 'who have sinned against my bidding, who teach others to take away or to add on, and who for their own glory work to make those turn away who really believe in me' (Ethiopic; Coptic similar); cf. further 60 (61); 37 (48).
[158] 3 (124) with echoes of Gen. 1.
[159] 3 (14); 5 (16).
[160] 13 (24).
[161] M. Hornschuh, *Studien zur Epistula Apostolorum* (1965), pp. 94f. says that the compiler puts 'at the beginning of the whole the hymnic confession of the Creator God, which turns into a confession of the saving God' only because his gnostic opponents divide the Creator from the Redeemer.
[162] 31 (42)f.; on this Campenhausen, *Die Entstehung der christlichen Bibel*, p. 211 (ET p. 217). That the opponents were Basilidians, as Hornschuh, pp. 86f., 94 suggests, seems to me highly unlikely. This identification, problematic in itself, would only be possible on the presupposition that the Epistula apostolorum originated in Egypt, for which Hornschuh pp. 99ff., makes a case. H. Lietzmann, *Geschichte der alten Kirche* II (1936), p. 87 (ET p. 93) also suggests an Egyptian origin, while the discoverer of the document, C. Schmidt, thought of Asia Minor as its place of origin: *Gespräche Jesu mit seinen Jungern nach der Auferstehung* (1919), pp. 364ff. That it came from Asia is maintained on good grounds by G. Kretschmar, *Studien zur frühchristlichen Trinitätstheologie* (1956), pp. 50f.; cf. also the observations of R. Staats, 'Die törichten Jungfrauen von Mt. 25 in gnostischer und antignostischer Literatur', in W. Eltester, *Christentum und Gnosis* (1969), pp. 98–115, pp. 104f.

Creatio Ex Nihilo

Ammonius – that the whole six days of creation pointed to Christ and the Church.[163] Clearly he was dependent on a widespread theological tradition in which Christ and the pre-existent Church, equated with Wisdom, were taken together,[164] but how Papias set out his thesis in detail and how he accounted for the literal meaning of the creation story, we do not know.[165] We can scarcely conclude from the notice of Anastasius that Papias wrote a whole commentary on the creation story;[166] perhaps it was only a matter of an occasional statement.[167]

Stemming from Syria, the Odes of Solomon, the theology of which is archaic rather than specifically gnostic,[168] do not go beyond the scope of the creation statements already known to us, which is hardly at all surprising in a text of such a strong Jewish-Christian character. Ode 16 praises the creator in Old Testament phraseology, and there is no suggestion to be found of a gnostic belittling or denigration of the creation.[169] It is held, without limitation, that God made everything.[170] Particular thoughts are reminiscent of popular philosophic ideas: God does not need men, but men need him;[171] in God there is no envy;[172] the world above is the original model for

---

[163] Contempl. anag. in Hexaem. I (PG 89, 860C) = fr. 6 Funk-Bihlm; this presumably refers to the Ammonius mentioned in Eusebius, H.E. VI 19.10; ep. ad Carp.

[164] Kretschmar, *Studien*, pp. 54–56.

[165] Papias had perhaps already had a hostile encounter with Marcion: fr. 13 Funk-Bihlm; cf. Harnack, *Marcion*, pp. 11*–14*.

[166] Thus correctly F. E. Robbins, *The Hexaemeral Literature. A study of the Greek and Latin Commentaries on Genesis* (Chicago, 1912), p. 36; E. Testa, 'La creazione del mondo nel pensiero dei SS. Padri', *Studii Biblici franciscani* liber annuus 16 (1965–66), pp. 5–68, pp. 5f. speaks again of the commentaries of Papias and Pantaenus.

[167] P. Nautin, 'Pantène', in *Tome commémoratif du millénaire de la bibliothèque Patriarcale d'Alexandrie* (Alexandria, 1953), pp. 145–152, p. 149 suggests that Anastasius took his statement about the Genesis-exegesis of Pantaenus from the Hypotyposen of Clement of Alexandria; did he find here also an allusion to Papias?

[168] Thus Chadwick, 'Some Reflections on the Character and Theology of the Odes of Solomon', in *Kyriakon* I Festschrift for J. Quasten (1970), pp. 266–270; A. Adam, *Lehrbuch der Dogmengeschichte* (²1970), pp. 142–146 attributes the Odes to an early Jewish-Christian gnosticism.

[169] 16.10ff.; cf. Epist. apost. 3.

[170] 4.15; cf. 4.7ff.; 7.8f., 11f.

[171] 4.9; cf. Dibelius, *Paulus auf dem Areopag*, pp. 42ff.; Conzelmann, *Die Apostelgeschichte*, pp. 98f. on Acts 17:25 (ET p. 142).

[172] 3.6; 7.3; 11.6; 17.12; 20.7; 23.4; cf. Plato, Tim. 29E. For Christian literature the absence of envy on God's part signifies the unconditional certainty of his pledge of salvation, as von Unnik has shown in a study based on the evidence of the Ode of Solomon 'De ἀφθονία van God in de oudchristelijke literatur', *Medelingen Nederl. Akad. Wetesch.* N. R. 35/2 (Amsterdam, 1973).

The Problem of the Creation of the World in Hellenistic Judaism 37

the world below.[173] Yet in their whole essence the Odes are unphilosophical. Their thought and diction are poetically descriptive, not speculative.

In the Gospel of Peter, a writing which represents for us the transition from early Christian mission preaching to specifically apologetic literature, it is said of God that 'he made the beginning of everything and that he has power over the end'. God is described with the negative predicates of philosophical theologians: he is without needs, but everything needs him and is there for his sake, and he has created everything through the Word of his power.[174] That is the popular philosophical language of the hellenistic synagogue.[175] But as far as the extant fragments allow us to judge, the creation was in the Gospel of Peter still not considered a philosophical problem.

The statements of non-gnostic theologians about the creation of the world offer, until the first decades of the second century, a uniform picture. The question of the possibility of the cosmos coming into being and the question of the 'How' of the creation process are not posed, not even under the pressure of the controversy with the growing gnostic movement. This need not surprise us. At a time when there was not yet any normative orthodoxy in the circles of Christian teachers, no doubt wide-ranging cosmological speculations were possible which people were not obliged to regard as unchristian or heretical.[176] In the congregations, on the other hand, the speculations of esoteric circles about the world and creation had

---

[173] 34.4f. But this very idea is also Jewish; cf. Adam I, p. 143; Harnack, *Ein jüdisch-christliches Psalmbuch aus dem ersten Jahrhundert* (1910), p. 66, refers to Acta Phil. 140 (34), van Unnik, 'A Note on Ode of Solomon 34, 4', JThS 37 (1936), pp. 172–175 on the similar-sounding passage Act. Petr. cum Sim. 38 (1936) (Mart. Petri 9), perhaps an agraphon, as a possible example; that would point to a wholly unplatonic idea.

[174] Clement of Alexandria, strom VI 39.2f. (= fr. 2a Dobschütz). In strom. VI 58.1 Clement notes that Peter by ἀρχή in connection with Gen. 1:1 means Christ, but this is surely an interpretation made by Clement, which does not correspond to the sense of the words; cf. E. v. Dobschütz, *Das Kerygma Petri* (1893), p. 19; Nautin, 'Les Citations de la "Prédication de Pierre" dans Clément d'Alexandrie, strom. VI 5, 39–41', JThS n.s. 25 (1974), pp. 98–105, pp. 101f. On the significance of 'In the beginning' in Gen. 1:1 for Christ cf. Harnack, *Die Altercatio Simonis Judaei et Theophili Christiani* (1883), pp. 130–134. The suggestion of C. F. Burney, 'Christ as the ARXH of Creation', JThS 27 (1926), pp. 160–177, that there is already in Col. 1:16–18 an exposition of the Hebrew b're'šît, is improbable, cf. Lohse, *Die Briefe an die Kolosser und Philemon*, p. 85, n. 1 (ET p. 46, n. 101).

[175] Cf. Dibelius, *Der Hirt des Hermas*, p. 498; Maria Grazia Mara, 'Il Kerygma Petrou', in *Studi in onore di Alberto Pincherle = Studi e materiali di storia delle religioni* 38 (1967), pp. 314–334), pp. 333f.; R. M. Grant, *The Early Christian Doctrine of God* (Charlottesville 1966), pp. 15f.

[176] On the body of Christian teachers, cf. Campenhausen, *Kirchliches Amt*, pp. 210ff. (ET pp. 192ff.).

probably scarcely become known. And even where people had noticed the deviating views, there was at first a lack of factual criteria and units of measurement by which they could be clearly and conclusively refuted. This accounts for the diffuse and imprecise character of the older anti-heretical polemic. The alien doctrines were dismissed as an expression of moral degeneration; they were rated as an eschatological phenomenon and it was thought sufficient for refuting them to refer to the firmly grounded, generally known and accepted tradition. The first great theological debate, in which the unity of the Church was seen to be at stake, broke out over the central point of Christian belief, over confession of Christ. Witnesses for this stage of the development are the First and Second Epistles of John and the Ignatian writings, which sharply contest a probably already gnostic docetism and give to the primitive Christian confession of Jesus as the Christ and the Son of God a new anti-heretical turn and stamp.[177] Here in Christology originates the division between orthodoxy and heresy which, as the second century ran its course, was to spread to the other debatable points of the Christian tradition. The anti-gnostic *regula fidei* is the result of this process of definition.

The fixing and ensuring of the tradition and the separation from gnosticism and other heresies was an unavoidable necessity, the further the Church moved in the course of history from her original roots and the wider the yawning gap became between the opinions held within her.[178] The controversy with gnostic cosmology came into play where the stir over the philosophical problems of the creation of the world was linked with adherence to traditional faith: in the circles around those Christian teachers and 'philosophers' who, like Justin, knew themselves to be obliged to uphold church orthodoxy. It is scarcely an accident that the two oldest campaign writings against the heretics that we know were composed by Justin.

---

[177] Cf. Campenhausen, 'Das Bekenntnis im Urchristentum', ZNW 63 (1972), pp. 210–153, pp. 234ff.; Beyschlag, p. 4.
[178] Cf. H.-D. Altendorf, 'Zum Stichwort: Rechtgläubigkeit und Ketzerei im ältesten Christentum', ZKG 80 (1969), pp. 61–74. The origin of the conflict between orthodoxy and heresy is treated from another point of view in M. Elze, 'Häresie und Einheit der Kirche im 2. Jahrhundert', ZThK 71 (1974), pp. 389–409.

2

The Question of the Origin of the World in Christian Gnosticism

Until the fourth decade of the second century the question of the creation of the world was not discussed seriously as a problem by church theologians. To the modern observer it seems almost inconceivable that, at a time when the gnostic movement was reaching its high point, the problems raised by the creation had not become a central issue in the orthodox Christian camp. But we have here a process which is frequently to be observed in history when new questions and new intellectual movements arise: the new is not recognised or grasped as such, its intellectual implications are not for the present to be measured, and the concepts and intellectual resources are lacking to do it justice. The process of taking up the new questionings and of the controversy with them comes about more slowly and hesitatingly, and runs less coherently, than one might have thought possible in retrospect over a long intellectual development.

I. The gnostic approach to the problem

In gnosticism the question of the origin of the world, of the 'Why' and 'How' of the creation, was accepted at once as a pressing problem and acquired the highest theological importance. The motive for this new questioning was not a sudden burst of philosophical interest in the cosmos – although this may have played a contributory role – but the specific gnostic rejection, or at least very negative estimate, of the world. It had to be explained how and to what purpose the cosmos, which is experienced as hostile, faulty and ungodly, came to be. In this sense the question about the creation is posed to the gnostic as the problem of theodicy.[1] The world is seen so negatively that one can no longer attribute its origin to a creative act of the true, the highest God. The gnostic myth teaches that it is to be understood as the work of heavenly beings of lesser rank and limited might, who did not know the true God or rebelled against him. In some gnostic outlines an unformed material principle, sometimes chaos or darkness, is postulated, which in one way or another has a part in the world's origin. But most gnostic theologians are engaged in striving to avoid a dualism of principles. They understand matter and the cosmos as something that has come into being, something secondary, which compared with the heavenly world of light possesses no full reality. The origin of the cosmos is conceived as a disturbance of the original plan, caused by the self-exaltation of the demiurgical powers, and the process of salvation has as its first goal the destruction of the material world. The intellectually significant, philosophically educated gnostics therefore not only rejected, with inner consistency, the doctrine of the eternity of the world but were also decisively opposed to the acceptance of an eternal matter. Only Marcion, who allowed no connection between the highest God and the demiurge, claims for the cosmic realm the pre-existence of matter.[2] Repeatedly church controversial-

---

[1] Ptolemaeus, ad Floram 7, 8–10.
[2] Plotinus is obliged to defend the eternity of the world against the gnostics: Enn. II, 9, 3f.; cf. V 8, 12, 20ff. For the Valentinians matter originated in a process of several stages; it is annihilated, as soon as the Pneumatics have entered the pleroma: see pp. 101ff. below. For the treatise 'The Hypostasis of the Archons' from the Nag Hammadi find (HNC II 4), matter originated but is distinguished from the apparently unoriginate Chaos (94, 9–32). On the other hand the related treatise 'On the Origin of the World' (NHC II 5) urges against the acceptance of an original chaos that this too is originate: 97, 24ff.; cf. A. Böhlig, 'Urzeit und Endzeit in der titellosen Schrift des Codex II von Nag Hammadi Mysterion und Wahrheit', (Collected Essays, 1968), pp. 135–148, pp. 136ff. In the Barbelo-gnostic 'Apocryphon of John' the existence of the 'Chaos of the underworld' seems to be simply presupposed: BG 41, 15; cf. NHC III 17, 19; II 11, 3–6. According to the teaching of the Ophites, of whom Irenaeus gives an account, there existed primaevally under the Holy Spirit the four elements Water, Darkness, Void (ἄβυσσος) and Chaos (Haer. I, 30, 1). So here Gen. 1:2 is referring to an eternal chaotic matter. The 'Docetists' too seem to accept an unoriginate chaos: Hippolytus, ref. VIII, 9, 3. Things are more complicated in the Three-Principle-systems known to us through Hippolytus: the Book of Baruch by the gnostic Justin (ref. V, 26f.) speaks of three uncreated principles of the All, two masculine beings, the 'Good One' and Elohim, the Father of things created, and one feminine being Edem, who is in form half maiden and half snake. Edem represents the earth and, indeed, her human part stands for 'psychic' substance and bestial part for matter (26, 7–9.14), but the idea of the eternity of matter differs from the usual gnostic scheme as follows: the origin of matter and of the world cannot be thought of as the result of a primaeval fall, but evil first originates after the creation when Elohim goes up to heaven (26.14ff.). The cosmos is thus evaluated in an unusually positive way; cf. M. Simonetti 'Note sul libro di Baruch dello

ists point out that the question of the origin of evil is the starting point of heretical errors. In so doing they recognised it as a basic problem for gnostic teaching; only it must be added that for the gnostics the question of evil is ultimately inseparable from the question of the origin of the cosmos.[3]

Likewise we must beware of over-estimating and isolating in the thought of the various more or less syncretistic schools and circles, what seems to us characteristically 'gnostic', the world-denying dualism and the denigration of the creator-God.[4] The distinction between the true God and the demiurge was neither put forward from the beginning nor always given the same radical emphasis; indeed it was rarely advanced controversially against the common Christian tradition, but was treated rather as esoteric knowledge. The great exception was Marcion who directed his frontal attack against the God of the Old Testament; through him were discredited all more subtle attempts to bridge the gap between the highest God and the world through subordinate divine powers. But in the confused theological situation of the thirties and forties of the second century the common ground and the intellectual factors making for unity between the 'gnostic' and the 'church' teachers seemed to prevail. Certainly the great and influential gnostic theologians like Basilides and Valentinus wished consciously and decisively to be Christians. Their doctrine made its appearance as a christocentric theology relying on Paul and John, in which speculation

---

gnostico Giustino', *Vet. Christ.* 6 (1969), pp. 71–89, pp. 82ff. By the Perates the Hyle, the third principle (ref. V, 17, 1) is expressly described as 'the originated' (12, 3). In the case of the third principle as the Naassenes saw it, the 'poured out chaos' (V 7, 9; 10, 2) it is again not clear whether it is thought of as originate or unoriginate. However, the third principle as seen by the Sethians, is certainly unoriginate. This is Darkness (V 19, 2), which is conceived as a 'fearful water' (19, 5f.; 20, 9f.); cf. the 'Paraphrase of Shem' (NHC VII 1, 26–28.36ff.), which is in extensive agreement with Hippolytus's source, and the doctrine of the Nicolaitans, Pseudo-Tertullian, adv. omn. haer. 1, 6; Epiphanius, panar. XXXV 5, 1. A. Orbe, *Estudios Valentinianos* I: 'Hacia la primera teologia de la procesion del verbo' (Rome, 1958), pp. 203–285 seeks to show that all gnosticism, including the Three Principles system, regarded the divine Ground as the only original principle. This thesis cannot be upheld so conclusively. But in any case the idea that matter was not there from the beginning, but originated in the course of the cosmogonic process, was more widespread and can be taken as characteristic of the more highly developed gnosticism (cf. H. Jonas, *Gnosis und spätantiker Geist*, 1964, pp. 328ff. on the 'Syrian-Egyptian' type). For our enquiry it is decisive that the leading Christian gnostics, especially the Valentinians, took matter to be originate. For the teaching of Marcion, which is only conditionally to be included in the scope of gnostic views, see pp. 55ff. below.

[3] Tertullian, praescr. 7, 5; adv. Marc. I 2, 2; Epiphanius, panar. XXIV 6, 1; Eusebius, H.E. V, 27. Confirmation is provided in Ptolemaeus, ad Flor. 7.8f.

[4] We are concerned exclusively with Christian-gnostic theology, and so with 'gnosticism', and we do not go into the debated question of the origin of gnosticism before or outside Christianity.

about aeons was only a construction to help in the solution of 'philosophical' questions like theodicy and the origin of the cosmos.[5] Already in their outward posture gnostic teachers were not to be distinguished from men like Justin, Tatian or Rhodon; they all worked as independent 'philosophers' without official church connections; they gathered a circle of students around them and found in the school their appropriate form of organisation. In the theological terminology of 'gnostics' and 'apologists' correspondences are to be seen which can only be explained by a common tradition of teaching.[6] Indeed from Rome we have various reports which show how ill defined are the fronts there around the middle of the century. Thus the Syrian gnostic Cerdo seems repeatedly to have aroused hostility in the congregation by his teaching, yet without coming to a lasting breach.[7] The assertion of Tertullian that Valentinus had once been a candidate for the Roman episcopal see but that a confessor had been given preferment, after which he resigned from the Church, is problematic and may be a slander typical of anti-heretical polemic.[8] But if the Christian teacher

---

[5] The most impressive example of debate within gnosticism about general Christian problems is afforded by the Letter of the Valentinian Ptolemaeus to Flora: it concerns the correct Christian view of the Old Testament 'law' and finds in the words of Jesus the criterion for its evaluation; the 'system' drops wholly into the background; cf. H. von Campenhausen, *Die Entstehung der Christlichen Bibel* (1968), pp. 98–104 (ET pp. 82–86). Reference should also be made to the Valentinian letter to Rheginos 'On the Resurrection'.

[6] W. C. van Unnik, 'Die Gotteslehre bei Aristides und in gnostischen Schriften', ThZ 17 (1961) 166–174; id., 'The newly discovered "Gospel of Truth" and the New Testament', in F. L. Cross, *The Jung Codex* (London, 1955), pp. 81–129, pp. 101f.; cf. also R. M. Grant, *Gnosticism and Early Christianity* (New York/London, 1966), p. 128.

[7] Irenaeus, haer. III 4, 3 (= Eusebius H.E. IV 11, 1) Tertullian reports similarly about Marcion and Valentinus (praescr. 30, 2). Or should this perhaps be regarded merely as a typical detail of ecclesiastical heretic-portraiture?

[8] Tertullian, adv. Val. 4, 1; Speraverat episcopatum Valentinus, quia et ingenio poterat et eloquio, sed alium ex martyrii praerogativa loci potitum indignatus de ecclesia authenticae regulae abrupit, ut solent animi pro prioratu exciti praesumptione ultionis accendi. The reproach that the later heresiarchs had first contended for appointment as bishops, and had separated from the Church when they were not successful, had been 'From the beginning a favourite form of stereotype for "Church" description of heretics': K. Beyschlag, 'Kallist und Hippolyt', ThZ 20 (1964), pp. 103–124, p. 107. But the first part of Tertullian's communication that a confessor had been preferred to Valentinus rings so true that it may well have been the fact. Only one cannot think of a monarchical bishopric yet existing in the Roman congregation at the time of Valentinus, as Tertullian naturally supposes. The confessor mentioned by Tertullian must, according to Irenaeus, haer. III 3, 3, have been Telesphorus: A. von Harnack, *Geschichte der altchristlichen Literatur* II 1 (²1958), pp. 178f., and in addition, E. Caspar, *Die älteste römische Bischofsliste* (1926, SKG 2/4), p. 225. Whether Valentinus had, at the time of the election of Telesphorus, finally separated from the Church, is open to doubt.

Ptolemaeus, mentioned by Justin, is, following Harnack's brilliant suggestion, identical with the Valentinian of the same name, then he died as a martyr of the Roman congregation.[9] Only the exclusion of Marcion from the congregation in 144 and his consequent founding of a church seems to have set efforts in motion in Rome to fence the Church off from heretical tendencies: now the controversy of Justin with the heresies is about to set in. But the theology of Tatian still contains many features of gnostic effect and, on the other side, the Valentinians lived at least until late in the second half of the century in close fellowship with the Great Church, to which they felt they belonged; the Pneumatics also are bound up with the 'psychic' church.[10]

The interest of the gnostics was not directed towards cosmology as such but in the foreground stood the question of God and redemption; only in that connection did the explanation of the origin of the world acquire its theological importance.[11] In the more advanced schools of higher reputation a certain striving after a philosophical understanding of the world may well have come into play, but we must not overestimate such approaches.[12] Knowledge of the origin and nature of the cosmos serves the gnostic only as a means of overcoming it. When he has known the true God and his

[9] Justin, Apol. II 2, 9–15; cf. Harnack, 'Analecta zur ältesten Geschichte des Christentums in Rom.' (*Texte und Untersuchungen* 13/2, 1905), pp. 3–5. The thesis was repeated – apparently without knowledge of Harnack's work – by H. Langerbeck, 'Zur Auseinandersetzung von Theologie und Gemeindeglauben in der römischen Gemeinde in den Jahren 135–165', in *Aufsätze zur Gnosis* (1967), pp. 167–179, p. 174. Langerbeck seeks to show in this article that in the middle of the century at Rome the decisive contradictions were not between gnosticism and orthodoxy but between philosophical theology and naive congregational belief. Valentinus, Ptolemaeus, Justin and Tatian were thus in the same camp, but on their part they had rejected Marcion, because they were not ready to give up, with him, the Old Testament. But surely this approach is overdone. I cannot place Tatian as near to Valentinianism as Langerbeck tries to, and above all Justin stands markedly nearer to the Christianity of ordinary members, but the wide possibilities which theological speculation still enjoyed at that time are clearly shown in Langerbeck's outline.

[10] Cf. Irenaeus, haer. I praef.; III 15, 2; Tertullian, adv. Val. 1; for the Church's estimate of the Valentinians cf. K. Müller, *Beiträge zum Verständnis der valentinianishen Gnosis*, NGG 1920, pp. 202f.; van Unnik, 'Die Gedanken der Gnostiker über die Kirche' in J. Giblet, *Von Christus zur Kirche* (1966), pp. 223–238.

[11] This was clearly formulated by E. Schwartz, *Aporien im vierten Evangelium* II, NGG 1908, pp. 115–148, p. 127, n. 1: 'The content of γνῶσις is not really metaphysics, but mystically induced redemption'; van Unnik, 'Die jüdische Komponente in der Entstehung der Gnosis', *Vig. Chr.* 15 (1961), pp. 65–82, p. 71 asserts, against modernising interpretations, that the central point in gnostic thinking is the question of God.

[12] Irenaeus, haer. II 32, 2 asserts, from admittedly a quite specific polemical viewpoint, the lack of interest on the part of the gnostics in secular knowledge and activity.

heavenly world, he becomes aware of the nothingness and ungodliness of the earthly cosmos and can do no other than turn away from it; indeed, he is in the fulness of that knowledge already removed from it. Thus in the 'Apocryphon of John' the disciple asks about the Redeemer, about the Father who sent him and about the being of the future aeon,[13] and when Christ appears to John, He tells him '[Now I have come], to reveal to you, [what] is, what has been; and what shall be, so that you [will know] the invisible things as well as [the] visible things, and to [teach you] about the perfect [man]'.[14] So teaching about God, the invisible and visible world and the drama of salvation is the content of gnosis. The same dominating interest in man's salvation appears in the writing 'The Hypostasis of the Archons', whose compiler introduces his teaching about the 'Powers' with a quotation from the Epistle to the Ephesians: 'The great apostle – referring to the powers of darkness – told us: "Our struggle is not against flesh and [blood]; rather against the powers of the universe and the spirits of wickedness"'.[15] After the descriptions of the archons, the matter from which sprang their Father and the world, have been concluded,[16] Norea, the woman receiving the revelation, asks: 'Lord, do I also belong to their matter?' She is then told that she belongs to the ultimate divine Father and that her soul and those of her children stem from the eternal Light.[17] Basilides names as content of the 'Gospel' the knowledge first vouchsafed to the archon of the ogdoad, the knowledge of the 'non-being' God, of the 'sonship' to be found with him, of the Holy Ghost, of the essence of creation and of the goal of the cosmic process.[18] The Valentinians can define the content of the gnosis as the knowledge of God,[19] but that is inseparable from the knowledge of the Pleroma and the whole cosmogony.[20] The basic

---

[13] BG 20, 8–14.
[14] BG 22, 2–9 Till; in agreement with the versions of NHC II 1, 2, 16–20 and IV 1, 3, 9–16; similarly the 'Sophia of Jesus Christ' 78, 2–10; 80, 1–3.
[15] 86, 21–25 (based on the translation of B. Layton); cf. Eph. 6:12.
[16] 96, 15–17; cf. 93, 33 – 94, 2; in this second part of the book a revelation of the angel Eleleth to Norea is dealt with: H. M. Schenke, 'Das Wesen der Archonten' in J. Leipoldt and H. M. Schenke, *Koptisch-gnostische Schriften aus den Papyrus-Codices von Nag Hammadi* V (1960), p. 69.
[17] 96, 18f.; 96, 19ff. The 'Apocalypse of Adam' from Codex V of Nag Hammadi (NHC V, 5), which is broadly connected with the first chapter of Genesis, deals exclusively with the release of the gnostics from the yoke of the world-god and offers no cosmogony.
[18] Hippolytus, ref. VII 26, 2; 27, 7.
[19] Evang. ver. 18, 4–11; 30, 23–34.
[20] Evang. ver. 18, 31ff.; Irenaeus, haer. I 6, 1: οἱ πνευματικοὶ ἄνθρωποι οἱ τὴν τελείαν γνῶσιν ἔχοντες περὶ θεοῦ καὶ <τὰ> τῆς Ἀχαμὼθ μεμυημένοι μυστήρια.

thought that through gnosis the world that originated out of 'unknowing' is overcome and destroyed, is expressed by the Valentinians in pregnant formal phrases: 'As through unknowing "want" and "passion" have come to be, so through knowledge everything that arose from unknowing shall be released'.[21] And the famous gnostic definition of being in the *Excerpta ex Theodoto* makes it clear how the whole purpose of the Valentinian myth consists in explaining the destiny of the individual gnostic and pointing out to him the way of redemption: 'It is not only the baptismal washing that liberates, but also the knowledge who we were, what we have become, where we were, whither we were cast; whither we hasten, whence we are redeemed, what birth is, and what rebirth'.[22]

Gnosis has essential features in common with the general religious notions of imperial times and also with contemporary Platonism. The longing for salvation and redemption and the emphasis on the transcendence of God are in both cases of basic importance.[23] Nevertheless there is a decisive difference between gnosis and philosophy, which is recognised and emphasised by the gnostics themselves: even in Middle Platonism, which had become so strongly theological, the only way to knowledge of God is still that of rational thinking,[24] while gnosis, in possession of its revelations and spiritual knowledge, knows itself to be just as superior to philosophy as

---

[21] Irenaeus, haer. I 21, 4; ὑπ' ἀγνοίας γὰρ ὑστερήματος καὶ πάθους γεγονότων, διὰ γνώσεως καταλύεσθαι πᾶσαν τὴν ἐκ τῆς ἀγνοίας σύστασιν. In agreement with Evang. ver. 18, 7–11; 24, 28–32; on this Jonas, *Gnosis und spätantike Geist* I, pp. 410f.

[22] Clement of Alexandria, Exc. ex Theod. 78, 2. For this and similar formulae cf. E. Norden, *Agnostos Theos* (1913), pp. 102ff.; A. D. Nock and A. J. Festugière, *Corpus Hermeticum* I (Paris, 1972), p. 90, n. 24 (on Corp. Herm. VIII 5); P. Courcelle, *Connais-toi toi-même de Socrate à Saint Bernard* I (Paris, 1974), pp. 69ff.

[23] Cf. H. Dörrie, 'Die platonische Theologie des Kelsos in ihrer Auseinandersetzung mit der christlichen Theologie', NAG 1967, pp. 23–25; id., *Von Platon zum Platonismus. Ein Bruch in der Überlieferung und seiner Überwindung* (1976), pp. 37–39. A. Toorhoudt, *Een onbekend gnostisch system in Plutarchus' de Iside et Osiride* (Louvain, 1942) seeks to unravel from De Is. et Os. 54 (373A-C) a gnostic system used by Plutarch, which is said to display a relationship with the Valentinian system in Hippolytus, ref. VI 30, 6 – 31, 6 (pp. 48–55). This attempt does not succeed, but the research shows how near Plutarch can come to 'gnostic' statements: cf. H. Schwabl, art. 'Weltschöpfung' in PW suppl. IX (1962) 1550. Gnostic features have been repeatedly emphasised in the thought of Numenius of Apamea in particular: cf. H. C. Puech, 'Numenius d'Apamée et les théologies orientales au second siècle', Annuaire de l'Institut de Philologie et d'histoire Orientales 2 (1934 = Melanges Bidez), pp. 745–778; cf. also E. R. Dodds, 'Numenios and Ammonios', in *Entretiens sur l'Antiquite classique V: Les sources de Plotin* (Vandoeuvres–Geneva 1960), pp. 3–61; R. Beutler, art., 'Numenius', PW suppl. VII (1940), pp. 664–678 has shown, on the contrary, that the thinking of Numenius can be understood on Middle Platonist assumptions alone.

[24] Dörrie, 'Die platonische Theologie des Kelsos', pp. 25f.

to common Christianity. A few examples will illustrate this attitude: the *Sophia Jesu Christi* puts into the mouth of the risen Christ a polemic against the attempts of the philosophers to draw conclusions about God from the world;[25] Christ alone knows and brings the truth. The position about philosophy is more complicated in the case of Isidor, the son and disciple of Basilides. He follows the example of Jewish apologetic in asserting the dependence of the philosophers on the prophets; thus he fundamentally acknowledges that philosophy also teaches the truth and presumably intends by this thesis to justify the use of heathen authors to combat Christian thinking.[26] Valentinus says in a sermon, quoted from Clement of Alexandria, that 'much that stands written in the profane books is also found written in the congregation of God', and gives as the basis of this agreement 'the law written in the heart'. Thus he seems to accept a common knowledge of truth.[27] But this way of looking at it remains an exception. In the later Valentinian school the judgment on philosophy is considerably more negative. Indeed it is justifiable to see in one version of the Valentinian myth, according to which Sophia through her boundless longing for knowledge comes to the Fall, an allegory on the philosophical striving for knowledge, which is condemned.[28] Also the 'Tripartite Tractate' of the

[25] 80, 4–81, 17; cf. 'On the Origin of the World', 125.28–32.
[26] Clement of Alexandria, Strom. VI 53, 2–5; cf. Campenhausen, *Die Entstehung der Christlichen Bibel*, p. 165 (ET p. 139).
[27] Clement of Alexandria, Strom. VI 52, 3f. Clement himself, though, is still in doubt whether the δημόσιαι βίβλοι signify the Jewish holy scriptures or the books of the philosophers (Strom. VI 53, 1). The contrast between the 'public books' and what 'is written in the congregation of God' suggests, however, that Valentinus had in mind the works of the philosophers; cf. T. Zahn, *Geschichte des neutestamentlichen Kanons* II (1890–92), pp. 953–956. A. Hilgenfeld, *Ketzergeschichte des Urchristentums* (1884), p. 301, and W. Foerster, *Von Valentin zu Herakleon* (1928), p. 96, think on the contrary that the Old Testament is meant. The Letter to Rheginus, which comes from the immediate circle of Valentinus, if not from his own hand, is critical of those 'who want to learn many things' and who, when they find the solution of problems that have confronted them, 'think very highly of themselves'; yet the truth comes from Christ (43, 25ff.). But later it says: 'There is one who believes among the philosophers who are in this world. At least he will arise. And let not the philosopher who is in this world have cause to believe that he is one who returns himself by himself – and (that) because of our faith!' (46, 8–13, English tr. by M. L. Peel). Who is this philosopher who believes in the resurrection? The editors of the editio princeps took various philosophical trends into account but could give no unambiguous answer: M. Malinine, H. C. Puech, G. Quispel, W. Till, assisted by R. McL. Wilson and J. Zandee, *De Resurrectione (Epistula ad Rheginum)* (1963) XVIIIf.; see now Peel's note in *Nag Hammadi Studies* 23 (1985), pp. 169f.
[28] Irenaeus, haer. I 2, 2; cf. Exc. ex Theod. 31.3; on this F. C. Burkitt, *Church and Gnosis* (Cambridge, 1932), pp. 44ff.; J. Zandee, 'Gnostic Ideas on the Fall and Salvation', *Numen* 11 (1964), pp. 13–74, pp. 24f.; also G. Quispel, 'Philo und die altchristliche Häresie', ThZ 5 (1949), pp. 429–36.

Codex Jung, only recently fully edited, expresses itself very negatively about philosophy.[29] And still the gnostics with whom Plotinus and his pupils were in controversy relied on their revelation texts and asserted that 'Plato did not penetrate the depth of intellectual being'.[30]

The declaration in principle of the difference does not, of course, exclude the gnostics from accepting and working on the philosophical stock of ideas. As far as we can tell from the extant fragments of their writings, Basilides, Isidor and Valentinus were men of considerable education, and were familiar with philosophical problems.[31] And for that very reason they wanted to make it clear that philosophy too could teach truth. Without a certain intellectual attainment gnostics would certainly have found no access to the circle of Plotinus's pupils.[32] But on the whole the gnostics were not seeking an academic controversy with philosophy. They did not, like the apologists, raise claims to be teaching the true philosophy. Use was made of philosophical concepts and ideas, but they were freely reshaped and adapted to the needs of gnostic thinking. What philosophy had to teach was allegorised by the gnostics, just as the biblical texts were, and with the same doctrinaire obstinacy.[33]

The unphilosophical character of gnostic thinking shows up very clearly in their exposition of Genesis. The gnostics take great pleasure in unfolding their cosmology and anthropology in connection with the biblical creation story and primaeval history.[34] This marked emphasis on Genesis is not

---

[29] Tract. Tripart. pp. 108, 36ff. On this passage cf. A. D. Nock, 'A Coptic Library of Gnostic Writings' JThS n.s. 9 (1958), pp. 314–324, pp. 318f.

[30] Porphyry, Vita Plotini 16.

[31] This was shown by H. Langerbeck in his attractive interpretations of individual fragments, 'Die Anthropologie der Alexandrinischen Gnosis', in *Aufsätze zur Gnosis*, pp. 38–82. The relation of Valentinianism to Middle Platonism is treated by P. Kübel, *Schuld und Schicksal bei Origenes, Gnostikern und Platonikern* (1973).

[32] Cf. now C. Elsas, *Neuplatonische und gnostische Weltablehnung bei Plotin* (1975). When listing the views of various philosophers about the activities of the soul, Iamblichus still includes the viewpoint of the gnostics: Joh. Stob. ecl. phys. I 49 (I 365, 9 Wachsmuth).

[33] Plotinus holds it against the gnostics that the innumerable spiritual beings whom they introduce do not correspond to the true gradation of Being in only three hypostases: Enn. II 9, 6; cf. II 9, 1.

[34] The view often advanced in the past that gnosticism rejected the Old Testament is untenable; it applies only to Marcion and his school; the gnostics merely used it very freely and critically: Campenhausen, *Die Entstehung der christlichen Bibel*, p. 94, n. 90 (ET p. 100). Cf. also G. Widengren, 'Die Hymnen der Pistis Sophia und die gnostische Schriftauslegung', in *Liber amicorum* Festschrift für C. J. Bleeker (Leiden, 1969), pp. 269–281; M. Krause, 'Aussagen über das Alte Testament in z.T. bisher unveröffentlichten gnostischen Texten aus Nag Hammadi', in *Ex Orbe Religionum*, Studia G. Widengren I (Leiden, 1972), pp. 449–456.

48   *Creatio Ex Nihilo*

confined to the gnostics: in church circles too the First Book of Moses is included among the most used books of the Old Testament.[35] And the gnostic interest in cosmogony naturally suggests starting with the biblical creation story.

The Holy Scriptures of the Jews, and above all the creation story were the subject of much wonder since they first became known in the Greek world.[36] But while the most striking character of the Old Testament creation story was for pagan readers its 'philosophical' content,[37] the gnostics on the contrary mythologised it.[38] In unbridled allegorising they took away from the biblical phraseology the details characteristic of its teaching; indeed some of the gnostic myths seem first to have been spun out of the Old Testament texts.[39] Repeatedly the interest of the gnostic exposition of Genesis is concentrated on particular verses which are

---

[35] Cf. G. Kretschmar, *Studien zur frühchristlichen Trinitätstheologie* (1956), p. 31; Campenhausen, *Die Entstehung der christlichen Bibel*, p. 94, n. 90 (ET p. 78).

[36] On this basically Harnack, 'Der Brief des Ptolemäus an die Flora', SAB 1902, pp. 507–545, pp. 507–510. From the time of Hecataios of Abdera's work 'Aegyptiaca' (around 300 BC), which devoted a section to the Jews, the latter were reckoned in the Greek world as a nation of philosophers, which adhered to a philosophical religion: cf. W. Jaeger, 'Greeks and Jews', in *Scripta minora* II (Rome 1960), pp. 169–183. The evidence is collected in M. Hengel, *Judentum und Hellenismus* ([2]1973), pp. 464–473.

[37] A neo-pythagorean writing of the second century before Christ, Ocellus Lucanus, de univ. nat. 46 already seems to relate to Gen. 1:28: R. Harder, *Ocellus Lucanus* (1926), pp. 128–132. The writing 'On the Sublime' 9, 9 quotes with full appreciation Gen. 1:3. (The quotation is not interpolated, as E. Norden has shown in 'Das Genesiszitat in der Schrift vom Erhabenen' (1955). But Norden's thesis that the author owed his knowledge of Genesis to personal contact with Philo, is scarcely tenable; he will have taken the bible passage from a Jewish apologetic writing thus W. Bühler, *Beiträge zur Erklärung der Schrift vom Erhabenen*, 1964, p. 34.) Galen praises the Mosaic creation story for its philosophical way of thinking, but misses the mention of the material principle in the creation process: De usu part. XI 14 (II 158 Helmreich); cf. R. Walzer, *Galen on Jews and Christians* (London, 1949), pp. 23–27. Numenius of Apamea relates Gen. 1:2 to the descent of the souls: fr. 30 des Places = Porphyry, de antro. nyph. 10; cf. J. G. Gager, *Moses in Greco-Roman Paganism* (Nashville/New York, 1972), pp. 65f.; P. Nautin, 'Genèse 1, 1–2 de Justin a Origene', in *In Principio. Interprétations des premiers versets de la Genèse* (Paris, 1973), pp. 61–94, p. 94. On the other hand, of course, Celsus naturally sharply criticises the creation story too: Origen, Cels. V 59; VI 49–51, 60f.); cf. IV 36.

[38] For the use of Jewish traditions in gnostic exegesis of Genesis cf. O. Betz, 'Was am Anfang geschah (Das jüdische Erbe in den neugefundenen koptisch-gnostishen Schriften)', in *Abraham unser Vater* Festschrift for O. Michel (1963), pp. 24–34; A. Böhlig, 'Der jüdische Hintergrund in gnostischen Texten von Nag Hammadi', *Mysterion und Wahrheit*, pp. 80–101; van Unnik, *Die jüdische Komponente*, pp. 75ff.

[39] Thus H. M. Schenke, *Der Gott 'Mensch' in der Gnosis* (1962), pp. 72–93.

The Question of the Origin of the World in Christian Gnosticism 49

interpreted again and again and must have counted as key sentences for esoteric speculation. Above all Genesis 1:2 is to be mentioned in this connection,[40] while for anthropology the basic passages Genesis 1:26f. and Genesis 2:7, have a special part to play.[41] But there exist also more or less coherent expositions and paraphrases of the first chapter of Genesis as a whole.[42] The fantastic mythology and the fanatical persistence of these exegeses offered nothing which Christian exposition of Genesis could have supported and taken further. It is characteristic that only with the Valentinians do we find an interpretation of Genesis 1:1–4, which shows any relationship with the Genesis exegesis of hellenistic Judaism, stamped as it was with philosophical ideas, or with the 'philosophical' expositions of Christian authors so closely connected with it.[43] The first continuous exposition of the creation story still extant from the writings of church theologians comes from Theophilus of Antioch. It places great emphasis on the literal sense of the biblical story, and bolts the door against any gnosticising interpretations.[44]

A straight historical explanation of the emergence of gnosticism and its view of the world does not seem to be possible. The intellectual state of affairs that led to the shaping and eventual complete severance of the unity

[40] The evidence is assembled in Schenke, *Der Gott 'Mensch'*, pp. 79–89 and in Orbe, 'Spiritus Dei ferebatur super aquas. Exegesis gnóstica de Gen. 1, 2b', *Gregorianum* 44 (1963), pp. 691–730. One may compare the exegesis of Genesis 1:2 of the Syriac Ququites, which Theodor bar Konai supplies in the eleventh book of his Scholia: H. Pognon, *Inscriptions mandaïtes des coupes de Khouabir* II (Paris, 1899), pp. 144, 209f. – on this H. Drijvers, 'Quq and the Quqites. An unknown sect in Edessa in the second century A.D.', *Numen* 14 (1967), pp. 104–129 – further the supposed Marcionite exposition in Ephraem, hymn, c. haer. 50, 8 (n. 89 below). On the influence of Gen. 1:2 on the cosmogony of the Mandeans cf. K. Rudolph, *Theogonie, Kosmogonie und Anthropogonie in den mandaïschen Schriften* (1965), pp. 166f.
[41] The gnostic exegesis of Gen. 1:26f. is treated by J. Jervell, *Imago Dei Gen. 1.26f. im Spätjudentum, in der Gnosis und in den paulinischen Briefen* (1960), pp. 122ff., the exposition of Gen. 2:7 by W. D. Hauschild, *Gottes Geist und der Mensch. Studien zur frühchristlichen Pneumatologie* (1972), pp. 263ff.
[42] Thus in the treatise 'On the Origin of the World' 100, 29 – 121, 35; on the Genesis exposition in the Apocryphon of John cf. S. Giverson, 'The Apocryphon of John and Genesis', *Stud. Theol.* 17 (1963), pp. 60–76; van Unnik, *Die jüdische Komponente*, p. 78. The 'Hypostasis of the Archons' and the 'Apocalypse of Adam' begin only with the creation of Man; on this Böhlig, *Der jüdische Hintergrund*, pp. 90ff. cf. also Justin's book of Baruch, Hippolytus, ref. V 26, 1–24.
[43] Exc. ex Theod. 47, 2–48, 1; see pp. 104ff. below.
[44] Autol. II 10–19; cf. Grant, 'Theophilus of Antioch to Autolycus', in *After the New Testament* (Collected Papers, Philadelphia, 1967), pp. 126–157, pp. 133–142.

between God and the world cannot be fixed at an exact point in history. Something new is breaking out, which can only be explained as the result of an intellectual and religious development of the presuppositions of hellenistic syncretism. For a methodical approach the attempt of R. M. Grant is particularly worth noting, which in contrast to all derivation of gnostic thought from the history of ideas alone, attributes its origin to the experience of a historical catastrophe which spelled at one and the same time the collapse of both religious ideas and religious expectations: he supposes the decisive shock which produced the world-denying gnostic dualism to be the frightful disappointment of Jewish apocalyptic hopes through the experience of the twofold overthrow of Jerusalem, which was bound to cast doubt on God's rule of the world.[45] Grant's thesis has the advantage that it gives a historical reason for the origin of the pessimistic gnostic attitude towards the world and its creator, that research limited to the history of motives could only partly derive from the comparative material available.

Unfortunately Grant's theory is not sufficiently supported by the sources, and it does not go far enough to solve completely the complex problem of the origin of gnosticism.[46] A historical account of gnosticism will have to start from the recognition that in its early history various motives were in play, some characteristic of particular places. Certainly an extreme dualism was not entertained right from the start. We saw just now that for primitive Christianity gnostic teaching first came into view as christological docetism.[47] The radical gnostic groups, world-denying and antinomian in their thinking, were not at all numerous and were perhaps already dependent on Marcion.[48] Indeed in the great systems of mature gnosticism, with their doctrine of various divine powers and entities, dualism is tempered. Basilides even brings forward the idea that the highest God himself created the cosmos and the Valentinians declare, far more strongly than the antagonistic contrast of God and world, that Being is in layers, ranging from the divine Ground itself down to matter.

---

[45] Grant, *Gnosticism*, pp. 27ff. On the problem of method cf. Jonas I 1–9; R. Haardt, 'Zur Methodologie der Gnosisforschung', in K. W. Tröger, *Gnosis und neues Testament* (1973), pp. 183–202.

[46] Cf. the controversy with Grant in G. Jossa, *La teologia della storia nel pensiero cristiano del secondo secolo* (Naples, 1965), pp. 52ff.

[47] See pp. 37f. above.

[48] Here the Ophites need special mention, of whom Origen reports (Celsus VI 27.28) and further the Cainites: Irenaeus, haer. I 31, 1; cf. H. C. Puech in E. Hennecke and W. Schneemelcher, *Neutestamentliche Apokryphen* I (1959), pp. 228f. The dependence of the radical antinomians on Marcion is suggested by Campenhausen, *Die Entstehung der christlichen Bibel*, pp. 92ff. (ET p. 87).

The doctrine of the creation of the world by angelic powers seems to belong to an earlier stage of gnosticism.[49] Only later is the God of the Old Testament distinguished from the highest God and seen as the actual creator of the world, while the demiurgical function of the angels recedes.[50] Of course gnosticism developed its doctrine of angels mostly from original Jewish ideas, but the specifically 'gnostic' view, that the angels created the world on their own and in an act of insurrection against God, is not to be derived from Judaism.[51] The relegation of Jahweh to the status of an inferior world-god could have resulted from the controversy between the early Christians and Jewry, but opposition to the synagogue was by no means the only motive for it, and again the sources permit of no certain conclusions.[52]

[49] The heresy at Colossae included the veneration of angels (Col. 2:18), but these angels were not conceived as having a part in the creation of the world. Creation of the world through angels was, according to Irenaeus, taught by the Simonians (haer. I 23, 2), Menander (I 23, 5), Saturninus (I 24, 1) and the Carpocratians (I 25, 1). The sequence in time of the schools and the schematic exposition of the teaching in Irenaeus, who seems to be following an older anti-heretical writing, present many difficulties. Thus the Simonians certainly do not belong to the beginning of the gnostic movement, and with them the lack of a single demiurge is not to be reckoned a particularly archaic feature: Beyschlag, *Simon Magus und die christlichen Gnosis* (1974), p. 145. Further evidence for the idea of the world-creating angels is offered by J. Michl, art. 'Engel III', RAC V (1962), 97–109, 104f.

[50] For Saturninus the God of the Jews is one of the angels, and so his part in the creation was not particularly emphasised (Irenaeus, haer. I 24, 2). But in the contemporary 'Apocryphon of John' Jaldabaoth, who corresponds to the Old Testament God, creates the angels: BG 39, 9ff. The Ophites had a similar doctrine: Irenaeus, haer. I 30, 4f. Pseudo-Tertullian, adv. omn. haer. 2.3; Epiphanius, panar. XXXVII 3, 6 – 4, 1. The demiurge still appears as an angel in the Valentinian Ptolemaeus: Irenaeus, haer. I 5, 2; cf. Michl, 100; Jonas I, pp. 227ff.

[51] Cf. Grant, 'Les êtres intermédiares dans le judaïsme tardif', in U. Bianchi, *Le origini dello Gnosticismo* (Leiden, 1966), pp. 141–154; J. Daniélou, 'Le mauvais gouvernement due Monde d'après le Gnosticisme', ibid. pp. 448–456 (on this Beyschlag, *Simon Magus*, pp. 204f.) Quispel, 'The origins of the gnostic demiurge' in *Kyriakon* I, Festschrift for J. Quasten (1970), pp. 271–276, would like to derive the idea of the angel-demiurge from heretical Judaism, but can only find a single witness and that from the 10th century. A starting-point for the doctrine of demiurgical angels is perhaps to be found in Philo, who, in order to be able to explain evil, allows the 'powers' a share in the creation of man: opif. 75; conf. ling. 179; fuga 68ff.; Abr. 143 (cf. Justin, dial. 62.3) Philo certainly has in view the under-gods of the Timaeus (41Cff.): P. Boyancé, 'Dieu Cosmique et Dualisme. Les archontes et Platon', in Bianchi, *Le origini*, pp. 340–356; cf. also W. Theiler, art. 'Demiurgos', RAC III (1957), 694–711, 708.

[52] Nock, *A Coptic Library*, p. 322 has suggested that the rejection of the Jewish law had been extended by gnosticism to creation by the Old Testament God and to God himself; Simone Petrément, 'Le mythe des sept archontes créaturs peut-il s'expliquer à partir du Christianisme?', in Bianchi, *Le origini*, pp. 460–466, pp. 476f. agrees. In a similar way L. Goppelt, *Christentum und Judentum im ersten und zweiten Jahrhundert* (1954), p. 193,

In any case this is a development that did not take place until the beginning of the second century.

The crude mythology and the syncretism of early gnosticism must have made too alien and too repulsive an impression to be recognised as really Christian and to have had a lasting influence on the faith of the churches. No theological progress in any case resulted from the fanciful cosmology of the early gnostics. Had their speculations been more broadly accepted, this would only have led to Christianity dissolving into a vague mythology. So far as the doctrines of the gnostic conventicles were known in church circles, they could only arouse sharp hostility and provoke at most a certain theological conservatism. Real historical importance attaches only to the two great gnostics, Valentinus and Basilides, and their schools, and to Marcion, standing alone as he does on the fringe of the gnostic movement. If we keep in view the fact that Basilides and the apologist Aristides must have been approximately contemporaries, then it becomes immediately clear what an astonishing educational standard and level of thought was attained by the leading gnostic teachers. But although gnosticism anticipated the church theologians in raising a number of problems, it only influenced the latter to a very limited degree, and the gnostic cosmology could not fail to rouse bitter opposition. The distinctions made between a crowd of divine beings; the doctrine of the Fall, before time, of a heavenly figure, which happened before the creation of the world and first led to it; the whole mythological imagery in which the gnostics presented their teaching about the origin of the world: all that was justly regarded as unchristian and was rejected. But the necessity of arguing with the theological fancies of the gnostics compelled their church opponents to tackle the questions the gnostics were raising, and to think through and establish their own understanding of creation.

The sharpest reactions on the Church side were provoked by the theology of Marcion. The distinction which he made with the most extreme coherence and in the most aggressive form between the Old Testament creator God and the 'alien' redeemer God revealed the dangers of the

---

wanted to explain the negative attitude of Saturninus towards the Old Testament and its God (cf. Irenaeus, haer. I 24, 2) by the hostility of Syrian Christianity to Judaism. On the other hand Antiochene Christianity certainly possessed very close links with Judaism. For this reason Grant, 'Jewish Christianity at Antioch in the second century', Rech. Sci. Rel. 60 (1972), pp. 97–108 sees Antiochene gnosis in double opposition to Judaism and to 'Jewish Christianity'. On the tense relationship between Christians and Jews in the years from 70 to 135 cf. W. H. C. Frend, *Martyrdom and Persecution in the Early Church* (Oxford, 1965), pp. 184ff.

dualistic gnostic approach and this was now decisively resisted in all its features. Correspondingly, the rejection of Marcion's ascetic hostility to the world led to a new emphasis on the gifts of the creation and to an affirmation of the world, the importance of which for the further development of Christian understanding of the world must not be underestimated.

The anti-heretical campaign literature of the second and third centuries shows that the Marcionites and the Valentinians exceeded all other gnostic schools in their influence and intellectual importance and thus in the danger they presented. Already, compared with them, the school of Basilides was in retreat. Marcion with his teaching stimulated innumerable polemical writings.[53] The great work of Irenaeus against the heresies is chiefly concerned with the controversy against the Valentinians, but also campaigns against other continuing heretical persuasions, especially the Marcionites. And Origen still sees the most dangerous unorthodoxy in the triad Marcion, Valentinus, and Basilides.[54]

II. Marcion

According to the testimony of Clement of Alexandria, which seems reliable, Basilides, Valentinus and Marcion taught at about the same time, in the later years of Hadrian's reign and under Antoninus Pius, say from 130 to 160, but Marcion seems to have been considerably older than the other two leaders.[55] Certainly Basilides and Valentinus had already taught for a fairly long time as Christian philosophers and teachers, when Marcion was expelled from the Roman congregation and founded his own church. Valentinus's pupil Ptolemaeus took up a position sharply opposed to Marcion and we must therefore reckon that Valentinus too was in controversy with him in Rome. So the Valentinian theology is already marked by the reaction against Marcion. Basilides, teaching in Alexandria, stands outside these debates. He seems to have emerged from the older Syrian gnosticism,[56] but he developed a highly independent doctrine. He may be

[53] Confirmation in Harnack, *Marcion. Das Evangelium vom fremden Gott* (^{2}1924), pp. 314*ff.
[54] Cf. e.g. princ. II 9, 5; hom. Jerem. X 5; XVII 2; Comm. Matt. XII 12, 13; hom. Luke (frag.) 166, 1.
[55] Strom. VII 106, 4.
[56] Irenaeus, haer. I 24, 1. Epiphanius, panar. XXIII 1, 2; XXIV 1,4 says expressly that Basilides came from Antioch, but this is only making more precise the statement of Irenaeus that Basilides and Saturninus were both dependent on the school of Menander in Syria.

placed in time a little earlier than Valentinus.[57] We turn now to Marcion and will treat the creation doctrine of Basilides and the Valentinians together in a later chapter.[58]

At the centre of Marcion's theology stands the message of salvation, which has appeared in Christ for men lost in the world and under the law. Marcion starts from Paul, but he understands the apostle one-sidedly as antinomian and world-denying. Not only do faith and law constitute for him an irreconcilable contradiction. Also the God who in Jesus Christ out of pure grace shows mercy to men is not the same as the Old Testament God of the creation and the law; and redemption can only consist in liberation from the world and from the rule of its creator. The doctrine of two Gods links Marcion with the gnostics, but he conceives the contradiction between the Redeemer-God and the world-creator more radically than any gnostic before him: Marcion opposed every connection between the 'alien' good God and the demiurge.[59] The creator-God and his world were not drawn away from the supreme God through a cosmogonic myth, but both Gods exist beside each other from eternity. The goodness of the alien God is manifest precisely in that he accepted the men whom he did not create and who do not belong to him. This hard and fast doctrine of two Gods was for biblical and Greek thinking alike intolerable. Neither could make anything of a God who stands in no relationship to the world. Marcion's doctrine could not but seem primitive and unphilosophical. At this point then the later Marcionite theology also strove to correct the master. His pupil Apelles, who had spent some time in Alexandria and had probably been influenced there by the prevailing religious and philosophical trends, taught

---

What Irenaeus says is in any case historically doubtful, as it could be the result of a construction in his source which tries to derive every heretical tendency from an older one; cf. Harnack, *Geschichte der altchristlichen Literatur* II 1, p. 290 n. 2.

[57] Cf. Harnack, *Geschichte der altchristlichen Literatur* II 1, pp. 290ff. H. Lietzmann, *Geschichte der alten Kirche* II (1936), p. 283 (ET II, p. 275).

[58] Harnack's classical work continues to form the basis of our portrait of Marcion. It will be cited below without repeating its title. Cf. now especially T. E. C. Blackman, *Marcion and His Influence* (London, 1948); Campenhausen, *Die Entstehung der christlichen Bibel*, pp. 173ff. (ET pp. 148ff.) and Barbara Aland, 'Marcion. Versuch einer neuen Interpretation', ZThK 70 (1973), pp. 420–447. Further literature is specified in Rudolph in 'Gnosis und Gnostizismus, ein Forschungsbericht', ThR 37 (1972), pp. 289–360, pp. 358–360.

[59] The term δημιουργός for a subordinate god seems first to have been used in the second century in Numenius (in Eusebius, praep. ev. XI 18. 6–10. 14; 22, 3.9.10) and in gnosticism. Concerning older stages of this usage cf. C. H. Dodd, *The Bible and the Greeks* (London, 1934), p. 137 n 2; Theiler, art. 'Demiurgos' col. 694ff.

in conscious contradiction of Marcion that there was only one ἀρχή.[60] Apelles conceived the demiurge as an angelic being created by the highest God, who creates the cosmos after the pattern of the upper world, and from him he distinguishes again the 'fiery' God of Israel, who had talked to Moses out of the burning bush, and the devil, as two more angels.[61] Thus Apelles led the way back to general gnostic lines. The question of the being and number of the principles remained a problem over which the Marcionite teachers reached no agreement. We find that in the Marcionite schools discussion went on as to whether two, three or four original principles were to be accepted.[62] Tertullian on the other hand in the first book of his great polemical work used all his rhetorical and dialectical skills to show up Marcion's doctrine of two Gods as absurd.[63]

Marcion's absolute world-denial determines and guides his whole theological thinking. It conditions his dualism and the further consequences are a strictly docetic christology, the rejection of the bodily resurrection and ascetic demands raised to the extreme, which were expressly motivated by the rejection of the creator of the world.[64]

The problem which kept gnosticism busy, namely how from a perfect divine principle the world with its imperfections could originate, no longer confronted Marcion. By the radical cut between the Redeemer-God and the world he makes the cosmogonic myth superfluous.[65] The world is only the visible evidence for the weakness of its creator.[66] With such assertions Marcion took the Stoic proof of providence, which sees in all spheres of

[60] Eusebius, H.E. V 13, 2.3. According to Pseudo-Anthimus, de sancta ecclesia 17 (published by G. Mercati, 'Noti di letteratura biblica e cristiana antica', *Studi e Testi* 5, 1901, pp. 87–98), what we have here is a writing by Marcellus of Ancyra: M. Richard, 'Un opuscule méconnu de Marcel d'Ancyre', *Mel. Sc. Rel.* 6 (1949), pp. 5–28. Apelles taught: ψεύδεται Μαρκίων λέγων εἶναι ἀρχὰς δύο· ἐγὼ δέ φημι μίαν, ἥτις ἐποίησε δευτέραν ἀρχήν. Similarly Epiphanius, panar. XXXXIV 1, 4. Cf. Harnack, pp. 177ff.; 404*ff.

[61] Tertullian, praescr. 34, 4; carn. Chr. 8, 2f.; Hippolytus, ref. VII 38, 1.

[62] Rhodon in Eusebius, H.E. V 13, 3f. (two and three principles); Dionysius of Rome in Athanasius, de decr. Nic. Syn. 26, 3; Hippolytus, ref. VII 31, 2; Adamantius, dial. I 3f. (three principles); Hippolytus, ref. X 19, 1 (four principles).

[63] To this now add E. P. Meijering, 'Bemerkungen zu Tertullians Polemik gegen Markion (Adversus Marcionem 1, 1–25)', *Vig. Chr.* 30 (1976), pp. 81–108.

[64] Clement of Alexandria, Strom. III 12, 2; 25, 1.

[65] This factual content has been strikingly formulated by U. Bianchi, 'Marcion: Théologien biblique ou docteur gnostique?' *Vig. Chr.* 21 (1967), pp. 141–149, p. 148: 'Cette péculiarité (the lack of gnostic myth) n'est, à son tour, que la conséquence de la radicalisation marcionienne du principe anti-cosmique, qui tranche toute connection ontologique de ce monde avec la Divinité, même au plan du problème cosmogonique, qui cesse même d'exister.'

[66] Harnack, p. 273*.

being the divine care at work, turned it upside down and applied it negatively.[67]

Marcion teaches that the demiurge formed the world out of the unformed, evil matter.[68] This idea is meant to explain why the world is faulty and evil, even though Marcion looks on the creator as just and not actually evil. But neither is matter simply the evil, ungodly principle, for alongside it Marcion still reckons with the devil as the author of evil.[69] Harnack suggested that Marcion had taken over the doctrine of eternal matter from the gnostic Cerdo, whose pupil Irenaeus and a series of later controversialists say he was;[70] but this is unlikely. That Marcion was Cerdo's pupil is to begin with by no means certain; the report of it might well arise from the well-known tendency to derive every heresy from an older one. But above all the acceptance of an unformed matter is no characteristic idea of early Syrian gnosticism, from which Cerdo stems intellectually. It is much more likely that Marcion's views about matter are dependent on the teaching of contemporary Platonism,[71] Marcion was an educated man, so that we may

---

[67] Cf. Jonas I, pp. 173–175. When M. Spanneut, *Le Stoicisme des pères de l'Eglise* (Paris, ²1957), p. 46 describes gnosticism as an 'anti-stoicism', this judgment falls in the first place on Marcion.

[68] Tertullian, adv. Marc. I 15, 4: Mundum ex aliqua materia subjacente molitus est innata et infecta et contemporali deo; V 19, 7: Collocans et cum deo creatore materiam de porticu Stoicorum; Clement of Alexandria, strom. III 12, 1: οἱ μὲν ἀπὸ Μαρκίωνος φύσιν κακὴν ἔκ τε ὕλης κακῆς καὶ ἐκ δικαίου γενομένην δημιουργοῦ (sc. ὑπολαμβάνουσιν). Cf. III 19, 4; later evidence in Harnack, p. 276*.

[69] Harnack, p. 97.

[70] Irenaeus, haer. I 27, 1; III 4, 3; cf. Harnack, p. 98.31*–39*.

[71] Representative of Middle Platonism is the statement of Celsus, in Origen, Cels. IV 65: τίς ἡ τῶν κακῶν γένεσις, οὐ ῥᾴδιον μὲν γνῶναι τῷ μὴ φιλοσοφήσαντι, ἐξαρκεῖ δ' εἰς πλῆθος εἰρῆσθαι ὡς ἐκ θεοῦ μὲν οὐκ ἔστι κακά, ὕλῃ δὲ πρόσκειται καὶ τοῖς θνητοῖς ἐμπολιτεύεται. Numenius can describe matter as 'wholly bad' (*plane noxia*): Chalcidius, in Timaeum 296. Clement of Alexandria asserted the dependence of Marcion on Plato, whom admittedly he completely misunderstood: strom. III 12–21. Against this Tertullian declares that Marcion's conception of matter is stoic: adv. Marc. V 19, 7 (n. 68 above); cf. also praescr. 7, 4. But this means nothing, for in the same context Tertullian reproaches Marcion for an epicurean idea of God. The Stoa envisaged matter as without qualities, so evil could not be attributed to it: cf. Plutarch, de an. procr. 6 (1015B); Comm. not. 34 (1076CD); on this C. Bäumker, *Das Problem der Materie in der griechischen Philosophie* (1890), pp. 364f.; E. U. Schüle, 'Der Ursprung des Bösen bei Marcion', ZRGG 16 (1964), pp. 23–42, p. 41 asserts in agreement with Harnack that Marcion's doctrine of matter was dependent on gnosis, and B. Aland, p. 429, compares, as E. W. Möller, *Geschichte der Kosmologie in der griechischen Kirche bis auf Origenes* (1860), pp. 385ff. had already done, the Marcionite scheme of Good God – demiurge – matter with the gnostic system of three principles. But the scheme as such is platonist, and the mythological notions characteristic of the gnostic cosmology are, as the significant silence of all the older witnesses shows,

without more ado assume his familiarity with Platonic conceptions. His criticism of the effects of the anthorpomorphic Old Testament God clearly betrays its philosophical source.[72] The Platonic thought that evil has its ground in matter – like the Stoic proof of providence – undergoes with Marcion a fundamental reversal. For the Platonists the referring of evil to matter is intended to solve the problem of theodicy; in this way it is explained why there is imperfection and evil in the cosmos, without dualistic consequences being drawn out: the presence of evil belongs necessarily to the earthly realm.[73] On the other hand for Marcion the creation of the world out of evil matter proves the imperfection and lowly status of the demiurge. A God who uses this material cannot be the true God.[74] Perhaps Marcion had also realised in this connection that the idea of an unformed matter excludes the idea of the almightiness of the creator, and made use of this insight for his criticism of the demiurge. Harnack says that Marcion declared in his 'Antithesis' that the demiurge completely absent from Marcion's statements about the creation. His opponents would certainly not have let the opportunity pass to draw attention to such features in his doctrine. Marcion thus apparently understood the creation of the cosmos in the sense of the prevailing philosophical conception of world-formation, without mythologising this doctrine in the gnostic manner. The exposition of the biblical creation story which was attributed to Marcion by the Armenian Eznik of Kolb in the fifth century and in which matter appeared personified as a female figure (Against the Sects IV 1) certainly does not go back to Marcion himself. But the text shows the kind of role matter could play in a late, obviously confused marcionite theology; cf. Harnack, pp. 169f., 372*ff.; C. S. C. Williams, 'Eznik's résumé of Marcionite Doctrine', JThS 45 (1944), pp. 65–73. A group called marcionite by Hippolytus, ref. X 19, 1 adds matter as a fourth principle.

[72] Cf. Pohlenz, *Vom Zorne Gottes* (1909), pp. 20–22; id., *Die Stoa* I (1970), pp. 410f.; II (1972), pp. 198f. Harnack, p. 24 n. 1, p. 18* n. 1, declares that his textual criticism shows Marcion to have been an educated man, but denies contemporary philosophical influences in his thinking (cf. p. 160). Harnack raised the matter of his basic rejection of philosophy, which emerges from Marcion's reading of Col. 2:8 (διὰ τῆς φιλοσοφίας ὡς κενῆς ἀπάτης: Tertullian, adv. Marc. V 19, 7; cf. Harnack, pp. 51, 93); but this was shared by most of the Christians of his day and in no way excludes dependence on philosophical teaching. J. G. Gager, 'Marcion and philosophy', *Vig. Chr.* 26 (1972), pp. 53–59, points out agreements between Marcion's critique of the demiurge and the epicurean critique of the gods (for the continuance of this in Christian apologetics, cf. W. Schmid, art. 'Epikur', RAC V 1962, cols. 681–819, 807ff.) Also J. Woltmann, 'Der geschichtliche Hintergrund der Lehre Markions vom "Fremden Gott"', in *Wegzeichen* Festschrift for H. Biedermann (1971), pp. 15–42, pp. 32ff. stresses in contrast to Harnack the philosophical problems tackled by Marcion and the arguments advanced.

[73] Cf. F. P. Hager, 'Die Materie und das Böse in antiken Platonismus', *Mus. Helv.* 19 (1962), pp. 73–103. Dörrie, *Gnomon* 29 (1957), pp. 188f. is opposed to talk of a platonist dualism.

[74] Cf. Harnack, p. 273*; id., *Neue Studien zu Marcion* (1923), p. 19 n. 1.

was not capable of creating without matter, while the true God – as far as he is creatively active – works through his word alone. Of course, Harnack can only call on the following antithesis: Elisha, the creator's prophet, needs 'matter', water, for the healing of the leper Naaman (2 Kings 5:14), but Christ healed a leper by his mere word (Luke 5:12–14).[75] It is a natural question whether from this statement about the healing of the sick it is possible to go straight back to Marcion's understanding of creation. In any case, Marcion was of the view that the true God had created the invisible heavenly world above the heaven of the demiurge. It is possible to think that when he emphasised the inequality of the two Gods, he was explaining that the true God had not been dependent in the creation of his heaven on any material substratum, as the weak demiurge had been. But that was to point out *a posteriori* that the true God had created the upper world 'out of nothing', and we should have to see in Marcion one of the earliest exponents of the idea of *creatio ex nihilo*, even if he did not use the corresponding formula. Unfortunately it is not possible with certainty to confirm that Marcion in fact taught this.[76] Nor has tradition retained any report of whether or how Marcion based the pre-existence of matter on Scripture. It might be suggested that he, like many expositors had referred Genesis 1:2 to formless matter, but safe points of reference are lacking.[77] Also from broad differentiations in Marcion's cosmology we learn nothing, and this is not surprising in him, for whom the doctrine of creation possessed no independent theological interest.

Marcion, as we have just established, could not think of the unknown God without a creation: He created the invisible.[78] This statement corre-

---

[75] Harnack, pp. 98 n. 2, 276*, 282*, cf. Tertullian, adv. Marc. IV 9, 7: Nam et hoc opponit Marcion: Heliseum quidem materia eguisse, aquam adhibuisse, et eam septies, Christum vero verbo solo et hoc semel functo curationem statim repraesentasse; cf. also IV 35, 4.

[76] The creation of the heaven of the alien God from nothing is expressly spoken of only by Ephraem, Ad Hypatium III: C. W. Mitchell, *S. Ephraim's prose refutations of Mani, Marcion and Bardaisan* I (London, 1912) LI (45). Nothing is to be got from Tertullian, Marc. I 15, 4–6 and in Adamantius, dial. II 19, the Marcionite Markos explains: ἐκεῖνοι οἱ τοῦ ἀγαθοῦ οὐρανοὶ ἀχειροποίητοι καὶ ἀγένητοι. Rufinus translates more briefly: illi coeli, qui sunt boni dei, non sunt manufacti.

[77] Basil, hexaem. II 4 (PG 29, 38B–D) asserts that Marcionites, Valentinians and Manichees applied the 'darkness' of Gen. 1:2 to the 'evil without beginning', but we cannot prove this from elsewhere in the case of Marcion.

[78] Tertullian, adv. Marc. I 15, 1: Cum dixeris esse et illi conditionem suam et suum mundum et suum caelum; I 16, 1: Non comparente igitur mundo alio sicut nec deo eius, consequens est, ut duas species rerum, visibilia et invisibilia, duobus auctoribus deis dividant et ita suo deo invisibilia defendant; cf. Justin, apol. I 26, 5; Clement of Alexandria, strom.

sponds to the fact that the Redeemer-God is unknown. The heaven of the good God, from which Christ descended, is that third heaven to which Paul was caught up.[79] Through his doctrine of the invisible world, which is superior to the earthly cosmos, Marcion approaches the gnostic scheme of Pleroma and Cosmos.[80] But unlike the rest of the gnostics Marcion seems scarcely to have speculated about the origin, creation and construction of the upper world. On the plane of the world-God just as much as on that of the Redeemer-God there is lacking the fundamental distinction between creator and created, and with that the tension by which the actual theological problem of the creation first arises. Marcion thinks of the heavenly world of the true God as the negation of the empirical cosmos. His hatred of the world must have forbidden him all sensuous enhancements of it.

The danger of Marcion's doctrine for the Church lay not so much in his extreme devaluation of the world and the flesh as in the fact – and here his stake in Paul counts – that he directed his attack squarely against the law and the God who had given it.[81] He aimed his polemic directly against the Old Testament. And as Marcion declined allegory or any form of 'spiritual' interpretation, he practised a merciless critique of the untempered anthropomorphisms of the old bible.[82] This writing had nothing to do with Jesus Christ. With the rejection of the Old Testament as the book of Christ, Marcion dealt the heaviest blow to the Church.[83] This is mirrored in the rapid growth of anti-Marcionite campaign literature, which in the first place sought to defend the Old Testament as the book inspired by the Father of Jesus Christ, to uphold its christological meaning, and to show the unity of God's dealings in the old covenant and in Jesus.[84] The controversy with Marcion was thus not conducted as a struggle about the right Christian metaphysics, but rather as a matter of upholding the Old Testament as Holy Scripture.

V 4, 4; Origen, hom. Ierem XVI 9; Jerome, comm. Eph. 3, 8f. (PL 26, 514B); Adamantius, dial. II 19; on this Harnack, p. 267*. B. Aland, p. 425, still refers to Ephraem, ad Hypatium III; C. W. Mitchell, *S. Ephraim's Prose Refutations* I, pp. LIff., pp. 44ff.

[79] Tertullian, adv. Marc. I 15, 1; IV 7,1.

[80] Bianchi, pp. 143f.

[81] Tertullian, adv. Marc. I 19, 4: Separatio legis et evangeli proprium et principale opus est Marcionis; cf. IV 1, 1; on Marcion's critique of the law cf. V. Hasler, *Gesetz und Evangelium in der alten Kirche bis Origenes* (1953), pp. 44–47.

[82] Marcion's reproaches are not in detail new; he attacks in the same texts which Philo already defended: Grant, 'Notes on Gnosis', *Vig. Chr.* 11 (1957), pp. 145–151, pp. 145ff.

[83] Campenhausen, *Die Entstehung der christlichen Bibel*, pp. 176–178, 194ff.

[84] Ibid., pp. 193ff. (ET pp. 148–150 for n. 83, p. 165 for nn. 83 and 84).

Stoicising expositions of the creation story, which were determined by hellenistic-Jewish traditions, had hitherto held their place in the liturgy and in the missionary proclamation, perhaps even in the apologetics that was beginning to appear.[85] Now the exegesis of Genesis gains new relevance in the controversy with Marcion. Eusebius mentions writings on the 'Six days' work'[86] by Rhodon, Candidus and Apion.[87] These works, which appeared in the second half of the second century, must have been to a large extent directed against Marcion.[88] The biblical account of creation had been able to offer Marcion little opportunity to attack the creator God.[89] We know only that he remarked of the creation of man, that human sin must be blamed on the creator, for the soul was his breath.[90] The starting point for Marcion's critique of the world creator seems to have been furnished by the story of the Fall, for here it was clear that the biblical God was lacking in goodness, in foreknowledge of the future, and in power to overcome evil.[91] On the other hand the exposition of the creation story offered Marcion's opponents the opportunity to point out the goodness and power of the Creator and the perfect and wise ordering of the cosmos.[92]

Marcion's teaching on the creation of the world out of eternal matter is conveyed to us in the first place through Clement of Alexandria and Tertullian. But we may well accept that it had been controversial earlier. In any case the question as to which principles constitute Being was one of the

---

[85] Cf. 1 Clem. 33, 3–6; Epist. apost. 3 (14); Athenagoras, suppl. 13, 2; on this R. Knopf, 'Die apostolischen Väter' 1 (HNT Supplementary Volume 1920), pp. 99–101. The Genesis exegesis of Theophilus of Antioch, strongly dependent as it is on Jewish traditions, is as much apologetic as it is anti-gnostic and anti-marcionite; Grant, *Theophilus of Antioch to Autolycus*, pp. 133ff.

[86] The expression ἑξαήμερον appears denoting the six-days work of creation for the first time in Philo, leg. all. II 12; decal. 100; cf. F. E. Robbins, *The Hexaemeral Literature. A Study of the Greek and Latin Commentaries on Genesis* (Chicago, 1912), p. 1 n. 2.

[87] Eusebius, H.E. V 13, 8; V 27.

[88] Thus also W. Bauer, *Rechtgläubigkeit und Ketzerei im ältesten Christentum* (²1964, ed. G. Strecker), pp. 150–152 (ET p. 155).

[89] Only on Gen. 1:2 have two marcionite meanings come down to us: Basil, hexaem. II 4 (PG 29, 38B–D; see n. 77 above; Ephraem, hymn. c. haer. 50, 8: 'And from the spirit (wind) which brooded over the waters in a natural way – they took a brooding, another, unlovely'. Perhaps we have here an interpretation by Syrian marcionites.

[90] Tertullian, adv. Marc. II 9, 1.

[91] Tertullian, adv. Marc. II 5, 1; cf. IV 41, 1; Theophilus of Antioch, ad Autol. II 26; Irenaeus, haer. III 23, 6; Pseudo Clement, hom. III 39, 1; further examples are offered by Harnack, p. 271*f. For the exposition of Apelles of the Paradise story cf. Harnack, pp. 413*–416*.

[92] Cf. Tertullian, adv. Marc. II 4, 2; 11, 1; 12, 2; V 11, 12.

[93] See pp. 154ff. below.

The Question of the Origin of the World in Christian Gnosticism

themes with which the Christian teachers of the second century were intensively occupied.[93] Marcion's teaching that matter and the world created from it were bad and hateful could only make it obvious in an impressive way what dangerous dualistic consequences could develop from the philosophical doctrine of the pre-existence of matter. While Justin Martyr still accepted that the world had arisen from unformed material, his pupil Tatian was already advancing the firm view that matter was created by God and could not count as a principle of being.[94] Perhaps we have, in this breakaway from Justin's Platonising understanding of the creation one result of the controversy with Marcion's doctrine of the principles.

[94] See pp. 149–152 below.

3

The Creation of the World in Basilides and the Valentinians

I. Basilides

The historical reconstruction and evaluation of the theology of Basilides depends on the solution of the problem of sources: in addition to the review which Irenaeus gives of the teaching of Basilides, there is the entirely different account by Hippolytus, as well as a few quotations from the writings of Basilides and his son Isidor to be found in Clement of Alexandria and Origen.[1] Shortly after the first publication, in 1851, of books IV to X of Hippolytus's great work against the heresies, a lively debate arose over the question whether Irenaeus's account or Hippolytus's gave the original teaching of Basilides.[2] This debate is even today not wholly settled, but in more recent research the conclusion has been widely accepted that Hippolytus's review is to be given preference,[3] which was the opinion adopted by F. C. Baur and G. Ullhorn in the fifties of the last century.[4] In

---

[1] Irenaeus, haer. I 24, 3–7; Hippolytus, ref. VII 20–27; X 14. A. von Harnack lists all further evidence, *Geschichte der altchristlichen Literatur* ([2]1958), pp. 157–161.

[2] A general view of the older literature on this question is given by A. Hilgenfeld, *Die Ketzergeschichte des Urchristentums* (1884), pp. 204–230: he finds the original system of Basilides in Irenaeus.

[3] Cf. J. H. Waszink, art. 'Basilides', RAC I (1950), 1220f.; G. Kretschmar, art. 'Basilides', RGG[3] I (1957), 909f.; W. Foerster, 'Das System des Basilides', NTS 9 (1962/63), pp. 233–255; G. Quispel, 'Gnostic Man; The Doctrine of Basilides', in *Gnostic Studies I* (Collected Papers, Istanbul, 1974), pp. 103–133.

[4] Cf. F. C. Baur, *Das Christentum und die christliche Kirche der drei ersten Jahrhunderten* (1853), pp. 187ff.; id. 'Das System des Gnostikers Basilides und die neuesten Auffassungen desselben', *Theol. Jahrbuch* 125 (1854), pp. 121–162; G. Uhlhorn, *Das Basilidianische System mit besonderer Rücksicht auf die Angaben des Hippolytus* (1855).

The Creation of the World in Basilides and the Valentinians   63

support of this view there is first a basic consideration Hippolytus retails a highly original and internally consistent body of doctrine, while the review of Irenaeus in many of its features coincides with his immediately preceding account of the Simonians and Saturninus, and offers a system, as it were, of gnostic normality. It is more probable that the intellectually more important system goes back to the great teacher himself rather than to his disciples of the second or third generation.[5] The decisive factor for the originality and authenticity of the system recounted by Hippolytus is the agreement between it and the fragments preserved by Clement of Alexandria, which can be traced in the very terminology.[6]

Hippolytus uses a written source which he quotes, sometimes word for word and sometimes in summary form; occasionally he inserts additional information, which does not come from the document before him, and makes passing remarks of a polemical nature.[7] Most striking is a series of contacts with reports on the teaching of other gnostic schools. G. Salmon, who in an article published in 1885 drew attention to these common features of fact and language in the various reviews of Hippolytus, concluded from his observations that the gnostic sources used by the Roman theologian had been extensively falsified, perhaps by the hand of a Valentinian.[8] H. Staehelin, in an exhaustive enquiry which started from

[5] Thus earlier Baur, 'Das System des Gnostikers Basilides', pp. 150f.; H. M. Schenke, 'Hauptprobleme der Gnosis', *Kairos* 7 (1965), pp. 114–123, pp. 119f. regards the system described by Hippolytus, on account of its philosophical character, as secondary or even pseudo-Basilidean. But Gnosis need not necessarily have developed from myth to a more philosophical way of thinking. We have also to reckon with the 'decline of a demanding philosophy of religion' (H. Langerbeck, 'Das Problem der Gnosis als Aufgabe der Klassischen Philologie', in *Aufsätze zur Gnosis*, 1967, pp. 17–37, p. 30).

[6] The most important correspondence is that between Hippolytus, ref. VII 26, 1f. and Clement of Alexandria, strom. II 35.5 – 36.1, which reproduces the Basilidean exegesis of Prov. 1:7, where decisive concepts of Hippolytus's report appear. A painstaking comparison of all the texts of question is provided by Baur in 'Das System des Gnostikers Basilides', pp. 153–157, and especially by Foerster, 'System', pp. 243ff. That Basilides relied on the apocryphal Matthias traditions is likewise confirmed by Clement: strom. VII 108.1.

[7] It is uncertain whether Hippolytus reproduced his source unaltered in its essentials, or whether he greatly shortened and recast it. J. Frickel, *Die 'Apophasis Megale' in Hippolyt's Refutatio (VI 9118): a Paraphrase on Simon's Apophasis* (Rome, 1968), pp. 30ff., tries to show that Hippolytus copied out his sources almost word for word. But the passages of the Refutatio that are dependent on Irenaeus, and which we can compare with the source (VI 19f.; 38–55; VII 28.32–37) show that Hippolytus did indeed often copy his material word for word, but that he is also capable of changing it, extending it and giving it a new emphasis; cf. K. Beyschlag, *Simon Magus und die christliche Gnosis* (1974), pp. 19ff. on ref. VI 19f., a text where Hippolytus has altered his source more drastically than in other cases.

[8] 'The Cross-Reference in the "Philosophumena" ', *Hermathena* II (1885), pp. 389–402. Salmon draws attention to the following parallels with the report on Basilides (pp.

Salmon's points, came likewise to the conclusion that the representations of outlines of gnostic teaching reworked by Hippolytus which lack the safeguard of parallel records are probably the work of a forger.[9] But this hypothesis of forgery is wholly untenable. In spite of the superficial agreements the systems reviewed by Hippolytus are much too original and much too different from each other to be the work of a forger, and there is no convincing motive for such a forgery. Furthermore in very recent times the situation over sources has changed: we now possess in the 'Paraphrase of Shem' among the finds at Nag Hammadi a writing which in terms of its content is closely related to the review of Hippolytus about the teaching of the Sethians, and its credibility is fully confirmed.[10] So there is no doubt that Hippolytus used good sources. But how then are the common features in his accounts to be explained? It might be suspected that Hippolytus himself in reproducing what lay before him used various stereotyped formulae and patterns, but it is much more likely that he had before him a collection of gnostic sources, which had already gone through a unifying redaction. The many clichés of concept and idea that arise would then be attributable to this editorial work.[11]

The New Testament quotations in the review, among them two from the Gospel of John, also give food for thought. If these go back to Basilides himself, we have here the earliest formal quotations from the Fourth Gospel that are known.[12] The Valentinians were the first to use it widely and to

401f.): in ref. VII 22, 8 is found a formulation similar to the one in V 9, 4; the 'Great Archon' (VII 23, 3 and above) appears also in VIII 9, 6; the image of the Naphtha (VII 25, 6f.) also in V 17, 9 (Doctrine of the Perates; here the image seems more firmly anchored in the text); in VII 26, 7 οἱονεῖ ἐκτρώματι is also presumably an interpretation (a Valentinian expression: VI 31, 2, and elsewhere).

[9] H. Staehelin, *Die gnostische Quellen Hippolyts in seiner Hauptschrift gegen die Häretiker* (1890); cf. the historical survey of research in Frickel, pp. 11–25.

[10] A comparison with ref. V 19.1–22 is made by C. Colpe, 'Heidnische, jüdische und christliche Überlieferung in den Schriften von Nag Hammadi' II, JAC 16 (1973), pp. 106–126, pp. 109–114. He comes to the conclusion that the paraphrase of Shem itself 'or a very similar text was what lay before the Church father or before the writer he was following' (p. 114).

[11] Beyschlag, ThLZ 95 (1970), p. 670, considers it possible that the compiler of the 'gnostic package of sources' might have been a Church Christian.

[12] 22, 4 (John 1:9); 27, 5 (John 2:4). T. Zahn, *Geschichte des neutestmentlichen Kanons* I (1888), p. 767, suspected that the three connected fragments in Clement of Alexandria, strom. IV 81–83 came from an exegesis of John 9:1–3; for a contrary view, H. Windisch, 'Das Evangelium des Basilides', ZNW 7 (1906), pp. 236–246, pp. 237f. L. Cervaux, 'Remarques sur le texte des Evangiles à Alexandrie au deuxième siècle', in *Recueil L. Cerfaux* I (Gembloux, 1954), pp. 487–498, pp. 489f. says that in strom. III 1, 1 an echo – albeit a very weak one – of John 9:1 is discernable. He is followed by F. M. Braun, *Jean le théologien et son évangile dans l' église ancienne* (Paris, 1959), p. 106. This cannot be proved.

The Creation of the World in Basilides and the Valentinians   65

expound it. In terms of time it is of course quite possible that Basilides knew John's Gospel.[13] And certainly he, who had written a gospel himself,[14] was greatly interested in the gospels that were available. It is therefore conceivable that Basilides made use of John's Gospel for his own gospel. But in all probability he only quoted from the latter. We must assume that his disciples were the first to quote in due form from the other gospels.[15] So we can hardly refer the gospel quotations in the review of Hippolytus back to Basilides himself. They must come from the tradition of his school.[16] That

[13] On the evidence of Pap. Ryl. Gk. 457 and Pap. Egerton 2 it can be accepted that the Gospel of St John was known in Egypt before the middle of the second century. G. D. Kilpatrick tells me (orally) that papyri were imported into Egypt, so the proof is not absolutely conclusive. All more or less certain testimonies to the knowledge of St John's Gospel in Egypt in the second century are collected in Braun, pp. 69–133. W. von Loewenich, *Das Johannes-Verständnis im zweiten Jahrhundert* (1932), p. 64, is not willing to claim the two quotations from John for Basilides, 'as Hippolytus in his account does not reliably distinguish between Basilides and his disciples'. On the other hand J. N. Sanders, *The Fourth Gospel in the Early Church* (Cambridge, 1943), p. 55, would like to regard the two passages, with reservations, as proof of the Alexandrian origin of the Gospel. Of course he thinks the quotation from John 1:9 (22, 4) was added later in particular circumstances (p. 52) and, in fact, the passage appears also in relation to the Naassenes, Hippolytus, ref. V 9, 20. M. F. Wiles, *The Spiritual Gospel. The Interpretation of the Fourth Gospel in the Early Church* (Cambridge, 1960), pp. 74 n. 5, 107, also considers the use of the Fourth Gospel by Basilides to be possible.

[14] Unfortunately nothing certain can be said about the form and content of the gospel compiled by Basilides, cf. H. C. Puech in E. Hennecke and W. Schneemelcher, *Neutestamentliche Apokryphen* I (1959), pp. 257f. (ET pp. 231ff.). H. von Campenhausen, *Die Entstehung der christlichen Bibel* (1968), pp. 164f. (ET pp. 139f.).

[15] The quotation formula with which John 1:9 is introduced: τὸ λεγόμενον ἐν τοῖς εὐαγγελίοις (22, 4) perhaps comes first from Hippolytus; cf. Zahn I, p. 162. Campenhausen, *Enstehung der christlichen Bibel*, p. 165 (ET pp. 139f.) takes it from the wording used by Hippolytus that the later Basilideans used other gospels beside that of Basilides. Basilides himself would surely have referred only to 'the Gospel' (his own) (cf. Agrippa Castor in Eusebius, H.E. IV 7, 7). Other quotation formulae in the report of Hippolytus 'show a distinctly modern stamp' (Zahn I, p. 765) and may stem from his own work or from that of the compiler of his source: thus 1 Cor. 2:13 is introduced as 'Scripture' (26, 3; cf. 25, 1; 26, 7). The Valentinians are happy to introduce the John-quotations with the words 'the Apostle says' (Ptolemaeus, ad Flor. 3, 6; Exc. ex Theod. 7, 3; 41, 3) John 2:4 is unreservedly quoted by Hippolytus as a 'word of the Lord' (27, 5: ὁ σωτὴρ λέγων). Further gospel quotations to be found are Lk. 1:35 (26, 9) and Mt. 2:1f. (27, 5); both passages also play a part with the Valentinians (Lk. 1:35: exc. ex Theod. 23, 3; 60; Hippolytus, ref. VI 35, 3; Mt. 2:2: exc. ex Theod. 74, 2; 75, 2).

[16] The linking in ref. VII 25, 9 of the doctrine of the 'enlightenment' of Jesus with the statements in Lk. 1:35 contradicts the original Basilidean Christology and surely represents a secondary development (see n. 107 below). By taking over the gospels of the Great Church the Basilideans were obliged to take account of the birth stories in their Christology; cf. the interpretation of Mt. 2:1f. in ref. VII 27, 5.

makes it clear that Hippolytus did not take his excerpts from an original writing by Basilides but used a résumé of the teaching of later Basilideans, which was contained in the collection of gnostic sources that he had before him.[17] Nevertheless it is established through the common features in the Basilides-quotations and the information about the teaching of Basilides contained in Clement of Alexandria that the essential basic thought in Hippolytus's review does go back to the founder of the school himself.

Irenaeus on the contrary, who likewise uses an older source, may be repeating the teaching of Basilideans who have given up the distinctive thought of the founder of the school and taken up in the broadest way the general notions of gnosticism.[18] It is particularly striking that in Irenaeus we are told of a system of pure emanations whereas in Hippolytus the rejection of the notion of emanation is said to be characteristic of the thought of Basilides.[19] The difference from the teaching of Basilides as we know it from Clement and Hippolytus is so great that one may not attribute the system described by Irenaeus even to personal disciples of Basilides, who must have been contemporaries of his son Isidor, who, it seems, adopted his father's doctrine unchanged.[20] How a branch of the Basilidean school could so rapidly come to complete abandonment of the original statements of the master, is one of the many riddles in the history of gnosticism which we cannot satisfactorily solve.[21]

---

[17] Hippolytus declares that he wants to set out the doctrine of Basilides, Isidor and their school: ref. VII 20, 1. In his report he speaks now of Basilides as an individual, now of the Basilideans as a group, obviously without wanting to make any distinction: 21, 5; 22, 3.6. 7; 25, 1; 27, 7; cf. P. Hendrix, *De Alexandrinsche Haeresiarch Basilides* (Amsterdam, 1926), pp. 27f. Neither does Clement of Alexandria distinguish in his statements between the doctrine of Basilides and that of his pupils (cf. strom. II 36, 1; 112, 1); he merely reproaches the Basilideans that their way of life does not correspond to the teachings of their founder (strom. III 3, 3), Clement thus appears not to have been aware of how the doctrine of Basilides had been modified as it was passed down to his successors (cf. Foerster, *System*, p. 243).
[18] Thus earlier Uhlhorn, pp. 54ff.; cf. Foerster, *System*, p. 255.
[19] Ref. VII 22, 2. Uhlhorn, p. 63, considers Valentinian influence on the Basilideans as of Irenaeus: cf. especially the series of Aeons, haer. I 24, 3.
[20] The single striking agreement between Irenaeus and Hippolytus consists in the fact that both draw attention to the Abraxas speculation of the Basilideans: Irenaeus, haer. I 24, 7; Hippolytus, ref. VII 26, 6. But in Hippolytus it is a matter of a clearly recognisable interpolation from another source, perhaps following Irenaeus. The 365 heavens, which the word Abraxas symbolises through its numerical value, cannot be fitted at all into the world-building of the system described by Hippolytus. Cf. on this subject, A. Dieterich, *Abraxas* (1891); Hendrix, pp. 61–63.
[21] Attempts have been made in various ways to attribute both systems to Basilides: Hendrix, pp. 80f., has suggested that Irenaeus emphasised the common gnostic features in

We must first briefly review the general outline of the system which plainly differs from all the other gnostic systems, so as to fix the position of creation within it.[22] In the beginning there is the pure, ineffable Nothing. It could be that Basilides already equated this original Nothing with God.[23] But Hippolytus does not bring that to clear expression; he brings in the 'non-being' God, without establishing a transition in his thought.[24] The description of God as 'non-being' can only be understood as *theologia negativa* pushed to the extreme, as is characteristic of gnostic thinking. It may be suspected that we have here a conscious link with the well-known saying of Plato in his parable of the sun in the *Politeia* that the Idea of the Good 'towers above being by its dignity and might'.[25] In any case this text

the doctrine of Basilides; a tendency of that kind is in fact to be observed in Irenaeus: he seeks to depict Basilides as a disciple of Menander and a friend of Saturninus (haer. I 24, 1). On the other hand he declares a peculiarity of Basilidean thought to be the enormous extension of speculation (haer. I 24, 3: ut altius aliquid et verisimilius invenisse videatur, in immensum extendit sententiam doctrinae suae); but for explaining the basic structures of the various systems this proposition does not cover the motives that guides Irenaeus in his exposition. The descriptions of heretics in haer. I 23–28 are thoroughly elaborated in a unitary scheme and show surprising common features. Only an enquiry based on redaction criticism into this whole passage could clarify the tendency and perhaps also the origin of the report on the Basilidean problem; cf. Beyschlag, *Simon Magus*, p. 16 n. 19. R. McL. Wilson, *The Gnostic Problem* (London, 1958), pp. 126f., claims to define the Irenaean system as the original teaching of Basilides brought from Antioch, while Hippolytus presents a later system fashioned in Egypt. Against this it may be argued that the system of emanations described by Irenaeus points to Egypt far more than the system in Hippolytus. A. Orbe, *Estudios Valentinianos* I: *Hacia la primera teologia de la procesion del Verbo* (Rome, 1958), pp. 706f., seeks in a methodically combative manner to show that the idea of emanation is compatible with the Basilidian doctrine described by Hippolytus. R. M. Grant, 'Gnostic Origins and the Basilidians of Irenaeus', *Vig. Chr.* 13 (1959), pp. 121–125, finds the original teaching of Basilides in Hippolytus and explains the origin of the system presented by Irenaeus in terms of his well-known theory of the origin of gnosticism in the shattered hopes of Jewish apocalyptic (see p. 50 above). Cf. also K. Rudolph, 'Gnosis und Gnostizismus, ein Forschungsbericht' [VII], ThR 38 (1974), pp. 1–25, pp. 2ff.

[22] Thorough accounts in Uhlhorn, pp. 5ff.; E. W. Möller, *Geschichte der Kosmologie in der griechischen Kirche bis auf Origenes* (1860), pp. 344ff.; Hendrix, pp. 67ff.; Waszink, RAC I, cols. 1220–1222; Quispel, *Gnostic Man*, pp. 109ff.; Foerster, *System*, pp. 236–242; H. J. Krämer, *Der Ursprung der Geistmetaphysik* (^{2}1967), pp. 234–238.

[23] Thus H. A. Wolfson, 'Negative Attributes in the Church Fathers and the Gnostic Basilides', *Harv. Theol. Rev.* 50 (1957), pp. 145–156, pp. 153ff. = *Studies in the History of Philosophy and Religion* I (Collected Papers, Cambridge, Mass., 1973), pp. 131–142, pp. 139ff.; cf. J. Whittaker, 'Basilides on the Ineffability of God', *Harv. Theol. Rev.* 62 (1969), pp. 367–371 (incidentally, rightly critical of Wolfson); Grant, *Gnosticism and Early Christianity*, pp. 144f.

[24] 21, 1: ἐπεὶ <οὖν> οὐδὲν <ἦν>... <ὃ> οὐκ ὢν θεός... κόσμον ἠθέλησε ποιῆσαι. Waszink, RAC I, col. 1221 distinguishes between Nothing and the non-being God.

[25] VI 509B.

plays a fundamental role[26] in the speculations of Platonists in imperial times over the relation between God and being. The 'non-being' God creates the cosmic seed, which contains within itself potentially the whole world, the seed-mixture (πανσπερμία) of the cosmos. The world-seed contains three 'sonships' which are consubstantial with the non-being God, but which possess a varying degree of purity. The first sonship, 'fine in its parts' (λεπτομερής) soars in the instant of the creation of the world-seed up to the non-being God; the second sonship – it is described as 'coarse in its parts' (παχυμερής) – is too heavy to soar alone; it is carried aloft as on wings by the Holy Ghost, who must himself remain behind and not achieve entry to the realm of God, because he is not equal in essence with him.[27] But the pneuma retains an exhalation of the second sonship which percolates down to the earthly realm[28] and becomes a 'firmament' (στερέωμα) which separates the cosmic from the supercosmic realm.[29] The formation of the cosmos proceeds in such a way that first the 'great archon' emerges from the primaeval seed. He rises to the firmament but does not realise that beyond there is a yet higher realm. He creates a son, who is greater and wiser than himself, and together they create the realm of the 'Ogdoad', the sphere of the fixed stars. Then there arises from the seed-mixture a second archon, less exalted than the first, whose realm is the 'Hebdomad' (the sphere of the

---

[26] Cf. J. Whittaker, Ἐπέκεινα νοῦ καὶ οὐσίας, *Vig. Chr.* 23 (1969), pp. 91–104; on Basilides p. 103. Of course Plotinus was the first clearly to formulate the idea that the highest divine Being, the One, in so far as he is above being, is non-being (cf. Enn. V 5, 6, 4ff.; VI 9, 3, 37–39). The systematic thinker Porphyry then brought the stages of being and non-being into an orderly scheme and placed God at the top as the 'non-being over the being' (μὴ ὂν ὑπὲρ τὸ ὄν): P. Hadot, *Porphyre et Victorinus* I (Paris, 1968), pp. 147–211. The negative theology of the gnostics is thus ahead of philosophical development: cf. H. Dörrie, 'Die platonische Theologie des Kelsos in ihrer Auseinandersetzung mit der christlichen Theologie', NAG 1967/2, p. 47, G. C. Stead, *JThS* n.s. 21 (1970), p. 485, refers, for the understanding of the predicate 'non-being', to a passage in the 'Apocryphon of James' in the Codex Jung: 'Further, I reprove you, you who are; become like those who are not, that you may be with those who are not' (13, 13–17, English translation by F. E. Williams). Is 'non-being', in the sense of the gnostic reversal of all values, perfection?
[27] 22, 10. This idea of the wings of the Spirit is, as Hippolytus remarks, surely dependent on the Platonic Phaedrus (246A): cf. Orbe, 'Variaciones gnósticas sobre las alas del Alma', *Gregorianum* 35 (1954), pp. 18–55, and on the history of the image of soul-flight especially P. Courcelle, *Connais-toi toi-même de Socrate à Saint Bernard* III (Paris, 1975), pp. 562ff.
[28] 22, 14f. On this idea cf. Irenaeus, haer. I 4, 1 and E. Lohmeyer, 'Vom göttlichen Wohlgeruch', SAH 1919/9, p. 39.
[29] 22, 13; 23, 1–3. On the thought that the Spirit lies deeper ontologically than the Sonships and, like the Valentinian Horos, forms the boundary between the supercosmic and the cosmic realms, cf. the similar conception of the Sethians in Hippolytus, ref. V 19, 4 and the remarks of A. Dihle, ThW IX (1973), p. 659.

planets). He likewise creates a son for himself, who is superior to him. The sublunary world consists of the rest of the unformed seed-mixture. It is subject to no archon, but in it all that happens is completed 'in accordance with nature', following the original plan of the supreme God.[30]

For the liberation of the third sonship, that of the 'children of God, for whose revelation the creation yearns',[31] that is, the chosen gnostics, the Gospel comes into the world. Through the mediation of the Holy Ghost it first reaches the son of the great archon and through him the archon himself, who now first becomes aware of the existence of the true God and of the sonships. He is terrified, recognises his ignorance and confesses the sin which he has committed in the arrogant belief that he was the supreme God.[32] After the great archon the whole Ogdoad receives the Gospel. The son of the archon of the Ogdoad gives the light of the gospel to the son of the archon of the Hebdomad, from him the archon himself receives it, and thereafter his whole dominion is enlightened. From here the light comes down to Jesus; he mediates it to the third sonship, which is now able to mount to the non-being God. The universal redemption consists in this, that the mixing in the cosmos is set aside and everything that is attains the

---

[30] In drawing the boundaries of the three cosmic realms there arises a problem of interpretation: the division between the Ogdoad and the Hebdomad points to the spheres of the Fixed Stars and the Planets, but Hippolytus asserts that the domain of the great Archon includes the whole world of the planets down to the moon (23, 7; 24, 3). Möller, *Kosmologie*, p. 356, therefore places the Ogdoad in the region of aether and the Hebdomad in the sphere of the moon. But that would be a wholly unusual scheme of division. Probably Hippolytus has created confusion here: as he wants to show that Basilides is dependent on Aristotle (ref. VII 14), he obviously constructs a link between the statements of his source about the great Archon and what passed in imperial times as Aristotelian doctrine, that the working of providence only extended as far as the sphere of the moon (cf. ref. I 20, 6; VII 19, 2 and A. J. Festugiére, *L'idéal religieux des Grecs et l'Evangile*, Paris, 1932, pp. 224ff.) So he reaches the conclusion that 'the whole region of the aether, which stretches as far as the moon' is governed and protected by 'the entelechy of the great Archon' (προνοούμενα καὶ διοικούμενα): ref. VII 24, 3. (There is definite agreement with the account of the supposed Aristotelian teaching in ref. VII 19, 2.) In reality Basilides taught that all things, including earthly events, were guided by the providence of the supreme God (Clement of Alexandria, strom. IV 82, 2; Hippolytus, ref. VII 24, 5; according to Clement of Alexandria, strom. IV 88, 3 the Pronoia of the supreme God also apparently works through the great Archon). Perhaps a second reason for Hippolytus's mistaken interpretation can be seen in the fact that his source referred to the Archons working also in the realms of being lying beneath them: cf. ref. VII 25, 2–4. In a similar way with the Valentinians Sophia reaches past her own realm of the Ogdoad into that of the Hebdomad, the realm of the demiurge (cf. Hippolytus, ref. VI 33).

[31] 25, 1.5 (combination of Rom. 8:19 and 22).

[32] 26, 1–4; Clement of Alexandria, strom. II 35, 5 – 36, 1.

realm that is appropriate to its nature. Jesus is the first-fruit of the cosmic 'separation' (φυλοκρίνησις) which is brought about through his sufferings.[33] After this process is complete, God brings the 'great ignorance' over the cosmos, so that everything remains in the condition appropriate to its nature. No being is aware of any higher realm of being than its own.[34] The cosmology of Basilides differs fundamentally from the teaching of the other gnostics. According to the prevailing view, at first only the heavenly world unfolds and only through the rebellion and fall of one of the heavenly beings does the cosmos emerge. Basilides, on the contrary allowed the whole of reality, from the sonships and the archons down to the terrestrial world, to come potentially into being through the single creative act of the supreme God; it only remains for it to unfold in space and time.[35] No precosmic catastrophe happens, but the whole cosmic process develops according to the original plan of God.[36] Creation results from pure, unconditioned Nothing. The source used by Hippolytus seems to have explained in a long, antithetically composed narrative, that in the moment of creation there was no matter, no substance, nothing without substance, nothing simple, nothing composed, in short no definite reality.[37] The world came without presuppositions out of nothing.

The creation of the world results from the will and the word of God. A series of negative statements is intended to exclude all anthropomorphic features from the notion of a decision of the divine will.[38] Even the expression 'God willed' is explained as only valid when not taken literally, since God knows no movements of will or understanding or feeling.[39] Nevertheless the saying that God created the world through his will is the most appropriate periphrasis for a basically inexpressible process.[40]

---

[33] 27, 8–12.
[34] 27, 1ff.
[35] 22, 1.
[36] 22, 6; 23, 6; 24, 5; cf. 27, 4.
[37] 21, 1.
[38] 21, 1f. For Quispel, 'Note sur "Basilide"', *Vig. Chr.* 2 (1958), pp. 115f. The statement that God willed to create the cosmos ἀνοήτως and ἀναισθήτως, signifies that God creates unconsciously and that before the creation things pre-existed unconsciously in him. But presumably the text really means to say that only figuratively and for want of a better expression can one talk of an act of divine will.
[39] 21, 1f.: ἀνοήτως, ἀναισθήτως, ἀβούλως, ἀπροαιρέτως, ἀπαθῶς, ἀνεπιθυμήτως κόσμον ἠθέλησε ποιῆσαι. τὸ δὲ ἠθέλησε λέγω, φησί, σημασίας χάριν, ἀθελήτως καὶ ἀνοήτως καὶ ἀναισθήτως.
[40] In the fragment given in Clement of Alexandria, strom. IV 86, 1 Basilides speaks of the 'so-called will of God'.

The cosmos created by the 'non-being' God is itself characterised as 'non-being'.[41] At first sight this description might be taken for a caricature on the part of Hippolytus or his immediate source. But a thoroughly good sense can be given to the statement: through the act of creation by the 'non-being' God arises merely the world-seed which unfolds as super-cosmic and cosmic reality only step by step. From the point of view that everything-that-is only exists potentially in the 'seed-mixture' of the world seed, it can be described as 'non-being'. The concept 'non-being' would in that case not mean, as with the supreme God, the transcendence of being, but the potentiality of what is not yet present reality.[42]

The figurative doctrine of the world seed is in no way naive. Philosophical echoes are clear. The figure of seed was especially used by the Stoics.[43] The world-logos contains within itself the 'spermatikos logos' and can, as the world-fire itself, be called the seed of the cosmos.[44] In the propagation of their doctrine of 'heimarmene' the Stoics often bring forward the figure of seed: the 'heimarmene', which appears under another aspect as the 'pronoia', is the sum of the causes proceeding from God and effective in the world. But in the causes the things that have not yet been realised in time are already present for God. This very thought can indeed be made comprehensible by comparison with the seed, in which everything that will come from it is already latent.[45] Similar ideas are found in Basilides: in the world-seed there already exists potentially everything which can come to be in time,[46] and the whole process of world-unfolding runs according to the established plan of the God who is above all.[47] In Basilides's doctrine of the

[41] VII 21, 4 (note 55 below); X 14, 1.
[42] On the pre-existence of reality in the world-seed cf. VII 21, 2–5; 22, 1.6; X 14, 2. The term 'seed-mixing' (*panspermia*) appears at VII 21, 4f. 22, 16; 23, 3.4.6; 24, 3.5; 25, 1; 27, 11; X 14, 5.
[43] On the concept of the seed in Epicurean physics cf. C. Bailey, *The Greek Atomists and Epicurus* (Oxford, 1928), pp. 343f.
[44] Cf. M. Pohlenz, *Die Stoa* I (1970), pp. 78f.; II (1972), p. 45.
[45] Cf. Cicero, de divin. I 128 (based on Poseidonius): Ut in seminibus vis inest earum rerum quae ex iis progignuntur, sic in causis conditae sunt res futurae; Seneca, nat. quaest. III 29, 3: Ut in semine omnis futuri hominis ratio comprehensa est et legem barbae canorumque nondum natus infans habet – totius enim corporis et sequentis actus in parvo occultoque liniamenta sunt – sic origo mundi non minus solem et lunam et vices siderum et animalium ortus quam quibus mutarentur terrena continuit; on this W. Theiler, 'Tacitus und die antike Schicksalslehre', in *Forschungen zum Neuplatonismus* (1966), pp. 46–103, pp. 55ff.
[46] See n. 42 above.
[47] The catch-word *pronoia* appears in two fragments given in Clement of Alexandria, strom. IV 88, 3; 82, 2; see pp. 81–83 below.

world-seed Stoic motives can thus be seen at work.[48] The term 'panspermia' has already a role in pre-Socratic philosophy[49] and is used by Plato in the *Timaeus* for the mixture of the elements, out of which the demiurge establishes the marrow of the human body.[50] Basilides could have got this concept also from the philosophical tradition.

After the rise of the first two sonships and the creation of the Ogdoad and the Hebdomad the rest of the panspermia then builds the terrestrial world, the 'formlessness', in which the third sonship attains its formation and purification.[51]

The process of the creation of the world-seed is denoted by the verb καταβάλλειν and the corresponding substantive καταβολή, the usual terms for the scattering or planting of seed. To be sure there is also a connection with one of the expressions favoured in Christian speech for the description of the creation of the world, namely καταβολὴ κόσμου. The sowing of the world-seed consists in its creation.[52] Furthermore καταβολή was a pregnant opposite of προβολή, the Valentinian term for emanation. Perhaps it was therefore chosen by Basilides who rejected the latter idea. The doctrine of the three sonships, however, remains difficult to explain. The third sonship is identical with (i.e. comprises) the elect gnostics. The function of the other two sonships consists in this, that after their ascent to the non-being God, which takes place immediately after the creation of the world-seed, they constitute the world above the sky and later send the light of the gospel, the gnosis, into the world.[53] The first two sonships could be brought into line with Christology and perhaps there are also uninterpreted philosophical notions worked into the whole of this piece of Basilidean speculation.[54]

---

[48] Thus earlier Uhlhorn, pp. 12–16; Möller, pp. 347f.
[49] Cf. Aristotle, de gen. et corr. I 1 (314a 29f.) on Anaxagoras and de caelo III 4 (303a 16); de an. I 2 (404a 4); phys. III 4 (203a 21f.) on Leucippus and Democritus.
[50] 73C; cf. A. E. Taylor, *A Commentary on Plato's Timaeus* (Oxford, 1928), p. 522; Festugière, *L'idéal religieux*, p. 247 n. 3.
[51] 22, 15f.; 24, 5; 25, 6; 26, 7.10; 27, 9f. 10.12.
[52] Mt. 13:35; 25:34; Lk. 11:50; Joh. 17:24; Eph. 1:4; Heb. 4:3; 9:26; cf. 11:11; 1 Pet. 1:20; Rev. 13:8; cf. Origen, De princ. III 5, 4: scripturae sanctae conditionem mundi novo quodam et proprio nomine nuncuparunt, dicentes καταβολήν mundi. On the meaning of the words cf. F. Hauck, ThW III (1938), p. 623; W. Bauer, *Griechisch-deutsches Wörterbuch zu den Schriften des Neuen Testaments* (⁵1958), pp. 808f.
[53] 22, 7–16; 25, 6 – 26, 1.
[54] M. Simonetti, *Testi gnostici christiani* (Bari, 1970), p. 105 n. 40, sees in the three sonships the Nous (the son of the highest God), the pneumatic Christ, and the pneumatics. Quispel, *Gnostic Man*, pp. 112–115, suggests a correspondence with the distinction 'divine nous, world nous and human nous' in the hermetic Asclepius 32; he finds the same

The Creation of the World in Basilides and the Valentinians 73

God creates the cosmos on the ground of the decisions of his will alone through his mighty word out of nothing.[55] Thus the world-seed originates neither by way of emanation nor through the fashioning of pre-existent material. Hippolytus's source achieved this double exclusion in two images: God neither brings out emanations as a spider its threads, nor does he need a substance, 'like a mortal man, who takes ore, wood, or some other part of matter, when he is making something'.[56] The rejection of the emanation idea is no doubt directed against other gnostics, probably against the Valentinians. The materialistic idea, closely linked with emanation, of a division and diminishing of the divine being, was apparently intolerable to the Basilideans, who declared any statement about God's being untenable.[57]

Basilides rejected the doctrine of world-formation out of pre-existent material because it is anthropomorphic and limits the omnipotence of God. God is not to be subject to the preconditions which apply to an earthly artist or craftsman. This critique by Basilides of the idea that God works like an artist on a raw material that is to hand represents the earliest clearly discernable explicit contradiction in the history of Christian theology of the

---

conception in the Chaldean Oracles (fr. 7.8.53 des Places) and in Arnobius II 25; Krämer agrees, p. 236; cf. also C. Elsas, *Neuplatonische und gnostische Weltablehnung in der Schule Plotins* (1975), pp. 138ff. W. Schmid, art. 'Epicurus', RAC V (1962), 800, suggests in agreement with H. Leisegang, *Die Gnosis* ([4]1955), p. 230, that the pre-Socratic terms λεπτομερής and παχυμερής, with which Basilides denotes the first and second sonships (22, 7.12; 25, 1; 26, 10; 22, 9f.) were passed on to him through the physics of Epicurus. An obvious contradiction exists between the statements about the creation of the sonships (cf. 22, 7) and the assertion of their homoousion with the highest God (22, 7. 12). Orbe, *Hacia la primera teologia*, pp. 199–709, therefore accepts that the sonships proceeded by emanation from the highest God and understands by the 'katabole' their transfer to the earthly-material realm.

[55] 21, 4: οὕτως ὁ οὐκ ὢν θεὸς ἐποίησε κόσμον οὐκ ὄντα ἐξ οὐκ ὄντων, καταβαλόμενος καὶ ὑποστήσας σπέρμα τι ἓν ἔχον πᾶσαν ἐν ἑαυτῷ τὴν τοῦ κόσμου πανσπερμίαν, cf. 22, 4.7.12; X 14, 1. Creation through the word: 22.3.

[56] 22, 2: ἐπεὶ δὲ ἦν ἄπορον εἰπεῖν προβολήν τινα τοῦ μὴ ὄντος θεοῦ γεγονέναι τὸ οὐκ ὄν – φεύγει γὰρ πάνυ και δέδοικε τὰς κατὰ προβολὴν τῶν γεγονότων οὐσίας ὁ Βασιλείδης –, ποίας γὰρ προβολῆς χρεία ἢ ποίας ὕλης ὑπόθεσις, ἵνα κόσμον θεὸς ἐργάσηται, καθάπερ ὁ ἀράχνης τὰ μηρύματα ἢ θνητὸς ἄνθρωπος χαλκὸν ἢ ξύλον ἤ τι τῶν τῆς ὕλης μερῶν ἐργαζόμενος λαμβάνει; cf. Baur, *Das System des Gnostikers Basilides*, p. 141 n. 1; Möller, *Kosmologie*, p. 346.

[57] On the concept of emanation and its problems cf. Dörrie, 'Emanation – ein unphilosophisches Wort im spätantiken Denken', in *Parusia. Studien zur Philosophie Platons und zur Problemgeschichte des Platonismus* Festschrift for J. Hirschberger (1965), pp. 119–141. Simonetti, *Testi*, p. 104 n. 37, draws attention to Origen's criticism of the emanation idea: princ. I 2, 6; IV 4, 1.

philosophical model of the formation of the world.[58] The earliest church theologian who declares that God's creativity must be thought of otherwise than that of a human artist, is Theophilus of Antioch, who belongs to the generation following that of Basilides. From now on the thesis that the divine creative activity must be superior to artistic creation has its firm place in the controversy with the doctrine of world-formation.[59] John Philoponus in the sixth century is still using this argument against Proclus, the Neo-Platonist, though in rather a different form: He distinguishes between the 'creation' of art and that of nature and contrasts both of them with God's creation. While *techne* is only able to fit elements together in a new way, *physis* brings forward the εἴδη of living being out of nothing. The superiority of the divine creation over both *techne* and *physis* must then consist in this, that God also creates the material out of nothing.[60]

The rejection of the model of world-formation might be thought a necessary consequence of the biblical idea of creation, which, at the moment when the Christians began to debate with philosophical ontology, must follow almost automatically. And in fact the impossibility of reconciling the biblical concept of creation with the idea of world-formation must soon have been realised in wide Christian circles, for otherwise the doctrine of *creatio ex nihilo* would not have been able to prevail so rapidly in the second half of the second century. But we have already seen that Philo and hellenistic Judaism in the confrontation with the philosophical tradition did not come to this conclusion; and the statements of Justin, Athenagoras, Hermogenes, and even Clement of Alexandria, about the creation of the world show that Christians educated in Platonism could hold that acceptance of an unformed matter was entirely reconcilable with biblical monotheism and the omnipotence of God, indeed that they were in no position to think of the creation of the world without that precondition.[61] Why, then, does Basilides, the earliest Christian thinker we know who was really at home with Platonism, reject the doctrine of world-formation so com-

---

[58] The Middle Platonist doctrine of three principles indeed presupposes the comparison between God and an artist: cf. Theiler, *Die Vorbereitung des Neuplatonismus* (1964), pp. 17ff.
[59] Theophilus of Antioch, Autol. II 4; cf. Irenaeus, haer. II 10, 4; Origen, comm. Gen. fragment in Eusebius, praep. ev. VII 20; Dionysius of Alexandria, adv. Sab. fr., ebd. VII 19, 6; Pseudo Justin, cohort. ad Graec. 22; Athanasius, de incarn., 2; or. c. Ar. II 22; Basil, hexaem. II 2; Theodoret, Graec. aff. cur. IV 36, 50–52, 68; Chalcidius, in Tim. 278; Augustine, Gen. c. Manich. I 6, 10; conf. XI 5, 7; John of Damascus, exp. fid. 8, 69–76 (I 8).
[60] De aet. mundi IX 9; cf. Simplicius, in phys. VIII 1 (p. 1142, 1ff. Diels).
[61] See pp. 120ff. below.

pletely? The decisive consideration is first that Basilides understands his supreme God in the common Christian sense as the almighty creator.[62] But to this basic view a further motive must be added which makes his rejection of the Platonic model fully comprehensible: the idea of God's absolute transcendence and superiority to the world forbids that his work of creation should be conceived according to analogies from within the world. Between the doctrine of the 'non-being' of God and the thought of creation out of nothing there is an undoubted correspondence. The gnostic supreme God produces in a simply wonderful way, corresponding to his boundless might. His 'act of creation' is exalted incomparably above all earthly processes of making and therefore can only be defined negatively. A corresponding, highly suggestive exposition of the working of the supreme God can be read in the Valentinian 'Tripartite Tractate' in the Jung Codex: 'No one else has been with him from the beginning; nor is there a place in which he is, or from which he has come forth, or into which he will go; nor is there a primordial form, which he uses as a model as he works; nor is there any difficulty which accompanies him in what he does; nor is there any material which is at his disposal, from which [he] creates what he creates; nor any substance within him from which he begets what he begets; nor a co-worker with him, working with him on the things at which he works. To say anything of this sort is ignorant.'[63] The statement that there is neither a pattern by which God works nor a pre-existent material is apparently directed against the Middle Platonist scheme of three principles[64] and corresponds to the saying of Basilides that God is not to be thought of as a human craftsman. The supreme God is the only principle of the Universe.[65] Of course this does not mean that in the 'Tripartite Tractate' the supreme God creates the world out of nothing or that an act of creation in the strict sense is ascribed to him. The Valentinian Fore-Father simply brings forth the Pleroma, and this happens exclusively by way of emanation.[66] Processes

---

[62] Also in the two fragments Clement of Alexandria, strom. II 36, 1 and IV 88, 3 it seems that the expressions 'the One who rules over all' and 'God of all' mean the supreme God.

[63] NHC I, 5, 53, 23–39: (English translation by H. W. Attridge and Elaine H. Pagels).

[64] This is accepted by the first editors of the Tripartite Tractate; I p. 315 (note to pp. 53, 31), and also by Attridge and E. H. Pagels: *Nag Hammadi Studies* 23, pp. 228f. (notes to pp. 53, 28.31).

[65] Thus Ptolemaeus, ad Flor. 7, 8; cf. 7, 6. Further material on the gnostic concept of God and its sources is to be found in W. R. Schoedel, 'Topological Theology and some Monistic Tendencies in Gnosticism', in *Essays on the Nag Hammadi Texts in Honour of A. Böhlig* (Leiden, 1972), pp. 88–108.

[66] Cf. Tract. Tripart. 56.1ff.

of creation take place first outside the Pleroma,[67] and these are conceived by the Valentinians according to the scheme of world-formation: the materialised affects of the Sophia are used by her and by the demiurge as stuff for the creation.[68] A similar distinction is found in Marcion, who thinks of the demiurge as world-former while he lets the alien God bring forth the heavenly world in an ineffable manner. Basilides, in contrast to the rest of the gnostics, looks on the supreme God, exalted over being and over all plurality, as being also the creator of the world and ascribes to the archons merely the function of under-demiurges.[69] From this statement he has to reach the conclusion that God can only have created the cosmos out of nothing.[70]

There is scarcely any doubt that Basilides started from the traditional Jewish and Christian statements about God's creating 'out of non-being'.[71] But we have seen that these formulae did not in themselves exclude the idea of the pre-existence of matter. Basilides is the first Christian theologian known to us who speaks in the strict sense of a creation out of nothing. So

---

[67] In the Tripartite Tractate the demiurge creates through the word: 101, 6f.; 102, 10f.

[68] See pp.102ff. below.

[69] From Hippolytus's account it is not clear how the creation of the archons is to be conceived: everything originated potentially with the creating of the world-seed, and indeed for the earthly realm this first creation is to suffice (24, 5); cf. Foerster, *System*, pp. 237f. and pp. 67ff. above.

[70] That Basilides really teaches a *creatio ex nihilo* is emphasised by Quispel, *Gnostic Man*, p. 122, and Kretschmar, art. 'Basilides', col. 909. On the other hand Uhlhorn, p. 10, and Möller, pp. 347f., decline to say that Basilides speaks of a *creatio ex nihilo* because the proposition that God created the world through his will (21, 1f.) is only figuratively valid and creation is thought of basically as a natural process. But Basilides is forced by his negative concept of God to restrict all specific statements about God. In Basilides the essential elements of the doctrine of *creatio ex nihilo* are present: the rejection of the emanation and world-formation models and, positively, the idea of creation 'out of nothing' through the will and the word of God. Creation through the world also plays a certain part in popular gnosticism but there it stands in no relation to a considered theory of creation and has the function of emphasising the miraculous character of the process cf. the treatise 'On the Origin of the World' 100, 14–19, 100, 33f.; 102, 14; Apocryphon of John, BG 31, 17; 43, 8; Sophia of Jesus Christ 115, 11–14. G. Scholem, 'Schöpfung aus Nichts und Selbstverschränkung Gottes', *Eranos-Jahrbuch* 25/1956 (1957), pp. 87–119, pp. 100f., claims to find in Basilides the first appearance of the mystical idea that God is Nothing and produces the creation out of himself. But he declares that the idea of Basilides is 'in no way thought out systematically or in principle' (p. 101). Basilides seems to have altered the theme of Non-being in a more refined way: God is non-being because he is above being, the cosmos pre-existing in the world-seed is non-being, because it has still to be realised in time and space (cf. Hippolytus, ref. VII 22, 1.6; X 14, 2), and the world-seed is created out of non-being in the absolute sense, out of nothing.

[71] Thus also Grant, *Gnosticism and Early Christianity*, pp. 143f.

The Creation of the World in Basilides and the Valentinians 77

the question arises whether Basilides developed the idea of *creatio ex nihilo* on his own or whether it was given him from some other quarter. The view that Basilides knew the doctrine of *creatio ex nihilo* from a given tradition might be supported by the following argument: we possess – though not beyond all doubt – the report of Irenaeus that Basilides originally came from Syria.[72] But the first theologian who, after Basilides, rejected the idea of world-formation and expressly asserted the *creatio ex nihilo* was Theophilus of Antioch. His lost work against Hermogenes, in which he thoroughly established the doctrine of *creatio ex nihilo*, and his books addressed to Autolycus were certainly not written before the seventies of the second century, but from his extant statements the impression can be gained that for him *creatio ex nihilo* counted among traditional Christian views.[73] When it is added that the Jewish prayer reproduced in Apostolic Constitutions VII, 34f., which certainly comes from Syria, shows at least the first beginnings of the idea of *creatio ex nihilo*,[74] then the conclusion becomes possible that even before Basilides, that is, at the beginning of the second century, the concept of *creation ex nihilo* could have been encountered in Antioch.

But it is in no way necessary to reconstruct such a hypothetical doctrinal tradition in order to be able to draw from it Basilides's concept of creation. The combination of the biblical creation-tradition with specific gnostic ideas of the incommensurability of the divine activity should make it clear how Basilides came to enunciate the thesis of *creatio ex nihilo*. One can certainly reckon with earlier stages of the doctrine, but one may not go on to ascribe them all to a common origin. The idea of *creatio ex nihilo* presented itself with an inner necessity as soon as people became conscious of the implicit dualism of the doctrine of world-formation and recognised that it contradicted the belief in God's omnipotence. Therefore it is superfluous to hunt at any price for immediate examples and sources for the *creatio ex nihilo* teaching of Basilides. We shall see that even Tatian, independently, as it seems, of any preceding traditions, refuted the eternity of matter for the sake of the monotheistic principle, but without yet talking of a creation 'out of nothing'.[75] The same can be true of Basilides. One can simply suppose that the older formulae, which spoke of a creation out of nothing, were known to him.

According to the report of Hippolytus the Basilideans found the creation of the world-seed set out in Genesis 1:3: The light came from nothing, for

---

[72] See p.53 above.
[73] See pp.156f. below.
[74] See p. 22 n. 96 above.
[75] See pp. 149ff. below.

it is not said whence it came, but simply that it came from the voice of him who spoke. 'Neither the speaker existed nor what came forth. The world-seed came out of nothing, it was the word "Let there be light".'[76] The train of thought, as reproduced either by Hippolytus or in his source, has certainly been abridged and perhaps consciously caricatured. Yet it must be recognised that the Basilideans tried, through a strict word-analysis of the verse in Genesis, to point out that the world-seed could only have been created out of nothing. If the world-seed was first equated with the light, it appears immediately afterwards to have been understood as the word of creation, and if in addition John 1:9 is brought in, both meanings coincide.[77] It is difficult to decide whether the world-seed was exclusively identified with the light of Genesis 1:3 at first and that the reference to the word of creation was only added later under the influence of the equating of Light and Logos in John's Gospel, or whether the interpretation of the Genesis verse now before us presupposes the connection with John's Gospel.[78] Basilides himself may have used the Fourth Gospel but he certainly did not formally quote it,[79] and we can therefore only claim the whole exegetical exercise for later Basilideans. If the world-seed is identical with the divine Logos, then it must – in contradiction of the statement about its creation – have been seen as an emanation from the supreme God.[80] This conception would explain how the three sonships originally to be found in the world-seed can be thought of as alike in being to the supreme God; on the other hand it is scarcely reconcilable with the view that the world-seed contains potentially within itself, not only the three sonships, but the whole cosmos and that it represents, after the archons have completed their work, the earthly-material world. Here we again come up

---

[76] 22, 3f.: ἀλλὰ 'εἶπε', φησί, 'καὶ ἐγένετο', καὶ τοῦτό ἐστιν, ὡς λέγουσιν οἱ ἄνδρες οὗτοι, τὸ λεχθὲν ὑπὸ Μωσέως· 'γενηθήτω φῶς, καὶ ἐγένετο φῶς'. πόθεν, φησίν, γέγονε τὸ φῶς; ἐξ οὐδενός· οὐ γὰρ γέγραπται, φησίν, πόθεν, ἀλλ' αὐτὸ μόνον ἐκ τῆς φωνῆς τοῦ λέγοντος· ὁ δὲ λέγων, φησίν, οὐκ ἦν, οὐδὲ τὸ γενόμενον ἦν. γέγονέ, φησιν, ἐξ οὐκ ὄντων τὸ σπέρμα τοῦ κόσμου, ὁ λόγος ὁ λεχθεὶς 'γενηθήτω φῶς'.

[77] 22, 4f.: καὶ τοῦτο, φησίν, ἔστι τὸ λεγόμενον ἐν τοῖς εὐαγγελίοις 'ἦν τὸ φῶς τὸ ἀληθινόν, ὃ φωτίζει πάντα ἄνθρωπον ἐρχόμενον εἰς τὸν κόσμον.' λαμβάνει τὰς ἀρχὰς ἀπὸ τοῦ σπέρματος ἐκείνου καὶ φωτίζεται.

[78] Orbe, 'A propósito de Gen. 1, 3 (fiat lux) en la exegesis de Taciano', *Gregorianum* 42 (1961), pp. 401–443, pp. 430–435, seeks to show that not only the Basilideans but also Tertullian and Origen were aware of a firm exegetical tradition in which Gen. 1:3 and John 1:9 were linked.

[79] See pp. 64f. above.

[80] Thus Orbe, 'A propósito de Gen. 1, 3', pp. 434f.

against an imbalance in the report of Hippolytus, which cannot be harmonised. From the fragments preserved in Clement of Alexandria we know that Basilides was intensively preoccupied with the problem of human sin and guilt.[81] The myth reproduced by Hippolytus surprisingly gives no explanation of the origin of evil. The goal of the salvation-process is the separation of what is mixed up;[82] but about the origin of the confusion that prevails in the cosmos we get no information – it seems already to have existed in the panspermia. Even so it is simply stated that the third sonship needs purification, without the reason for this being specified.[83] But in reality Basilides seems to have understood the 'original confusion and disorder' as a turning against God and as the ground of evil.[84] Its originator was obviously for him the great archon.[85] Two items in the report of Hippolytus suit this interpretation: the great archon considers himself the supreme God – here we have the well-known gnostic theme of the overweening presumption of the demiurge[86] – and it is his rule of the world that is meant in a modification of the Pauline saying: 'From Adam to Moses sin reigned'.[87]

[81] Strom. IV 81, 1 – 83, 1; III 1, 1 – 3, 2; II 113, 3 – 114, 1 (Isidor).
[82] 27, 8–12.
[83] 22, 7.16; 26, 10; X 14, 2.5.
[84] The passions are a kind of spirits which κατά τινα τάραχον καὶ σύγχυσιν ἀρχικήν cling like appendages to the rational soul: Clement of Alexandria, strom. II 112, 1; cf. E. Mühlenberg, 'Wirklichkeitserfahrung und Theologie bei dem Gnostiker Basilides', KuD 18 (1972), pp. 161–175, p. 173. On the doctrine of the appendages of the soul (also in Isidor, Clement of Alexandria, strom. II 113, 3 – 114, 1) cf. E. des Places in *Numenius, Fragments* (Paris, 1973), p. 122 n. 3 on fr. 43. The alleged Basilides fragment in Hegemonius, Acta Archel. 67, 7–11, in which light and darkness are juxtaposed as principles, is certainly not authentic; it even seems to take the Manichaean myth as given. A remote relationship with the doctrine of Basilides attaches to the view expressed in the pseudo-Clementine documents that the four elements were produced by God without qualities and only through their mingling did evil and the devil originate: hom. XIX 12; XX 3, 8f.; XX 8. H. J. Schoeps, 'Die Dämonologie der Pseudoklementinen', in *Aus frühchristlicher Zeit* (1950), pp. 38–81, pp. 40ff. and: 'Der Ursprung des Bösen und das Problem der Theodizee im pseudoklementinischen Roman', in *Judéo-Christianisme* Festschrift for J. Daniélou (Paris, 1972), pp. 129–141, claims to derive this theory from Jewish tradition.
[85] Thus Mühlenberg, *Wirklichkeitserfahrung*, pp. 172ff. who concludes from Clement of Alexandria, strom. IV 165, 3f. that Basilides regarded the archon as a counter-god; cf. also strom. V 74, 3.
[86] Ref. VII 23, 4f.; 25, 3.
[87] 25, 2 (cf. Rom. 5:13f.) the archon of the Ogdoad, who is obviously imagined as the God of the heathen, rules from Adam to Moses, while the archon of the Hebdomad, the God of the Jews, rules from Moses to Christ (25, 3f.); cf. Heracleon, fr. 20, Origen, comm. Joh. XII 16, 95–97.

Nevertheless Basilides evaluates the world and what happens in it in a relatively positive way: the archons are in fact powerful and wise,[88] and their creating is no act of rebellion or self-overestimation, but realises the plan of the transcendent God.[89] The Gospel, which is none other than the gnosis, comes first to the sons of the archons, then to the archons themselves and is willingly accepted by them.[90] Even the sojourn on earth of the third sonship has a positive meaning: the elect are in the world to do good and to receive good.[91] Their well-doing is more exactly defined as 'the ordering, shaping, improving and completing' of those souls which must remain in the earthly world when the gnostics ascend to God[92] and the latter are also 'formed' in the earthly life.[93] With the ascent of the third sonship the 'apocatastasis' finally reaches its goal.[94] The cosmos will not be dissolved and annihilated, but will 'find mercy'. God spreads the 'great ignorance' over the cosmos, and that extinguishes all 'unnatural' yearning and striving after higher realms. Everything now rests in the place appropriate to its being, and is thus not transitory.[95] Here Basilides's view of the world, in decisive points ungnostic, begins to count: the cosmos is created by God and evil is not essentially immanent in the material, but arises from a disorder contrary to nature in what exists, a confusion and overturning of the original order. To overcome evil and root it out there is need to overcome the confusion, not to annihilate the material world as such.

Basilides's understanding of the world and of creation is essentially different from the Christian conception. True, the world comes into being through a single divine act of creation, but the unfolding of what is in time follows according to a plan laid down at the creation of the world-seed, and in this God takes no further part.[96] Even Christ is formed beforehand in the 'seed-heap' and comes into reality[97] at the hour ordained for him, and the Gospel simply consists in the teaching about the organisation and determi-

---

[88] 23, 4.7; 24, 3f.
[89] 23, 5f.
[90] 26, 1–6.
[91] 25, 1; 26, 10; 27, 11f.; X 14, 9; cf. Clement of Alexandria, strom. IV 82, 1 and Foerster, *System*, p. 242.
[92] 25, 2; X 14, 10.
[93] 26, 10.
[94] Apocatastasis: 25, 1; 26, 2; 27, 4.5.10.11; Clement of Alexandria, strom. II 36, 1; on this A. Méhat, 'ΑΠΟΚΑΤΑΣΤΑΣΙΣ chez Basilide', in *Mélanges d'histoire des religions* Festschrift for H. C. Puech (Paris, 1974), pp. 365–373.
[95] 27, 1–4.
[96] 22, 1.6; 24, 5; 27, 4f.
[97] 27, 5.

The Creation of the World in Basilides and the Valentinians   81

nation of the Universe.⁹⁸ The world thus becomes real in a determined process which strives for the cosmic 'division of natures' and the ascent of the third sonship. Even the disobedience of the archons seems a necessary stage in this sequence. One gets the impression from Hippolytus's exposition that a God acting in history was inconceivable to Basilides. In the end his supreme God is much more like the 'heimarmene' of the Stoics than like the God of the Bible.⁹⁹

His teaching about the pronoia, which determines everything that happens in the world, was maintained by Basilides in the face of persecution and martyrdom.¹⁰⁰ Basilides will give up everything before admitting that Providence can be called unjust.¹⁰¹ His discussion of this theme affords us a rare opportunity of seeing how gnostic thought copes with the experience of reality. To be sure the answer which Basilides gives to the question about the ground of suffering is not 'gnostic' at all: he does not divide the world in which Christians are persecuted from the true God and he also declines to attribute the sufferings of the martyrs to the attacks of an evil power;¹⁰² and he will hold fast unconditionally to the goodness of God. Basilides affirmed martyrdom and took it seriously, and he certainly did not regard denial under persecution as permissible, something with which the church controversialist Agrippa Castor reproaches him.¹⁰³ Basilides indicates that the sufferings of the martyrs are punishment for sin; the punishment is either for a sin which has remained hidden, or, if anyone has not outwardly sinned, for the secret tendency towards the sinful.¹⁰⁴ And indeed Basilides

---

⁹⁸ 26, 1f.; 27, 7.
⁹⁹ Quispel, *Gnostic Man*, pp. 118ff., claims to find in Basilides a salvation-history conception and a philosophy of history, but in reality Basilides thinks in a completely unhistorical way; he transforms salvation-history into a cosmic process, which passes like a natural event.
¹⁰⁰ Clement of Alexandria takes up a position thoroughly opposed to Basilides over martyrdom: strom. IV 81–88. Basilides had treated this question in the 23rd book of his 'Bible expositions' (81, 1).
¹⁰¹ Clement of Alexandria, strom. IV 82, 2; cf. Plato, polit. II 380B. The Platonic way of arguing used by Basilides has been pointed out by W. H. C. Frend, *Martyrdom and Persecution in the Early Church* (Oxford, 1965), p. 246, and especially Mühlenberg, *Wirklichkeitserfahrung*, pp. 165ff.
¹⁰² Strom. IV 81, 3.
¹⁰³ In Eusebius, H.E. IV 7, 7.
¹⁰⁴ The assertion of Clement of Alexandria that Basilides taught that the souls were punished for sins they had committed in an earlier life (strom. IV 83, 2; 85, 3; 88, 1; cf. exc. ex Theod. 28: the Basilideans apply Deut. 5:9 to re-incarnations) seems to be an unjustifiable inference; Origen who, in comm. Matt. ser. 38 (pp. 73, 12f. Klostermann); comm. Rom. V 1 (VI 336f. Lomm.), likewise explains that Basilides taught re-incarnation, may have got

understands martyrdom, in Platonising fashion, as a 'favour' from God, as an honourable opportunity for atonement, which is especially appropriate for the 'elect souls', from whom other forms of penalty are thereby withheld.[105] He pursues the results of his explanation of suffering as atonement for sin so far as not to exempt Jesus from sin, since he suffered.[106] Basilides could assert this comparatively easily, because for him Jesus counted as a mere man, on whom the heavenly light only descended at his baptism.[107]

In the account which Basilides gives of martyrdom the fundamental difference between his understanding of the reality of the world and of human existence and that of the early Christians is given clear expression. Martyrdom is no longer the unique situation in which the Christian has to bear witness to his Lord and protect his faith; rather is it a beneficent opportunity for atonement and purification, made available by Providence. The account of the sufferings of martyrdom as a divine favour deprives it of its pressing seriousness; and Clement in his controversy with Basilides

this from Clement: cf. P. Nautin, 'Les fragments de Basilides sur la souffrance et leur interprétation par Clément et Origen', in *Mélanges d'histoire des religions* Festschrift for H. C. Puech (Paris, 1974), pp. 393–403.

[105] Strom. IV 81, 1 – 83, 2; cf. Campenhausen, *Die Idee des Martyriums in der alten Kirche* (²1964), p. 94; Frend, *Martyrdom*, pp. 245–247; Langerbeck, 'Die Anthropologie der alexandrinische Gnosis', in *Aufsätze zur Gnosis*, pp. 38–82, pp. 46f.; Mühlenberg, *Wirklichkeitserfahrung*, pp. 164ff.

[106] Strom. IV 83, 1; cf. 85, 1.

[107] The Basilidean Jesus (in the source used by Hippolytus Christ is called only the son of the great archon) is composed of four elements which belong to the earthly world, to the Hebdomad, to the Ogdoad, and to the boundary Spirit (27, 10). There is no mention of an element essentially similar to the third sonship which 'follows' Jesus in his ascent (26, 10). The bodily part of Jesus suffers and dies and is returned to the earthly world, to the Amorphia. The resurrection consists in his other elements ascending to the realms of being appropriate to them (27, 10). Jesus is 'the first-born of the separation' (τῆς φυλοκρινήσεως ἀπαρχή: 27, 12). The third sonship is purified through him, in it turn experiences a 'separation' and ascends to the other two sonships (27, 11f.; X 14, 9). The redemption of the third sonship begins with the descent of the 'Gospel', of the 'Light' from the 'blessed' sonship (25, 5ff. The equation of Gospel and Light arises from 26, 5). The Gospel is mediated through the boundary Spirit (25, 5–7). According to one of the fragments preserved in Clement the Gospel is 'the speech of the serving spirit' (strom. II 36, 1; cf. II 38, 1f.; Hippolytus, ref. VII 26, 3 corresponds exactly to this). The Gospel comes down to Jesus through the Ogdoad and the Hebdomad and enlightens him (26, 8). From this account one gets the impression that the enlightenment of Jesus through the Spirit takes place at his baptism. But immediately afterwards the enlightenment linked with Luke 1:35: the Light is equated with the Spirit, which is to come upon Mary, and the 'power of the Most High' which is to 'overshadow' Mary, is to be the power of the separation (26, 9). Obviously the source used by Hippolytus combined two different traditions about the enlightenment of

rightly emphasises the element of personal decision and testing, which is what matters in the situation of confession.[108]

We turn again to the problem of *creatio ex nihilo*. About the middle of the second century a surprising picture emerges: the gnostic Basilides advances a thoroughly thought out doctrine of the creation of the world out of nothing, while the contemporary church Christian teachers either pay scant attention to the problem of the creation of the world or – if they have a certain intellectual formation – can talk unthinkingly about the shaping of the world from eternal matter; we shall see this in the case of Justin. A generation later the situation has fundamentally changed. By then the church theologians are asserting the *creatio ex nihilo* and reproaching the gnostics for falsifying the Christian conception of the creation of the world through their attachment to the cosmology of the philosophers. Is it anything more than a curious accident of history, that the doctrine of the *creatio ex nihilo* first meets us in unambiguous form in the work of a gnostic theologian? Even if Basilides is dependent on an older tradition and the impression that he is the earliest exponent of the doctrine of *creatio ex nihilo* is mistaken, it remains striking that we find no comparable statements in non-gnostic theologians before Tatian. We have found the *creatio ex nihilo* doctrine of Basilides to be based on three components: on the traditional conception that God creates 'out of nothing'; on the conviction that the supreme God is the sole creator, in which Basilides departs from the usual gnostic views; and on the radical negative concept of God which excludes

Jesus. It is to be accepted that Basilides himself put forward the older idea of the enlightenment of Jesus at his baptism and this is confirmed by Clement's statements that the Basilidians celebrated the day of the baptism of Jesus (strom. I 146) and that in the pericope of the baptism they described the dove as the 'servant' (exc. ex Theod. 16; the 'servant' is the Spirit, who brings the enlightenment: strom. II 38, 1f.; cf. II 36, 1). The idea that the enlightenment occurred at the moment of conception certainly goes back only to later Basilidians who were seeking, after taking over the gospels of the Great Church, to link the doctrine of the Virgin Birth with the christological traditions of their own school; cf. Campenhausen, 'Die Jungfrauengeburt in der alten Kirche', SAH 1962, pp. 16–18. H. Usener, 'Das Weihnachtsfest' *Religionsgeschichtliche Untersuchungen* I (³1969), pp. 140f., noted the contradiction in the report of Hippolytus, but sought nevertheless to reconcile the two conceptions of the enlightenment of Jesus. On the other hand K. Holl, 'Der Ursprung des Epiphanienfests', in *Gesammelte Aufsätze zur Kirchengeschichte* II (1928), pp. 123–154, pp. 143f., objected that the Basilideans celebrated exclusively the baptism of Jesus and not, at the same time, his birth; the birth of Jesus thus seems to have played originally no part in their thinking. Simonetti, 'Note die cristologia gnostica', in *Riv. di storia e lett. rel.* 5 (1969), pp. 529–553, pp. 532f., thinks on the contrary that the Basilideans exclusively taught that the enlightenment of Jesus occurred at conception. But this interpretation is explicitly ruled out by the statements of Clement, which Simonetti does not take into account.

[108] Strom. IV 85f.

the explanation of God's creation in terms analogous to those used of any forms of activity within the world. The doctrine of *creatio ex nihilo* thus arises with Basilides out of a singular knitting together of common Christian and gnostic motifs. Or one could even say: the biblical ideas of creation and omnipotence are overstated in Basilides in a gnostic way; thus, as the being of the gnostic God explodes all concepts, so his creation can only be described, in a manner paradoxical for Greek thinkers, as creation out of nothing.

Two or three decades later the church theologians founded the doctrine of *creatio ex nihilo* in detail on arguments similar to those of Basilides: the acceptance of further unformed principles alongside God would take away his divinity, and his creation cannot merely consist, as in the case of a human artist or craftsman, in the shaping of a stuff previously given. Only the concept presented of God is different. The doctrine of *creatio ex nihilo* is therefore not in itself gnostic, but it is characteristic of theological development in the second century that although it was first developed by a gnostic at least in the first half of the century the gnostics are educationally more advanced: philosophical doctrines and problems play a role earlier and to a greater extent with them than with the conservative upholders of the traditions of the local churches. So it need not be surprising that Basilides is the first to controvert explicitly the Greek model of the formation of the world and to formulate the thesis of *creatio ex nihilo*, at a time when the same conclusions emerged from the biblical as from the gnostic ideas.

So far as we know, the idiosyncratic creation doctrine of Basilides remained without historical effect. As Irenaeus's exposition shows, a section of the later Basilideans gave up almost entirely the characteristic ideas of the founder of their school, and on the Church side the whole theology of Basilides must have soon encountered mistrust and rejection. Relatively early on, a church controversialist, Agrippa Castor, wrote against Basilides.[109] Only Clement of Alexandria looked more closely at the writings of Basilides and Isidor and debated with them in, so to speak, an academic style, but he was concerned mainly with ethical questions. If we did not have the report of Hippolytus, the speculations of Basilides on the creation would remain unknown to us.

---

[109] Eusebius, H.E. IV 7, 5–8. Whether Agrippa Castor really wrote in Hadrian's day, as Eusebius maintains, cannot be proved; cf. Harnack, *Literaturgeschichte* II I, pp. 290f.

II. Valentinus

The theology of Basilides can be regarded as an attempt to unite common Christian and gnostic ideas in a synthesis. With Valentinus and his disciples the motives which appear to us more characteristically gnostic begin to count. The few fragments that have survived of the words of Valentinus himself[110] show high literary quality and reveal the unusually high educational standard of their writer.[111] But it is impossible from this scanty material to get an overall picture of Valentinus's doctrine. Irenaeus sets out the supposed system of Valentinus in concise form and points out the differences from the doctrine of Ptolemaeus, yet this sketch does not conform at all points with what we otherwise know of Valentinus's doctrine.[112] Tertullian reports that the school of Valentinus moved a long way from the doctrine of the founder.[113] The only pupil who, according to Tertullian, remained true to the master, Axionicus in Antioch, is for us a mere name.[114] If it is desired to reconstruct the original theology of Valentinus, then the double presupposition must be made the starting-point, that Valentinus probably taught more simply than his disciples, but that at the same time the essential lines of thought of the second generation were laid down by him, as a complete abandoning of the leading ideas of the head of the school after so short a time would be inconceivable. Perhaps Valentinus did not produce a closed system, but rather experimented with various forms of the myth without bringing them together into a whole.[115]

---

[110] The material is assembled in Harnack, *Literaturgeschichte* I, pp. 174–184.

[111] Cf. E. Norden, *Die antike Kunstprosa* II (1909), pp. 545–547.

[112] Irenaeus, haer. I 11, 1. The system of thirty Aeons, which is found in the same form in Ptolemaeus, and the acceptance of a second Horos, who separates the original divine Ground from the aeons that have originated from it, are scarcely to be reconciled with the statement of Tertullian, that Valentinus understood the aeons as spiritual events within the Godhead and no one before Ptolemaeus had understood them as 'personal substances' (adv. Val. 4, 2; n. 152 below). On the other hand, the acceptance of only one Sophia (as in exc. ex Theod. 23, 2) might be more original than her doubling in Ptolemaeus. The idea that Christ was born of Sophia but deserted her and ascended to the Pleroma is also found in exc. ex Theod. 32, 2 – 33, 1. 3; cf. G. C. Stead, 'The Valentinian myth of Sophia', JThS, n.s. 20 (1969), pp. 75–104, pp. 84f.

[113] Ad. Val. 4.

[114] He is mentioned again by Hippolytus, who describes him as the representative of the oriental school of Valentinianism; ref. VI 35, 7.

[115] This is the thesis of the essay by Stead mentioned above (n. 112). Through this research the attempt by Quispel, 'The original doctrine of Valentinus', *Vig. Chr.* 1 (1947), pp. 43–73, to reconstruct the original doctrine of Valentinus from the agreements between the systems of Ptolemaeus and Theodotus, has been superseded.

86 *Creatio Ex Nihilo*

One can only try, therefore, to interpret the genuine fragments from themselves and then to draw out general lines of connection with the doctrine of the greater members of the Valentinian school.[116] The source problem has been changed by the attribution to Valentinus of two writings in the Codex Jung, the so-called 'Gospel of Truth' and the Letter to Rheginos 'On the Resurrection'. While Valentinus's authorship of the 'Gospel of Truth' seems far from probable,[117] it is in the case of the 'Letter to Rheginos' quite acceptable.[118] What we have here is not the usual gnostic revelation-document, but a genuine letter from a teacher, who possesses high authority, to his pupil, and we know that Valentinus wrote such letters.[119] The letter stems in any case from a respected Valentinian teacher, whose theology seems to be older than that of Heracleon and Ptolemaeus – why should the writer not be Valentinus himself?[120]

---

[116] So argue, more or less, W. Foerster, *Von Valentin zu Herakleon* (1928), pp. 91–97; A. J. Festugière, 'Notes sur les Extraits de Théodote de Clément d'Alexandrie et sur les Fragments de Valentin', *Vig. Chr.* 3 (1949), pp. 193–207, pp. 203ff. On the contrary F. M. M. Sagnard, *La gnose valentinienne et le témoignage de Saint Irénée* (Paris, 1947), pp. 559–561, interprets the fragments of Valentinus from the start by reference to the views of his pupils.

[117] The compilation of this by Valentinus and the identity of the writing with the 'veritatis evangelium' mentioned by Irenaeus, haer. III 11, 9 was first put forward by van Unnik, 'The recently discovered "Gospel of Truth" and the New Testament', in F. L. Cross, *The Jung Codex* (London 1955), pp. 81–129, pp. 90–104. The hypothesis that this is an early work, in which Valentinus has not yet distinguished between the demiurge and highest God, is however without proof; we have no knowledge of the intellectual development of Valentinus. Also Grant, *Gnosticism and Early Christianity*, pp. 128ff., regards the 'Gospel of Truth' as an early work by Valentinus.

[118] The first editors accept Valentinus as the compiler: M. Malinine, H. C. Puech, G. Quispel, W. Till, R. McL. Wilson, J. Zandee, *De Resurrectione, Epistula ad Rheginum* (1963) XXIV–XXXIII, also van Unnik, 'The newly discovered Gnostic "Epistle to Rheginos" on the Resurrection' I, JEH 15 (1964), pp. 141–152, p. 144. M. L. Peel, *The Epistle to Rheginos. A Valentinian Letter on the Resurrection* (London, 1969), pp. 156ff., contests that it was compiled by Valentinus. He points out contradictions of content between the Letter and on one hand the 'Gospel of Truth' and on the other the system of Valentinus, as Quispel has reconstructed it. But this line of argument has no weight, for the composition of the 'Gospel of Truth' by Valentinus is improbable (see n. 117 above) and Quispel's attempt at reconstruction has proved to be inadequate (see n. 115 above).

[119] This is stressed by van Unnik, 'The newly discovered Gnostic "Epistle to Rheginus"' I, pp. 145–147; cf. Clement of Alexandria, strom. II 36, 2; 114, 3; III 59, 3.

[120] Thus also G. Kretschmar, 'Auferstehung des Fleisches. Zur Frühgeschichte einer theologischen Lehrformel', in *Leben angesichts des Todes* Thielicke Festschrift (1968), pp. 101–137, pp. 118f.; P. Kübel, *Schuld und Schicksal bei Origenes, Gnostikern und Platonikern* (1973), pp. 69–71.

The Creation of the World in Basilides and the Valentinians   87

We possess no utterances of Valentinus on the process of the creation of the world. The demiurge and his relationship with the highest God are dealt with in some sentences from a sermon, which Clement of Alexandria quotes and illustrates from the context: 'In what follows he is alluding to this God (i.e. the demiurge), when hè writes in so many words: "In the same way as a portrait falls short of the living face, so is the cosmos weaker than the living Aeon. What is now the cause of the portrait? The majesty of the countenance that delivers the pattern to the painter, whereby the copy can be honoured with his name; for the form was not found corresponding to reality, but the name completed what was lacking in the picture. But it contributes the invisible being of God to the attestation of the formed".[121] For he (i.e. Valentinus) described the demiurge, in so far as he is called God and Father, as the copy of the true God, and as his prophet, but Wisdom, as painter, who has formed the copy for the glorification of the invisible; for all beings which proceed from a syzygy are pleromata, but those which spring from an individual are only copies.'[122] Thus Sophia brought forth the demiurge as a copy of the highest God, in order to glorify the latter thereby. The copy frankly falls very short of the original but the Name of God makes up for what is lacking in the copy: as God and Father of the cosmos and of mankind, the demiurge represents, on the lowest step of being, the true, the highest God.[123] It is surprising how positively Valentinus sees the creator and his world.[124] To be sure, the statement, that the picture produced by

[121] Cf. Rom. 1:20.
[122] Strom. IV 89, 6 – 90, 2. The last sentence is also found in exc. ex Theod. 32, 1. As Clement obviously had the sermon of Valentinus before him, it is to be assumed that he interpreted accurately the passage reproduced verbatim. According to Hilgenfeld, *Ketzergeschichte* p. 300, however, Clement misunderstood what Valentinus had to say, and, according to E. Preuschen, art. 'Valentinus', RE 20 (1908), pp. 399f., he used a later Valentinian writing, in which the homily was only cited. Neither the one nor the other is likely.
[123] That the demiurge 'as image of the Father becomes a Father himself' is stated also in exc. ex Theod. 47, 2f.; cf. 33, 3; otherwise exc. 7.5; Irenaeus, haer. I 5, 1; II 7, 2. (On the inscriptions of the names on images of the gods cf. Justin, dial. 35, 6.) It is questionable whether behind the statement of Valentinus there lie the speculations about the 'name' in exc. 22, 6; 26, 1; 31, 3, as Sagnard, *La gnose Valentinienne*, p. 561, suggests. Festugière, *Les Extraits*, p. 205, understands the 'name of God' in the Old Testament sense of his 'glory', but gives no evidence for this interpretation.
[124] The sentences 'But it also contributes the invisible being of God to the attestation of the formed' (εἰς πίστιν τοῦ πεπλασμένου) (90, 1) is difficult. Perhaps it has also the meaning that the 'invisible being of God' works with belief in the original conception exhibited in the image, i.e. the true God himself (cf. Festugière, *Les Extraits*, p. 205). Simonetti, *Testi gnostici*, p. 129, has yet another rendering: 'Cosi l'invisibilità di Dio coopera alla fede di ciò che è stato creato'. Both interpretations would in any case be referring here to the origin of Pistis.

Sophia to glorify God is not really like its original, presupposes the myth of the hybris and the fall of Sophia. But the thought of the fall comes in the fragment far behind the idea that the demiurge copies the highest God and that it is possible to see through the cosmos the heavenly reality.[125]

In a comparable way the fragment preserved by Hippolytus of a psalm composed by Valentinus speaks of the ladder of being which reaches from matter upwards to the pleroma and to the highest God. Every step depends on the one above, and there is no indication of any break between the pleroma and the cosmos.[126]

However, negative utterances about the world and creation are also not lacking in Valentinus. In the same sermon in which he spoke of the pictorial character of the demiurge and the cosmos, he also, according to Clement, spoke of the fact that the pneumatics, chosen from the beginning to be immortal, annihilated death. When they let go of the world, without themselves being let go of, they become lords over creation and over everything transitory.[127] Creation, death and passing away are thus brought closely together. But the origin of death must be the work of the world-creator, about whom it is therefore said in the Old Testament: 'No one can see the face of God and live'.[128] We cannot fit these fragments together into a general picture of the doctrine of Valentinus. His thought must at any rate have been characterised by a deep split: on the one side the world is a pictorial indication of the reality of the pleroma, on the other side it is dominated by death and must be conquered and annihilated by the pneumatics – perhaps through severe asceticism. It might be that Valentinus was not yet in a position to bring together these two aspects into a unified

---

[125] Cf. Stead, *Myth*, pp. 92f., 95. The singular Aeon used in the sense of Pleroma (89, 6) is also found in Heracleon, fr. 1 = Origen, comm. Joh. II 14, 100; 18 = XIII 11, 70; 22 = XIII 19, 114; ev. Phil. 11 (p. 102, 1); tract. tripart. 74, 1ff. The statement of Tertullian (adv. Val. 4, 2; n. 152 below) that Valentinus had not yet separated the Aeons from God, fits in with this usage; cf. K. Müller, 'Beiträge zum Verständnis der Valentinianischen Gnosis' I, NAG 1920, pp. 179–184, pp. 182f. Festugière, *Les Extraits*, p. 205, suggests that Aeon here means a semi-divine being, and refers to corp. herm. XI 15: 'Thus the aeon is an image of God and the cosmos an image of the aeon'. Cf. the analysis of the Tractate and the investigation of the Aeon-concept by Festugière, *La révélation d'Hermès Trismégiste* IV (Paris, 1954), pp. 152–199. Following this, Aeon is in the Hermetica 'the cosmic God personified, and together the ἀπέραντος world and infinite time' (p. 199). But that is not the conception the Valentinians had. A good survey of the meanings of Aeon is given by W. Scott, *Hermetica* III (Oxford, 1926), pp. 188f.

[126] Ref. VI 37, 6–8.

[127] Strom. IV 89, 2f.; on this passage cf. Beyschlag, 'Christentum und Veränderung in der Alten Kirche', KuD 18 (1972), pp. 26–55, pp. 40f.; id., *Simon Magus*, pp. 206–208.

[128] Strom. IV 89, 4f. (Ex. 33:20).

The Creation of the World in Basilides and the Valentinians 89

theological design.[129] In any case, the ambivalence indicated dominates also the later Valentinian system and, according to whether one side or the other is emphasised, world denial can preponderate, but there an astoundingly positive evaluation of human and cosmic reality is possible.

The ascetic inclinations of Valentinus are also mirrored in his christological ideas. In a further fragment preserved by Clement of Alexandria it says that the divinity of Jesus was manifest in his complete abstinence: Although he bore everything, he was abstinent. He ate and drank and did not give the food back from himself. The strength of his abstinence was so great that even the food he ate was not destroyed, because he himself was not subject to destruction.[130] Clement passes on these sayings without criticism; they are related to his own views.[131]

The peculiar ambivalence of affirming the earthly reality and denying the world which the extant fragments of Valentinus display, is also known in the Rheginos Letter. In a train of thought surprisingly close to Paul's for something written in the middle of the second century and with an express appeal to the 'Apostle',[132] the writer deals with the problem of the resurrection. He affirms and defends the resurrection of the flesh[133] and gives no thought to the antithesis between immortal soul and mortal flesh.[134] The resurrection becomes effective in the faith-bond with Christ; the believer's

---

[129] According to Stead's hypothesis Valentinus was trying to combine two different wisdom-traditions, without being able fully to equate them (*Myth*, pp. 93ff.).

[130] Clement of Alexandria, strom. III 59, 3.

[131] Cf. Paid. I 4, 1f.; strom. VI 71, 2. The food of the Logos and the angels (Gen. 18:8) is another problem for Justin: dial. 57, 2. It is doubtful whether we should presuppose for Valentinus himself the Christology of the later Valentinians, who hold one Christ composed of four different substances and understand his human nature as psychic substance, though it seems merely hylic. The Rheginus letter puts forward a kind of two-natures Christology: 'The Son of God, Rheginus, was Son of Man, He embraced them both, possessing the humanity and the divinity' (44, 21–26, translation by Peel). These statements could well come from Valentinus himself; cf. Kretschmar, 'Christliches Passa im 2. Jahrhundert und die Ausbildung der christlichen Theologie' in *Rech. Sc. Rel.* 60 (1972), pp. 287–323, pp. 312ff. On the other hand it seems to me that the supposed fragment of Valentinus cited by Eulogius of Alexandria in Photius, bibl. 230 (273B), which contests the two-natures doctrine of the 'Galileans' with 'one nature of the visible and the invisible', is not authentic, in spite of Usener's attempt to rescue it (*Weihnachtsfest*, p. 145).

[132] 45, 24f. On the Pauline parallels cf. especially R. Haardt, '"Die Abhandlung über die Auferstehung" des Codex Jung aus der Bibliothek gnostischer koptischer Schriften von Nag Hammadi' II, *Kairos* N.F. 12 (1971), pp. 237–269.

[133] 47, 1–8; 44, 6–10; 46, 14–16.

[134] Van Unnik, *The newly-discovered Gnostic 'Epistle to Rheginos'* I, p. 151: 'The soul is not imprisoned in the body, as was held by many non-Christian thinkers. The fetters that are spoken of are the fact that one lives in the world.'

fellowship with Christ is already in itself the resurrection.[135] But the resurrection is not exhausted in the fulfilment of faith; the whole person, not just a spiritual kernel of being, will be included in the expected perfection after death.[136] In this train of thought, therefore, the bodily reality of man seems to be given a thoroughly positive value. It corresponds to this conception that it is said of Jesus too, without limitation, that he was 'in the flesh'.[137] But now on the other hand the flesh which the believer puts on at the resurrection is by no means identical with the empirical bodiliness of the person, for it is quite removed from that body which is subject to transitoriness.[138] And it can further be said that the spiritual resurrection embraces that of the soul and the flesh.[139] Through such statements the phrase about the resurrection of the flesh loses all its concrete significance and there seems to remain of its particular content only the idea that the believer, who has put on Christ, will after death ascend to the pleroma.[140] The 'flesh' is thus regarded one-sidedly in its relation to Christ and not in its attachment to the reality of the world. In addition to this, the resurrec-

---

[135] 45, 23–39; cf. 44, 30–33; on this Kretschmar, *Auferstehung des Fleisches*, pp. 124f.

[136] 48, 3–12; cf. Kretschmar, *Auferstehung*, pp. 126–128. Alongside the emphasis on belief and its decisive meaning there stands also the typically gnostic notion of a predestination to knowledge: 46, 25–29; cf. van Unnik I, p. 150; Haardt II, pp. 249–251.

[137] 44, 15; cf. van Unnik I, pp. 148f. Simonetti, 'Note di cristologia gnostica', p. 547, n. 58, wants to understand the 'flesh' here too in the later Valentinian sense of a pseudosubstance; similarly Haardt II, pp. 251ff., who refers to Tertullian, carn. Chr. 15, 1: licuit et Valentino ex privilegio haeretico carnem Christi spiritalem comminisci.

[138] 47, 38 – 48, 3; cf. 47, 17–24; Haardt II, pp. 262f., considers that by the flesh which rises the compiler understands the pre-existent pneuma of the gnostic.

[139] 45, 39 – 46, 2. J. Zandee, 'De opstanding in de brief aan Rheginos en in het Evangelie van Philippus', *Nederl. Theol. Tijdschr.* 16 (1961/62), pp. 361–377, pp. 371f., thinks of a change of the somatic body into pneuma. Haardt II, pp. 266–268, gathers from this passage that we see here 'a stamp of gnosis, which will not concede salvation to the psychic element' (p. 268) and he suggests, with the editors of the editio princeps (pp. xxiiif.) that the Letter could have been related to the eastern school of Valentinianism. On the other hand, according to Kretschmar, the Letter of Rheginos like the Gospel of Philip does not understand the flesh as the 'physical being of the individual' but as 'a dimension of reality', which would be a 'specific extension of the Pauline, and perhaps also the Old Testament usage' (*Auferstehung* p. 125, cf. pp. 122f.). The sarx is the substratum of the fallen world which in the Apocatastasis (44, 31) will be, in both senses of the word, 'replaced'. The fact that the Risen ones at every time 'will have the use of their "flesh"' (pp. 126ff.) is also part of this. Similarly Kübel, pp. 69–71. This attractive interpretation would have to be demonstrated systematically from all the Valentinian sources; cf. also A. H. C. van Eijk, 'The Gospel of Philip and Clement of Alexandria', *Vig. Chr.* 25 (1971), pp. 94–120.

[140] Van Unnik II, p. 165, suggests that the writer basically held the idea that souls ascend to heaven after death (with reference to Justin, dial. 80, 4; Irenaeus, haer. V 31, 2).

tion moves into sharp contradiction with the cosmos. It is not the resurrection that is an illusion, to a much greater extent the cosmos is a deception. To the believer who receives the resurrection the transitoriness of the world is revealed.[141] So the thought of the writer is shown to be distinctly alien to history and in the last resort hostile to the world: its interest in the 'flesh' is limited to the believers, who are indeed identical with the pneumatics. But what is special about the Letter is that the writer, who is drawn from his gnostic ways of thought to a radical spiritualism, is determined to hold fast unconditionally to the Christian idea of the resurrection of the body and therefore does not completely devalue the earthly, bodily life of men.[142]

The myth of the Valentinian school
Valentinus's own views on the origin and construction of the heavenly world of the Aeons and on the origin of the cosmos remain to a large extent obscure to us. For these questions we must refer to the systems of his immediate disciples, who are comparatively well known to us. As the foundation of the exposition we shall be primarily served in what follows by the best preserved system, that of Ptolemaeus (known to research as System A), with which the system derived from the fragments of Heracleon is virtually identical.[143] Beside it stands the system passed on by Hippolytus, which in its fundamental outline coincides with that of Ptolemaeus, but diverges from it in a series of characteristics (System B).[144] The 'Tripartite Tractate' from the find at Nag Hammadi finally sets out a system in which elements from A and B are combined.[145]

The task of the cosmogonic myth is precisely stated by Ptolemaeus, when at the end of his Letter to Flora he proposes to give his correspondent

---

[141] 48, 10 – 49, 6; cf. 45, 14–17; 46, 35–38.
[142] The immediate juxtaposition of specifically gnostic and Christian ideas is emphasised by van Unnik II, p. 165, 'It is the great question, to which I see no answer, at present, why this Valentinian with *this* idea of the deity was so deeply attached to Christianity.'
[143] Irenaeus, haer. I 1, 8; exc. ex Theod. 43–65; on Heracleon cf. Foerster, *Von Valentin zu Herakleon*, pp. 67ff.
[144] Ref. VI 29–36. But Irenaeus occasionally mentions views from B, while conversely Hippolytus sometimes draws on A.
[145] Cf. Puech and Quispel, 'Le quatrième écrit gnostique du Codex Jung', *Vig. Chr.* 9 (1955), pp. 65–102 and the note to p. 75, 17, in the editio princeps: I pp. 337f. In the Excerpta ex Theodoto the self-contained passage 29–43, 1 agrees to a large extent with the system attributed by Irenaeus to Valentinus himself (haer. I 11, 1; but cf. also exc. 23, 2); cf. Sagnard's analysis in his edition of the Excerpta: *Clément d'Alexandrie, Extraits de Théodote* (SC 23, Paris, ²1970), pp. 28–49.

instruction, at a later date, on how from the simple, ungenerate, intransitory and good principle there could arise 'The nature of corruption' – the material – and 'the nature of the middle' – the demiurge and all psychic substances – although the Good itself can only bring forth what is of like kind with itself.[146] The problem at issue is not that of the philosophical question about the principle on which all being is based. To the Valentinians the thought of the earthly world as such has become questionable. They are troubled by the question how from the highest God, thought of as the principle of being, any less perfect being could originate. Thus it is a matter of concern to find the answer to the religious question about the origin of the imperfect, of the transitory and of evil. The myth shows how God first communicated with the world through emanations, but the origin of the cosmos, outside the pleroma, can only be explained by a breach, through the fall of Sophia, who arose as the last emanation, and thus is furthest removed from God.

System A, transmitted by Irenaeus, gives no grounds for the beginning of the process of emanation; it says in passing that the divine Abyss willed to allow the All to come into being.[147] An attempt is made to explain how God first allowed the Aeons to be imperfect – from the second stage of emanation downwards they lacked knowledge of the Father: The first emanation, the Nous, wants to pass on his gnosis to the other Aeons, but is hindered in this by his mother Sige, because the Aeons must first be led to an independent longing for gnosis.[148] The original withholding of the knowledge has thus an educational significance.[149] A passage of the *Excerpta ex Theodoto* gives as the Father's motive for bringing forth the Aeons the wish to be known by them,[150] and System B gives the grounds that the Father decided to bring forth the most beautiful and the most perfect that he had within him, since he is wholly love, but there can be no love without the beloved.[151] The decision of the Fore-Father to let the pleroma come into being is thus the expression of his divine goodness.

---

[146] Ad Flor. 7, 8f.
[147] Irenaeus, I 1, 1.
[148] Irenaeus, I 2, 1.
[149] The Evangelium Veritatis (18, 38–40) and the Tractatus Tripartitus (62, 20) stress in this connection that the ultimate Father did not withhold knowledge from the aeons out of envy (cf. Timaeus 29E); on this van Unnik, 'De ἀφθονία van God in de oudchristelijke literatur', *Mededel. Nederl. Wetensch.*, N.R. 36/2 (Amsterdam, 1973), pp. 17ff.
[150] Exc. 7. 1.
[151] Hippolytus, ref. VI 29, 5.

Tertullian reports that Valentinus himself understood the Aeons as 'thoughts, strivings and excitements within the divine Being' and that Ptolemaeus, the great systematiser of the Valentinian school, was the first to make of them independent 'personal' beings.[152] But the doctrine of Aeons was already given to the Valentinians in a fairly fixed shape through older forms of the gnostic myth which they used.[153] Perhaps they understood the Aeons by analogy with the Platonic Ideas and took this into account both in the naming and in the ordering of them.[154] Yet the doctrine of the Aeons, of whose names and two-by-two procession there are various detailed versions, can scarcely lay claim to serious philosophical meaning. Such pseudo-learned speculations belong to the apparatus of gnostic system-making. Only the fall of Sophia is decisive for the further unfolding of being.[155] Here alongside the weakening depiction of the trespass of Sophia in systems A and B – in A Sophia seeks to know the being of the Father, in B she wants to bring something forth without syzygy as the Father does – a broader difference comes into view: in B the fall derives solely from Sophia and from her longing to imitate the Father; on the other hand in system A the passion of Sophia which drives her to want to know the Father, already takes its beginning on the first step of emanation, Nous – 'Truth'.[156] Ptolemaeus thus in no way follows the tendency to place the origin of the fall as far as possible away from the highest God, but puts it in the pleroma itself.[157] Ptolemaeus must have regarded it as esoteric knowledge that the fall, from which evil takes it origin, had its beginning in the immediate presence of God. But the idea is quite coherently developed from the presuppositions of Valentinian thought: the process which leads to the

---

[152] Val. 4, 2: eam (sc. viam) postmodum Ptolemaeus intravit, nominibus et numeris Aeonum distinctis in personales substantias, sed extra deum determinatas, quas Valentinus in ipsa summa divinitatis ut sensus et affectus (et) motus incluserat.

[153] This dependence is already asserted by Irenaeus, I 11, 1, probably using an earlier source; cf. N. Brox, Γνωστικοί als häresiologischer Terminus', ZNW 57 (1966), pp. 105–114, pp. 111f. Such a preliminary stage of the Valentinian myth is exhibited especially by the Apocryphon of John.

[154] Cf. Krämer, *Ursprung der Geistmetaphysik*, pp. 242ff.

[155] System A: Irenaeus, I 2, 2 (Sophia falls through her hybrid striving after knowledge); B: Irenaeus, I 2, 3; Hippolytus, VI 30, 6 – 31, 2 (Sophia wants, in imitation of the Father, to bring forth a new being without a partner).

[156] Irenaeus, I 2, 2; cf. II 17, 7.

[157] On the theme that Sophia, from whom stems the Fall, is distanced from the Father, cf. H. M. Schenke, 'Nag Hammadi Studien III. Die Spitze des dem Apokryphon Johannis und der Sophia Jesu Christi zugrundeliegenden gnostischen Systems', ZRGG 14 (1962), pp. 352–361.

origin of the world and of matter begins with the origin of the first imperfect being, differentiated from God. Irenaeus, with his assertion that for the Valentinians the world came into being only through the ignorance and 'diminution' of the Aeons, had thoroughly grasped the meaning of the Ptolemaic myth.[158]

We do not need here to go over again the whole Valentinian myth, so often described, but shall confine ourselves to directing our attention to the structure of the processes in which the stages of being are unfolded, and so to acquainting ourselves with the inner mechanism of the myth. The pleroma goes forth, by way of emanation, from the original Ground. The fixed term by which the Valentinians denote both the process of emanation and the beings that emanate is προβολή.[159] It corresponds to the specific nature of the emanation idea that every προβολή contains the being of the Father who sends it out, but with a diminution equivalent to the increasing distance from God.[160] The imperfection and remoteness from God of each

---

[158] Haer. II 19, 9.

[159] Cf. Clement of Alexandria, strom. III 1, 1; V 126, 2; Tertullian, Prax. 8, 1. The reason for this choice of words is not clear. Perhaps the image of the shooting and fruiting of plants played a part. (On the meanings 'shoot' and 'fruit' of προβάλλειν and 'shooting, shoots, growth' of προβολή cf. F. Passow, *Handwörterbuch der griechischen Sprache* II 1 [1852] 1093, 1096. In any case ideas from this area are relatively plentiful in Valentinian texts: the primaeval Father and the higher aeons are described as 'roots of the all' (Irenaeus I 1, 1; 2, 1; Hippolytus, VI 30, 7; tract. tripart. 51, 3f. 18; 66, 18; 74, 11; cf. Sagnard, *La gnose valentinienne*, pp. 436f.) and emanation is often compared with the production of fruit (cf. Valentinus, fr. 8 in Hippolytus, ref. VI 37, 7; Irenaeus, I 2, 4.6; 4, 5; 8, 5f.; 11, 1f.; 14, 5; Hippolytus, VI 32, 1f.; cf. 55, 1; tract. tripart. 51, 17–19; 74, 10–13; on this Sagnard, *La gnose*, pp. 432–436; cf. also tract. tripart. 62, 9–11, p. 96 below. Later authors understand the προβολή expressly from the shooting and fruiting of plants: cf. Basil, ep. 52.3; Socrates, H.E. I 8, 32. J. Ratzinger, art. 'Emanation', RAC IV (1959), cols. 1218–1228, col. 1220, suggests on the contrary that with this choice of words the image of light was decisively adopted. On the meaning and history of the emanation idea cf. with Ratzinger's article Dörrie, art. 'Emanation', RGG³ II (1958), pp. 449f.; id., 'Emanation, Ein unphilosophisches Wort im spätantiken Denken', in *Parusia, Studien zur Philosophie Platons und zur Problemgeschichte des Platonismus* Festgabe for J. Hirschberger (1965), pp. 119–141.

[160] Cf. Dörrie, 'Emanation', p. 131. This factor of diminution of being in emanation is surely the reason why the Valentinians seem not to have applied the term ὁμοούσιος, which they otherwise favoured, to the relationship between the aeons and the Fore-Father: the pneumatic substance which is born of the Sophia-Achamoth pairing is alike in being to this (Irenaeus, haer. I 5, 1.6; Tertullian, Val. 18, 1); the (pneumatic) body of Jesus is alike in being to the Church (i.e. the pneumatics) (exc. ex Theod. 42, 3; cf. Sagnard, *La gnose valentinienne*, pp. 523, 532); in the same way that which is alike in being to Him will be saved by the pneumatic and psychic body assumed by Christ according to Rom. 11:16 (exc. 58, 1; cf. Müller, *Beiträge* III, pp. 200f.). The 'psychic man' which the demiurge at his creation breathed into the 'hylic man' (exc. 50, 2; cf. Gen. 2:7) – in both cases it is a matter of souls,

pair of Aeons, increasing step by step, explains how in the end the last Aeon could fall. It is against this thought of separation and distancing of the emanations from God, although they stem from his being, from which must arise the idea of a division of the divine being, that the church controversialists especially direct their criticism.[161] For the Valentinians themselves the emanation images were indeed only symbols and pointers in oblique language to the process that was inconceivable and therefore only to be expressed in myth, namely that out of God beings can proceed which are related to him and yet at the same time are so distant from him that they are no longer in a position to know him.[162] What is said of the Aeons is basically the destiny of the pneumatics in the world.[163] Irenaeus reports that he had questioned Valentinians in personal conversation about the essence

which only later will be clothed in earthly bodies (cf. exc. 55, 1; Irenaeus, I 5, 5) – is alike in being to the demiurge. The 'hylic man' to the animal souls (exc. 50, 1) and to the devil (exc. 53, 1). The man who does wrong becomes alike in being to the devil (Heracleon, fr. 44–46 = Origen, comm. Joh. XX 20, 168–170; 23, 198–201; 24, 211–219. In this case the homoousion is not the result of a natural relationship but of human conduct: cf. Langerbeck, *Die Anthropologie der Alexandrinischen Gnosis*, pp. 67–70). Also Ptolemaeus, ad Flor. 7, 8 excludes a consubstantiality in the fullest sense between the aeons and the original Ground. In all these passages ὁμοούσιος likeness of being on the level of the same stage of being, thus the word expresses, so to speak, a horizontal relation. On the connection between emanation and consubstantiality see Ratzinger, col. 1225.

[161] Cf. Origen, Princ. I 2, 6: observandum namque est, ne quis incurrat in illas absurdas fabulas eorum, qui prolationes quasdam sibi ipsi depingunt, ut divinam naturam in partes vocent et deum patrem quantum in se est dividant, cum hoc de incorporea natura vel leviter suspicari non solum extremae impietatis sit, verum etiam ultimae insipientiae, nec omnino vel ad intelligentiam consequens, ut incorporeae naturae substantialis divisio possit intellegi; further princ. IV 4, 1; Jerome, apol. adv. libros Rufini II 19 (on the disputation of Origen with the Valentinian Candidus); Tertullian, Prax. 8; on this Ratzinger, col. 1221ff.

[162] Dörrie in his investigation of the idea of emanation starts from the concept ἀπόρροια, which evokes the image of a spring and the flow from it. With the Valentinians, however, this particular term only plays a subordinate part. Marcus alone seems to have applied it to the emanation of the pleroma (Irenaeus, I 14, 5). Elsewhere, in the excerpta ex Theodoto (2, 1) the pneumatic soul is called an ἀπόρροια ἀγγελικοῦ and in Ptolemaeus it is said of the soul which the demiurge breathes into the hylic man that it comes from a 'pneumatic outflow' (Irenaeus, I 5, 5; in exc. 50, 3, where the same source is reproduced, this expression is lacking); cf. again the letter from Alexander of Alexandria to Alexander of Thessalonica in Theodoret, H.E. I 4, 46. The problem raised by Dörrie, that emanation could mean a gradual withdrawal of the substance of God, was in all probability scarcely noticed by the Valentinians on account of the different kind of terminology they used (otherwise Dörrie, 'Emanation', pp. 131f.).

[163] Müller, *Beiträge* IV, p. 200, declares that whatever happens in the Pleroma is 'only a reflection of what is going on in the gnostic, a projection from the world of men into that of the aeons'.

Creatio Ex Nihilo

of the emanation process, but that they had not been able to give him any more precise explanation or basis for it.[164]

The Valentinian emanation idea takes various forms. In the 'Tripartite Tractate' it says that the Fore-Father brings forth the Aeons 'like a little child, like a drop from a spring, like a blossom from a [vine], like a [flower], like a shoot'.[165] The syzygy idea draws upon the analogy of procreation and birth, so that the coming forth of the emanations can be depicted naturally as a process of birth.[166] But alongside this pictorial way of imagining it, a striving towards abstraction is also visible. In a system about which Irenaeus reports, it can be said that the divine Duality brought forth a further Pair of beings 'without bringing it forth'.[167] The most astonishing example of the use of massive mythological imaginings which are continually reinterpreted in psychological and intellectual terms, is afforded by the Letter of the 'intransitory Nous', presumably the document of later, less restrained Valentinianism, which has again taken up ideas of popular gnosticism to an increased extent. Here the origin of the emanations is depicted as the result of sexual unions of the Aeons, but the union is described as the 'will' and it is 'intransitory' and timeless.[168]

---

[164] Haer. II 17, 9: hoc autem solum dicunt, quoniam emissi sunt unusquisque illorum et illum tantum cognovisse qui se emisit, ignorans autem eum qui ante illum est. Iam non autem cum ostensione progrediuntur, quemadmodum emissi sunt, aut quomodo capit tale quid in spiritualibus fieri. On oral discussions as the source of Irenaeus's knowledge of Valentinian doctrine cf. Sagnard, *La gnose valentinienne*, pp. 94–99. Irenaeus tries to describe the relation of the emanations to God through various similes: sun–sunbeam; person–person; animal–animal; tree–twig; (II 17, 2); star–star (17, 5): hand–finger (17, 6). Sagnard, p. 97, suggests that Irenaeus borrowed these images from Logos-speculation; but the Valentinians may have used them themselves: in the Tripartite Tractate it is said of the Fore-Father that he 'is like a root, with tree, branches and fruit' (51, 17–19, English translation by Attridge and E. H. Pagels; similarly 74, 10–13); the image of the sun and the sunbeam appears in the Letter of Rheginos, though applied to the relation of the Redeemer to the pneumatics (45, 28–39).

[165] 62, 7–11 (English translation by Attridge and E. H. Pagels); cf. 74, 6ff.

[166] Irenaeus, I 1, 1. Hippolytus reports the school debate over the question whether the Fore-Father brought forth the aeons with or without a female partner: ref. VI 29, 3.

[167] Irenaeus, I 11, 3 (Marcus?): προήκαντο μὴ προέμεναι.

[168] Epiphanius, panar. XXXI 5, 6.7; 6, 5.7; cf. O. Dibelius, *Studien zur Geschichte der Valentinianer* II: 'Der valentinianische Lehrbrief', ZNW 9 (1903), pp. 329–340, pp. 338–340; that this comes from a later period of Valentinianism is emphasised by A. J. Visser, 'Der Lehrbrief der Valentinianer', *Vig. Chr.* 12 (1958), pp. 27–36, pp. 35f. On the contrary Holl says in his edition of Epiphanius I (p. 390) that the Letter is 'one of the oldest documents of Valentinianism'.

The terms προβολή and προβάλλειν can in addition to the bringing forth of the Aeons also denote processes of emanation outside the pleroma. Thus the pneumatic seed as well as the cosmos put together from the substances of the psychic and hylic are described as emanations of Sophia.[169] In both cases the emanative origin is clear: the pneumatic seed is born of Sophia, and the psychic and hylic emerge through changes from the affects of Sophia. It is, however, worthy of note that in the Ptolemaic strand of sources of the *Excerpta ex Theodoto* the demiurge also can appear as an emanation of Sophia, for she formed him, according to the exposition given by Irenaeus, from psychic material.[170] Moreover it even says here that the demiurge 'emanates' the psychic Christ, the angels and the archangels, although it is expressly stated that he created them out of the psychic material.[171] Presumably Clement of Alexandria reproduced inexactly what lay before him, for otherwise the Valentinians were terminologically and factually exact in distinguishing between emanation and creation.[172]

Church theology decisively rejected the gnostic doctrine of emanation,[173] and yet in Christology the term προβολή was used,[174] as the relation of the Son to the Father was in general described under various emanational images. The word ἀπόρροια was given in Wisdom 7:25 and could therefore appropriately play a role in church Christology.[175] But the decisive difference consisted in this, that church theology used comparisons of this kind to indicate the essential unity of Christ with the Father, while the gnostics used the image of emanation to describe the decline of the divine being and ultimately its fall, as a result of which the cosmos came into being.

A special part is played in the unfolding of the pleroma by the first emanation of the Fore-Father, the Nous: he is indeed called 'father' and is 'the principle of the All', in which all further Aeons are already present as

[169] Exc. 53, 3.5; 67, 1.4; in the passage exc. 29–42, which is clearly deviating from the Ptolemaic system, there emanate from Sophia Christ, the 'left' and 'right powers' and the pneumatic seed: 34, 1; 39–41; cf. Irenaeus, I 11, 1.

[170] Exc. 47, 2; otherwise Irenaeus, I 5, 1; cf. also exc. 33, 3f.

[171] Exc. 47, 3; cf. Irenaeus, I 5, 1.

[172] Cf. exc. 41, 1f. and Ratzinger, col. 1221.

[173] Cf. Ratzinger, cols. 1221ff.

[174] Tertullian distinguishes his use of the concept precisely from that of the Valentinians: Prax. 8; cf. Ratzinger, cols. 1223–1225; a survey, rich in material, of the use of the term προβολή in Christian literature from the second to the fourth century is given by Orbe, *Estudios Valentinianos* I; 'Hacia la primera teologia de la procesion del Verbo' (Rome, 1958), pp. 519–754.

[175] Cf. Grant, 'The Book of Wisdom of Alexandria', in *After the New Testament* (Collected Papers, Philadelphia, 1967), pp. 70–82, pp. 72ff.; Marguerite Harl, 'A propos d'un passage du Contre Eunome de Grégoire de Nysse: Aporroia et les titres du Christ en théologie trinitaire', *Rech. Sc. Rel.* 55 (1967), pp. 217–226.

98   *Creatio Ex Nihilo*

seed.[176] The exalted position of the Nous becomes even more significant in that the Fore-Father through him brought forth the Horos as well as Christ and the Holy Ghost.[177] Through Christ the Aeons come to know that the cause of their eternal situation is their inability to comprehend the Father, but the cause of their origin and forming is his 'ability to be known', the Son-Nous.[178] These statements about the Nous and his function in the system of Aeons are obviously influenced by the views of Middle Platonism.[179] Certainly, the particular philosophical problems of the Nous-concept remain without importance for Valentinian speculation. The idea that the Nous is the immediate originator and sustainer of the unfolding of the rest of the pleroma merely serves to give expression to the transcendence of the primaeval Ground.

Beside the idea of emanation the thought of 'forming' is constitutive for the Valentinian system. This concept also derives its meaning from various spheres of thought. Ptolemaeus distinguishes between a 'forming according to being' and a 'forming according to knowledge'.[180] For the 'forming

---

[176] Irenaeus, I 1, 1; 8, 5; similarly Hippolytus VI 29, 6. In system A the Logos, brought forth from the Nous, is described as 'principle' and 'Father of all'; he includes in himself the substance of the other aeons, who are later formed by him (Irenaeus, I 1, 1; 8, 5); cf. Sagnard, *La gnose valentinienne*, pp. 311–315. The Logos is probably 'to be conceived mainly as a modification (variation) of the Nous': Krämer, p. 251 n. 210.

[177] Irenaeus, I 2, 4f. In this passage the version B of the myth is partly used: Stead, *Myth*, pp. 78f. According to Hippolytus VI 31, 2 the pair of aeons Nous and 'Truth' bring forth at the Father's behest Christ and the Holy Ghost.

[178] Irenaeus, I 2, 5; the possibility of knowing the unknowable Father through the 'only-begotten' is also asserted in exc. 7, 1.

[179] It is difficult to decide whether the Valentinians carry over into the pleroma the Platonic notion that God orders the cosmos through the world-soul (cf. Albinus, did. 10, pp. 164, 19ff.; on Numenius cf. Krämer, pp. 72ff.; M. Baltes, 'Numenios von Apamea und der platonische Timaeos', *Vig. Chr.* 29, 1975, pp. 241–2701, pp. 263–267) or whether they know a neo-pythagorean-platonist scheme, in which a supreme One stands over the Nous. Krämer suggests the latter; he draws attention to the report of Porphyry about the doctrine of Moderatus of Gades, preserved in Simplicius, in which is to be found the series: One – Ideas – World-soul – Hyle (Simplicius, in phys. I 7; 230, 36 – 231, 5). A corresponding scheme, in Krämer's opinion, determines the construction of the Valentinian system (Bythos – Aeons – Demiurge – Hyle); Kübel agrees, pp. 79f. Of course Porphyry in his reproduction of the doctrine of Moderatus might well have given it a wholly neo-platonist style: P. Hadot, *Porphyre et Victorinus* I (Paris, 1968), pp. 165–167. But Albinus also takes into consideration the possibility that God is above the Nous (did. 10, pp. 164, 18f.); cf. further Clement of Alexandria, strom. VII 2, 2f.; V 38, 7; otherwise IV 162, 5.

[180] Μόρφωσις κατ' οὐσίαν (Irenaeus, I 4, 1; 7, 2) and κατὰ γνῶσιν (Irenaeus, I 4, 1; exc. ex Theod. 45, 1; 59, 1); Heracleon, fr. 2 = Origen, comm. Joh. II 21, 137 talks of a first forming κατὰ τὴν γένεσιν.

The Creation of the World in Basilides and the Valentinians 99

according to being' the cosmological picture of the shaping of unformed matter is the model. In Irenaeus' account it seems that in the Ptolemaic system in the case of the Aeons the origin of their substance and their forming coincide.[181] But in his exposition of St John's prologue Ptolemaeus says that the substance of the Aeons that came into being after the Logos was at first present in the Logos and only later was formed from him. The emanation of the divine substance through the Nous and its formation through the Logos are thus two successive processes.[182] The origin of the Sophia-Achamoth pair is quite clearly depicted on the analogy of the forming of cosmic matter: the Horos strips from the first Sophia, who has tried in vain to know the divine Father, her enthymesis and her passion and removes them both from the pleroma. What is stripped away is assuredly a pneumatic substance but without form or figure.[183] Ptolemaeus thus describes the material, out of which the second Sophia is formed, with the standard predicates which in Platonism are characteristic of matter.[184] The shapeless Enthymesis receives from the Christ 'above' formation according to being and is from then on called Sophia. Having become intelligent through her forming, she begins to seek after Christ who has again left her though she is still filled with affects.[185] Finally the pneumatic seed also receives a forming which, according to Heracleon, brings to the pneumatics 'shape, illumination, and individuation'.[186]

'Forming according to knowledge' is thought of as an intellectual process: it consists in the lending of gnosis to the heavenly beings and to the pneumatics on earth.[187] This is depicted as an act of instruction or – on the

---

[181] Yet it says in haer. I 1, 1 that the Logos is the 'principle' and the 'forming' of the whole pleroma; similarly I 2, 5; the Nous is the cause of the origin and forming of the aeons. Origin and forming are thus distinguished, in words at least.

[182] Irenaeus, I 8, 5. Inexactly Foerster, 'Die Grundzüge des ptolemäischen Gnosis', NTS 6 (1959/60), pp. 16–31, p. 18: 'shaping according to being is simply the divine process of creation'.

[183] Irenaeus, I 2, 4: εἶναι μὲν πνευματικὴν οὐσίαν, (ὡς) φυσικήν τινα Αἰῶνος ὁρμὴν τυγχάνουσαν, ἄμορφον δὲ καὶ ἀνείδεον διὰ τὸ μηδὲν καταλαβεῖν. Cf. I 4, 1.

[184] Cf. for example Albinus, did. 8 (pp. 162, 31). Stead, *Myth*, pp. 100f., suggests that one of the original elements of the gnostic Sophia myth is the equality of wisdom with the evil material principle.

[185] Irenaeus, I 4, 1.

[186] Heracleon, fr. 2 = Origen, comm. Joh. II 21, 137; cf. Sagnard, *La gnose valentinienne*, pp. 485ff.; Yvonne Janssens, 'Héracléon. Commentaire sur l'Evangilie selon Saint Jean' I, *Le Muséon* 72 (1959), pp. 101–151; p. 126 n. 7; II, pp. 277–299, pp. 280f.

[187] The expression could have been derived from Rom. 2:20, but a reference to this passage cannot be proved.

plane of earthly being – as a long drawn out process of education. The Aeons receive their forming in knowledge after the fall of Sophia; the Aeon Christ instructs them that the Fore-Father is in himself unknowable and is only to be known indirectly through the Nous, and the Holy Ghost makes them all equal, teaches them to be thankful, and brings in true peace.[188] The second Sophia receives her forming according to knowledge, which heals her from her affects, through the Saviour sent out from the pleroma, who shows her everything 'which is in the pleroma and down as far as her'.[189] The forming of the pneumatics according to knowledge is depicted as a slow, only gradually completed process of education and perfection.[190] The cosmos lasts until the entire pneumatic seed has attained its perfection.[191]

A further variant of the idea of forming, which we find in System B, is dependent on a widespread theory about the origin of the embryo. According to this conception, which goes back to Aristotle, the father's sperm determines the principle of form and the mother's menstrual blood provides the substance of the foetus.[192] The need to unite a masculine and a feminine Aeon into a syzygy is in system B based on the idea that in the multiplication of every formed being the feminine partner provides the material which the masculine forms.[193] The emanation is thus depicted here as a matter wholly of begetting and birth. Sophia, who wants to give birth without a partner, can therefore only bring forth an unformed miscarriage, but which, in agreement with system A, is described with the characteristics of unformed matter. Genesis 1:2a ('the earth was without form and void'), the passage which pointed to a Platonising exegesis of the unformed material in Genesis, is here applied to the formless offspring of Sophia.[194] Cosmological and embryological understanding of the form-matter relationship thus come together.[195]

---

[188] Irenaeus, I 2, 5f.

[189] Irenaeus, I 4, 5; exc. 45, 1.

[190] Irenaeus, I 5, 6; 6, 1.4; 7, 5; II 19, 1.5; exc. 59, 1; cf. Sagnard, *La gnose valentinienne*, pp. 401–403.

[191] Irenaeus, I 6, 1; 7, 1; exc. 57.

[192] Proof in J. H. Waszink, *Tertulliani de Anima* (Amsterdam, 1947), pp. 342–344; H. I. Marrou in *Clément d'Alexandrie. Le Pédagogue* I (SC 70, Paris, 1960), p. 197 n. 5 (on paid. I 48, 1); J. Behm, ThW IV (1942), pp. 760–762; Erna Lesky, art. 'Embryologie', RAC IV (1959), cols. 1230–1232, cols. 1241ff.

[193] Hippolytus, ref. VI 30, 8; cf. also exc. 68, 79.

[194] Hippolytus, ref. VI 30, 8f. Conversely in Irenaeus the unformed Achamoth is described as a miscarriage: I 4, 1; 8, 2 (exposition of 1 Cor. 15:8).

[195] Cf. Behm, ThW IV, p. 161: The use of μορφοῦσθαι taken over into the language of gnosis, is to be explained partly from cosmogony, partly from the process in a mother's womb.

While in the A version of the Valentinian myth also the Father has a feminine Aeon beside him, in system B he is alone the principle of being. So he must contain within himself both the form and the material for the first pair that he brings forth.[196] In the unformed Ground, 'everything is together'.[197] Before the ingenerate Father decides to bring something forth, he is alone; there was nothing formed, no space, no time, no counsellor, not even, in any thinkable way, being.[198] A plurality of principles is excluded. The Father brings forth the Aeons alone, and in a wonderful way that can be compared with no other process of birth or creation. Similar ideas are developed with even greater thoroughness, and in express polemic against the Platonist doctrine of three principles, in the 'Tripartite Tractate'.[199] From the refusal of a plurality of principles we cannot draw the conclusion that in system B the production of the highest God is conceived as a *creatio ex nihilo*. For the Father does not call something essentially different from himself from nothing into being, but rather allows divine being to proceed from himself. It is a process of emanation, not an act of creation. A creation by the highest God is expressly denied by the Valentinians.

The realm outside the pleroma in which the cosmos comes to exist is the region of emptiness and shadow, the Kenoma.[200] In Theodotus' account the emptiness owes its existence to Sophia: the 'emptiness of knowledge' which she suffers becomes Space.[201] Whether the Ptolemaic sources used by Irenaeus gave such an account of the origin of Kenoma, we do not know. In the report of Irenaeus its existence is presupposed.[202]

---

[196] Hippolytus, VI 29, 1–5; Irenaeus, I 2, 4; on the question already raised by Hippolytus of neo-pythagorean influence on Valentinian speculation, cf. Stead, *Myth*, p. 79; Krämer, pp. 243ff., 248ff.

[197] Hippolytus, VI 30, 8: ἐν μὲν γὰρ τῷ ἀγεννήτῳ, φησίν, ἐστὶ πάντα ὁμοῦ, ἐν δὲ τοῖς γεννητοῖς τὸ μὲν θῆλύ ἐστιν οὐσίας προβλητικόν, τὸ δὲ ἄρρεν μορφωτικὸν τῆς ὑπὸ τοῦ θήλεως προβαλλομένης οὐσίας.

[198] Hippolytus, VI 29, 5.

[199] 51, 1ff.; see pp. 75f. above.

[200] Irenaeus, I 4, 1f.; exc. 31, 4. In Hippolytus, VI 31, ὑστέρημα appears with a similar meaning; cf. evang. ver. 24, 22–26.

[201] Exc. 31, 4; cf. evang. ver. 24, 28 – 25, 3.

[202] Mühlenberg, *Die Unendlichkeit Gottes bei Gregor von Nyssa* (1966), p. 181, suggests that the 'total substance', into which Sophia in her striving after knowledge risks being poured out and dissolved (Irenaeus, I 2, 2; 3, 3) is the Kenoma, the 'indeterminate being'. But from haer. I 8, 5 (τὴν ὅλην τῶν Αἰώνων οὐσίαν) it emerges unambiguously that it is the substance of the Aeons which is involved (thus also Sagnard, *La gnose valentinienne*, p. 149; Holl, *Epiphanius* I, p. 403 App. to Z. 19, is not clear: 'in the total, i.e. the common substance'; cf. also Tertullian, adv. Val. 9, 3; Prax. 8, 2: in reliquam substantiam). According to Stead's ingenious suggestion (*Myth*, p. 102 n. 5), underlying the thought that Sophia nearly dissolves into the substance of the pleroma is a spiritualising interpretation of Phaidros

Creatio Ex Nihilo

The passage from Irenaeus's main source which deals with cosmogony is also reproduced in the *Excerpta ex Theodoto*. This parallel transmission is in part more reliable than Irenaeus; especially the *Excerpta* offer the Scripture references of the original at the right places, where Irenaeus often passes them over and gives them only in appendices.[203] As far as can be checked from extant fragments, Heracleon agrees with this source. The writing which Irenaeus and Theodotus had before them must have been a representative exposition of the doctrine of the origin of the cosmos held in the Italian school of Valentinianism.[204]

The lower Sophia, after receiving the 'forming according to being' which Christ has brought her, gets into passions and affects, and strives after Christ who has again left her.[205] Thereupon the Soter is sent who forms Sophia

---

252A. According to the corrupt text of Irenaeus I 3, 1 Sophia is very nearly lost in matter: ἡ τοῦ πεπονθότος Αἰῶνος καὶ μετὰ μικρὸν ἀπολωλότος, ὡς ἐν πολλῇ ὕλῃ διὰ ζήτησιν τοῦ Πατρός, συμφορά. Holl suggests that ὕλη may be an old mistake for λύπη (*Epiphanius* I, p. 406 App. to Z. 10; the reverse mistake has crept into the Greek that underlies the Latin text of I 5, 4). But in haer. II 19, 4 Irenaeus says of the second Sophia, that she almost choked in matter; quomodom autem non ridiculum, matrem quidem ipsorum in materiam periclitatam dicere, uti pene suffocaretur (cf. I 4, 5: cum igitur peregrasset omnem passionem mater ipsorum et vix cum elata esset): and with similar expressions he sketches what happens in the myth of first Sophia: illa enim quae passa est virtus extensa et in immensum effluens, ita ut periclitaretur per omnem substantiam dissolvi (II 20, 1). The idea that Sophia risks sinking into matter is also found in the report of Irenaeus on the doctrine of the Ophites: haer. I 30, 3; comparison may further be made with Heracleon, fr. 23 = Origen, comm. Joh. XIII 20, 120, where, with reference to the pneumatics, 'the one related to the Father' is 'lost in the deep matter of error'. But Ptolemaeus surely did not teach that the first Sophia almost perished in matter, as matter first originates from the affects of the second Sophia. Irenaeus may have regarded as matter the 'total substance', of which there was talk in his source, on the basis of a mistaken analogy.

[203] Exc. 43, 2–65 corresponds to Irenaeus I 4, 5–7, 5. On the question of sources the basic information is in O. Dibelius, 'Studien zur Geschichte der Valentinianer I. Die Excerpta ex Theodoto und Irenäus', ZNW 9 (1908), pp. 230–247; cf. also Carola Barth, *Die Interpretation des Neuen Testaments in der valentinianischen Gnosis* (1911), pp. 11–21, and the accounts given by Sagnard in his edition of the Excerpta ex Theodoto, pp. 28–49. The differences between the Irenaean view and the one offered in the Excerpta ex Theodoto, to which Luise Schottroff, 'Animae naturaliter salvandae. Zum Problem der himmlischen Herkunft des Gnostikers', in W. Eltester, *Christentum und Gnosis* (19679), pp. 69–97, pp. 86–90 draws attention, are too trifling to call the identity of the sources into question.

[204] The Tripartite Tractate agrees essentially in its account of the cosmology with Ptolemaeus and Heracleon; cf. Zandee, 'Die Person der Sophia in der vierten Schrift des Codex Jung', in U. Bianchi, *Le origini dello Gnosticismo* (Leiden, 1967), pp. 203–212, pp. 203–207.

[205] Irenaeus, I 4, 1.

'according to knowledge' and strips off her passions.[206] These passions form the first, still incorporeal substratum, out of which, after numerous intermediate steps, two materials, the psychic and hylic, originate. For the hylic material the passions λύπη, φόβος, ἀπορία / ἔκπληξις are available, to all of which – their symbolical meaning is again obvious – the ἄγνοια is basic.[207] The psychic material originates from ἐπιστροφή, the turning of Sophia to the pleroma, which already forms the presupposition for the forming according to knowledge. Thus it already possesses an ontologically higher rank than the other passions and is specifically distinguished from these as the ἑτέρα διάθεσις.[208] The first reshaping of the passions is taken in hand by the Saviour himself, who has loosened them from Sophia; thereby he becomes the highest creator of the world, was exclusively held by the Italian school. We shall consider its systematic significance separately.[209] And indeed the Saviour changed the three original passions of Sophia on the one hand and the epistrophe on the other hand into materials which at first are still incorporeal but to which he lends the quality of being able to take on form and body. Out of the first three passions there originates the evil hylic substances, and out of the epistrophe the psychic substance tending towards passions. Both these find themselves currently in a state of mixing.[210]

[206] Exc. 43, 2 – 45, 1; Irenaeus, I 4, 5. In system B the place of the Enthymesis is taken by the miscarriage of the higher Sophia, which is formed into the second Sophia.
[207] On ignorance as the basis of the cosmos see also evang. ver. 24, 28ff.
[208] Irenaeus, I 4, 1; exc. 45, 2. The denotations of the affects are inconsistent in detail. The series φόβος, λύπη, ἀπορία / ἔκπληξις appears in exc. 48, 2f.; Irenaeus, I 5, 4; 8, 2; (in the last two cases without ἔκπληξις). Deviating series are found in Irenaeus, I 2.3 (of the first Sophia); 4, 2 (certainly from another source). In system B the affects are called φόβος, λύπη, ἀπορία, to which are added δέησις, ἱκετεία or ἐπιστροφή (Hippolytus, VI 32, 5f.); cf. Hippolytus VI 31, 1f. (first Sophia). These differences are not important for the understanding of the basic ideas of Valentinianism, for they show how intensively these gnostics worked on the details of the myth; cf. Sagnard, *La gnose valentinienne*, pp. 178f.; Stead, *Myth*, pp. 83f. In part the Valentinians clung to the philosophical doctrine of the affects, in which since Plato, Laches 191D the series ἡδονή, λύπη, φόβος, ἐπιθυμία was firmly established; this theory was then markedly developed by the Stoa; cf. SVF III 377– 420. The Valentinians found the particular affects of Sophia also in the Passion story: cf. Irenaeus, I 8, 2; on this Orbe, *Estudios Valentinianos IV; La teologia del Espiritu Santo* (Rome, 1966), pp. 421–427.
[209] Exc. 43; 45, 3; 47, 1; Irenaeus, I 4, 5; 5, 1; 8, 6; Heracleon, fr. 1 = Origen, comm. Joh. II 14; 22 = XIII 19, 118; see pp. 112f. below.
[210] The texts differ considerably from each other at this point: exc. 40, 6: πρῶτον οὖν ἐξ ἀσωμάτου πάθους καὶ συμβεβηκότος εἰς ἀσώματον ἔτι τὴν ὕλην αὐτὰ μετήτλησεν καὶ μετέβαλεν, εἶθ' οὕτως εἰς συγκρίματα καὶ σώματα· ἀθρόως γὰρ οὐσίαν ποιῆσαι τὰ πάθη οὐκ ἐνῆν· καὶ τοῖς σώμασι κατὰ φύσιν ἐπιτηδειότητα ἐνεποίησεν. Irenaeus, I 4, 5: ἀποκρίναντα χωρίσει συγχέαι καὶ πῆξαι καὶ ἐξ

The Saviour is the first creator; the further shaping of the creation is taken over by Sophia.[211] She cannot form the pneumatic seed born from herself as it is alike in essence with her. So she turns to the forming of the psychic material and brings forth 'what she has learned from the Saviour'.[212] First she forms the demiurge, who becomes father and king of the All[213] and through him she creates everything else, while he thinks he is creating

ἀσωμάτου πάθους εἰς ἀσώματον [τὴν] ὕλην μεταβαλεῖν αὐτά· εἶθ' οὕτως ἐπιτηδειότητα καὶ φύσιν ἐμπεποιηκέναι αὐτοῖς, ὥστε εἰς συγκρίματα καὶ σώματα ἐλθεῖν, πρὸς τὸ γενέσθαι δύο οὐσίας, τὴν φαύλην (ἐκ) τῶν παθῶν, τήν τε τῆς ἐπιστροφῆς ἐμπαθῆ· καὶ διὰ τοῦτο δυνάμει τὸν Σωτῆρα δεδημιουργηκέναι φάσκουσι. According to the version in Excerpta ex Theodoto the Soter lends corporeality to the incorporeal stuff and creates out of it both simple and composite bodies, to which he gives their appropriate qualities. But it cannot have said that in the source, for the corporeal world only originates at a later stage of the cosmogony, as the order of the account in the Excerpta shows: it is not the Soter but the demiurge, found later by Sophia, who divides the psychic stuff from the hylic and then gives corporeality to the incorporeal (47, 3 – 48, 1; cf. Irenaeus, I 5, 2); thereupon he forms the elements and only then does he create the composite bodies (48, 2–4). The Soter can therefore only have brought about the possibility of the origin of bodies. This is also the train of thought in Irenaeus, on which Tertullian, Val. 16, 3 provides the best commentary: Sed enim exercitata vitia et usu viriosa confudit atque ita massaliter solidata defixit seorsum, in materia incorporalem paraturam commutans ex incorporali passione, indita habilitate atque natura, qua pervenire mox posset in aemulas aequiperantias corpulentiarum, ut duplex substantiarum condicio ordinaretur, de vitiis pessima, de conversione passionalis (ed. J.-C. Fredoville). If the Soter had indeed created the bodies, then he would not only have been a potential creator (Irenaeus, I 4, 5) but the demiurge himself: Quispel, *The Original Doctrine*, p. 62, also considers the Irenaean version to be the original one. Dibelius I, p. 232 n. 7, suggests that the Excerpta had preserved the original order as compared with Irenaeus, since the individual beings must first come to be 'before there can be talk of the distribution of natural characteristics'. In this, however, he overlooked the fact that κατὰ φύσιν ἐπιτηδειότης in the Excerpta and ἐπιτηδειότης καὶ φύσις ὥστε εἰς συγκρίματα καὶ σώματα ἐλθεῖν in Irenaeus have a different sense: in the first case the expression is to be translated 'natural characteristic', in the second 'capacity to become bodies'. Clement (or Theodotus before him) has reinterpreted what his source said. (Quispel, *The Original Doctrine*, p. 62, corrects Irenaeus from the Excerpta: ἐπιτηδειότητα κατὰ φύσιν – the sense remains unchanged.)

[211] Exc. 47, 1: πρῶτος μὲν οὖν δημιουργὸς ὁ Σωτὴρ γίνεται καθολικός·'ἡ δὲ Σοφία' δευτέρα 'οἰκοδομεῖ οἶκον ἑαυτῇ καὶ ὑπήρεισεν στύλους ἑπτά' (Prov. 9:1).
[212] Irenaeus, I 5, 1.
[213] Irenaeus, I 5, 1. The title βασιλεύς is not found in the parallel passage Exc. 47, 2f. Irenaeus puts it more precisely:τῶν μὲν δεξιῶν πατέρα λέγοντες αὐτόν, τουτέστιν τῶν ψυχικῶν, τῶν δὲ ἀριστερῶν, τουτέστιν τῶν ὑλικῶν, δημιουργόν, συμπάντων δὲ βασιλέα. Cf. Heracleon, fr. 40 = Origen, comm. Joh. XIII 60, 416.425. Calling God βασιλεύς is Platonic: Plato, ep. 2, 312E; polit. X 597E; nom. X 904A; Numenius, fr. 12 des Places; Maximus of Tyre, 11, 12; Porphyry, vita Plot. 3, 32. On describing the demiurge as father and creator (also Ptolomaeus, ad Flor. 3, 2) cf. Timaeus 28C; on this e.g. Plutarch, plat. quaest. 2 (1000E–1001C).

The Creation of the World in Basilides and the Valentinians 105

independently.²¹⁴ In that way the popular gnostic idea of the unconsciousness of the demiurge is taken over in a milder form, and the latter becomes merely the unsuspecting tool of Sophia.

The creation of the demiurge took in the source the form of an exposition of Genesis 1:1–4.²¹⁵ We have in this text the only extant 'scholarly' commentary on the biblical account of creation by a gnostic author. While popular gnosticism finds its mythological figures in the first verses of Genesis and is not interested in a continuing and systematic exegesis, our Ptolemaic source expounds Genesis 1:1–4 consistently in the light of the Valentinian doctrine of primaeval matter, and in this the relationship with the philosophical exposition of Genesis in hellenistic Judaism becomes evident.

Sophia creates through the demiurge 'the heaven and the earth', by which is to be understood 'the heavenly and the earthly'. This is later specified as 'the right and the left', in Valentinian terminology the psychic and the hylic.²¹⁶ First the demiurge brings out of the psychic matter the psychic Christ, the archangels and the angels. The psychic matter is still mixed with the hylic, but the psychic is light and therefore soars upward in the mixture, while the hylic, on account of its weight, sinks to the bottom – the source finds this state of affairs described in Genesis 1:2b.²¹⁷ But even the heavy hylic matter is still incorporeal: this is derived from the statement that the earth, which is equated with the hylic, is described in Genesis 1:2a, as 'invisible'. This predicate cannot be understood literally, as there were not

---

²¹⁴Exc. 49, 1; Irenaeus, I 5, 1.3.
²¹⁵Exc. 47, 2 – 48, 1; Irenaeus, I 5, 2 only gives an abbreviated summary.
²¹⁶Exc. 47, 2 (cf. Phil., 2:10; Col. 1:16); Irenaeus, I 5, 1.
²¹⁷Exc. 47, 2f.: οὗτος ὡς εἰκὼν πατρὸς πατὴρ γίνεται καὶ προβάλλει πρῶτον τὸν ψυχικὸν Χριστὸν υἱοῦ εἰκόνα, ἔπειτα τοὺς ἀρχαγγέλους Αἰώνων εἰκόνας, εἶτα ἀγγέλους 'ἀρχ-' ἀγγέλων ἐκ τῆς ψυχικῆς καὶ φωτεινῆς οὐσίας, ἥν φησιν ὁ προφητικὸς λόγος· καὶ πνεῦμα θεοῦ ἐπεφέρετο ἐπάνω τῶν ὑδάτων', κατὰ τὴν συμπλοκὴν τῶν δύο οὐσιῶν τῶν αὐτῶν πεπεισμένων τὸ εἰλικρινὲς 'ἐπιφέρεσθαι' εἰπών, τὸ δὲ ἐμβριθὲς καὶ ὑλικὸν ὑποφέρεσθαι, τὸ θολερὸν καὶ παχυμερές. Cf. Irenaeus, I 5, 1f. In exc. 47.3 the passage τῶν δύο οὐσιῶν τῶν αὐτῶν πεπεισμένων is corrupt. O. Ruben's improvement, taken over by Stählin, τῶν αὐτῷ πεποιημένων is surely not to the point, for the stuff was not created by the demiurge. The conjecture of J. Bernays, attained with the minimum change of letters, οὕτως (or ἐς ταὐτό) πεπιεσμένων is, however, not convincing either. I suggest that the text ran something like ἀ(δια)κρίτως μεμειγμένων (cf. Athenagoras, suppl. 10, 3). The creation of the psychic Christ, of the archangels and angels seems in this passage to fit in badly with the context, as first the division of the stuff is reported. But the sequence is also supported by Irenaeus, I 5, 1f. It could be that in the Excerpta, as in Irenaeus, an originally more thorough account of the source has been compressed.

yet any human beings to whom the earth could have been invisible, and it cannot have been invisible to the demiurge who was fashioning it. Thus only the incorporeality and the formlessness of the hylic can be meant.[218] The demiurge now separates the pure psychic from the heavy hylic matter – so apparently is interpreted the separation of light and darkness (Gen. 1:4) – and gives to both these substances their form. This process of form-giving is depicted in the creation of light (Gen. 1:3). The verse must not be understood literally, since the creation of the heavenly bodies is only described later.[219]

The exposition of the creation story does not seem to have been pursued in the source beyond this point. But a few later allusions show that Ptolemaeus interpreted the whole biblical creation story strictly in the sense of his own cosmology and anthropology.[220]

The interpretation of Genesis 1:2 of the still unformed matter is firmly in the tradition of the philosophical-physical Genesis exegesis, which goes back to hellenistic Judaism.[221] The idea that the primitive substances, which were at first in a state of chaotic mixture, were separated and put in order by the demiurge, in the course of which first the light was separated from the heavy, corresponds to the cosmological ideas of Middle Platonism and to many authors of the same period influenced by Platonism.[222] In the close intellectual environment of Valentinianism we find a similar conception of the origin of the world to the one in Philo, in the Hermetic Corpus or in Athenagoras.[223] The idea that the hylic matter is incorporeal but has the

---

[218] Excerpta 47.4: ἀσώματον δὲ καὶ ταύτην ἐν ἀρχῇ αἰνίσσεται τῷ φάσκειν 'ἀόρατον' οὔτε γὰρ ἀνθρώπῳ τῷ μηδέπω ὄντι ἀόρατος ἦν οὔτε τῷ θεῷ· ἐδημιούργει γάρ· ἀλλὰ τὸ ἄμορφον καὶ ἀνείδεον καὶ ἀσχημάτιστον αὐτῆς ὧδέ πως ἐξεφώνησεν. Sagnard refers in his translation of this sentence to the 'mixing' (47, 3); p. 159. But Bernays has hit on the right solution, when he adds to ταύτην, in accordance with Gen. 1:2, τὴν γῆν. The predicates used show that matter is what is meant; cf. Albinus, did. 8 (pp. 162f.).

[219] Exc. 48, 1: διακρίνας δὲ ὁ Δημιουργὸς τὰ καθαρὰ ἀπὸ τοῦ ἐμβριθοῦς, ὡς ἂν ἐνιδὼν τὴν ἑκατέρου φύσιν, φῶς ἐποίησεν, τουτέστιν ἐφανέρωσεν καὶ εἰς φῶς καὶ ἰδέαν προσήγαγεν, ἐπεὶ τό γε ἡλιακὸν καὶ οὐράνιον φῶς πολλῷ ὕστερον ἐργάζεται. Cf. Irenaeus, I 5, 2. In the Ptolemaic exposition of St John's prologue in Irenaeus, I 8, 5 one finds the related statement that 'enlighten' means the same as 'form' and 'make visible'.

[220] Cf. Exc. 49, 2 (Gen. 2:3); 50, 1 (Gen. 1:9); 50–55 (creation of mankind).

[221] See p. 6 n. 24 above, 10f. and pp. 144f. below.

[222] Cf. W. Spoerri, *Späthellenistische Berichte über Welt, Kultur und Götter* (1959), pp. 69–113, on the 'diacrisis cosmogonies'.

[223] Philo, plant. 3; heres. 133f. 140.146; corp. herm. III 2 (cf. on this J. Kroll, *Die Lehren des Hermes Trismegistos*, 1914, pp. 178ff.); Athenagoras, suppl. 10, 3; 15, 2.

The Creation of the World in Basilides and the Valentinians 107

capacity to become bodies, finds a parallel in the Middle Platonist doctrine that matter is only potentially bodies.[224] The Valentinians of the Italian school, like other Christian theologians of the second century, thus interpret the creation story in Platonist concepts, but at the same time fit their cosmogonic myth into the Bible text. No doubt this Platonising exegesis attached itself widely to Jewish-Hellenistic traditions.[225]

In the source, after the separation of the psychic and hylic matter, the creation of the angels and of heaven was perhaps next described,[226] and then in any case the further shaping of the hylic: out of the affects of Sophia the demiurge creates the demons, the souls of animals and the elements of the cosmos.[227] Only the three elements earth, water and air form the particular building blocks of the corporeal world, while fire is present in all of them as the material locus of transitoriness.[228] Fire corresponds to the lowest plane of being, the ignorance which was basic to the affects of Sophia-Achamoth.[229]

This exposition of the last stage of the creation of the world is surprising after what goes before. It merely presupposes the stripping of the affects or passions from Sophia and takes no notice whatever of the complicated process by which they were gradually changed into the substances of the psychic and hylic. Obviously the source has worked on two traditions about the origin of the psychic and hylic materials, without being able effectively to sort them out and combine them. According to the simpler tradition the

---

[224] Albinus, did. 8 (pp. 163, 7); Apuleius, de Plat. I 5; Hippolytus, ref. I 19, 3.

[225] In respect of Valentinus's Alexandrian origin it is quite conceivable that he knew and used the writings of Philo. His dependence on Philo has already been suggested by Quispel, 'Philo und die altchristliche Häresie', ThZ 5 (1949), pp. 429–436; new arguments were put forward by H. Chadwick, 'St Paul and Philo of Alexandria', *Bull. John Ryl. Libr.* 48 (1965/ 66), pp. 286–307, p. 305; more cautiously Stead, *Myth*, pp. 90ff.

[226] Irenaeus, I 5, 2.

[227] Exc. 48, 2f. Irenaeus, I 5, 4 is much more thorough, but, through partly differing interpretations of the passions and different repetitions, reveals the use of probably two further sources, of which one also used I 4, 2 and the other could have been system B (cf. Hippolytus, VI 32, 6); on this Dibelius I, p. 233 n. 5.

[228] Exc. 48, 4; cf. Irenaeus, I 5, 4; 7, 1. Probably this is a borrowing from the Stoic doctrine of the world fire which admittedly has been completely altered: the Stoic world fire is identical with the primaeval substance worked on by the Logos and as such is indeed the basis of all being and distinct from the element 'fire'. But the Valentinians had to find a way of relating the four elements to the three passions of Sophia, all of which were underlain by 'agnoia'; cf. H. Jonas, *The Gnostic Religion* (Boston, 1958), pp. 197–199; id., *Gnosis und spätantiker Geist* II 1 (1966), p. 160 n. 3. On the influence of the Stoic doctrine of the world fire on gnostic and early Christian thinking cf. also van Unnik, 'The "Wise Fire" in a Gnostic Eschatological Vision', in *Kyriakon* I Festschrift for J. Quasten (1970), pp. 277–288.

[229] Irenaeus, I 5, 4; cf. I 4, 1.

108   *Creatio Ex Nihilo*

epistrophe and the three original affects of Sophia seem to have been directly transformed into the psychic and hylic substance. The attempt to make the myth fit the Platonist doctrine of the origin of the world, which was already playing a decisive role in the hellenistic-Jewish exposition of the creation story, obviously led to the more complicated version. The more primitive tradition is seen, with various deviations, in the report of Hippolytus: here Jesus, the 'common fruit of the pleroma' – he corresponds to the Saviour of system A – strips the passions from Sophia and transforms them immediately into independent substances. Fear becomes psychic, λύπη becomes hylic, ἀπορία the material of the demons, and the epistrophe becomes 'the ascent and penitence and power' of the psychic.[230] The distribution of the substances among the passions seems very problematical, but all that concerns us now is that the simpler exposition of the origin of the substances is here retained.

The oldest account of the transformation of the passions is offered however by a passage in Irenaeus which assuredly comes from a special source. According to this tradition all soul-substance, including the soul of the demiurge, originates from the epistrophe; from Sophia's tears came the moist substance, from her laughter the light substance, while from the λύπη and ἔκπληξις originated the somatic elements in the cosmos. 'Now she wept and mourned, so they (i.e. the Valentinians) say, because she was left alone in darkness and emptiness (the Kenoma); now she remembered the light that had left her, and became cheerful and laughed; now again she suffered fear, and at other times she was bewildered and beside herself.'[231] The notion that the world originated from the passions and from the laughter and weeping of a god, is probably of Egyptian provenance and may have been taken up by the Valentinians in the syncretistic milieu of Alexandria.[232] Unfortunately we cannot follow over any length of time the

---

[230] Hippolytus, VI 32, 6.

[231] Irenaeus, I 4, 2; the statements of Irenaeus about the role of the affects in this version of the cosmogony are inconsistent (cf. II 10, 3), only the meaning of weeping and laughing remains constant.

[232] The best-known example of this form of cosmogony is the so-called 'Leiden Kosmopoiia', in K. Preisendanz, *Papyri Graecae Magicae* II (1974), pp. 93–97, 109–114 (P XIII 139–206 = 443–564). Here the creation of various divine beings and cosmic powers through the sevenfold laughter of a god is outlined, in the course of which the mood of the creator changes (bitterness, sadness, joy, weeping, terror): ll. 161ff., 472ff.; cf. A. Dieterich, *Abraxas* (1891), pp. 20–31; Barth, p. 99; H. Schwabl, art. 'Weltschöpfung', PW Suppl. IX (1962), cols. 1433–1582, cols. 1565f. Foerster, *Von Valentin zu Herakleon*, p. 79, recalls the weeping and laughing of the soul in the Naassene psalm (Hippolytus, ref. V 10, 2), but his suggestion that Irenaeus took the idea from that and inserted it into the Valentinian myth himself is entirely unlikely.

history of the reception and reinterpretation of this idea by the Valentinians. All that is clear is that Ptolemaeus modified and elaborated in a Platonist sense the doctrine he had before him of the origin of the world. And we can also see, in the account given in the *Excerpta ex Theodoto*, how he contrived to interpret the biblical creation story as the last phase of this cosmogony. If we take a general view of the Valentinian system, no special explanation is required why matter is thought of as something that became. The world originated through the fall of an Aeon, its existence does not correspond to God's original plan. Therefore its material substratum cannot possibly be eternal.[233] The whole account of the origin of the terrestrial world follows the design of showing that everything corporeal and material has proceeded by several intermediate steps from the immaterial passions of Sophia and belongs to the lowest rank of the hierarchy of being. The same tendency dominates the anthropology and also the Christology of the Valentinians: the demiurge does not first create the earthly human body, but prepares from the incorporeal hylic substance a soul without reason which is like the souls of animals; in this the Valentinians see the man 'made in the image' of Gen. 1:26. To this the demiurge breathes in the man 'according to the likeness', which is the 'divine' soul consubstantial to himself. In the fourth heaven, where the creation of mankind takes place, the hylic soul serves the psychic soul as flesh, 'for the earthly flesh does not ascend so high'.[234] (This is the psychic soul in the narrower sense, stemming from the demiurge.) Only later, in a last act of creation, is the incorporeal man clothed in 'tunics of skin' (Gen. 3:21), the visible earthly flesh.[235] These complicated speculations serve to show that the bodily existence of man is only what is not peculiar to him. The Valentinian Christ takes on nothing at all that is hylic.

---

[233] On the problem of the origin of matter in the other gnostic schools see p. 40 n. 2 above. Krämer, pp. 238–264, tries to prove that the outline of the Valentinian myth is dependent on a neo-pythagorean or an academic system of derivation, in which matter also is derived from the One. But in fact the basic framework of the myth is taken, as the 'Apocryphon of John' shows, from the older gnostic speculation in which the stock of philosophical ideas only plays a subordinate part. That, of course, does not settle Krämer's question how far Valentinianism belongs to the pre-history of neo-platonism: both the emanation-idea and the placing of the highest deity above the Nous seem to anticipate Plotinus; cf. Harnack, *Lehrbuch der Dogmengeschichte* I (⁴1909), p. 274 n. 1; Cornelia J. de Vogel, 'On the Neoplatonic character of Platonism and the Platonic character of Neo-platonism', in *Mind* 62 (1953), pp. 43–64, pp. 48f.
[234] Exc. 50f.; Irenaeus, I 5, 5.
[235] Exc. 55, 1; Irenaeus, I 5, 5; Julius Cassianus, according to Clement of Alexandria, strom. III 95, 2. The idea is Philo's; cf. post. Caini 137.

He receives a body from the invisible psychic substance, which is miraculously made visible and susceptible of suffering.[236] Although the Valentinians upheld that matter had come into being, the idea of *creatio ex nihilo* in this connection was quite remote from them. Matter is not created by a sovereign divine act, but comes into being, so to speak, as a byproduct of the fall of Sophia. The affects of the second Sophia cannot simply be destroyed, and so they are transformed by the Soter, by Sophia and by the demiurge in a series of successive acts of formation into the substances from which the demiurge, as an unwitting tool of Sophia, then creates the angels and spirits, the cosmos and men.[237] The idea of forming, which, as we have seen, plays in various versions a decisive role in the whole Valentinian myth, is also constitutive for the cosmogonic process. The creation of the world is simply understood as the formation of given material. Over and above that, the common Ptolemaic source of Irenaeus and the *Excerpta ex Theodoto* in its account of the origin of the world is clearly dependent on the cosmological ideas of Middle Platonism; but changes these in a remarkable way. We have just established that the mixing of the psychic and hylic substance and their separation by the demiurge is depicted in connection with the model of the 'Diakrisis-cosmogony'. It is said of the demiurge that he is unaware of the Ideas of the things he created; he brought forth what Sophia gave him, but for her the pleroma served as the original pattern of the creation.[238] So the Platonist scheme of world-formation is here rearranged: the deity specifically creating is Sophia and the demiurge is reduced to an executing instrument. But even this correction is kept within the framework of the Platonist model. And the hylic substance, out of which not only the classical elements but also the demons, the souls of animals and the human souls which are animal like them, has the same predicates with which the Platonists described matter.[239] The

---

[236] Exc. 59, 4; Irenaeus, I 6, 1; 7, 2.

[237] Cf. Ratzinger, col. 1221: 'The visible world is indeed, as far as its stuff goes, a product of emanation, but the shaping of the stuff is "creation".' The Valentinians use various verbs to denote creation, without substantial difference of meaning: ποιεῖν (exc. 47, 2; 48, 2; Irenaeus, I 5, 3); δημιουργεῖν (exc. 47, 4; 49, 1; Irenaeus, I 4, 5; 5, 2.5; exc. 51, 1); μορφοῦν (Irenaeus, I 5, 1; 8, 5); κατασκευάζειν (Irenaeus, I 5, 2f.); κτίζειν (exc. 37; 38, 1; 43, 3; 45, 3; 48, 2; Irenaeus, I 4, 5). On the use of προβάλλειν in the sense of 'create' in exc. 47, 2f. see p. 97 above. Heracleon also describes the demiurge as κτίστης: fr. 20 = Origen, comm. Joh. XIII 16, 95–97.

[238] Irenaeus, I 5, 3 (ἠγνοηκέναι αὐτὸν τὰς ἰδέας ὧν ἐποίει); exc. 47, 3; Irenaeus, I 5, 1.

[239] Exc. 47, 3f. (n. 218 above); Irenaeus, I 5, 5 (τὸ ῥευστὸν τῆς ὕλης): cf. Albinus, did. 11, pp. 166, 27; Numenius, fr. 3.11 des Places.

The Creation of the World in Basilides and the Valentinians 111

church controversialists who criticised the Valentinians for their philosophical conception of matter, had already seen the dependence of this on Platonism, but at the same time derided them because they still claimed to know the origin of this matter.[240] There is no way from the Valentinian cosmogony to the church doctrine of *creatio ex nihilo*.

The distinctive ambivalence of Valentinus over his judgment of the world determines also the thought of his school. For Irenaeus the greatest blasphemy of the Valentinians consisted in the doctrine that the world arose because of a 'mistake' and out of ignorance.[241] The phraseology of 'The Gospel of Philip' shows that Irenaeus did not exaggerate.[242] The 'Gospel of Truth' also, in particularly ambivalent language, calls matter a work of error; the man of knowledge will extinguish it like a flame.[243] The devil can be described as cosmocrator[244] and counts as a 'part of matter'.[245] As soon as the pneumatic seed has ascended into the pleroma with Sophia and the souls of the righteous psychics have entered the Ogdoad with the demiurge, the hidden world fire will break out to destroy all matter and to dissolve with this into nothing.[246]

But by means of the idea, already put forward by Valentinus, that every grade of being depicts a higher one by which it is determined, a more positive evaluation of the cosmos is also possible. Indeed one may interpret the conception of the world as an image in a negative way too, by

---

[240] Irenaeus, II 10, 2f.; 14, 4; Tertullian, Val. 15, 1; 16, 3. In the dialogue 'De autexusio' of Methodius two Valentinians put forward the view that matter is unoriginate and forms the ground of evil (cf. also the Adamantius dialogue VI 4f., which is dependent on Methodius). Harnack, *Literaturgeschichte* I, p. 183, draws attention to the possibility that Methodius might have used the proceedings of the disputation between Origen and the Valentinian Candidus (cf. Rufinus, de adulter. libr. Origenis 8, pp. 11–23ff. Simonetti; Jerome, apol. adv. Ruf. II 18ff.). But the Platonising views contested by Methodius show no specifically Valentinian features. Probably Methodius puts them in the mouths of Valentinians only because Valentinianism was known as a heresy influenced by philosophy.

[241] Haer. II 3, 2; 19, 8; cf. also Tertullian, praescr. 34, 4.

[242] Ev. Phil. 75, 2–11: 'The world came about through a mistake. For he who created it, wanted to create it imperishable and immortal. He fell short of his desire. For the world never was imperishable, nor, for that matter, was he who made the world. For things are not imperishable but only intransitoriness of children' (English translation by W. W. Isenberg); cf. 84, 23–24.

[243] Evang. ver. 17, 15; 25, 12–19.

[244] Irenaeus, I 5, 5; Hippolytus, VI 33; 34, 1.

[245] Heracleon, fr. 20 = Origen, comm. Joh. XIII 16, 95; Ptolomaeus, ad Flor. 7, 7; Hippolytus, VI 34, 4f.

[246] Irenaeus, I 7, 1.

emphasising that it is no more than an image, a mere reflection,[247] but that is outweighed by the positive understanding. In the Ptolemaic source used by Irenaeus it said, basically, that Sophia willed to produce the cosmos in honour of the Aeons, which goes back to an idea of Valentinus himself.[248] A decisive move to a strong affirmation of the world was made by Ptolemaeus and Heracleon, the two leading figures in the Italian school of Valentinianism, and this found its systematic expression in a changed account of the origin of the world. Valentinus himself clearly allowed creation to proceed from Sophia, who creates the demiurge;[249] the same idea is also found in a passage from the *Excerpta ex Theodoto*, which probably reproduces Theodotus' own teaching.[250] Ptolemaeus and Heracleon on the other hand bring into the process of creation the Saviour also, sent out from the pleroma,[251] who works as the first universal demiurge,[252] and is 'the head of all things after the father'.[253] This apparently trivial change in the myth has important theological consequences: on the one hand the creation of the world now proceeds from the powers of the pleroma and ultimately from the Fore-Father himself, who hands over to the Soter his whole might;[254] thereby the idea that the cosmos is the result of a fall loses weight for the understanding of earthly reality. On the other hand, and this is even more important, through the participation of the Soter in the process of creation a link is established between creation and redemption. For this same Soter descends as the particularly divine element onto the pneumatic Christ at his baptism.[255] Of course these ideas are limited in their bearing by the doctrine peculiar to Valentinianism of the gradation of divine beings and powers.

---

[247] Cf. exc. 7, 5. The creation of time after the pattern of eternity (cf. Timaeus 47DE) by the demiurge can, in a characteristically gnostic reversal of the values of the Platonic conception, be regarded as a pitiful bungling: Irenaeus, I 17, 2 (Marcus? cf. Jonas, *Gnosis und spätantiker Geist* I, 1964, p. 416 n. 1); cf. Apocr. Joh. BG 71, 14 – 72, 12; on this Puech, 'la gnose et le temps', *Eranos-Jahrbuch* 20/1951 (Zurich, 1952), pp. 57–113, pp. 97–99.

[248] Irenaeus, I 5, 1; cf., Valentinus in Clement of Alexandria, strom. IV 89, 6 – 90, 2 (pp. 87f. above); on this Müller, *Beiträge* IV, p. 220.

[249] fr. 5 = Clement of Alexandria, strom. IV 89, 6 – 90, 2; Irenaeus, I 11, 1.

[250] Exc. 33, 3.

[251] Heracleon, fr. 1 = Origen, comm. Joh. II 14; 22 = Origen, XIII 19, 118 (cf. Foerster, *Von Valentin zu Herakleon*, p. 69); Ptolomaeus, ad Flor. 3, 6; Irenaeus, I 8, 6; exc. 43, 2 – 47, 1; Irenaeus, I 4, 5; 5, 1; also Hippolytus, VI 32, 5f.

[252] Exc. 47, 1 (n. 211 above).

[253] Exc. 43, 2. In 43. 3 Col. 1:16 is referred to the Soter, leaving out 'in heaven and on earth' and in place of 'authorities and power' reading βασιλεῖαι, θεότητες and λειτουργίαι (cf. Irenaeus, I 4, 5); on this Dibelius I, p. 231 n. 5.

[254] Exc. 43, 2; Irenaeus, I 4, 5; cf. Hippolytus, VI 32, 4.

[255] Irenaeus, I 6 1; 7, 2; exc. 59f.

The Saviour does not conduct the work of creation alone, but only introduces this process, which is carried further and completed by Sophia and the demiurge, and even so he only forms the highest element in Christ, to which are still to be added the pneumatic and psychic Christ and the substance of his docetic body, prepared from psychic substance. The world in its concrete appearance is thus the work of Sophia and the demiurge. But the activity of these lower powers is directed by the heavenly Soter and so ultimately by the Fore-Father who sent him. So, just as Ptolemaeus and Heracleon look upon the Soter as the real redeemer, he counts also for them as the true creator. And as they identify the Saviour with the Logos of St John's Gospel, they manage to achieve statements which on the surface correspond fully to the propositions of the church Logos-doctrine.[256]

This reshaping by Ptolemaeus and Heracleon of the Valentinian cosmology can be understood in general as an adaptation to church doctrine.[257] But it is worth asking whether it is not rather a reaction directed especially against the dualism of Marcion, which was in complete contradiction to the Valentinian thought of images and steps. Ptolemaeus, anyhow, in his Letter to Flora, turned decisively against the Marcionite denigration and damnation of the creation.[258] The occasion of this writing is the question about the origin and validity of the Old Testament law. Ptolemaeus rejects on the one hand the church conclusion that the law was given by God the Father, but on the other hand takes up much more sharply a position against the Marcionite assertion which he characterises in polemical caricature, that the law stems from the devil, who is also responsible for the creation of the world.[259] To the idea that a 'destructive god' created the world Ptolemaeus opposes his own teaching of creation through the 'Saviour' and the demiurge; Sophia, who stands between the two, is not mentioned in the simpler version of the Letter. The creation of the world goes back to the Saviour, for 'the Apostle' expressly says that 'all things were made by him'.

---

[256] Ptolomaeus, ad Flor. 3, 5f.; Irenaeus, I 8, 5; exc. 45, 3; Heracleon, fr. 1 = Origen, comm. Joh. II, 14; fr. 22 = Origen XIII 19, 118.
[257] So Quispel, *Ptolémée, Lettre à Flora* (SC 24, Paris, ²1966), pp. 14–17.
[258] Beside Harnack's account, 'Der Brief des Ptolemäus an die Flora', SAB 1902, pp. 507–45, and the annotated edition by Quispel mentioned in the previous note, the most important work to consult on the Letter is Campenhausen, *Die Entstehung der christlichen Bibel*, pp. 98–104 (ET pp. 82–86).
[259] In reality Ptolemaeus stands nearer to Marcion in some respects than he himself realised: like him he puts forward the idea that the true God was unknown and only revealed through Jesus (3, 7), and also in the determination of the nature of the demiurge as righteous Ptolemaeus comes very close to Marcion (7, 5); cf. Harnack, *Marcion* (1924), p. 112 n. 2; Quispel, SC 24, pp. 14f.

And it is at once the work of a righteous God who hates evil. Anyone who does not recognise the providence of the creator of the world is not only blind in soul, but in body as well.[260] Ptolemaeus thus goes back to the well-known Stoic doctrine that the providence of God is to be seen in the cosmos, and this he turns against Marcion.[261] To be sure, he talks only of the providence of the demiurge, but the latter is for his part subordinated to the Saviour, and in the end Ptolemaeus can describe the highest God as 'the Father of All, from whom all things are'.[262] Ptolemaeus does not attempt to explain more precisely the nature of the collaboration between the two creators, just as in the introductory letter probably addressed to a Catholic woman he refrains from fully developing the system of stages of being and the divine powers associated with them. Because of this simplification his arguments sound more orthodox than they actually are. But there can be no doubt that Ptolemaeus decisively rejects the antagonism maintained by Marcion between creation and the true God; he declares on the contrary that the righteous creator is an image of the perfect God.[263]

Starting from the systematic presuppositions indicated, the Valentinians are able to affirm a positive judgment of the world and of humanity. Yet their theological interest is wholly directed to the other-worldly reality which is mirrored in this world. The world is seen, just as is the Bible, as a great allegory of the figures and events of the pleroma, and salvation consists in liberation from the earthly-material world. Everything historical is merely superficial, and its deeper meaning is revealed to the pneumatic.[264]

As the goal of the creation of the world can be postulated the education of the pneumatics, which must occur in connection with the psychic in the

---

[260] 3, 6 (cf. Joh. 1:3).
[261] On the elsewhere distinctive narrowing of providence by the gnostics to the divine plan of salvation cf. Jonas, *Gnosis und spätantiker Geist* I, pp. 172ff. Most noteworthy, in the 'Sophia of Jesus Christ' the idea of a cosmic providence is expressly rejected: 80, 7f.; 81, 9; 82, 6f.; 106, 8f.; 122, 2.
[262] 3, 7; 7, 6 (cf. 1 Cor. 8:6); 7, 8; the expression πατὴρ τῶν ὅλων is of course ambiguous: as a Valentinian technical term it means God as the Father of the Aeons: cf. Quispel, SC 24, p. 55 n. 1. But variable meaning is intended; cf. Irenaeus, IV 33, 3: lingua quidem confitentur unum deum patrem et ex hoc omnia ipsum autem qui fecit defectionis sive labis fructum esse dicunt.
[263] 7, 7.
[264] In an essay which deals with the surprising theme 'La théologie de l'histoire dans la gnose valentinienne' (in Bianchi, *Le origini dello Gnosticismo*, pp. 215–225) Marrou was basically able to indicate only that the Valentinians judged events in the world in a more friendly way than is commonly supposed of the gnostics; but that is no 'theology of history'.

cosmos.²⁶⁵ Therefore the chain of births in the world may not be broken until the decreed number of the pneumatics has been born.²⁶⁶ In Ptolemaeus's view the demiurge already in pre-Christian times, without knowing the true reason for it, especially loved the souls of the pneumatics, and so ordained them to be prophets, priests and kings.²⁶⁷ Thus Ptolemaeus in no way achieves a total re-evaluation of history, but rather the pneumatics take a prominent place in it.²⁶⁸ The content of truth in Old Testament prophecy and in the law is not in principle contested, but the Valentinians distinguish different elements in the traditions, which are referred according to their provenance to the pneumatic seed, to Sophia and to the demiurge.²⁶⁹ The Old Testament is not read as a document of historically ongoing divine activity, but it falls into separate layers which, with more or less clarity, convey heavenly truth or announce the coming of the Redeemer.

All salvation is brought through Christ.²⁷⁰ Of course, his human reality is only the necessary earthly phenomenon which veils his true being. The psychics know him as the 'psychic' Christ, the son of the demiurge, and only to the pneumatics does he reveal himself in his full divinity, as the Soter who descended from the pleroma.²⁷¹ But the whole story of Jesus can also be treated as a mere copy of the fate of Sophia.²⁷² In spite of their relative

---

[265] Irenaeus, I 6, 1.

[266] Exc. 67, 2f.

[267] Irenaeus, I 7, 3. Ptolemaeus seems to think only of the history attested by the Old Testament, otherwise there would be no lack of poets and philosophers. Heracleon distinguishes between pagans and Jews according to their awareness of God: men before the Law and pagans honour the cosmos, the Jews honour the demiurge, but the true gnostics honour the Father of Truth (fr. 20 = Origen, comm. Joh. XIII 16; cf. fr. 21 = XIII 17, 102ff.; 22 = XIII 19). The Law is thus, as also in Ptolemaeus, regarded relatively favourably. Very strongly, but not in a historical context, the Gospel of Philip emphasises the contrast between Christians on the one hand and Jews, Romans, hellenes and barbarians on the other: 62, 26–35. Valentinus himself had thought more positively about the pagans; cf. Clement of Alexandria, strom. VI 52, 3f. (see p. 46 n. 27 above).

[268] On the other hand, according to Theodotus (exc. 38, 3), the demiurge is hostile to the pneumatics.

[269] Cf. exc. 59, 2; Irenaeus, I 7, 3; IV 35, 1.4; exc. 24, 1; 43, 1 and above all the Letter to Flora. A more negative conception is offered by Hippolytus, ref. VI 35, 1f.: all prophecy stems from the foolish demiurge, the message of salvation is totally hidden from it.

[270] Cf. ad Rheg. 43, 35 – 44, 3: Ptolomaeus, ad Flor. 3, 7; exc. 3, 1; 58, 1; 76, 1; ev. Phil. 62, 5f.; Hippolytus, VI 35, 3.

[271] Cf. exc. 23, 3f.; 66; Irenaeus, I 7, 3; ev. Phil. 57, 28 – 58, 10; 80, 23 – 81, 14. On the idea that Christ himself variously exhibits the stages of spiritual understanding, cf. Beyschlag, *Die verborgene Überlieferung von Christus* (1969), pp. 99ff. This, work is also of the greatest importance for the Christology of Origen: cf. Cels. VI 77.

[272] Irenaeus, I 8, 2; cf. I 7, 2.

Creatio Ex Nihilo

affirmation of human reality, the Valentinians entertain in their Christology a strict docetism,[273] which seems in comparison with Valentinus's own views to have been intensified by his disciples.[274] The Church plays a positive role in Valentinian thinking. The pneumatic and the psychic are of necessity bound together in her until the pneumatic seed is finally formed.[275] In the time of the Church the psychic Christ sits on the right hand of the demiurge,[276] until the pneumatic seed is perfected, its 'gathering' takes place, and it enters with the Lord into the pleroma.[277]

The meaning of historical existence in the world is in Valentian thinking reduced to the forming and perfecting of the pneumatics. For the pneumatic, world and history are transparent and become symbols of truth. The inclination of the Valentians to distinguish everywhere, in Christian communication and in experienced reality, steps and levels of thought, which in varying degrees approach the truth that can never be fully grasped, weakens and relativises the significance and weight of the historical. Thus also the problem of the meaning of history before Christ and the question of the truth known by the Greek philosophers, which preoccupied Justin were for the Valentinians almost unimportant. With their exclusive claim to revelation and truth, they could only allow to the church psychics a limited, relative knowledge of divine truth.[278]

---

[273] Cf. excerpta 59, 4; Irenaeus, I 6, 1; exc. 61, 6f.; 62, 2f.; Irenaeus, I 7, 2; on this Puech, 'La Gnose et le Temps', pp. 108f. The 'Apocryphon of James' (NHC I, 2) which puts forward a striking theology of the Passion and the Cross (cf. especially 4, 32ff.) is probably not Valentinian; cf. van Unnik, 'The Origin of the Recently Discovered "Apocryphon Jacobi",' *Vig. Chr.* 10 (1956), pp. 149–156. Passion theology and docetism are united in the 'Apocalypse of James' (NHC V, 3) which probably does come from Valentinian circles: Jesus is afraid of the wrath of the 'powers', who have taken up arms against him (27, 18 – 28, 4): James mourns over the sufferings of his Lord (30, 13–15; 31, 6–8) but the Risen One tells him: 'I am he who was within me. Never have I suffered in any way, nor have I been distressed (31, 17–20; English translation by W. R. Schoedel).

[274] See n. 131 above. According to a note of Clement of Alexandria, the Valentinians taught a repetition of the incarnation (ecl. proph. 23, 3).

[275] Cf. exc. 24, 1; 58, 1; 59, 1; 61, 2f.; 63, 1; 64; on this Müller, *Beiträge* III, pp. 202f. Cf. also van Unnik, 'Die Gedanken der Gnostiker über die Kirche', in J. Giblet, *Vom Christus zur Kirche* (1966), pp. 223–238.

[276] Exc. 62, 1f. (Ptolemaeus); turned into the negative the thought is found in Theodotus (exc. 38, 3): Jesus must appease the demiurge, in order to assure to the pneumatics ascent into the pleroma.

[277] Irenaeus, I 7, 1.5; exc. 49, 1; 26, 3.

[278] In the Tripartite Tractatus it is expressly said of the philosophers that they do not know 'the cause of the things which exist' (p. 109, 3–5), and the contradictions between the doctrines of the philosophical schools serve as a proof of the inner disruption of hylic humanity (109, 5). Valentinus himself had thought more liberally; see p. 46, above.

Valentinianism left far behind the speculative fantasy and the unrestrained syncretism of primitive gnosticism. The generation of significant teachers following the founders of the school held firm to the theological questions posed by the latter and developed by sustained intellectual effort several comprehensive systems of impressive unity. In the Valentinian theology the common Christian tradition took a much greater part than it did in the thinking of most gnostic schools. The faith of the 'psychic' church was recognised as relative truth and acknowledged as a necessary stage to be passed through by the pneumatics. In their judgment of the demiurge and his creation they knew themselves to be essentially nearer to the Catholic Christians than to the Marcionites. Yet the problematic basis of the gnostic position was in no way surrendered. The separation of the various divine powers and the corresponding grades of being and knowledge were, like the myth of the fall of Sophia, not to be reconciled with the primitive Christian understanding of God and creation. Justifiably the Valentinian teaching was quickly rejected by the Catholic Church as heretical.

Like Basilides the Valentinians asserted that matter had come into being. True, from the other presuppositions of their system they never reached the conclusion of *creatio ex nihilo*, but the idea that the affects of Sophia, cut off and made corporeal, are provided to the demiurge as material for the creation, amounts to a characteristic compromise with the model of world-formation. The attempts of the great gnostics to explain the origin and nature of matter hardly influenced in a direct way the inception and general prevalence of the church doctrine of *creatio ex nihilo*, for the general systematic conceptions with which they were bound up had to be regarded as unacceptable by correct theology. But there is no doubt that the gnostic speculations about the origin of matter provided an essential spur to the church theologians to seek on their part an answer to this problem. In the long run it was impossible to ignore the questions the gnostics were asking. In addition to this, after the middle of the second century the controversy with philosophy steadily increased in importance in the orthodox camp and made it unavoidable that the belief in creation should be thought through again from new points of view.

4

Christian and Platonist Cosmology

Christianity as the true philosophy
The gnostics put forward the claim that Christian truth, as it was understood and taught by them, was something essentially other than the insights of philosophy and plainly superior to them. A similar attitude to philosophy was adopted, around the turn of the first and second centuries, by most Christians. But at the same time the gnostics made great use of philosophical concepts and schemes, even if unmethodically at times and with curious reinterpretations. This inner contradiction is characteristic of the unhistorical, syncretistic thinking of gnosticism. A rational approach to the problem that was decisive for the intellectual future of Christianity, its relation to philosophy, was not to be achieved on the basis of gnostic presuppositions. But in the first half of the second century, at the time when the most important gnostic theologians built their systems, individual Christian teachers forged a new way of controversy with philosophy; they understood the Christian message itself as the true philosophy, went deliberately into philosophical questions, and sought to show that Christian teaching, new in appearance only, but in reality older than all barbarian or hellenic wisdom, conveyed that truth with which the whole classical tradition had, with only very limited success, concerned itself.

Aristides
The oldest work of the new 'apologetic' literature that has come down to us completely comes from the 'philosopher' Aristides. The clumsiness of thought and style shown by this apology reveals that what we have here is the document of an intellectual new beginning.[1] In connection with his

---
[1] On the problems of transmission see cf. B. Altaner, art. 'Aristides', RAC I (1950), cols. 652–654 and the work by Cost. Vona, *L'apologia di Aristide* (Rome, 1950) in which the whole of the known text material is assembled.

Christian and Platonist Cosmology 119

polemic against the veneration of the elements Aristides, according to the Greek version of the text, makes it clear that he wants to show that 'the elements are not gods, but transitory and mutable, brought out of nothing through the commandment of the true God'.[2] The writing of Aristides probably appeared in the time of Hadrian. The only theologian of that period, in whose work we can surely detect the idea of *creatio ex nihilo* is Basilides. Justin, writing somewhat later, taught the creation of the world from unformed matter. Tatian and Theophilus of Antioch are the first non-gnostic theologians expressly to reject the idea of world-fashioning. It is thus somewhat surprising to find in Aristides the idea of *creatio ex nihilo* in a nearly classical formulation: God created the elements out of nothing through his commandment. The Greek text of the *Apology* of Aristides is, however, only known to us as it was repeated in the novel of Barlaam and Joasaph, probably written by John of Damascus.[3] In the Syriac translation the passage runs differently: here Aristides wants to show that the elements 'are not gods, but a transitory and mutable creation like humanity'.[4] The comparison of the elements with humanity is more likely to be original than the statement that God made the elements out of nothing. For the formulation given in the Greek text, which underlines the distinction between creator and creation, corresponds much more closely to the aspirations of a later age to theological precision and academic correctness than does the statement of the Syriac version. Supposedly the Greek rendering arose from the attempt to bring the text of Aristides theologically into line.[5] If, nonetheless, the Greek text is held to be original, then in spite of its apparently unambiguous assertions, one ought not to read more from it than from corresponding statements of Hermas or of hellenistic-Jewish literature: Aristides means that the elements are created by God; but it does

---

[2] 4, 1: ἔλθωμεν οὖν, ὦ βασιλεῦ, ἐπ' αὐτὰ τὰ στοιχεῖα, ὅπως ἀποδείξωμεν περὶ αὐτῶν ὅτι οὐκ εἰσὶ θεοί, ἀλλὰ φθαρτὰ καὶ ἀλλοιούμενα, ἐκ τοῦ μὴ ὄντος παραχθέντα προστάγματι τοῦ ὄντως θεοῦ.

[3] In addition there are extant two papyrus fragments (printed by Vona, pp. 115–117), which do not, however, include the text of apol. 4, 1.

[4] Literally 'which is in accordance with the image of man'. This presumably means indeed that the elements are just as transitory and mutable as men are (cf. 7, 1f.). Vona, p. 142, applies the passage to the human figure of the images of the gods. But it is unlikely that there is an allusion to Rom. 1:23, as Vona in agreement with most earlier editors suggests.

[5] The originality of the Syriac version is suggested, on the ground of similar considerations, by R. Seeberg, 'Die Apologie des Aristides' in T. Zahn, *Forschungen zur Geschichte des neutestemantlichen Kanons und der altkirchlichen Literatur* V (1893), pp. 159–438, p. 339; E. Hennecke, *Die Apologie des Aristides* (1893), p. 12; Vona, p. 142. Conversely, J. Geffcken, *Zwei griechische Apologeten* (1907), p. 52, gives the Greek version of the process, with reference to 2 Macc. 7:28 and Hermas 26, 1.

not appear from his book that he consciously distanced himself from the philosophical model of world-formation and that he had formulated the conceptual difference between world-formation and creation. But only when the nature of the problem is to that extent grasped can one speak of a doctrine of *creatio ex nihilo* in the full and strict sense. Aristides does not seem to have reached this awareness of the problem.

Justin

Justin Martyr is a theologian who must not be undervalued. By contrast with the claim to secret knowledge implied in gnostic speculation, he seeks to give full value to what is believed and accepted by Christians in general. Justin knows and mentions deviations from what he considers to be correct Christian views, but which it is legitimate to express,[6] but he emphatically separates himself from the heresies which falsify Christianity and bring it into disrepute.[7] Justin sees it as a sign of the truth and divine origin of the Christian message that simple and uneducated Christians, who cannot even read and write, are in possession of that knowledge after which the philosophers strive without being able to attain it.[8]

Justin considers himself a philosopher. Christianity is for him the true philosophy, resting on the age old wisdom of the prophets. The classical philosophy of the Greeks also stands in a tradition connected with that of the prophets, but in the course of history it has increasingly distanced itself from the one ancient truth, so that it now possesses the latter only in an obscure and broken form.[9] This idea is by no means a mere postulate. Justin has philosophical training and his thinking is determined by the questions asked by philosophers, even if he never completed a formal course of philosophical study.[10]

---

[6] Dial. 47, 1–4; 48, 4; 80, 2.5; cf. 128, 2–4; cf. H. Chadwick, 'Justin Martyr's Defence of Christianity', *Bull. John Rylands Libr.* 47 (1965), pp. 275–297, p. 293.

[7] Apol. I 26; dial. 35; 80, 3f.

[8] Apol. I 60, 11; II 10, 8.

[9] Dial. 2.1f.; 7, 1 – 8, 2. On the idea of Christianity as the original philosophy cf. N. Hyldahl, *Philosophie und Christentum. Eine Interpretation der Einleitung zum Dialog Justins* (Copenhagen, 1966), pp. 114ff., and now especially J. C. M. van Winden, *An Early Christian Philosopher. Justin Martyr's Dialogue with Trypho, Chapters One to Nine* (Leiden, 1971), pp. 111ff., who partly corrects Hyldahl's interpretation.

[10] In Apol. II 12, 1 Justin remarks that before his conversion to Christianity he had found solace in Plato's teachings, and in his trial before the city prefect Junius Rusticus he explains that he tried 'to get to know all doctrines', until he turned to Christianity: acta Just. A 2, 3.; B 2, 3; cf. C 2, 2. The famous Preface to the Dialogue with Trypho, in which Justin outlines how his quest for truth led him to various philosophical doctrines, until he met a mysterious

Intellectually Justin is above all indebted to Platonism.[11] But on account of his conviction that in his Christian faith he possesses the whole truth, Justin can express himself very independently on the subject of philosophical views prevalent in the schools.[12] He is not in thrall to academic Platonism and can use peripatetic arguments to criticise Platonist ways of seeing things.[13] In his doctrine of the Logos spermatikos Justin connected Stoic and Platonist ideas with the image of the Sower, provided for him by the synoptic parable.[14] Even Justin's keen assertion that the teaching of the prophets is the original philosophy, from which the Greeks have moved ever further away, is the original reinterpretation of an idea widely current in imperial times. The view that long before the Greeks philosophy had reached its zenith among barbarian peoples, probably goes back to Poseidonius.[15] Among these peoples who were in possession of the original, uncorrupted truth, were to be counted the Jews. Thus Numenius thought it necessary to get behind Plato to Pythagoras and still further to the teaching of the Brahmins, the Jews, the Magi and the Egyptians.[16] Justin on

old man, who told him of the teaching of the prophets (dial. 2ff.), is a literary composition and must not be understood as simple autobiography. But from the text it emerges that Justin before his conversion was an adherent of Platonism; cf. van Winden, *An Early Christian Philosopher*, pp. 108f. The Preface to the Dialogue has been in recent times the subject of much thoroughgoing research; cf. in addition to the works already mentioned of Hyldahl and van Winden, the essay by W. Schmid, 'Frühe Apologetik und Platonismus. Ein Beitrag zur Interpretation des Prooms von Justins Dialogus', in EPMHNEIA Festschrift for O. Regenbogen (1951), pp. 163–182 and now R. Joly, *Christianisme et Philosophie. Etudes sur Justin et les Apologistes grecs du deuxième siècle* (Brussels, 1973), pp. 9ff.

[11] On this especially C. Andresen, 'Justin und der mittlerer Platonismus', ZNW 44 (1952/53), pp. 157–195; through this research the older work of I. M. Pfättisch, *Der Einfluss Platons auf der Theologie Justins des Martyrers* (1910) has been rendered obsolete.

[12] The intellectual independence of Justin has been emphatically declared by Chadwick, *Early Christian Thought and the Classical Tradition* (Oxford, 1966), pp. 12–22.

[13] Dial. 6, 1; cf. R. M. Grant, 'Aristotle and the Conversion of Justin' in *After the New Testament* (Collected Papers, Philadelphia, 1967), pp. 122–125; van Winden, *An Early Christian Philosopher*, p. 101.

[14] On this active significance of the Logos spermatikos concept as the 'sowing Logos' cf. R. Holte, 'Logos Spermatikos. Christianity and Ancient Philosophy according to St Justin's Apologies', *Stud. Theol.* 12 (1958), pp. 109–168, and especially J. H. Waszink, 'Bemerkungen zur Justins Lehre vom Logos Spermatikos', in *Mullus* Festschrift for T. Klauser (1964), pp. 380–390.

[15] Waszink, 'Some Observations on the Appreciation of the "Philosophy of the Barbarians" in Early Christian Literature', in *Mélanges offerts à Mademoiselle Chr. Mohrmann* (Utrecht/Antwerp, 1963), pp. 41–56, pp. 51ff.

[16] Fr. 1a des Places = Eusebius, praep. ev. IX 7, 1; cf. fr. 1b = Origen, Cels. I 15; on this H. C. Puech, 'Numenius d'Apamée et les théologies orientales au second siècle', *Annuaire de l'Inst. de Philol. et d'Hist. Orient.* 2 (1934 = *Mélanges* J. Bidez, pp. 745–778), pp. 767ff.

the contrary finds the sole approach to the original truth in the writings of the prophets as interpreted by the Christians. The opposite proposition was put forward some decades later by Celsus, perhaps in direct controversy with Justin's idea: the 'true doctrine', the one true tradition about God and the gods, has been handed down from the oldest and wisest peoples; only Judaism fell away from this enlightened tradition and Christianity is again a revolutionary split from Judaism.[17] So, while Justin finds the break in the common pagan tradition, Celsus says that Judaism and Christianity distanced themselves from the unified stream of pagan tradition.[18]

In his statements about creation Justin is heavily dependent on Platonist ideas. His preferred epiphet for God is 'Creator' and repeatedly we hear echoes of the formula from the *Timaeus*: 'Creator and Father of this universe'.[19] The statement that God in the beginning through the Logos 'created and ordered everything' is in general accord with the language of older Greek Christianity.[20] But in Platonising phraseology Justin can also say 'God in his goodness created everything from formless matter'.[21] Justin expressly declares that Plato and the Christians agree in holding that everything came to be through God,[22] and he sets out in parallel – for the first time, so far as we can ascertain, in the history of Christian theology – the biblical creation story and the creation myth in the *Timaeus*. Plato, he says, took over the doctrine that God made the cosmos out of unoriginate matter from the opening verses of Genesis.[23] Justin does not say, in agreement with the exegesis of the *Timaeus* by Plutarch or Atticus, that Moses and Plato both taught that the world began in time. But Justin does understand Genesis 1:2 as a statement about unordered, preexistent matter. It has been asserted that Justin, as a Christian, naturally took

---

Waszink, 'Some Observations', pp. 53–55, accepts influence of Numenius on Clement of Alexandria, strom. VI 57, 2–3.

[17] Origen, Cels. I 14; cf. I 16. On this A. Wifstrand, 'Die wahre Lehre des Kelsos', *Bulletin de la Société Royale des lettres de Lund* 1941–42/5, pp. 391–431, pp. 398ff.; Chadwick, *Early Christian Thought*, pp. 23, 132f.

[18] The thesis that Celsus had read Justin and is contesting him is put forward by Andresen, *Logos und Nomos. Die Polemik des Kelsos wider das Christentum* (1955), pp. 308ff.; Chadwick, *Early Christian Thought*, pp. 22, 132f., is in agreement.

[19] Timaeus 28C; cf. dial. 7, 3; 56, 1; 60, 2f.; 117, 5. The passage is given word for word in apol. II 10, 6; on the form of the text cf. Andresen, *Justin*, pp. 167f.; Hyldahl, pp. 278–80.

[20] Apol. I 20, 4; II 6, 3; dial. 11, 1.

[21] Apol. I 10, 2: πάντα τὴν ἀρχὴν ἀγαθὸν ὄντα δημιουργῆσαι αὐτὸν (sc. τὸν θεόν) ἐξ ἀμόρφου ὕλης δι' ἀνθρώπους δεδιδάγμεθα. Similarly apol. I 67, 7; cf. Andresen, *Justin*, pp. 164f.

[22] Apol. I 20, 4.

[23] Apol. I 59, 1–5.

it for granted that matter was created by God.[24] But there is no evidence to support this postulate. Justin by no means seeks to make apologetic points at any price. Elsewhere he points out the differences between Christian and philosophical views.[25] Thus, specifically in the case of the creation, he would certainly not have failed to correct Plato and to point out that in the true Christian understanding matter was to be considered as having come into being. Obviously at this point Justin had not perceived any difference between Christian and Platonist teaching.[26]

Again, in another context, Justin goes into the Platonist views of the origin of the cosmos. In the conversation with the mysterious old man which Justin describes at the beginning of the *Dialogue with Trypho*, one of the central themes is the Platonic doctrine of the immortality of the soul. The stranger opposes this doctrine with the argument that an immortal soul would also have to be thought of as unoriginate, but that the soul is no more unoriginate than the cosmos. Justin remarks in the course of this conversation that he knew of philosophers – obviously Platonists – who held the cosmos to be unoriginate, but that he did not himself agree with them.[27] The old man goes on to say that, even so, not all souls die: to the good ones God grants immortality, the bad he allows to die after punishment.[28] Justin now establishes once more through a question the relationship between the doctrine of souls and cosmology: Plato says in the *Timaeus* that the cosmos, in so far as it has come into being, is indeed transitory, but that it is protected from dissolution by the will of God – and this conception his interlocutor probably applies to the soul.[29] Justin thus shows that he is familiar with the Platonist debate over the origin of the world in time and he takes a stand for the literal understanding of the *Timaeus*.[30] In connection with his question

[24] Thus finally again Hyldahl, p. 283.
[25] Apol. II 7, 3.4.8.9; cf. I 20, 2; dial. 4–6.
[26] Thus, more or less, R. A. Norris, *God and World in Early Christian Theology* (London, 1966), p. 52; L. W. Barnard, *Justin Martyr. His Life and Thought* (Cambridge, 1967), pp. 111–113; Chadwick, *Early Christian Thought*, p. 12.
[27] Dial. 5, 1f.; cf. van Winden, *An Early Christian Philosopher*, pp. 84ff. The argument that the cosmos, as a body which is still, refractory and compounded, changing, failing and being renewed daily, cannot be without a beginning, is dependent on Timaeus 28BC; cf. Plutarch, de animae procr. 9 (1016DE). Hyldahl, p. 203, asserts without compelling proof that the idea is stoic; on that cf. van Winden, pp. 87f.
[28] Dial. 5, 3.
[29] Dial. 5, 4; cf. Timaeus 41AB.
[30] Cf. Andresen, *Justin*, pp. 163f. Of course one can scarcely conclude from this statement of Justin's that he belonged, in academic terms, to the persuasion of Plutarch and Atticus, as Andresen suggests. The whole speech is composed with reference to the peripeteia, the transition to Christianity; cf. Dörre, *Gnomon* 29 (1957), pp. 189f.; Hyldahl, pp. 202f.

124 Creatio Ex Nihilo

Justin develops the following train of thought: God alone is not originate and not transitory. His unoriginate and intransitory character constitute his being. Everything after him is originate and transitory. Between a number of unoriginate beings no distinction would be conceivable; they would all have to be perfectly alike and therefore there can only be one single unoriginate being. Yet if one wished to accept the existence of various unoriginate beings, it would be impossible to give any reason for their variety. In the attempt to find this reason, thinking would fall into an infinite regress, and finally one would have arbitrarily to explain any ἀγένητον as God, the cause of all.[31] About a century after Justin, Porphyry in his commentary on the *Timaeus* with almost identical reflections advances against Atticus the proposition that matter is originate: if one were to establish matter as a second ἀγένητον alongside the divine, there would have to be a cause for the difference between God and matter. This cause can neither be something originate nor something unoriginate, and so the search for it would peter out – exactly Justin's conclusion – in an infinite regress.[32] But unlike Porphyry, Justin is only maintaining that the soul is originate and transitory; he does not go into the question whether matter is originate or unoriginate. No doubt the logical consequence of his train of thought would be the thesis that matter could not be unoriginate either. But Justin did not formulate this proposition in the prologue to the Dialogue, and in his explicit statements about matter he seems to consider it an eternal, uncreated substratum of the cosmos. One gets the impression that for Justin the idea that the creation of the world must have resulted from matter given in advance was so self-evident that he saw no problem in it.[33] It is not to be concluded that Justin had taken over his thesis that there

---

[31] Dial. 5, 4–6; ὅσα γάρ ἐστι μετὰ τὸν θεὸν ἢ ἔσται ποτέ, ταῦτα φύσιν φθαρτὴν ἔχειν, καὶ οἷά τε ἐξαφανισθῆναι καὶ μὴ εἶναι ἔτι· μόνος γὰρ ἀγέννητος καὶ ἄφθαρτος ὁ θεός καὶ διὰ τοῦτο θεός ἐστι, τὰ δὲ λοιπὰ πάντα μετὰ τοῦτον γεννητὰ καὶ φθαρτά... τὸ γὰρ ἀγέννητον τῷ ἀγεννήτῳ ὅμοιόν ἐστι καὶ ἴσον καὶ ταὐτόν, καὶ οὔτε δυνάμει οὔτε τιμῇ προκριθείη ἂν θατέρου τὸ ἕτερον. ὅθεν οὐδὲ πολλά ἐστι τὰ ἀγέννητα· εἰ γὰρ διαφορά τις ἦν ἐν αὐτοῖς, οὐχ ἂν εὕροις ἀναζητῶν τὸ αἴτιον τῆς διαφορᾶς, ἀλλ', ἐπ' ἄπειρον ἀεὶ τὴν διάνοιαν πέμπων, ἐπὶ ἑνός ποτε στήσῃ ἀγεννήτου καμὼν καὶ τοῦτο φήσεις ἁπάντων αἴτιον.

[32] As said by Proclus in Timaeus 119 B-C (I 391, 6 – 392, 2 Diehl) = *Porphyrii in Platonis Timaeum commentariorum fragmenta*, ed. A. R. Sodano (Naples, 1964), pp. 34f. (fr. 51).

[33] From the statement that God alone is unoriginate H. A. Wolfson, 'Plato's Pre-existent Matter in Patristic Philosophy', in *Studies in the History of Philosophy and Religion* I (Collected Papers, Cambridge, Mass., 1973), pp. 170–181, pp. 173f. and E. F. Osborn, *Justin Martyr* (1973), pp. 46ff., both conclude that Justin also taught the creation of matter. But this conclusion, which impresses the modern reader of Justin, is not to be read from the

could not be a plurality of unoriginate beings from any particular philosophical tradition.[34] Probably he developed his line of argument independently from the conventional supposition that God is unoriginate.[35] Unlike the Platonists, Justin never connects the origin of evil with matter. The created beings possess from their nature the freedom to choose good or evil.[36] Creation as such is good, yet the demons have brought evil into the world.[37] The notion that matter could impose a limit on God's good activity or that evil could find its basis in matter, is found nowhere in Justin's work. So when Justin presupposes an eternal material as the stuff of creation, this conception simply has the function of explaining how the creation of the world was possible; Justin obviously cannot but represent it as only the formation of a material substratum. Beyond that the doctrine of uncreated matter plays no part in Justin's thinking.

texts. Passages like Apol. I 10, 2 and 59, I show that Justin accepted without reflection the pre-existence of matter. Philo too, who in any case held matter not to be created, can say that God as the Unoriginate stands over against all originate things: cf. leg.all. III 100; sacrif. 101; gig. 42; deus imm. 56; heres 98; congr. 48; spec. leg. II 166; virt. 180. E. W. Möller, *Geschichte der Kosmologie in der griechischen Kirche bis auf Origenes* (1860), pp. 148f., and now again Joly, pp. 59f., suggest that Justin regarded matter as 'non-being' and therefore could define God as the only unoriginate and intransitory being. Cf. also Norris, pp. 50–53.

[34] Thus, against Hyldahl, pp. 211f., who above all draws aristotelian and stoic parallels, van Winden, *An Early Christian Philosopher*, p. 98: 'One would prefer rather to see the present passage as an awkwardly construed argument. No need for searching further external sources.' In another way Athenagoras argued in the context of a proof that God was One from the concept of the 'unoriginate being': if there were several unoriginate beings, then they would have to be unlike each other, as they would not be copied from an ideal paradigm (suppl. 8, 2); cf. Grant, *The Early Christian Doctrine of God* (Charlottesville, 1966), pp. 105–110; A. J. Malherbe, 'Athenagoras on the Location of God', ThZ 26 (1970), pp. 46–52.

[35] The predicate 'unoriginate' (ἀγένητος) applied to God occurs in the language of Christian theology from early in the second century: J. Lebreton, 'ΑΓΕΝΝΗΤΟΣ dans la tradition philosophique et la littérature chrétienne du IIe siècle', *Rech. Sc. Rel.* 16 (1926), pp. 431–443. For the antithesis 'unoriginate God – the originate' cf. in addition to the examples offered by Lebreton, Irenaeus, haer. IV 38, 1 (from an older source, which is worked over in IV 37–39: M. Widmann, 'Irenäus und seine theologischen Väter', ZThK 54, 1957, pp. 156–173, pp. 163–165), the gnostic statements Ptolomaeus, ad Flor. 7, 6–8; Irenaeus, haer. I 11, 1; Hippolytus, ref. VI 29, 2.5.7.8 and as non-Christian parallels corp. herm. XIV 2.3.6.9.

[36] Apol. I 10, 3–6; 28, 3; 43; 44; II 7, 3ff.; 14, 1f.; dial. 88, 4f.; 102, 4; 124, 4; 141, 1; cf. Chadwick, *Justin Martyr's Defence*, pp. 287f.

[37] According to dial. 5, 4 the human body constitutes a hindrance to knowledge of God, but the thought is not emphasised and nothing elsewhere in Justin corresponds to it.

Justin considers the Logos to be the agent of creation, but this idea is not greatly emphasised; the decisive factor is God's role as creator.[38] Nor does he express himself more precisely about the idea of the Logos as agent in the creation. But it emerges from Justin's exposition of the theophanies of the Old Testament that in his view the transcendent God cannot enter into immediate contact with the world. God cannot himself appear on earth, therefore the theophanies reported in the Old Testament must be attributed to the Logos.[39] All anthropomorphic images of God must be avoided, such as that he moves or gets anywhere;[40] he remains always in his place above the sky and cannot appear to men in the limitations of earthly space, since the whole cosmos cannot contain him.[41] Were God to intervene actively at a specific point in the world, he would not at that moment be in heaven.[42] This idea of transcending space is indeed philosophically naive, but other Platonists of the period think likewise, so Justin should not be underestimated on account of these statements.[43] For us it is essential to see that Justin bases the agency of the Logos on the fact that God does not leave his place above the sky, and not on the idea that God cannot touch matter, which we found in Philo.[44] Justin's statements about the transcendence of God are thus not motivated by a dualistic devaluation of the earthly-material world.

In a few isolated passages Justin describes the function of the Logos in the cosmos by analogy with the Platonist world-soul,[45] and perhaps the Middle Platonist conception that the Ideas are the thoughts of God had an influence on his concept of the Logos.[46] But these statements have no

---

[38] Apol. II 6, 3; I 64, 5; dial. 62, 1; 84, 2; 114, 3; cf. 113, 5. The strong affirmation of God's role as creator could also have an anti-gnostic point.

[39] Dial. 56–62; 127; cf. apol. I 63, 1ff.; on that Chadwick, *Justin Martyr's Defence*, pp. 295f.; id., *Early Christian Thought*, pp. 15f.

[40] Dial. 127, 1f.

[41] Dial. 56, 1; 60, 2; 127, 2f.

[42] Dial. 127, 5. This view corresponds to the thought that God has handed over providence for the whole world under heaven to the angels: apol. II 5, 2. Here Justin seems to be dependent on the Middle Platonist doctrine of demons; cf. Celsus in Origen, Cels. VIII 28.35; Apuleius, de Plat. I 12.

[43] Cf. Schmid, *Frühe Apologetik*, p. 178, which refers to Maximus of Tyre, or. 11.10. The Platonist character of Justin's statements on the transcendence of God is wrongly contested by Hyldahl, p. 287.

[44] A. von Harnack, *Lehrbuch der Dogmengeschichte* I (1909), p. 530, asserts this of the apologists in general; cf. Philo, spec. leg. I 329 (p. 11 n. 41 above).

[45] Apol. I 55.60; cf. Andresen, *Justin*, pp. 188ff.

[46] Andresen, *Justin*, p. 190 n. 131 refers to dial. 62, 1: καὶ τοῦτο αὐτό, ὦ φίλοι, εἶπε καὶ διὰ Μωϋσέως ὁ τοῦ θεοῦ λόγος, μηνύων ἡμῖν ὃν ἐδήλωσε τὸν θεὸν λέγειν

central importance for Justin and are rather in the first place to be understood as apologetic points of contact.[47] For Justin the most difficult problem of Christology is posed by the incarnation. He in no way conceals the paradox and difficulty of his doctrine, but he still holds fast to it, without weakening.[48] Justin seeks to base the incarnation, at least for a start, on a general view of the history of salvation, and so to make it comprehensible; the appearance of the Logos as a man is the culmination and conclusion of the Old Testament theophanies; prophecy as a whole points to Jesus, and in him the knowledge of truth and salvation is finally brought to the whole world.[49] But as a basis for the possibility of the incarnation Justin constantly returns to the will of God, who has decreed it so.[50] The virgin birth of Christ is something Justin can directly compare with the creation: through the power and the will of God Eve was created from Adam's rib, and in the same way, through the Word of God all other living beings originated. Just so, through the power and the will of the creator, could the 'first-born of all creation' be born as

τούτῳ αὐτῷ τῷ νοήματι ἐπὶ τῆς ποιήσεως τοῦ ἀνθρώπου, λέγων ταῦτα Ποιήσωμεν κτλ'. (Gen. 1: 26–28). But the text does not seem to have been incontestably transmitted; perhaps we should read with the old English editor of Justin, S. Thirlby, *Iustini Philosophi et Martyris apologiae duane et Dialogus cum Tryphone Iudaeo* (London, 1722), p. 268 on dial. 62, 4; 129, 4 γεννήματι instead of νοήματι. Certainly there is an allusion here to the notion of the Ideas as the thoughts of God in apol. I 64, 5, where Justin asserts that the demons had named Athene as the first thought of God after the pattern of the Logos through whom God planned and created the world. This equation of Athene with the Platonic Ideas, the paradigm of the world, is first mentioned by Varro (in Augustine, civ. Dei VII 28); cf. Dörrie, 'Die Frage nach dem Transzendenten im Mittelplatonismus', in *Entretiens sur l'Antiquité classique* V; *Les sources de Plotin* (Vandoeuvres–Geneva, 1960), pp. 191–223, p. 206. This idea was already found in apol. I 64, 5 by P. Maran, *S. P. N. Justini Philosophi et Martyris opera quae exstant omnia* (Venice, 1747), p. 84; he refers to Themistios, or. 13 (167A).

[47] Cf. Andresen, *Justin*, p. 194: 'However, these speculations of Middle Platonism did not gain constitutive importance for Justin's Logos-doctrine. For Justin the Logos is always the personal bearer of the divine revelation in history. That is what is wholly un-Greek and, if you like unphilosophical about the Logos-doctrine of Justin.'

[48] Cf. dial. 38, 2; 68, 1; apol. I 53, 2.

[49] Apol. I 63; dial. 75, 4; 87, 3–5; also the ideas, later so important for Irenaeus of the correspondence of Adam to Christ and of Eve to Mary, are already found in Justin: dial. 103, 6; 100, 5; cf. Chadwick, *Defence*, p. 290; Campenhausen, 'Die Entstehung der Heilsgeschichte. Der Aufbau des christlichen Geschichtsbildes in der Theologie des ersten und zweiten Jahrhunderts', *Saeculum* 21 (1970), pp. 189–212, p. 205.

[50] Dial. 41, 1; 48, 3; 68, 1; 75, 4; 76, 1; 84, 2; 87, 2; 95, 2–4; 103, 3; 127, 4; apol. I 63, 10; II 6, 5. Next Justin seeks to clarify the 'two natures problem' by the acceptance that the blood of Christ had its origin in the 'power of God' and exhibited the divine element in him: dial. 54, 2; 63, 2; 76, 2; apol. I 32, 9; on the meaning and origin of this idea cf. Chadwick, *Defence*, p. 289 n. 13.

the child of a virgin.[51] One must not doubt that God can do anything that he wills.[52] With this declaration of the unlimited omnipotence of God, which achieves the apparently impossible, Justin decisively breaks through the Platonist concept of God.[53]

In specific opposition to the Platonist understanding of the world, Justin advances his anthropocentric doctrine of creation: God created the cosmos for the sake of man.[54] To men, however, is given the task of imitating God's perfection in moral behaviour.[55] In such formulations there is an echo of the basic teleology of Platonist ethics, the challenge to imitate God.[56] Conversely, however, God sustains the world for the sake of the Christians and of those people who will yet come to salvation. He postpones the Last Judgment until their number, which he foreknows, is complete. Only for that reason can the demons, the wicked angels and wicked men pursue their course, and only so is the persecution of Christians possible.[57] The stoicising idea that the whole world was created for the sake of men thus has in Justin a sense related specifically to the history of salvation. In this way he is also able to characterise the Eucharist as thanksgiving for the creation of the world, and for liberation from sin and the vanquishing of the demonic powers through Christ.[58]

Justin's positive relation to the created reality is to be seen finally in his statements about the resurrection. He is a chiliast and advances his eschatological ideas with determination as the right conception against such

---

[51] Dial 84,2. For Justin's thoughts on the virgin birth cf. Campenhausen, *Die Jungfraugeburt in der alten Kirche* (1962), pp. 15f., 23–26.

[52] Dial. 84,4.

[53] In dial. 5, 3f.; 6, 1f. where Justin accepts the statements of Timaeus 41AB about the will of the demiurge, the difference is especially clear: Justin declares the sovereign freedom of the divine will, while Plato's demiurge acts almost under the compulsion of his will: cf. Hyldahl, pp. 206f.; van Winden, *An Early Christian Philosopher*, pp. 93f. On the will of the demiurge in Timaeus 29E; 41AB cf. also W. J. Verdenius, 'Platons Gottesbegriff' in *Entretiens sur l'Antiquité classique* I: *La notion du devin* (Vandoeuvres – Geneva, 1954), pp. 241–293), p. 248.

[54] Apol. I 10, 2; II 4, 2; 5.2; dial. 41, 1.

[55] Apol. I 10, 1f.; II 4, 2.

[56] On this H. Merki, Ὁμοίωσις θεῷ. *Von der platonischen Angleichung an Gott zur Gottännlichkeit bei Gregor von Nyssa* (1952); Dörrie, *Die Frage nach dem Transzendenten*, p. 214.

[57] Apol. II 7, 1f.; I 28, 2; 45, 1; dial. 39, 2. Celsus reproaches both Jews and Christians for asserting that divine providence works in the first place for them and that the rest of the cosmos came into being for their benefit (Origen, Cels. IV 23).

[58] Dial. 41, 1; cf. apol. I 13, 2; on this W. Bousset, 'Eine jüdische Gebetssammlung im siebenten Buch der apostolischen Konstitutionen', NGG 1915, pp. 435–489, p. 463.

Christians as do not at this point share his views.⁵⁹ Justin finds the decisive argument for the resurrection again in the omnipotence of God, to whom the impossible is possible.⁶⁰ And he sees the resurrection in the context of continuing creation, as its advancement and completion: just as God in the beginning created man out of non-being, so he will also give him in the Last Days incorruptibility and eternal fellowship with himself.⁶¹

Justin several times in his extant works takes a stand against the gnostics and especially against Marcion. As early as his first Apology Justin reports that Simon Magus and his disciple Menander had with the help of the demons accomplished miracles and that Simon on the strength of these magical arts had been taken for a god and have even enjoyed divine veneration in Justin's own time.⁶² Against Marcion Justin brings the reproach that he taught a second God, who stands over the creator of the world and that he likewise brings in a second Christ. Justin also emphasises the success and spread of Marcion's teaching, whom he seems to envisage as still alive.⁶³ In his Dialogue written at a later date, Justin counts as exponents of heresy – alongside the Marcionites who are, scarcely by accident, mentioned first – the Valentinians, the Basilidians and Satornilians, whom he had not previously mentioned in the Apology. Possibly in the interval between the composition of the two writings in Rome, the controversy with the gnostic schools had intensified.⁶⁴ But the comprehensive description of heretical doctrine that Justin gives in two passages of the Dialogue seems in the first place again directed against the Marcionites: the false teachers slander the creator of the world, the God of Abraham, Isaac

---

⁵⁹ Dial. 80f.; cf. 138, 3; 139, 4f.
⁶⁰ Apol. I 18, 6; 19, 5f. Celsus again opposes basing the resurrection on God's omnipotence. Origen, Cels. V 14.
⁶¹ Apol. I 10, 2f.(οὐκ ὄντας ἐποίησε). In dial. 113, 5 Justin seems to set side by side Christ's function as intermediary in the creation and in the new creation, but the meaning of the passage, hardly transmitted without some distortion, is by no means clear. Justin parallels the creation and the resurrection of Jesus, when he explains that the Christians hold divine service on Sundays because on that day God created the world and Christ rose from the dead (apol. I 67,7); cf. W. Rordorf, *Die Sonntag. Geschichte des Ruhe- und Gottesdiensttages im ältesten Christentum* (Zurich, 1962), pp. 285f. (ET p. 290).
⁶² Apol. I 26, 1–4; 56; cf. dial. 120, 6. Analysis of the text in Beyschlag, *Simon Magus und die christliche Gnosis* (1974), pp. 9–13.
⁶³ Apol. I 26, 5; 58; cf. Harnack, *Marcion. Das Evangelium vom fremden Gott* (²1924), pp. 6*–10*, 314*.
⁶⁴ Dial. 35, 6; cf. G. Kretschmar, 'Auferstehung des Fleisches. Zur Frühgeschichte einer theologischen Lehrformel', in *Leben angesichts des Todes* Festschrift für H. Thielicke (1968), pp. 101–137, p. 128.

and Jacob, as well as Christ, and they deny the resurrection of the dead.[65] Justin's anti-heretical writings have not come down to us.[66] The reason why these works have not remained extant is certainly not that they failed to match up to the stricter theological standards of a later age, but that they had simply lost their relevance.[67] The intensive efforts of research in the last century to reconstruct Justin's 'Syntagma against all heresies' from his own statements and from the writings of later authors who used this work, have brought meagre results.[68] We may assume that the Syntagma was in form a tidy, catalogue-like survey of a series of deviations. Besides, there is a certain likelihood that Irenaeus in his doxographical presentation of the pre-Valentinian heresies (Haer. I 23–27) used Justin's text. But Irenaeus

[65] Dial. 35, 5; 80, 4; that here it is the Marcionites who are mostly meant is accepted also by W. Bauer, *Rechtgläubigkeit und Ketzerei im ältesten Christentum* (^{2}1964, ed. by G. Strecker, p. 133 (ET p. 129); cf. the similar sounding characterisation of the heretics in the apocryphal Epistle of the Corinthians to Paul 9–15, which clearly also has the Marcionites in view: Harnack, *Marcion*, p. 315*.

[66] Justin himself mentions a writing against all heresies: apol. I 26, 8. Irenaeus quotes from a work against Marcion (haer. IV 6, 2 = Eusebius, H.E. IV 18, 9), which he probably also uses at haer. V 26, 2 (= Eusebius, H.E. IV 18, 9). It has been suggested that the writing against Marcion was identical with the Syntagma against all heresies, which is in fact mainly devoted to opposing Marcion: thus Harnack, *Marcion*, p. 10*; P. Prigent, *Justin et l'Ancien Testament* (Paris, 1964), pp. 12, 66; but for this equation there is no certain evidence; cf. F. Loofs, *Theophilus von Antiochien adversus Marcionem und die anderen theologischen Quellen bei Irenaeus* (1930), p. 225 n. 4. Tertullian, adv. Val. 5, 1 names Justin as the opponent of the Valentinians (cf. also Irenaeus, haer. IV praef. 2: hi qui ante nos fuerunt, et quidem multo nobis meliores, non tamen satis potuerunt contradicere his qui sunt a Valentino, quia ignorabant regulam eorum). But should Justin already have taken position against the Valentinians in the work against all heresies? (Kretschmar, *Auferstehung des Fleisches*, p. 128 is opposed to this.) Or did he produce a work solely directed against the Valentinians? But since it cannot be proved that Tertullian had read the Syntagma against the heresies (see n. 71 below), it is to be supposed that his statement rests only on the common knowledge that Justin had engaged in literary controversy with the heresies.

[67] H. Langerbeck, 'Theologie und Gemeindeglauben in der römischen Gemeinde in den Jahren 135–165', in *Aufsätze zur Gnosis* ed. H. Dörrie (1967), pp. 167–169, p. 172, is of the view that Justin's Syntagma against the heresies soon became theologically suspect. But this suggestion lacks any foundation. H. D. Altendorf, 'Zum Stichwort: Rechtgläubigkeit und Ketzerei im ältesten Christentum', ZKG 80 (1969), pp. 61–74, pp. 66f., rightly rejects the view that the Christian literature of the second century fell partly victim to a later ecclesiastical 'censorship'.

[68] Above all should be named: R. A. Lipsius, *Zur Quellenkritik des Epiphanios* (1865); id., *Die Quellen der ältester Ketzergeschichte* (1875); Harnack, 'Zur Quellenkritik der Geschichte des Gnosticismus', *Zeitschrift f. d. histor. Theologie* 44 (1874), pp. 143–226; A. Hilgenfeld, *Die Ketzergeschichte des Urchristentums* (1884); critically against these older works Joh. Kunze, *De historiae gnosticismi fontibus novae quaestiones criticae* (1884); cf. the research report of P. Nautin in *Hippolyte, Contre le hérésies* (Paris, 1949), pp. 22–28.

certainly drew on other sources and in addition worked up his material from a specific point of view: he wanted to show that the older deviations were the 'mothers, fathers and forefathers' of the Valentinians.[69] The main source used by Irenaeus cannot be easily uncovered.[70] In later authors traces of a use of Justin's Syntagma can no longer be confirmed. Even Tertullian and Hippolytus seem to be based only on Irenaeus.[71]

In the 'Dialogue with Trypho' Justin presumably drew on his piece against Marcion of which Irenaeus tells us.[72] A reconstruction is frankly not possible in this case either, for Justin undoubtedly used other sources, among them perhaps collections of proof-texts, and made his choice of material from the older writing from the altered point of view of the

---

[69] Haer. I 31, 3; IV praef. 2.

[70] Harnack, *Geschichte der altchristlichen Literatur* I, p. 145, remarks on the writing used in haer. I 23–27 that 'over its relationship to the Justinian Syntagma agreement has not so far been reached'. Beyschlag expressly renounces research into the source-problem of haer. I 23ff. (p. V 16 n. 19) but considers it probable that the Irenaean report on Simon Magus (haer. I 23) goes back in its 'essential core' to Justin's Syntagma against the heresies (pp. 17f.). G. Lüdemann, *Untersuchungen zur simonianischen Gnosis* (1975), pp. 35f., following Hilgenfeld pp. 46ff., conjectures that Justin's work formed the source of haer. I 11.23.24.27.

[71] The proof that Harnack sought, *Zur Quellenkritik* I, pp. 67–76, that in De Anima 23.34.50 Tertullian used Justin's treatise on heresy has not been confirmed: Kunze, pp. 40–45; cf. also Waszink, *Tertulliani de Anima* (Amsterdam, 1947) on the relevant passages. The view that Hippolytus used it was indeed refuted by Harnack himself: *Zur Quellenkritik* II, pp. 216ff. Harnack's suggestion (*Zur Quellenkritik* I, pp. 36–41), that Hegesippus took over his list of heresies (in Eusebius H.E. IV 22, 5) from Justin, is not capable of proof either: such genealogies of heresy belong to the refutation of conflict of error; cf. Campenhausen, 'Die Nachfolge des Jakobus', in *Aus der Frühzeit des Christentums. Studien zur Kirchengeschichte des ersten und zweiten Jahrhunderts* (1963), pp. 135–151, pp. 144f.

[72] This seems to me to arise from the researches of Prigent. Of course Prigent holds that the works against heresies in general and against Marcion in particular are identical (see n. 66 above), and given this presupposition his reconstruction is in any case untenable: Beyschlag correctly criticises him for ignoring the problem of the list of heresies in apol. I 26, just as he ignores also (p. 10 n. 8) the relationship of Irenaeus, haer. I 23–27 to the Syntagma (p. 17 n. 20). But if one maintains the distinction between the two documents, then it is entirely possible that the work which Prigent reconstructs in outline, which served as a model for Justin, could have been the Syntagma against Marcion. The goal of the work described in the dialogue, the defence of the Old Testament, was of course unambiguously anti-Marcionite; but with the polemic against Marcion there naturally went also the refutation of other heretics: cf. dial. 35, 5f.; 80, 4. On the special interpretation of Justin, in contrast to Marcion, of the Old Testament law, cf. Campenhausen, *Die Entstehung der christlichen Bibel* (1968), pp. 112ff. (ET pp. 100ff.). Marta Müller, *Untersuchungen zum Carmen adversus Marcionitas* (Diss. Würzburg, 1936), pp. 70ff., tries to show through a comparison of the pseudo-Tertullian's poem 'Against Marcion' with Irenaeus that both to a large extent used Justin's work against Marcion; but the agreements show rather that the anonymous poet is dependent on Irenaeus.

controversy with the Jews. In any case it can be accepted that Justin in the work against Marcion demonstrated with thoroughgoing exegetical exposition the unity of the God to whom the Old Testament testifies with the Father of Jesus Christ, and defended the right to interpret the old scripture christologically, as happened elsewhere in the anti-Marcionite literature of the time.[73]

In Justin's statements about the creation of the world philosophical and specifically theological trains of thought stand side by side, which are not truly assimilated to each other. Justin understands the process of creation itself as the shaping of a pre-existent unordered material. But after that the Platonist model no longer has any importance for him. The possibility of incarnation and resurrection Justin sees as based on the omnipotent will of the creator, who can do anything. In such formulations it becomes evident that for Justin the activity of God is not limited by the presupposition, in the Platonist sense, of a superimposed concept of Nature and of what is possible and conceivable within its framework.[74] The critique which Celsus advanced against this concept of omnipotence is sufficient to show how inadequate it was philosphically.

The conception so emphatically declared by Justin of the unlimited creative power of God and the thought that God, as the sole unoriginate being stands over against the originate, the creation, are mutually supportive in their bearing and seem to urge the doctrine of *creatio ex nihilo*. But Justin did not take the last step towards its formulation; in that he was obviously hindered by the Platonist preconceptions of his thinking. In Justin's philosophical theology two things can be observed: on the one hand that the dynamic of the Christian concept of God practically compelled acceptance of the doctrine of *creatio ex nihilo*, on the other hand how monstrously difficult it was for thought stamped with the philosophical tradition to take in the biblical idea of creation in its full implications. Justin

---

[73] Chadwick, *Defence*, pp. 281f. reckons with the revision of the collection of proof-texts. It might be supposed that Justin in his work against Marcion embarked on an explanation of the morally repulsive passages in the Old Testament, which was not necessary when debating with Trypho: cf. the exegeses of the anti-Marcionite 'elders' in Irenaeus, haer. IV 28, 3–31.

[74] On one occasion Justin says expressly that we must believe that even what is impossible by its nature (τὰ τῇ ἑαυτῶν φύσει) and what is impossible to men are possible for God: apol. I 19, 6. Otherwise the concept of nature for Justin plays a part relating only to ethics: cf. apol. II 2, 4 ('Law of Nature'; on this Andresen, *Justin*, p. 179); dial. 93, 1–3. He is particularly concerned with the relationship between the Old Testament law and the 'naturally good, pious and righteous': dial. 45, 3f.; 47, 2. The natural seems to coincide with what is given by creation: cf. dial. 29, 3.

was not fully aware of the tension between his statements about the omnipotence of God and those about the creation of the world from pre-existent matter, but the whole outcome of his thought shows that he had freed himself from the ontological presuppositions of the world-formation model. The generation of theologians following Justin would already draw from the biblical idea of creation the necessary conceptual conclusion and would formulate in contradiction of traditional metaphysics the proposition that God created the world out of nothing.

Justin defines the theological meaning of creation by reference to God's work of salvation: God creates and sustains the cosmos so that men can turn to him and grasp the salvation offered in Christ. This understanding of creation points firmly in the direction of the theology of Irenaeus who consistently understands the creation as the first datum in the many-faceted history of salvation.[75]

Justin is not yet in a position to solve the problems with which he is grappling within a unified theological scheme. But with the questions he poses and with the provisional answers which he reaches he becomes a decisive pioneer of future theological development. With his syllabus of a philosophical theology he formulates one of the great themes of western thought. With his approaches to an understanding of the Old Testament in terms of salvation-history he prepares the way for the theology of Irenaeus,[76] and in his doctrine of the Logos spermatikos he opens up a view of history which draws in secular history as well and so announces a future theological interpretation of universal history.[77]

The treatise 'On the Resurrection'
John of Damascus in his *Sacra Parallela* reproduced some considerable fragments from a work apparently by Justin 'On the Resurrection'.[78] If we could take this writing into account for Justin, our knowledge of his theology would be significantly extended. But in spite of far-reaching agreements between Justin's authentic works and the *De Resurrectione*, which was used by Irenaeus, yet there are also such obvious differences in

---

[75] Andresen, *Logos und Nomos*, p. 316, declares that already in the story of creation 'the Logos appears as a historical-theological principle of revelation'; but the salvation-history aspect of the Logos doctrine is not so expressly worked out by Justin as Andresen supposes.
[76] Cf. Campenhausen, *Die Entstehung der christlichen Bibel*, pp. 106ff. (ET p. 98).
[77] Chadwick, *Justin Martyr's Defence*, p. 297.
[78] I give page and line references to the edition of K. Holl, *Fragmente vornicänischer Kirchenväter aus den Sacra parallela* (1899), pp. 36–49, and give besides the chapters of the older edition by J. C. T. Otto, *Corpus Apolog. Christ. Saec. Sec.* III (1879), pp. 210–248.

the way of thinking and in the intellectual stance, that to me the attribution to Justin seems untenable.[79] Nevertheless, the nearness of the work to Justin in both time and thinking suggests that it would be right to give attention to it at this point.

The compiler of *De Resurrectione* is an ascetic,[80] but he decisively affirms the bodily nature of men; while in the work of the gnostic opponents whom he is combatting, asceticism and devaluation of the flesh are associated in quite a different way.[81] For their conclusion that the dead do not rise the opponents appeal to the creation of mankind out of dust; this stuff is not worthy of resurrection and of heavenly life.[82] Against this the compiler makes the point that it is precisely the man of flesh who is created after the image of God, so the flesh can in no circumstances be devalued.[83] Yes, he can even bring in the challenge of asceticism as an argument for the resurrection of the flesh.[84] A further proof is afforded by the thesis that the world was created for the sake of men – we have already met this idea in Justin – so man consisting of flesh is the most valuable of all creatures.[85] God will not let this creature perish, for if he did his creation would be null and void.[86]

---

[79] A thorough proof of the authenticity of the work has been provided by Prigent, *Justin et l'Ancien Testament*, pp. 50ff.; Kretschmar, *Auferstehung des Fleisches*, p. 119, agrees with him in essentials. But in spite of the impressive number of parallels which Prigent has assembled, it seems to me that the whole way of thinking in the De Resurrectione is so different from that in the genuine works of Justin that I cannot consider Justin to be the author. Following an allusion by Harnack (*Die Überlieferung der griechischen Apologeten des zweiten Jahrhunderts in der alten Kirche und im Mittelalter*, 1882, p. 163 n. 147), W. Delius, 'Ps. Justin "Über die Auferstehung"', *Th. Viat.* 4 (1952), pp. 181–204; pp. 201ff., suggests Melito of Sardis as the author of De Resurrectione, but offers no convincing grounds for this attribution.
[80] Cf. 3, pp. 38, 71ff.; 10, pp. 49, 35ff.
[81] 3, pp. 38, 66ff.; cf. Delius, pp. 192f. In particular the following arguments of the opponents are mentioned: the flesh is the cause of sin: 2, pp. 38, 46f.; cf. 7, pp. 44, 235f. 251; a resurrection of the flesh is basically impossible; 5, pp. 40, 124f.; it is not worthy of God to awaken the evil and despicable flesh: 5, pp., 40, 125–127; cf. 7, pp. 44, 233f.; only the soul, which as the breath of God is a part of Him, possesses intransitoriness, 8, pp. 46, 303ff.; there is only one resurrection, spiritual: 9, pp. 47, 5f. (about this more must have been said in the preceding lacunae); Matt. 22:30 excludes resurrection in full fleshliness; 2, pp. 38, 55ff.; there is no promise of a resurrection of the flesh: 5, pp. 40, 127f.; 8, pp. 45, 265ff.
[82] 7, pp. 44, 234.
[83] 7, pp. 44, 236ff.; cf. 5, pp. 41, 144ff.
[84] 10, pp. 49, 35ff.
[85] 7, pp. 44, 250ff.
[86] 8, pp. 45, 268ff.

But in addition the compiler also seeks to give philosophical assurance to the belief in resurrection. He asks the 'children of truth' to excuse him for undertaking to argue the proof of the possibility of the resurrection of the flesh on philosophical grounds, but this is permissible, 'for nothing is outside God' and because he is dealing with unbelievers.[87] Talking to believers one could indeed dispense with all proofs.[88] In this the compiler seems to presuppose that the objections of his opponents to the resurrection of the flesh are philosophically based.[89] There follows a short doxography of cosmologists of the Platonists, Stoics and Epicureans.[90] All agree in the view that nothing comes from nothing, nothing dissolves into nothing, and the elements are not transitory. From these presuppositions he finds it without more ado conceivable that human bodies, originating out of matter or – to speak in Epicurean terms – out of the union of atoms, after their destruction arise again new. But then it is in no case to be doubted that God can reconstitute the body he created after its dissolution.[91]

The whole way in which the philosophical proof is brought in is not one that we should expect to find in Justin. If the excuses and the special justification for the introduction of philosophical arguments are understandable if the mistrust of church circles was to be overcome, still the author of *De Resurrectione* seems to have a fundamentally different attitude to philosophical thinking than Justin's. The latter is, of course, fully convinced that only Christians possess the full truth. But because he understands Christianity to be the true philosophy, all Christian propositions must also make sense philosophically. This thesis, it must be admitted, remains in many respects no more than a postulate, but basically there is for Justin no difference between philosophical and specifically 'Christian' argumentation. For the compiler of the resurrection treatise on the other hand the philosophical proof is only something supplementary and indeed superfluous, possessing for the Christian nothing of intellectual impor-

---

[87] 5, pp. 41, 154–159.
[88] 5, pp. 41, 159f.; cf. also the explanation of truth, which surpasses all proofs, 1, pp. 36, 1ff.
[89] 5, pp. 42, 165f.
[90] 6, pp. 42, 171–181; the mention of only two principles for Plato (God and matter) also in Diogenes Laertius III 77; the characterising thus of the epicurean doctrine also in Irenaeus, haer. II 14, 3; Hippolytus, ref. I 22, 1; the comparison of the stoic matter with the four elements also in Diogenes Laertius VII 137; cf. Philo, cherub. 127; on this C. Bäumker, *Das Problem der Materie in der griechischen Philosophie* (1890), pp. 333f. The writer has used one of the current doxographical manuals.
[91] 6, pp. 42, 181ff.

tance. It is scarcely to be imagined that the Justin whom we know from the Apologies and from the 'Dialogue with Trypho' spoke in this way.[92]

Theologically the central foundation of the resurrection is for the compiler of *De Resurrectione* the proof from Jesus: his life in the flesh, his resurrection and ascension show the reality of the resurrection of the flesh.[93] God's promise is valid for the whole man, who consists of body and soul,[94] soul and body have both believed and received baptism[95] and the miracles of healing and raising of the dead performed by Jesus announce the resurrection of the flesh.[96] This christological argument for the Christian hope makes it considerably clearer than do the authentic works of Justin, where the theological point of connection lies between awakening the dead and creation: God has created man, consisting of body and soul, as the most precious of his works,[97] and the plan of salvation which he is following with him reaches its goal in the resurrection.[98] From this understanding of the resurrection as the completion of the divine work of salvation, the statement that God can do the impossible, which is less strongly asserted in the *De Resurrectione* than in the assured works of Justin,[99] gets its precise theological sense: God's godhead is shown by the fact that he keeps faith with his creatures, preserving them through death and renewing them.

The biblical evidence for the resurrection of the flesh is central to the *De Resurrectione*. Only for the sake of completeness, to answer a criticism which obviously used philosophical arguments, is it shown that a bodily resurrection is conceivable also from the presuppositions of philosophical ontology. The doctrine of the eternity of matter is decisive for this demonstration: if the substratum of the body is not transitory, then the body, after its dissolution into the elements, can be put together again. The compiler of the *De Resurrectione* makes it emphatically clear that he is confining himself to the refutation of his opponents' objections to the principles of philosophical ontology and does not identify himself with them. But it is striking

---

[92] More reminiscent of Justin is the statement that the immortality of the soul had been taught by Pythagoras and Plato; the new thing that Christ brought was the promise of the resurrection of the flesh: 10, pp. 48, 13ff.; cf. apol. I 18, 5. In dial. 5, 6–6, 1, however, Justin distances himself from the two earlier philosophers, opposing their teaching of the essential immortality of the soul (Otherwise Joly, p. 54).
[93] 9, pp. 47, 5ff.; Kretschmar, *Auferstehung*, pp. 132ff.
[94] 8, pp. 46, 289–291.
[95] 8, pp. 46, 297ff.
[96] 9, pp. 47, 1–5.
[97] 7, pp. 44, 236ff.
[98] 8, pp. 45, 273–278; cf. Kretschmar, *Auferstehung*, p. 135.
[99] Cf. res. 5, pp. 40, 128ff.

that he makes no direct criticism of the doctrine of the eternity of matter or of the basic proposition 'Ex nihilo nihil fit'. He contents himself with the remark that the believer needs no proof of the resurrection of the body.[100] Nowhere in the comparatively comprehensive fragments of the treatise which are extant is to be found the assertion that God created the world out of nothing. So it looks as if the compiler, although he has no doubt about the omnipotence of God and his absolute role as creator, nevertheless possessed no clear conception of the *creatio ex nihilo*. It again becomes clear how little we are entitled to presuppose that the fully thought-out doctrine of *creatio ex nihilo* had become by the middle of the second century part of the common stock of orthodox theology. Tertullian is the first to adduce creation out of nothing as a proof that God had the power to awaken the dead.[101]

Athenagoras

Athenagoras, writing in the seventies of the second century, shows himself more heavily dependent in his cosmology on the contemporary Platonist scheme of concepts than Justin.[102] Indeed it is not easy to discern, under the veil of a deliberately ostentatious presentation and a contrived style, what his theological position or his intellectual motivation are.[103] Athenagoras is much more of an 'apologist' than Justin. But otherwise his views are not remote from those of Justin, whom he had probably read.[104]

[100] 5, pp. 41, 159–161.
[101] Res. mort. 11, 5–10.
[102] I quote the Apology of Athenagoras from the edition of W. R. Schoedel, whose paragraphing does not accord with that of Goodspeed: *Athenagoras, Legatio and De Resurrectione* (Oxford, 1972). The treatise 'On the Resurrection of the Dead', which is included in the Paris Arethas Codex likewise as a work of Athenagoras, is presumably not his. As R. M. Grant, 'Athenagoras or pseudo-Athenagoras', *Harv. Theol. Rev.* 47 (1954), pp. 121–129, has shown, this work, since it seems directly to oppose Origen, cannot have originated before the third or fourth century. To be sure, there is a striking series of agreements with the pseudo-Justin's treatment of the resurrection (Grant, p. 128). Here a link with the history of tradition must be taken into account: the anti-spiritualising arguments, which were originally directed against gnostic opponents of a physical resurrection, are now turned against Origen.
[103] The significance of Middle Platonism for the thought of Athenagoras has been especially traced by A. J. Malherbe, 'The structure of Athenagorus, "Supplicatio pro Christianis"', *Vig. Chr.* 23 (1969), pp. 1–20; 'Athenagoras on the pagan Poets and Philosophers', in *Kyriakon* I Festschrift for J. Quasten (1970), pp. 214–225.
[104] Athenagoras 7, 1f. conceives the relationship between Christianity and philosophy as Justin does: the philosophers have, 'in the strength of a sympathy with the breath (πνοή) of God', sought the truth and so arrived at a miscellany of doctrines, while the Christians possess the God-inspired prophets as witnesses of the truth. Only here the doctrine of the

God created everything through the Logos and through his Spirit it is held together.[105] The Pneuma is here described with the features of the Platonist World Soul.[106] But in Athenagoras there is an inconsistency in his teaching about the Logos and about the Spirit. In the passage adduced the creation of the world is ascribed to the Logos, its sustaining and guidance to the Spirit. But Athenagoras can also ascribe both functions to the Logos, while the Pneuma is seen simply as an inspiring power.[107] Athenagoras does not succeed in developing a unified pneumatology; like his contemporary Theophilus of Antioch he is unable to draw a clear line between the functions of the Spirit and those of the Logos.[108]

The Logos is the Nous of God, which contains within itself the totality of the Ideas. As in Philo, the Logos functions as the ideal paradigm of creation and at the same time as the agent of creation.[109] God lets him emerge from the godhead, in order that through him and according to the pattern of the Ideas contained within him he may order matter so that it becomes the cosmos.[110] Athenagoras understands the creation of the world

---

Logos spermatikos is replaced by the inspiration-doctrine characteristic of Athenagoras; on this cf. 9, 1. That Athenagoras had read Justin is suggested by Harnack, *Geschichte der altchristlichen Literatur*, I, p. 100; Schoedel, p. XIII.

[105] 6, 2; cf. 5, 3.

[106] Cf. Albinus, did. 10 (pp. 164, 16–20); Atticus in Eusebius, praep. ev. XV 12, 3; on that Andresen, *Justin*, p. 193, and especially Malherbe, 'The Holy Spirit in Athenagoras', JThS n.s. 20 (1969), pp. 538–542.

[107] A similar split finds expression perhaps in the exposition of Prov. 8:22: Athenagoras, differing from Justin who applies the passage to the Logos (cf. dial. 61; 129, 3f.) seems to refer it to the Spirit (10, 4; cf. Malherbe, *The Holy Spirit*, pp. 538f.), but can also describe the Logos as the wisdom of the Father (24, 2). Obviously he knows two different interpretations of wisdom, which he uses side by side: equating it on the one hand with the Logos, on the other with the Pneuma. On these conceptions of wisdom cf. Kretschmar, *Studien zur früchristlichen Trinitätstheologie* (1965), pp. 27–61.

[108] On Theophilus cf. Grant, 'Theophilus of Antioch to Autolycus' in *After the New Testament* (Collected Papers, Philadelphia, 1967), pp. 126–157, pp. 152f.

[109] 10, 2; ἀλλ' ἐστὶν ὁ υἱὸς τοῦ θεοῦ λόγος τοῦ πατρὸς ἐν ἰδέᾳ καὶ ἐνεργείᾳ· πρὸς αὐτοῦ γὰρ καὶ δι' αὐτοῦ πάντα ἐγένετο. Cf. 10, 3. 'Energeia' has here the same meaning as 'organon' in Philo: W. Theiler, art. 'Demiurgos', RAC III (1957), col. 707; id. 'Philo von Alexandrien und der Beginn des kaiserzeitlichen Platonismus', in *Parusia. Studien zur Philosophie Platons und zur Problemgeschichte des Platonismus*. Essays in honour of J. Hirschberger (1965), pp. 199–218, pp. 215f. Suppl. 10, 2; 24, 2 will describe the Logos as the Nous of God.

[110] 10, 3: ὡς τῶν ὑλικῶν ξυμπάντων ἀποίου φύσεως καὶ γῆς ὀχίας ὑποκειμένων δίκην, μεμιγμένων τῶν παχυμερεστέρων πρὸς τὰ κουφότερα, ἐπ' αὐτοῖς ἰδέα καὶ ἐνέργεια εἶναι προελθών. Perhaps, hidden beneath the incomprehensible γῆς ὀχίας there is an allusion to Gen. 1:2; otherwise the attempted emendation of E. Schwartz and Geffcken. On the idea of the mixing of the heavy and the light in the original chaotic state of matter see p. 106 above.

Christian and Platonist Cosmology 139

unambiguously as the mere shaping of the unoriginate matter.[111] Quite naturally he compares the process of creation with the shaping of clay by the potter.[112] The material is assumed to be given, and nowhere are questions raised about its origin.[113] Obviously the Platonist scheme of world-formation possesses for Athenagoras unquestioned validity.[114] Athenagoras asserts an affinity of the devil and the fallen angels with matter; the power hostile to God had originally been created by God to have control over matter, just as the angels were created to undertake providence for regions of the cosmos, while God himself exercised universal providence for the whole world.[115] The 'Archon of Matter' and a part of the angels fell, because they had been created as free beings and so also possessed the possibility of turning away from God.[116] They were all no longer capable of rising above the earthly atmosphere and they are now disturbing the divine government in the earthly realm.[117] The demonic powers raged most of all against men, who succumb to the attack when they become materialist.[118] In these ideas the influence of a negative conception of matter, which brings it into close connection with evil, is unmistakeable. But it is significant that Athenagoras never describes matter directly as evil or the ground of evil. The possibility of evil is given with the freedom of moral choice which God has granted to his creatures.[119]

---

[111] The elements emerge through 'diacrisis' from the original matter: 22, 2; on this Platonist idea cf. Albinus, did. 12 (pp. 167, 15–18) and the numerous parallels given in W. Spoerri, *Späthellenistische Berichte über Welt, Kultur und Götter* (1959), pp. 69ff.

[112] 15, 2f.; cf. 19, 4. The comparison with the potter is also in Albinus, did. 8 (pp. 163, 1ff.).

[113] Cf. 10, 3 (n. 110 above); 15, 2f.; 22, 2; on this Möller, pp. 149ff. But from 4, 2 it is not to be taken that Athenagoras describes matter as μὴ ὄν: against Möller, pp. 121–123.149 and H. Schwabl, art. 'Weltschöpfung', PW Suppl. IX (1962), cols. 1433–1582, cols. 1574f.

[114] Athenagoras can indeed describe matter as originate and transitory (4, 1), but he then clearly means in a broader sense the corporeal and the visible, not the formless original substratum: cf. Möller, p. 152; for similar statements by Philo, see p. 11 n. 42 above. When Athenagoras speaks of the transitoriness of the elements (16, 4f. also 22, 3, where the Hyle is identical with the elements), he seems to be thinking of the possibility of their dissolution into the primaeval matter, out of which they came at the creation of the world (22, 2; see n. 111 above).

[115] 24, 2f.; cf. 10, 5. On this doctrine of providence and of demons cf. A. J. Festugière, 'Sur une traduction nouvelle d'Athénagore', REG 56 (1943), pp. 367–375, pp. 371ff.

[116] 24, 4f.

[117] 25.

[118] 25, 3; 27.

[119] 24, 4f.; 25, 4.

Hermogenes

It was Hermogenes who went furthest in taking over the cosmological ideas of Middle Platonism. In the last decades of the second century he lived first in the East, probably in Antioch, and later in North Africa, at Carthage. We are only aware of these biographical details because Theophilus of Antioch and Tertullian both wrote against him.[120] By accepting an unoriginate matter Hermogenes not only wishes to make the process of creation understandable: in the first place he is concerned to explain the origin of evil. So he does not settle for the gnostic solution of the problem: while the gnostics explain the presence of evil in the cosmos by the imperfection of the demiurgic powers, Hermogenes holds firmly to the unity of God in the Platonist manner, and understands uncreated matter as the ground of evil. This view which, in spite of all the qualifications and limitations that Hermogenes proposes, sets up matter as an evil principle alongside God, could not but appear intolerable to church theology which in the struggle against Marcion had become fully aware of the dangers of dualism. When Hermogenes put forward his ideas, literary polemic against him seems to have begun almost immediately.[121]

Our most complete and reliable source for the cosmology of Hermogenes is the treatise written against him by Tertullian,[122] which is supplemented on certain points by the report of Hippolytus.[123] Tertullian and Hippolytus could both have used the lost polemical work of Theophilus of Antioch.[124]

According to Tertullian's account, Hermogenes started from the proposition that God must have created the world either out of himself or out of

---

[120] For the non-extant work of Theophilus cf. Eusebius, H.E. IV 24, 1. In addition to the 'Adversus Hermogenem', Tertullian compiled a work lost to us, 'De censu animae adversus Hermogenem', in which he contested Hermogenes' doctrine of the soul: an. 1, 1; 3.4; cf. Waszink, *Tertulliani de Anima* (Amsterdam, 1947), pp. 7*ff.

[121] Theophilus of Antioch had perhaps written his work against Hermogenes as early as the seventies; at the time of the compilation of Tertullian's treatise (after 200) Hermogenes was still alive: herm. 1, 2.

[122] The most important contribution for the understanding of this work and the thought of Hermogenes in general has been made through the works of Waszink: beside his edition of the Tractate (1956) one may mention the essay 'Observations on Tertullian's Treatise against Hermogenes', *Vig. Chr.* 9 (1955), pp. 129–147, and the annotated translation 'Tertullian, The Treatise against Hermogenes' (Westminster, MD/London, 1956); cf. also G. T. Armstrong, *Die Genesis in der alten Kirche* (1962), pp. 102–111. The older work of E. Heintzel, 'Hermogenes, der Hauptvertreter des philosophischen Dualismus in der alten Kirche (Diss. Erlangen, 1902) is still worth reading, though naturally superseded today at many points.

[123] Ref. VIII 17; X 28.

[124] Harnack, *Die Überlieferung der griechischen Apologeten des zweiten Jahrhunderts in der alten Kirche und im Mittelalter* (1882), pp. 294–297; Waszink, *Trans.*, pp. 9–12.

nothing or out of a 'something' distinct from himself.[125] He could not create the world out of himself because his being is indivisible and immutable, nor out of nothing because as perfect Goodness he could only have created good, so the origin of evil would not be explained. There remains as the only possibility that God created the world out of a 'something', out of preexistent matter.[126]

It may be asked whether Hermogenes in this train of thought was seeking to refute specific cosmological models; he could have had in mind the emanation idea, the doctrine of *creatio ex nihilo* and the Platonist scheme of world-formation. But it is more likely that what we have here is simply an abstract discussion of the basic conceptions of the world's origin.[127]

Hermogenes emphatically declared that matter cannot be a principle of equal rank ontologically with God.[128] God is Lord over matter, and this proposition is turned into an argument for the eternity of matter: God was in his unchangeableness always Lord, and so there must have been from eternity something for him to be Lord of.[129] He is not comparable with any other being, the first, the sole Lord and creator of everything,[130] and in the power of his lordship he uses matter for his creation.[131] Hermogenes finds the biblical basis for his doctrine, as might be expected, in Genesis 1:2: in the sentence 'But the earth was without form and void'. 'Earth' means matter, the imperfect tense 'was' expresses its eternal duration, and by

---

[125] Tertullian, Herm. 2, 1: Praestruens aut dominum de semetipso fecisse cuncta aut de nihilo aut de aliquo, ut, cum ostenderit neque ex semetipso fecisse potuisse neque ex nihilo, quod superest exinde confirmet, ex aliquo eum fecisse atque ita aliquid illud materiam fuisse.

[126] Herm. 2, 2–4.

[127] Cf. Plutarch, Plat. Quaest. 4 (1003AB) on Timaeus 30B: the world-soul created the world-body neither out of itself nor out of nothing (οὐδ' ἐκ τοῦ μὴ ὄντος), 'but out of an unordered and unformed body it made an ordered and governable one'. Somewhat differently Methodius, autex. 2, 9: the 'Valentinian' explains: the world must either have come into being out of something existing eternally alongside God or have come out of himself: for it is unthinkable that anything should arise out of nothing. In the sequel the 'Orthodox' proves that God has created the world out of nothing.

[128] Herm. 5, 1; 7, 1: Minorem et inferiorem materiam deo et idcirco diversam ab eo et idcirco incomparabilem illi contendit, ut maiori, ut superiori. P. Nautin, 'Genèse 1, 1–2 de Justin à Origène, in *In Principio. Interprétations des premiers versets de la Genèse* (Paris, 1973), pp. 61–94, p. 74 n. 44, suggests that Hermogenes described the material not as 'unoriginate' like God but merely as coming eternally into being.

[129] Herm. 3, 1. On the further history of this argument cf. H. Kusch, 'Studien über Augustinus II: Der Titel Gottes "Dominus" bei Augustinus und Thomas von Aquino', in Festschrift für Fr. Dornseiff (1953), pp. 184–200, pp. 185ff.

[130] Herm. 5, 2.6.

[131] Herm. 9, 3: Ex dominio defendit (sc. Hermogenes) deum materiam usum.

'without form and void' its unordered, chaotic state is described.[132] Hermogenes also relates the idea of 'beginning' in Genesis 1:1 to matter,[133] while in this verse he applies the word 'earth' to the already formed earth.[134] Finally Hermogenes interprets Genesis 1:2b as the four elements which make up the parts of which the original matter consists.[135]

Matter itself before its ordering is without qualities, neither corporeal nor incorporeal.[136] It is also neither good nor evil, although Hermogenes derives evil from it.[137] But matter cannot be essentially evil, otherwise God would have been unable to create anything out of it.[138] It even bears in itself the demand to be ordered by God.[139] As matter is infinite, God has only partly formed it.[140] Through this forming it has undergone a change for the better, but even the ordered cosmos is still a mirror and copy of matter in its original uniformed state.[141] Hermogenes seems to have considered the traces of the original disorder of matter remaining in every created thing as the specific ground of the evil present in the world.[142] God shaped matter

---

[132] Herm. 23, 1: Nam et terrae nomen redigit (in) materiam, quia terra sit quae facta est ex illa, et erat in hoc dirigit, quasi quae semper retro fuerit, innata et infecta, invisibilis autem et rudis, quia informem et confusam et inconditam vult fuisse materiam; cf. 28. On the reading 'invisibilis et rudis' (cf. 25, 1; 26, 2) Waszink, *Trans.*, p. 140 n. 202. The interpretation given by Hermogenes to the 'erat' (cf. also 27, 1) is contested by Ambrose, exam. I 7, 25; cf. J. Pépin, 'Echos de théories gnostiques de la matière au début de l'Exameron de Saint Ambroise', in *Romanitas et Christianitas* Festschrift for J. H. Waszink (Amsterdam, 1973), pp. 259–273, pp. 261ff. Procopius of Gaza treats it as an exegesis of the Manichaeans: Comm. Gen. I, PG 87, 1 41C. In a similar way Plotinus, Enn. III 7, 6, 50ff. concludes from the imperfect ἦν in Timaeus 29 E 1 (the demiurge 'was good') that the intellectual cosmos, which was for him identical with the demiurge, was without a beginning in time; cf. M. Baltes, *Die Weltentstehung des platonischen Timaios nach der antiken Interpreten* I (1976), pp. 133f.

[133] Herm. 19, 1; cf. Waszink, *Trans.*, p. 5. Tertullian ascribes this interpretation to 'the heretics', but is no doubt implying that Hermogenes also uses it; cf. Nautin, 'Genèse 1, 1–2', p. 68 n. 27.

[134] Herm. 25, 1–3.

[135] Herm. 30, 1; cf. 28, 1; 31, 1. It is a matter surely of the interpretation of Hermogenes and not merely of a possible exegesis which Tertullian circumspectly refutes, as Nautin, 'Genèse 1, 1–2', p. 69, n. 0 says: cf. Waszink, *Trans.*, p. 5; 92 n. 22.

[136] Herm. 35, 2; cf. 36, 1f.; Waszink, *Trans.*, p. 6.

[137] Herm. 37, 1; 41, 1; 43, 2; cf. 11, 1; 12, 1.

[138] Herm. 14, 1; cf. Waszink, *Trans.*, p. 6.

[139] Herm. 42, 1.

[140] Herm. 38, 2–4; Hippolytus, ref. VIII 17, 2.

[141] Herm. 40, 1f.; cf. 17, 2; 38, 4; 39, 2. Ambrose seems to be at variance with this view: exam. I 2, 7 (pp. 6, 14–16 Schenkl); cf. I 2, 5 (pp. 5, 1–3); on this Pépin, pp. 259–261.

[142] Cf. Waszink, 'Observations', p. 134; *Trans.*, p. 7, and earlier Uhlhorn, art. 'Hermogenes', RE VII (1899), p. 757.

into the cosmos without touching it. The creation of the world was accomplished through the mere appearance of God on the scene and through his approach to the matter, just as beauty is effective through its mere appearance and the magnet by its proximity.[143] Hermogenes probably thought of the creation of the world as an eternal process; in any case he taught that God is eternally Lord and creator, but that matter is eternally his servant and in process of becoming.[144] Tertullian and Hippolytus in their day described Hermogenes as a Platonist.[145] This judgment is to the point. Waszink has shown in detail that practically every statement of Hermogenes about the nature of matter has parallels in Middle Platonism.[146] Even the decisive idea for his explanation of evil, that matter is only to be given form to a limited extent, was taken over by Hermogenes from the Platonist tradition.[147] The idea of God creating by his mere presence goes back to the Aristotelian teaching on the Unmoved Mover, but Hermogenes will have taken this thought also from a Platonist source, as Middle Platonism was decisively influenced by the Aristotelian teaching about God.[148] Hermogenes expressly distanced himself from Stoic views: he rejected the idea that God is immanent in matter,[149] and his polemic against 'the arguments of certain people who say that evil is necessary to illuminate the good, so that the latter may be known by

---

[143] Herm. 44, 1: Non, inquis, pertransiens illam (sc. materiam) facit mundum, sed solummodo apparens et adpropinquans ei, sicut facit quid decor solummodo apparens et magnes lapis solummodo adpropinquans. M. Poblenz, *Die Stoa* II (⁴1972), p. 189, understands 'decor' here mistakenly as the reflection of God present in the matter.

[144] Hippolytus, ref. VIII 17, 1; cf. Waszink, *Trans.*, p. 6.

[145] Tertullian, Herm. 1, 4 (the words 'a Stoicis' were rightly struck out as glosses by Waszink; cf. 'Observations', pp. 129f.); Hippolytus, ref. VIII 17, 2.

[146] 'Observations', pp. 129ff.; *Trans.*, p. 9.

[147] Cf. Numenius on Chalcidius, in Timaeus 298 = fr. 52 des Places: Sed postquam silvae ornatus accesserit, ipsam quidem matrem esse factam corporeorum et nativorum deorum, fortunam vero eius prosperam esse magna ex parte non tamen usque quaque, quoniam naturale vitium limari omnino nequiret (pp. 300, 20 – 301, 3 Waszink); cf. R. Beutler, art. 'Numenius', PW Suppl. VII (1940), col. 674; van Winden, *Caldidius on Matter. His Doctrine and Sources* (Leiden, 1959), p. 118; further information in Waszink's edition of Chalcidius, *in loco*. In Methodius, de autex. III 9 the Valentinian attributes evil to the unformed 'yeast' of matter.

[148] Waszink, 'Observations', pp. 135f.; cf. Dörrie, *Die Frage nach dem Tranzendenten*, p. 204; Beutler, col. 671.

[149] Tertullian, Herm. 44, 1 (n. 143 above); cf. SVF II 1028–1048; this idea is often criticised by Christian authors: M. Spanneut, *Le stoicisme des pères de l'Eglise de Clément de Rome à Clément d'Alexandrie* (Paris, 1957, 2nd undated ed.), pp. 88–90.

reference to its opposite'[150] is probably aimed at the thesis put out by Chrysippus of the Stoic theodicy that evil is necessary because without its opposite there could be no good.[151]

In the exegesis of Genesis 1:2 Hermogenes follows a widespread expository tradition which goes back to hellenistic Judaism. This is true not only of the meaning given to Genesis 1:2a, on unordered matter,[152] but also of the equating of 'darkness', 'deep', 'Spirit of God', and 'water' (Gen. 1:26) with the four elements. Related interpretations of Genesis 1:2b are to be found in Philo, Justin and Theophilus of Antioch.[153] In this connection should also be remembered the Jewish-hellenistic exposition given in the midrash Genesis rabba, which sees in Tohuwabohu, darkness, water, wind, and 'deep' the original materials of creation.[154] Only the reference of the term 'beginning' in Genesis 1:1 to matter[155] and the thesis that the imperfect tense 'was' in Genesis 1:2a denotes the eternity of matter and its lack of a beginning,[156] seem to be without parallels.

Waszink misses in Hermogenes a reference to Wisdom 11:17, where it expressly says that God created the world out of unformed matter.[157] But this passage, as far as we can ascertain, was first quoted by Origen.[158] Even

---

[150] Tertullian, Herm. 15, 4: Nam et Hermogenes expugnat quorundam argumentationes dicentium mala necessaria fuisse ad inluminationem bonorum ex contrariis intelligendorum.

[151] Cf. SVF II 1169.1181; on this Heintzel, p. 59; Pohlenz II, p. 189. Chrysippus's idea was contested by Plutarch: Stoic rep. 36 (1051AB); comm. not. 13ff. (1065Aff.); cf. D. Babut, *Plutarque et le Stoicisme* (Paris, 1969), pp. 294–298. The notion that evil is a necessary component of the world is to be found in Theaet. 176A and was taken over by Middle Platonism: Numenius in Chalcidius on Timaeus 297 (fr. 52 des Places); Celsus in Origen, Cels. IV 62.65.69.70; VIII 55; cf. van Winden, *Calcidius*, pp. 112f. But, at variance with Chrysippus, the stress here is on the inevitability of evil. J. B. Gould, *The Philosophy of Chrysippus* (Leiden, 1970), p. 157, asserts against this the fundamental agreement between Chrysippus and Plato.

[152] Cf. p. 6 n. 24 above; further: Clement of Alexandria, strom. V 90, 1; Origen, princ. IV 4, 6 (33); comm. Gen. fr. in Eusebius, praep. ev. VII 20, 9; Chalcidius on Timaeus 278 (after the Genesis commentary of Origen: van Winden, *Calcidius*, pp. 54–66); gnostic variants in Clement of Alexandria, exc. ex Theod. 47, 4; Hippolytus, ref. VI 30, 8f.; cf. Ilona Opelt, art. 'Erde', RAC V (1962), cols. 1169–1172.

[153] Philo, prov. I 22; Justin, apol. I 59, 5; Theophilus of Antioch, Autol. II 13; on the last-named passage cf. Waszink, 'Observations', p. 138; Nautin, 'Ciel, pneuma et lumière chez Théophile d'Antioche (Notes critiques sur ad Autol. II 13)', *Vig. Chr.* 27 (1973), pp. 165–171.

[154] Gen. rabba I 9; see p. 23 above.
[155] Tertullian, Herm. 19, 1; see n. 133 above.
[156] Tertullian, Herm. 23, 1; 27, 1; see n. 132 above.
[157] 'Observations', pp. 133f.
[158] Origen, princ. IV 4, 6 (33).

Clement of Alexandria makes no reference to it, although he otherwise turns to 'wisdom' comparatively often; so it is not surprising that Hermogenes too does not seem to have had recourse to this passage of Scripture.[159] Hermogenes obviously came, as Justin did, from Platonism to Christianity. But as a Christian he remains much more of a Platonist than the latter.[160] About his relationship to the intellectual trends and developments within Christianity we can only make conjectures. He interprets the opening verse of the creation story as many educated Christians understood it, while his speculations about soul and spirit, about which we know mainly through Tertullian's critical remarks in the *De Anima*, show a certain relationship with the teaching of Tatian.[161] The polemic against alien doctrines to which Tertullian refers in two passages of the *Adversus Hermogenes*, deals with Stoic theorems.[162] We find no evidence, however, of any direct controversy between Hermogenes and Christian views. Tertullian's statements show that Hermogenes in his teaching about creation was in the first place concerned to explain the origin of evil. This question was not only philosophically important, but was also the great theme of the gnostic theologians. So Hermogenes was taking a position in relation to a problem which was of burning relevance to the educated Christians of his time.

As we have no direct statements we cannot simply say whether the opposition to the doctrine of *creatio ex nihilo* had any significance for the thinking of Hermogenes. The idea of *creatio ex nihilo* seems to have played a role in Antioch comparatively early,[163] so that Hermogenes could have known about it and opposed it from the beginning. But it is not very probable that he conceived his teaching on creation directly as a campaign against the doctrine of *creatio ex nihilo*.[164] In the event this doctrine was not

[159] On the use of 'wisdom' cf. T. Zahn, *Geschichte des Neutestamentlichen Kanons* II (1890/92), p. 99 n. 2. The first volume issued by the Strasburg 'Centre d'Analyse et de Documentation Patristiques', of the Repertory of patristic biblical quotations, which covers the literature as far as Clement of Alexandria and Tertullian, gives no quotation of Wisdom 11:17: *Biblia Patristica* I (Paris, 1975), p. 220.

[160] Cf. Waszink, 'Bemerkungen zum Einfluss des Platonismus in frühen Christentum', *Vig. Chr.* 19 (1965), pp. 129–162, pp. 144f.; similarly Grant, *Miracle and Natural Law in Graeco-Roman and Early Christian Thought* (Amsterdam, 1952), p. 144.

[161] The evidence for Hermogenes's doctrine of soul and spirit is collected and interpreted by Waszink, *Tertulliani De Anima*, pp. 7a–14a. On the agreements with Tatian cf. Heinzerl, pp. 54f.; W. D. Hauschild, *Gottes Geist und der Mensch. Studien zur frühchristlichen Pneumatologie* (1973), pp. 198ff.

[162] See pp. 143–144 above.

[163] See p. 77 above.

[164] This is the thesis of Heintzel, who puts it somewhat anachronistically: 'Hermogenes seeks to refute dialectically the dogma of creation out of nothing' (p. 78; cf. p. 83).

commonly entertained in the seventies by church theologians, and furthermore the traditional belief about creation was then in competition with the various gnostic doctrines of the origin of the world. Hermogenes was thus scarcely confronted in Antioch by a unified Christian understanding of creation. He, who was so emphatically anxious to ensure the absolute goodness of the creator God, no doubt found, however, the gnostic myth of emanation and fall and the closely linked devaluation of the demiurge no less intolerable than the idea of creation through the will and word of the one God alone. If Hermogenes developed his teaching from the beginning in opposition to other views – of which we have no evidence – there is no reason for his opposition to have been fixed solely by the *creatio ex nihilo*, but it could equally have been provoked by gnostic speculations about the origin of the cosmos and the basis of evil.

The ideas of Hermogenes hardly had a great effect on the Christianity of his time. It has been suggested that his doctrine of matter could have influenced the speculations of Bardesanes on the elements, but this is wholly improbable.[165] But all the same, Hermogenes must have gained so much publicity with his teaching that theological controversy with him became unavoidable. In the last decades of the second century the process by which the Catholic Church fenced itself off from the gnostic heretics was in full swing, and with it there was a critical reaction against philosophical reinterpretations of Christian doctrine and especially against all forms of intellectual syncretism. In this historical situation a synthesis of Christianity and Platonism, such as Hermogenes was attempting, could no longer be pursued; to undertake it was, in the atmosphere of anti-gnostic theology, immediately to incur the verdict of heresy. The controversy with Hermogenes

---

[165] Such a dependence of Bardesanes on Hermogenes is in the mind of H. Lietzmann, *Geschichte der Alten Kirche* (1936), pp. 270f. (ET p. 264) and more recently of T. Jansma, *Natuur, lot en vrijheid. Bardesanes, de filosoof der Arameeers en zijn images* (Wageningen, 1969), pp. 157–159. But the doctrine of Bardesanes on the creation of the world from the mixing of darkness with light, wind, fire and water separates him fundamentally from the creation theory of Hermogenes, wholly dependent on Middle Platonism and is more closely related to gnostic ideas: cf. Barbara Ehlers, 'Bardesanes von Edessa – ein syrischer Gnostiker', ZKG 81 (1970), pp. 334–351, pp. 340ff.; B. Aland, 'Mani und Bardesanes – Zur Entstehung des manichäischen Systems', in *Synkretismus in syrisch-persisches Kulturgebiet* AAWG 3, F. 96 (1975), pp. 123–143, pp. 127ff. Furthermore Bardesanes hardly had to rely on Hermogenes in order to acquire the Middle Platonist doctrine of matter. This dependence was also energetically disputed by H. J. W. Drijvers against Jansma: cf. Drijvers, 'De schilder en de kunstcriticus. Discussies rind een portret van Bardesanes, de filosoof der Armeeers', *Nederl. Theol. Tijdschr.* 24 (1969/70), pp. 89–104, pp. 103f.; Jansma, 'Bardesanes van Edessa en Hermogenes van Carthago' ibid., pp. 256–259; Drijvers, 'Het image van Bardesanes van Edessa', ibid., pp. 260–262.

no doubt contributed to a further clarification of the concept of creation and eased the way for the adoption of the doctrine of *creatio ex nihilo*. Theophilus of Antioch, the earliest opponent of Hermogenes, is the first church theologian known to us – and this is certainly no accident – to use unambiguously the substance and the terminology of the doctrine of *creatio ex nihilo*. His manifesto was read by Tertullian and Hippolytus; so it seems to have attracted relatively wide notice.[166] And Tertullian in his broadsheet again delivered a penetrating case for and defence of *creatio ex nihilo*.

All the same, throughout the second century and the early part of the third the doctrine of the pre-existence of matter was firmly held by philosophically educated Christians. We have observed this in Athenagoras, and Clement of Alexandria still seems to accept unformed matter.[167] Tertullian mentions Christians to whom the *creatio ex nihilo* is an impracticable idea.[168] At the same time these Christian Platonists are convinced of the unlimited freedom and omnipotence of God and put themselves on guard against the ontological equating of God and matter. Clement expressly declines to allow matter to count as a second principle of being and even expresses the opinion that that was Plato's own view too.[169] The world-formation model is thus simply left with the limited task of making the origin of the world understandable. Soon the world-formation schema will be connected with the *creatio ex nihilo*: it is accepted that God created formless matter out of nothing and shaped this into an ordered cosmos.[170]

---

[166] Also Clement of Alexandria (ecl. proph. 56, 2) and Origen (sel. in ps., XII 73 Lomm., otherwise without mention of names) know about Hermogenes; perhaps they knew the work of Theophilus: Nautin, 'Genèse 1.1–2', p. 90.

[167] Photius, bibl. 109; cf. Clement of Alexandria, strom. V 89, 6; 92, 3; on this S. Lilla, *Clement of Alexandria* (Oxford, 1971), pp. 193–196.

[168] Res. mort. 11, 6; cf. adv. Marc. II 5, 3. Tertullian reckons Hermogenes among the larger group of 'materiarii heretici': Herm. 25, 2; cf. Val. 16, 3.

[169] Strom. V 89, 5–7.

[170] Cf. the thorough discussion in Augustine, de gen. c. Manich. I 5, 9 – 7, 12; de gen. ad litt. op. imperf. 3, 10 – 4, 18; conf. XII; de gen. ad litt. I 14, 28 – 15, 30.

5

The Church Doctrine of Creatio Ex Nihilo

Conflict on two fronts against gnosticism and philosophy
In the second half of the second century the theological development begins which leads directly to the formulation of the church doctrine of *creatio ex nihilo*. The intellectual resistance to the gnostic movement gains momentum and in the debate with philosophy a more strongly critical tone now prevails. The oft repeated thesis that heresy is dependent on philosophical teaching – we have already found this in the treatise *De Resurrectione*[1] – results in the polemic against gnosticism being extended to its ostensible philosophical foundations. In this situation the defence of the omnipotence and unity of God inevitably demands the proposition that matter also is created by God. This conclusion is reached at almost the same time by Tatian and Theophilus of Antioch, and soon with Irenaeus the doctrine of *creatio ex nihilo* achieves its essentially permanent form.

I. Tatian

In a position similar to Justin's, his pupil Tatian worked as a freelance teacher first in Rome and later in the East.[2] In his fundamental conception

---

[1] See p. 134 above.
[2] The 'Oratio ad Graecos' cannot be dated with certainty. M. Elze, *Tatian und seine Theologie* (1960), pp. 41ff. considers it possible that it was composed in Rome before the death of Justin (162/168), but a later origin is also not to be excluded. The arguments which R. M. Grant, 'The Date of Tatian's Oration', *Harv. Theol. Rev.* 46 (1953), pp. 99–101 advances for a date after 176 are however not compelling: cf. G. W. Clarke, 'The Date of the Oration of Tatian', *Harv. Theol. Rev.* 60 (1967), pp. 123–126. L. W. Barnard, 'The

of the nature of Christianity Tatian allies himself with Justin: he also understands Christianity as the original 'barbarian' philosophy, from which all later philosophy arose. But in contrast to his teacher, Tatian gives this idea a sharp twist against the philosophical tradition of the Greeks.[3] The contradiction and strife between the schools, as well as the dubious lifestyle of individual philosophers, shows that the Greeks had missed the truth and fallen totally into error.[4]

In his *Oratio ad Graecos* Tatian gives a sketch of his teaching on the Logos and on cosmology.[5] The Logos comes forth from God to order matter into the cosmos.[6] The matter which the Logos shapes cannot, however, have been, like God, without a beginning, as in that case it would have to be thought of as a second, godlike principle, but it is brought into being by God himself.[7] Creation thus proceeds in two stages: first God produces directly the material substratum, and then the Logos shapes this into the cosmos.[8] Tatian does not speak of a 'creation' of matter, but uses the term προβάλλεσθαι which the Valentinians used to denote the process of

Heresy of Tatian – Once Again', JEH 19 (1968), pp. 1–10, pp. 1–3 claims to place the work before 160.

[3] Cf. J. H. Waszink, 'Some Observations on the Appreciation of "the Philosophy of the Barbarians"' in Early Christian Literature', in *Mélanges offerts à Mademoiselle Christine Mohrmann* (Utrecht/Antwerp, 1963), pp. 41–56, pp. 51ff.; N. Hyldahl, *Philosophie und Christentum. Eine Interpretation der Einleitung zum Dialog Justins* (Copenhagen, 1966), pp. 235ff. has correctly recognised that Tatian took over Justin's thesis but made it more radically anti-Greek: cf. also Elze, pp. 19ff., especially p. 26.

[4] Proofs in Elze, pp. 59f.

[5] Or. 5. I refer here basically to the thorough account of Tatian's theology in Elze, pp. 63–105. All the same it seems to me that Elze greatly overestimates the systematic importance for Tatian's thought of the idea of the unity of truth (cf. pp. 34–40).

[6] On the statement in or. 5, 1, pp. 5, 19–21 Schwartz (on the text cf. Elze, pp. 72f.), that before the creation all things existed with God, in so far as he is 'the foundation (ὑπόστασις) of the universe' and 'all power over the visible and invisible things' is with him, M. Spanneut, *Le stoicisme des pères d'l'Eglise de Clément de Rome à Clément d'Alexandrie* (Paris, 1957, 2nd undated ed.), p. 352 n. 15 refers to corp. herm. 8, 5; 10, 2; cf. again F. Erdin, *Das Wort Hypostasis, seine bedeutungsgeschichtliche Entwicklung in der altchristlichen Literatur bis zum Abschluss der trinitarischen Auseinandersetzungen* (1939), p. 19; H. Dörrie, 'Hypostasis, Wort- und Bedeutungsgeschichte', NGG 1955/3, pp. 35–92, p. 75 and the Scholion of Arethas in the edition of Schwartz, pp. 44f. (on pp. 5, 16ff.)

[7] Or. 5, 3, pp. 6, 12–15: οὔτε γὰρ ἄναρχος ἡ ὕλη καθάπερ καὶ ὁ θεός, οὔτε διὰ τὸ ἄναρχον ἰσοδύναμος τῷ θεῷ, γενητὴ δὲ καὶ οὐχ ὑπὸ ἄλλου γεγονυῖα, μόνου δὲ ὑπὸ τοῦ πάντων δημιουργοῦ προβεβλημένη. Cf. or. 12, 1, pp. 12, 22–26; 4, 1f., pp. 4, 29ff.

[8] The peculiar idea that first God himself, without bringing in the Logos, created matter and that after that the Logos merely shapes it, appears at a later time in Methodius, de creatis 9 (Photius, bibl. 235).

emanation.⁹ It is, however, inconceivable that he should have looked on matter as an emanation from God.¹⁰ The meaning of his statements can only be that God caused matter to come into being without any outward precondition, that he created it – even if the corresponding formula is lacking – out of nothing.

Tatian is the first Christian theologian known to us who expressly advanced the proposition that matter was produced by God.¹¹ We are concerned here with an idea which sooner or later had to be drawn from the biblical belief in creation, as soon as Christian thought engaged in a critical debate with the philosophical doctrine of principles. At the same time it is impossible to be satisfied with the simple confirmation that with Tatian this very point was reached. We must enquire into the special reasons which led Tatian to oppose the acceptance of an eternal matter, while other Christian teachers then and after him, who were, like him, under the influence of Middle Platonism, were still able to hold fast to that idea. First Tatian's relationship as a pupil to Justin must be noted: Justin's theses that there could be nothing unoriginate except God and that no limits existed to God's creative capability, had to lead, when thought through consistently, to accepting that matter also had been created. Justin himself had not got as far as this conclusion, but it must have suggested itself to Tatian, who saw and emphasised much more sharply than his teacher the contradiction between Christian and Greek thought.¹² Further, we may well ponder whether Tatian was not under pressure to deny the pre-existence of matter by reason of the demands of actual controversies within the Church.

In Rome especially there was a multiplicity of heretical groups.¹³ Teach-

---

⁹ Or. 5, 3, pp. 6, 15 (n. 7 above); 12, 1, pp. 12, 24; Drawn by the act of human speech, the Verbum appears Or. 1, 2 pp. 1, 17; 5, 2, pp. 6, 6.

¹⁰ Thus also Elze, p. 84; on the contrary A. Adam, *Lehrbuch der Dogmengeschichte* I (1970), p. 155 says that Tatian conceived matter as 'an emanation of God, comparable to the word of a speaker'.

¹¹ Basilides had merely asserted negatively that the 'non-being' God is not limited to matter for his creation. Indeed Krämer, *Der Ursprung der Geistmetaphysik* (Amsterdam, ²1967), p. 237, says that in the system of Basilides the world-seed, created out of nothing, 'plays to a large extent the role of the material principle'; but this is very much more than the mere material substratum of the cosmos; see pp. 68ff. above.

¹² See pp.122ff., 148f. above.

¹³ Cf. A. von Harnack, *Die Mission und Ausbreitung des Christentums in den ersten drei Jahrhunderten* II ⁴(1924), p. 929 (ET II p. 308). W. Bauer, *Rechtgläubigkeit und Ketzerei im ältesten Christentum* (²1964, ed. G. Strecker), pp. 132f. (ET p. 132), may have somewhat underestimated the danger that heresy posed in Rome; cf. the exciting sketch by H. Langerbeck, 'Zur Auseinandersetzung von Theologie und Gemeindeglauben in der römischen Gemeinde in den Jahren 135–165', in *Aufsätze zur Gnosis*, ed. H. Dörrie (1967), pp. 167–179.

The Church Doctrine of Creatio Ex Nihilo   151

ers of the various persuasions were feuding among themselves.[14] Justin was in conflict with Marcionites and gnostics, the Valentinian Ptolemaeus took up a position against Marcion,[15] and we learn from Rhodon, a pupil of Tatian's, about a debate which he had with Apelles, the most important theologian of the Marcionite school.[16] We may be quite sure that Tatian also took part in this kind of academic disputation. So it is to be supposed that his thesis that matter was created was directed against the Marcionites, who counted matter as one of the ἀρχαί.[17] Admittedly we possess no direct evidence that Tatian engaged in controversy with the Marcionites, but it is likely that even in the compilation of the *Diatessaron* opposition to the gospel of Marcion played a part.[18] In any case Tatian is sure to have come into contact with Marcionite teachers in Rome, for they were extremely active there, and if he wanted to defend Christian monotheism against them, he would have to reject the notion that matter was an unoriginate principle. Tatian's assertion that matter is directly created by God and 'originates through no other'[19] could also have been directed against the Valentinian view that matter derives from Sophia.[20] Indeed Tatian's statements about the creation of the world show some agreements with the views of the Valentinians: the Logos in his function as the One who orders matter previously created by God reminds us of the divine intermediaries in the Ptolemaic system, who out of the likewise already existing psychic and hylic substance create the cosmos,[21] and the use of the term προβάλλεσθαι is scarcely to be understood without the example of Valentinian usage, even if the word has a quite different meaning in Tatian. Yet the thesis that God directly produces matter stands in sharp contrast with the Valentinian cosmogony.[22] This partial contact with the ideas and language of the

---

[14] Cf. G. Bardy, 'Les écoles Romaines au second siècle', RHE 28 (1932), pp. 502–532.
[15] See pp. 112ff. above.
[16] See pp. 154ff. below.
[17] See pp. 54ff. above.
[18] H. von Campenhausen, *Die Entstehung der christlichen Bibel* (1968), p. 206 (ET p. 179).
[19] Or. 5, 3, pp. 6, 14 (note 7 above).
[20] On the Valentinian doctrine of the origin of matter see pp. 101ff. above.
[20] Ptolemaeus and Heracleon place the Soter, from whom the process of creation proceeds (see pp. 102f. above), on an equality with the Logos and refer John 1:3 to him: Ptolemaeus, ad Flor. 3, 6; Irenaeus, haer. I 8, 5; exc. ex Theod. 45, 3; Heracleon, fr. 1 = Origen, comm. John II 14; fr. 22 = Origen, XIII 19, 118.
[22] The idea that the Logos creates 'in imitation of the Father who begot him' (or. 7, 1, pp. 7, 7f.; cf. 5, 2. pp. 6, 8) corresponds to Platonist thought. We may compare Tatian's Logos not only with the world-creating powers of the Valentinian system, but also with the demiurge of Numenius, who is the 'imitator' of the first God; fr. 16 des Places = Eusebius,

Valentinians is best explained by recognising that Tatian developed his teaching about the creation of matter in the course of controversy with gnostic positions and in doing so to a certain extent appropriated his opponents' ways of putting questions and formulating answers.

The older tradition of the statement, which spoke of creation by God 'out of nothing' seems to have played no part in Tatian's creation doctrine. We established earlier that the assertion 'God created the world out of nothing' or created 'non-being' in no way necessarily implied that matter also was something created. Thus Philo could speak of the creation of the world 'out of nothing' and at the same time suppose the pre-existence of matter. In Rome less than a generation before Tatian, the prophet Hermas had spoken in these traditional phrases of the creation of everything out of nothing, but the philosophical problems felt by educated teachers over principles were clearly beyond his ken.[23] The unexamined idea of creation out of nothing and the thesis that matter is created by God thus do not necessarily belong together. The latter is not simply to be derived as a conceptual consequence of the former; rather does the argument run the other way: only when one has achieved the insight that for the sake of the unity and omnipotence of God matter must be considered created, does one find the proposition of creation out of nothing to be the pregnant formula for this. Tatian apparently was not familiar with the strongly Jewish traditions on which Hermas was dependent. So it is not surprising that he did not yet speak of a creation out of nothing, and did not go beyond the statement that matter is 'produced' by God.

Otherwise the cosmological statements of the *Oratio ad Graecos* agree largely with the views of Justin and Athenagoras,[24] though it is doubtful whether in this writing we get to know the whole Tatian. Both Clement of Alexandria and Origen report that Tatian interpreted the words 'Let there be light' (Gen. 1:3) not as a command but as a request from the creator to the first God.[25] It would be quite possible that Tatian let the Logos make this request to God and that would tally with the statements in the writing to the Greeks,[26] but Clement and Origen found in him in any case the

---

prep. ev. XI 22, 3–5; 18 = XI 18, 24; cf. Elze, p. 80. Waszink, 'Observations', pp. 55f. suggests in another connection a direct influence of Numenius on Tatian.

[23] Hermas 1, 6; 26, 1; see p. 27 above.
[24] Cf. Elze, pp. 79–88.
[25] Clement of Alexandria, ecl. proph. 38. 1; Origen, orat. 24, 5; cf. Celsius VI 51; on that A. Orbe, 'A propósito de Gen. 1, 3 (fiat lux) en la exegesis de Taciano', *Gregorianum* 42 (1961), pp. 401–443.
[26] Thus Elze, pp. 119f.; Adam I, p. 155.

The Church Doctrine of Creatio Ex Nihilo 153

gnostic distinction between the creator and the highest God.²⁷ Perhaps Tatian wrote a commentary on the creation story,²⁸ but he might also have advanced his individual interpretation of Genesis 1:3 in the writing mentioned by Rhodon entitled *Problemata* which was devoted to the clarification of difficult and obscure Bible passages and must have contained all manner of curiosities, for Rhodon says he would have liked to write a book of 'solutions' to Tatian's 'Problems'.²⁹ Tatian's ostensible doctrine of two Gods is mentioned by Clement of Alexandria in another connection: Tatian is said to have attributed the law to 'another God', when expounding Romans 7:2f.³⁰ Irenaeus reproaches Tatian for his encratistic views, but also for having accepted the Valentinian invisible aeons and having denied the redemption of Adam.³¹ These assertions of Tatian's gnosticising views cannot simply be dismissed as misunderstandings or malicious allegations, even if it is impossible to obtain from them and from the *Oratio ad Graecos* a coherent general account of Tatian's theology.³² It indeed looks as if the reproaches levelled at Tatian's heretical doctrines had

---

²⁷ Orbe, pp. 425ff., suggests that Tatian equates the light with Christ (cf. or. 13, 1f. pp. 14, 16ff.); the sense of his interpretation of Gen. 1:3 would then be that the demiurge asks the supreme God to send the Saviour into the world.

²⁸ This is suggested by Elze, 119f.

²⁹ Eusebius, H.E. V 13, 8; see Orbe p. 402 and generally on Tatian's 'Problemata' Campenhausen, *Die Entstehung der christlichen Bibel* p. 190 (ET p. 161). A new witness to the independent exegesis of scripture by Tatian is found in the Zechariah commentary of Didymus of Alexandria, which came to light in the papyrus find at Tura: Tatian is said to have asserted, with reference to Ps. 119:91, that days in the past were longer than in his present (In Zach, I 323 = Didymus the Blind, *Sur Zacharie*, ed. L. Doutreleau I [SC 83, Paris, 1962], p. 364).

³⁰ Strom. III 82, 2. On this not very clear passage cf. Langerbeck, *Zur Aufeinandersetsung von Theologie und Gemeindeglauben*, p. 177.

³¹ Irenaeus, haer. I 28, 1; III 23, 8. Hippolytus, who in other matters seems to be dependent on Irenaeus, ascribes to Tatian the view that the world was created by one of the aeons (ref. X 18).

³² Elze, pp. 106ff. goes too far when he says that the statements of Irenaeus and Clement on Tatian's gnosticising ideas were completely beside the point. On the other hand Grant in several papers drew attention to the relationship of Tatian's thought with gnosticism: cf. 'The Heresy of Tatian', JThS n.s. 5 (1954), pp. 62–68; 'Tatian and the Bible', *Stud. Patr.* I (1957), pp. 297–306; 'Tatian and the Gnostics' in *After the New Testament* (Collected Papers, Philadelphia, 1967), pp. 208–213. Langerbeck, *Zur Aufeinandersetzung*, pp. 176ff., places Tatian very close to a Valentinianism not yet degenerate. More cautious is the judgment of Barnard, *The Heresy of Tatian*, pp. 1ff. The attempt of Adam I, pp. 154–156 to derive the doctrine of Tatian largely from pre-gnostic Aramaic ideas is questionable: to the pupil of Justin, who thinks in Middle Platonist terms, the intellectual traditions of his Syrian homeland were not very important: cf. Elze, pp. 120ff. For the influence of Tatian

as their main aim the discrediting of his ascetic rigorism.[33]

Tatian stands between the two fronts of orthodoxy and heresy, neither of which was yet firmly established,[34] but certainly his view that matter was directly created by God was ungnostic and probably developed in his controversies with gnostic theologians. It constitutes the decisive step to the final formulation of the doctrine of *creatio ex nihilo*.

Academic debates at Rome

The fragments preserved by Eusebius from Rhodon's writing against Marcion's heresy give an impression how lively the debate was, not only between Catholics and Marcionites but also between the various schools of Marcionites, about the question of the principles of being.[35] In the lack of unity between the Marcionite theologians Rhodon finds the proof of the untenability of their views. Apelles teaches one principle only, Pottus and Basilicus accept two, so remaining true to the original teaching of Marcion, others even set up three 'natures': the head of this group was Synerus.[36] Rhodon's manner of expression when he speaks of the ἀρχαί shows that he was here consciously using the academic language of philosophy. Rhodon even formulated his critique in philosophical concepts: the Marcionites, who accept a plurality of principles, have not found the 'diairesis of things'. That is Platonist terminology.[37] In the report about his disputation with Apelles, Rhodon also declares his own superiority over his opponent, who holds that you cannot prove doctrine, and everyone should stick to his own convictions; anyone who believes the Crucified and abounds in good works will attain salvation. Rhodon demands from Apelles proofs of his doctrine and in particular wants to know how he comes to accept only a single principle. But Apelles assures him that he does not know why there is only

---

on later Syrian Christianity cf. E. Peterson, 'Einige Bemerkungen zum Hamburger Papyrus-Fragment der Acta Pauli', in *Frühkirche, Judentum, Gnosis* (Collected Papers, 1959), pp. 183–208; A. F. J. Klijn, 'Das Thomasevangelium und das altsyrische Christentum', *Vig. Chr.* 15 (1961), pp. 146–159, pp. 157f.

[33] This is emphasised by H. Chadwick, art. 'Enkrateia', RAC V (1962), 352f.

[34] Thus Bauer, p. 196 (ET p. 207); H. E. W. Turner, *The Pattern of Christian Truth* (London, 1954), pp. 85–89; Barnard, *The Heresy of Tatian*.

[35] Eusebius, H.E. V 13.

[36] Eusebius, H.E. V 13, 2–4. When acceptance of two principles is attributed to Marcion, matter is not counted. Synerous and his school seem to have expressly added matter as a third principle, which is what Hippolytus, ref. X 19, 1f. asserts of Marcion: cf. Harnack, *Marcion. Das Evangelium vom fremden Gott* (²1924), pp. 160f., 322*, 333*.

[37] Eusebius, H.E. V 13, 4: μὴ εὑρίσκοντες τὴν διαίρεσιν τῶν πραγμάτων. Cf. Philo, heres. 235f.; Albinus, did. 4 (pp. 154, 15f.).

one unoriginate God, he just believes this. At that Rhodon laughs at him, because he wants to be a teacher but cannot prove what he teaches.[38] Harnack made known his sympathy for the unspeculative Christianity of Apelles,[39] but the conclusion that man becomes aware of the existence of God through faith could well be entertained by philosophers too.[40] It is decisive for us that in the second half of the second century there was philosophical discussion among the Christian teachers in Rome about the problem of principles. There can be no doubt that in these controversies the question of the nature of matter and of the 'How' of creation also played a part, even if we lack direct evidence of this.[41]

As late as the year 190 the presbyter Florinus left the orthodox Church in Rome and joined the Valentinians.[42] Eusebius reports that before the defection of Florinus Irenaeus wrote a letter to him 'On the Monarchy; or that God is not the author of evil' and later drew up another piece on his

---

[38] Eusebius, H.E. V 13, 5–7. Already Justin criticises Marcion for being unable to offer proof of his doctrine: apol. I 58, 2. Naturally the pagan opponents of Christianity also reject *pistis* and demand *apodeixis*: cf. J. C. M. van Winden, 'Le Christianisme et la Philosophie, Le commencement du dialogue entre la foi et la raison', in *Kyriakon* Festschrift for J. Quasten I (1970), pp. 205–213, pp. 206ff.

[39] *Marcion*, p. 187: Apelles 'is the only Christian theologian before Augustine with whom we can come to terms today without painstaking accommodation'.

[40] W. Theiler, *Die Vorbereitung des Neuplatonismus* (^{2}1964), p. 143 goes back to Poseidonius for the origin of the statement made by Apelles, that acceptance of a single divine principle rests on inner emotion ('Bewegtwerden', κινεῖσθαι) and faith (Eusebius, H.E. V 13, 6f.). On the proposition of Porphyry, adv. Marc. 24, that faith forms the condition and the basis of the ascent of the soul to God, cf. E. R. Dodds, *Pagan and Christian in an Age of Anxiety* (Cambridge 1965), pp. 122f.

[41] In any case Rhodon wrote a piece on the 'Six days' work': Eusebius, H.E. V 13, 8. Galen in his work 'De usu partium' which was written in Rome between 169 and 176 expresses his view on the subject of the Bible story of creation: he accords a relative acknowledgement to the doctrine of creation found in Moses, by regarding it as superior to the views of Epicurus, but he finds lacking in Moses any mention of the principle of matter and rejects the idea that God could create everything that he willed (XI 14); cf. R. Walzer, *Galen on Jews and Christians* (Oxford 1949), pp. 11–13, 23–37. Perhaps the great physician knew a work by a Roman Christian – anti-gnostic, of course – in which the doctrine of *creatio ex nihilo* was put forward: this is suggested by Langerbeck, 'Die Verbindung aristotelischer und christlicher Elementen der Philosophie des Ammonius Saccas', in *Aufsätze zur Gnosis*, pp. 146–166, p. 160; otherwise Grant, *Miracle and Natural Law in Graeco-Roman and Early Christian Thought* (Amsterdam, 1952), p. 130.

[42] Eusebius, H.E. V 15.20. Also in the introduction to the Syrian Irenaeus fragment no. 28 (Harvey II, p. 457) Florinus is described as an adherent of the errors of Valentinus; cf. Bardy, p. 457.

account, 'On the Ogdoad'.[43] The themes of these lost writings show that there were also cosmological questions involved in the controversy with Florinus.[44] The communication 'On the Monarchy' obviously dealt with the question how the reality of evil could be reconciled with belief in one creator God, and we can accept that Irenaeus in this connection founded and defended with special consistency the doctrine of *creatio ex nihilo*, through which the problem was taken to extreme lengths.

Thus the doctrine of creation and of first principles remains the subject of bitter controversy at Rome until the end of the second century. Orthodox teachers like Rhodon no doubt pursued in these discussions the thesis of Tatian's that matter is created by God and probably ventured before long the pregnant formulation that creation had been achieved 'out of nothing'.[45]

II. Theophilus of Antioch

Only a little later than Tatian and much more thoroughly than he, Theophilus of Antioch tackles the problem of creation. In his second book addressed to Autolycus he offers a complete commentary on the primitive history in the Bible. This is the oldest continuous exposition of the opening chapters of Genesis by a church theologian which has come down to us.[46] Going beyond Tatian, Theophilus speaks in settled terminology of creation 'out of nothing': 'God has created everything out of nothing into being'.[47] In view of the clear unambiguity and definiteness with which Theophilus presents the doctrine of *creatio ex nihilo* and in view also of the almost formal stamp given by him to the declaration that God created the world out of nothing, we are inclined to think that he owed his concept of creation to an older tradition. We established above that one of the Jewish prayers edited in the Apostolic Constitutions showed tendencies to the idea of *creatio ex*

---

[43] Eusebius, H.E. V 20, 1.
[44] A. Baumstark, 'Die Lehre des römischen Presbyters Florinus', ZNW 13 (1912), pp. 306–319 refers to the report of the Arab historian Agapius of Hierapolis (10th century) who attributes gnostic views to Florinus, which in point of fact only partly coincide with Valentinian teaching, but are thoroughly characteristic of the second century.
[45] In the early third century Hippolytus puts forward the doctrine of *creatio ex nihilo* in a relatively sophisticated form: ref. X 32f.; cf. c. Noet. 10.
[46] Autol. II 9–33.
[47] Autol. I 4: τὰ πάντα ὁ θεὸς ἐποίησεν ἐξ οὐκ ὄντων εἰς τὸ εἶναι. Likewise II 4.10.13; cf. also I 8.

nihilo in the narrower sense,[48] and Basilides, who taught the creation of the world-seed 'out of nothing' probably also came from Antioch.[49] These clues certainly suggest that the idea of *creatio ex nihilo* had already been formulated at Antioch before Theophilus, but we cannot say precisely at what date or in what circles – whether Jewish, 'orthodox' Christian, or gnostic – this first happened.[50] On the other hand it is certain that Theophilus through his controversy with Hermogenes was obliged to think through the doctrine of pre-existent matter. In his pamphlet, no longer extant, against that Platonising heretic the systematic unfolding and justification of the *creatio ex nihilo* must have taken a great deal of space. It would be conceivable that Theophilus in the books to Autolycus went back to the work against Hermogenes, or at least that his observations about creation out of nothing were written with that opponent in mind.[51]

The writing against Hermogenes may well have been used by Tertullian and also by Hippolytus: on the one hand there are striking agreements between Tertullian's work *Adversus Hermogenem* and the extract which Hippolytus in his *Refutatio* devotes to the Syrian teacher; on the other hand Hippolytus offers further statements, which must come from a good source, but are not found in Tertullian. To accept that Hippolytus is directly dependent on Tertullian's work is thus not viable, and it is not far-fetched

---

[48] See pp. 21f. above.
[49] See p. 53 above.
[50] See p. 77 above.
[51] We possess no points of information which would allow a sure answer to the question which came first, the books against Autolycus or the piece against Hermogenes: cf. Harnack, *Geschichte der altchristlichen Literatur* II: Die Chronologie I (1958), pp. 319f. Grant, 'Theophilus of Antioch to Autolycus', in *After the New Testament*, pp. 129–169, p. 134 claims to see in the Genesis-exposition of Autol. II a first draft of the work against Hermogenes. Waszink on the contrary takes account of the other possibility, that the work against Hermogenes came before Ad Autol. and that Theophilus in the later piece was harking back to the older one: Tertullian, *The Treatise against Hermogenes* (Westminster, MD and London, 1956), p. 10. This second solution is decisively advocated by P. Nautin, 'Genèse 1, 1–2 de Justin à Origène', in *In Principio. Interprétations des premiers versets de la Genèse* (Paris 1973), pp. 61–94, pp. 69f. The three books to Autolycus are, as their prefaces show, independent works (cf. Grant, *Theophilus*, p. 127). In Autol. III 27 is mentioned the historical work of Chryserus Nomenclator (only known to us through Theophilus) (cf. H. Schenkl in PW Suppl. III, 1918, pp. 248f.) which went as far as the death of Marcus Aurelius, and Theophilus also gives the chronology of the Roman emperors down to that point; so the book originated after 180. The two preceding books in the list that has come down to us could be a few years older. In that case the work against Hermogenes, if it came before the three books to Autolycus, could without more ado be assigned to the seventies. This dating would still fit in with the fact that Tertullian in his dispute with Hermogenes, conducted after 200, confronted him as a living contemporary (Herm. 1, 2).

to look for the common source by which both were inspired in the lost work of Theophilus.[52] Various contacts, also, between the statements of Tertullian and characteristic ideas of Theophilus, as found in *Ad Autolycum*, point to a use of the work against Hermogenes.[53] It is, of course, impossible to reconstruct the lost writing of Theophilus out of Tertullian's book and Hippolytus's report; the comparable material does not suffice for that. Nevertheless we can pick up certain clues as to how the Antiochene bishop conducted his polemic against Hermogenes.

In his second book to Autolycus Theophilus criticises, comparatively thoroughly, the Platonist model of world-formation and opposes it with the doctrine of *creatio ex nihilo*. As Tertullian and Hippolytus also characterise the cosmology of Hermogenes as Platonist, it is to be concluded that Theophilus has already campaigned against his opponent as Platonist and in so doing has used arguments similar to those he brings into play against Platonist teaching in *Ad Autolycum*.[54] But in the lost work Theophilus may have also delivered a thorough-going biblical foundation for the doctrine of *creatio ex nihilo*. At one point this is demonstrated with some probability: Eusebius mentions that Theophilus in his work against Hermogenes quoted from the Apocalypse of John.[55] Now there is to be found in the

[52] Cf. Harnack, *Die Überlieferung der griechischen Apologeten des zweiten Jahrhunderts in der alten Kirche und im Mittelalter* (1882), pp. 294–297.

[53] Tertullian seems to have used the Ad Autol. in his Apologeticum: C. Becker, *Tertullians Apologeticum. Werden und Leistung* (1954), pp. 136, 160f., 354f.; cf. Grant, *Vig. Chr.* 9 (1955), p. 255; conversely Harnack, 'Tertullians Bibliothek christlicher Schriften', SAB 1914, pp. 303–334, p. 320, who thought that it was not surely proven that Tertullian knew the Ad Autol. G. Quispel, *De bronnen van Tertullianus' Adversus Marcionem* (Diss. Utrecht 1943), pp. 34–55 tries to show that Tertullian in Adv. Marc. II used what Theophilus had written against Marcion. Frankly this does not seem to me convincingly demonstrated. In any case, taking into account the totality of the evidence, it is most probable that in his Adv. Herm. Tertullian used Theophilus's work against Hermogenes; cf. Waszink in Tertullian, *The Treatise against Hermogenes*, pp. 9–12. Tertullian, Herm, 18, 1 utters the thought that God, if he needed material for the creation, had his wisdom available, and quotes in this connection Proverbs 8:27ff. M. Simonetti, 'Sull' interpretazione patristica di Proverbi 8, 22', in *Studi sull' Arianesimo* (Rome, 1965), pp. 9–87, p. 15 n. 18 draws attention to the fact that the same thought, equally associated with the quotation of Prov. 8:27, is also found in Marcellus of Ancyra: fr. 59 Klostermann = Eusebius, c. Marc. II 2; de eccl. theol. II 15. Simonetti prefers to see the common source of Tertullian and Marcellus in the work of Theophilus against Hermogenes. Waszink also had previously suggested influence of Theophilus on Tertullian, Herm. 18, 1: Tertullian, *The Treatise*, pp. 11f.

[54] II 4. That this criticism could also be aimed at Hermogenes is suggested by Grant, *Theophilus*, p. 141; cf. before him E. Heintzel, *Hermogenes, der Hauptvertreter des philosophischen Dualismus in der alten Kirche* (Diss. Erlangen, 1902), p. 57.

[55] Eusebius, H.E. IV 24.

books to Autolycus only one somewhat dubious echo of the Apocalypse.[56] On the other hand Tertullian's tractate contains five quotations from the Apocalypse, which appear in no other work of Tertullian's.[57] Three of these passages stand in connection with the same argument: a chain of biblical passages which deal with the end of the world are intended indirectly to prove creation out of nothing, for if in the plan of God everything is to be dissolved into nothing then it must have originated from nothing too.[58] The supposition is not remote that Tertullian took over the whole argument with the biblical references from the work of Theophilus.[59] In all probability the statements of Hippolytus about the Christology of Hermogenes also go back to Theophilus.[60] So one gets the impression that the lost writing must have offered a total refutation of the views of Hermogenes and probably was a large book. Unfortunately we can say nothing about its outer or inner construction.

Another lost book of Theophilus, his work against Marcion[61] was very probably used by Irenaeus.[62] There can be little doubt that in it Theophilus also treated the doctrine of *creatio ex nihilo*. But this would mean that not only Tertullian but also Irenaeus, the first Catholic theologian in the West to speak in the pregnant sense of a creation out of nothing, knew the train of thought of Theophilus about *creatio ex nihilo*. Obviously the anti-heretical writings of Theophilus played a decisive role in the breakthrough of the doctrine of *creatio ex nihilo* in Catholic theology which occurred as the second century drew to a close.[63]

Theophilus opens the discussion about creation, which fills a large part of his second book to Autolycus, with a short review of the different philosophical conceptions of the relation of God to the world, which, to be frank, is somewhat confused.[64] He deals with the Stoa, Epicurus and Plato,

---

[56] II 28 (Rev. 12:9); cf. Grant, *Theophilus*, p. 134; G. Kretschmar, *Studien zur frühchristlichen Trinitätstheologie* (1956), p. 48.
[57] Herm. 7, 2 (Rev. 1:17); 11, 3 (20:3); 34, 1 (20:11); 34, 2 (6:13; 21:1). Herm. 22, 3 does not allude to Rev. 22:18f., but we are concerned here with a traditional formula: cf. W. C. van Unnik, 'De la règle Μήτε προσθεῖναι μήτε ἀφελεῖν dans l'histoire du canon', *Vig. Chr.* 3 (1949), pp. 1–36.
[58] Herm. 34, 1f. (Rev. 6:13; 20:11; 21:1); the passages Isa. 34:4 and 42:15 are also quoted by Tertullian only here; cf. Waszink in his translation of Adv. Herm., p. 156 nn. 292, 302.
[59] Similarly before him Harnack, *Die Überlieferung der griechischen Apologeten*, p. 297.
[60] Ref. VIII 17, 3f.
[61] Eusebius, H.E. IV 24.
[62] See n. 90 below.
[63] Thus also Nautin, 'Genèse 1.1–2', p. 78.

mainly in connection with the well-known doxography of Aetius, but also using other sources.[65] The refutation that follows of the world-formation doctrine is directed exclusively at Plato, and here perhaps there is a link with the controversy with Hermogenes.[66]

Theophilus opposes the acceptance of an unoriginate matter basically on the same lines as Tatian, but his argumentation is carried further and displays new aspects. Three main arguments can be distinguished: 1. If in the Platonist conception not only God but also matter is unoriginate, then God can no longer be thought of as in the fullest sense creator of everything and the divine 'monarchy' is not preserved.[67] 2. God is unoriginate and therefore by his nature immutable; if matter were also unoriginate, it would also be immutable and in that godlike. We have already found this argument in Tatian.[68] 3. It would be nothing great if God had made the cosmos out of pre-existent matter.[69] There would be no difference between him and a human craftsman who out of a given material fashions what he wants.[70]

---

[64] II 4.
[65] Cf. Grant, 'Irenaeus and Hellenistic Culture', in *After the New Testament*, pp. 158–169, pp. 159f.; also A. Elter, *De Gnomologiorum Graecorum historia atque origene commentatio* III (1893), pp. 131–138.
[66] II 4; see n. 54 above.
[67] On the concept of the μοναρχία of God cf. Philo, decal. 51; spec. leg. I 12; II 256; virt. 220; Justin, dial. 1.3; Tatian, or. 14, 1. p. 15, 9; 29, 2, p. 30, 11. Eusebius mentions a treatise of Justin's on the Monarchy of God: H.E. IV 18, 4.
[68] Or. 5, 3; p. 6, 12f.
[69] Ἐξ ὑποκειμένης ὕλης. The rendering 'out of an underlying material' would also be possible. This seems to have been the usage of Hermogenes; cf. Tertullian, Herm. 38, 1: subiacentem facis deo materiam; on that Waszink in the introduction to his translation of Tertullian's treatise, p. 10.
[70] The Christian polemic against the idea that God works like a craftsman on material that he finds to hand (for further evidence see p. 74 n. 59 above), shows a certain relationship with the Epicurean and Stoic criticism of the demiurge-myth of the Timaeus, taken literally: cf. on the one hand the Epicurean Velleius in Cicero, nat. deorum I 18–20 and Aetius I 7, 7 (H. Diels, *Doxographi Graeci*, 1879, p. 300), on the other hand SVF II 307.323a; on this J. Pépin, 'Théologie cosmique et théologie chrétienne' (Ambroise exam. I 1, 1–4) (Paris, 1964), pp. 48–50; on the epicurean critique of Plato see also M. Baltes, *Die Weltentstehung des platonische Timaios nach den antiken Interpreten* I (Leiden, 1976), pp. 25–28, 30–32. But while the Epicureans reject the idea of a creating God in general and the Stoics uphold the immanence of the creative principle in matter, the Christians of course reject the thought that God is limited in his creating by any kind of external conditions. In the Platonism of imperial times the comparison of God with a craftsman or artist first plays a great role. But the attempt is made to overcome this model systematised in the doctrine of three principles, and that leads to the conclusion which sets the highest divine principle over the demiurge; cf. Dörrie, 'Die Frage nach dem Transcendenten im Mittelplatonismus', in *Entretiens sur l'Antiquité classique* V; *Les sources de Plotin* (Vandoeuvres–Geneva, 1960), pp. 191–223, pp. 206ff.

The Church Doctrine of Creatio Ex Nihilo

God's power is shown precisely in that he creates out of nothing what he wills, just as he alone confers life and movement. Theophilus thus puts *creatio ex nihilo* in parallel with the conferring of life. A man can of course put together an image, but he cannot give reason, breath and sensual awareness. God on the other hand creates beings who possess all these faculties. It also reflects his superior power that he creates and did create being out of nothing and that he creates what and how he wills.[71]

Theophilus indeed brings forward all the essential arguments with which the Christian theologians of the succeeding centuries would contest the doctrine of the eternity of matter.[72] In two aspects Theophilus goes further than Tatian: on the one hand with the significant statement that God creates 'out of nothing', on the other hand with the thesis that the sovereign divine will is the sole ground of creation.[73] Justin had based the possibility of incarnation and of the resurrection on the almighty will of God, but he had not yet asked the question how the unlimited omnipotence of God was to be reconciled with acceptance of an unoriginate matter as the stuff of creation. Only with Theophilus is the decisive distinction fully grasped and declared between the biblical God creating an omnipotent freedom and the platonic demiurge who is restricted in his creative activity by the precondition of matter and its possibilities.[74] Now with the thesis of *creatio ex nihilo* and the corresponding positive statement that the free decision of God's will is the sole ground of creation, the biblical idea of free creation is properly formulated and validated within the ambit of philosophical thought. With this sharper appreciation of its peculiarity, the biblical concept of God now to an increasing extent was bound to become a philosophical problem. But that is a question far beyond Theophilus, which in its full implications did not become important until Origen.

The other statements that Theophilus made about creation out of nothing add nothing essentially new to what is said in *Ad Autolycum* II, 4. In II, 10 Theophilus introduces the exposition of the biblical creation story

---

[71] II 4: ὥσπερ οὖν ἐν τούτοις πᾶσιν δυνατώτερός ἐστιν ὁ θεὸς τοῦ ἀνθρώπου, οὕτως καὶ τὸ ἐξ οὐκ ὄντων ποιεῖν καὶ πεποιηκέναι τὰ ὄντα καὶ ὅσα βούλεται καὶ ὡς βούλεται.

[72] Cf. Pépin, pp. 52ff.

[73] Tatian merely explains of the Logos that he 'springs forth' from God through an act of God's will (θελήματι) (or. 5, 1, p. 5, 21f.). Further it says in his work that the cosmos has received a share of the material spirit through the will (θελήματι) of the creator (or. 12, 3 p. 13, 10f.). Elze, p. 73, emphasises the agreement with the Platonist concept of will.

[74] Basilides attributes the creation of the world exclusively to the will of God (Hippolytus, ref. VII 21, 1f.), but the idea of the freedom of God is excluded; see p. 81 above.

by saying that according to the united witness of the prophets[75] God created everything out of nothing. Nothing existed which was co-eternal with God; he was himself space,[76] was self-sufficient and was before all times. God willed to create man, in order to become known by him, and so he first prepared the cosmos for him.[77] In II, 13 Theophilus declares again that the power of God comes to expression in that he creates out of nothing and how he wills. God can do what is impossible to men. Thus for Theophilus the 'monarchy' of God, his unlimited almightiness, and the freedom and contingence of his creation are the decisive ideas. But a differentiated philosophical and theological reflection on these ideas is still lacking.

Theophilus comments on Genesis 1:2 that Scripture here teaches 'a matter in a way originate, made by God, out of which God created and shaped the cosmos'.[78] According to Theophilus this verse describes the following situation: the earth is covered by the waters which are equated with the 'deep'. As the sky lies like a lid over the water and the earth, darkness reigns. But between the water and the sky the Spirit hovers, which Theophilus in the Stoic manner understands as the life-force of creation. Before the creation of light the Spirit has the task of keeping the darkness away from heaven.[79] Finally it says that heaven surrounded matter, which 'resembled a lump of earth', like a vault.[80] As Theophilus has said shortly before that the sky covers water and earth like a lid, it is to be assumed that for him matter consisted of these two elements.[81] Thus Theophilus showed himself to be dependent, like his opponent Hermogenes, on the Platonising tradition of exposition, which finds in Genesis 1:2 a description of the world matter before it was shaped.[82] For Theophilus, however, it is clear from Genesis 1:1 that matter is created by God out of nothing.[83]

---

[75] Cf. II 9.
[76] This idea also appears in Philo, leg. all. I 44; somn. I 63; Tertullian, Prax. 5, 2; cf. Pépin, pp. 108f.
[77] Cf. also I 4.
[78] II 10: ταῦτα ἐν πρώτοις διδάσκει ἡ γραφή, τρόπῳ τινὶ ὕλην γενητήν, ὑπὸ θεοῦ γεγονυῖαν, ἀφ' ἧς πεποίηκεν καὶ δεδημιούργηκεν ὁ θεὸς τὸν κόσμον.
[79] II 13.
[80] II 13; cf. Isa. 40:22.
[81] Perhaps the spirit must be reckoned as a third element; cf. Nautin, 'Genèse 1.1–2', pp. 73f.; id. 'Ciel, pneuma et lumière chez Théophile d'Antioche (Notes critiques sur Ad Autol 2.13)', *Vig. Chr.* 27 (1973), pp. 165–171.
[82] Cf. Waszink, 'Observations on Tertullian's Treatise against Hermogenes', *Vig. Chr.* 9 (1955), pp. 129–147, p. 138 and pp. 141ff. above. If Theophilus considered the mass made up of the earth and the waters as matter, he is of course far from the philosophical concept of matter.
[83] II 10, 13.

The Church Doctrine of Creatio Ex Nihilo 163

The turn of phrase 'to create out of nothing'[84] Theophilus no doubt took over from the traditional theological language,[85] but it now has a new, a pregnant sense. The sentence about creation out of nothing is formulated as an antithesis to the world-formation idea of the Greek philosophers and calls in question the axiom 'Ex nihilo nihil fit'.[86] Theophilus did not of course fully realise that a radical break with the theological tradition the doctrine of *creatio ex nihilo* constituted. He can even himself still talk of creation out of nothing in the older undifferentiated sense: as a proof of the possibility of the resurrection he points out that God created man out of nothing, in that he formed him from a tiny drop of seed which did not exist before.[87] Theophilus takes no account of the question whether in that case one can talk of a *creatio ex nihilo* in the real sense at all. He simply wants to exalt the miraculous factor in the process of begetting and developing human beings, while in his statements about the creation of the world out of nothing the decisive factor is the idea of absolute unconditionality.

Within the scope of this research we need not go further into the cosmology of Theophilus. Here it would first be a matter of pointing out the strong dependence of the Antiochene bishop on Jewish traditions. This is true as much of his exegesis of Genesis[88] as it is of his mainly cosmologically orientated understanding of the figure of Wisdom: she stands beside the Logos as the second of the two powers by which God created the world.[89] But for the controversy with the Greek model of world-formation these ideas lead to no new aspects.[90]

---

[84] Theophilus consistently uses the formula ἐξ οὐκ ὄντων. Only at I 8 does it say of man that God brought him into being ἐξ οὐκ ὄντος.

[85] Cf. E. W. Möller, *Geschichte der Kosmologie in der griechischen Kirche bis auf Origenes* (1860), p. 158. The suggestion made by Grant, *Theophilus*, p. 141, that Theophilus could have taken over the expression from Hermas (26, 1) is unprovable.

[86] Cf. Walzer, pp. 26f.

[87] I 8; cf. Grant, *Theophilus*, p. 131. The reference to the development of man out of the drop of seed as a proof of the possibility of resurrection is also found in Justin, apol. I 19, 1f. and Athenagoras, resurr. 17, 2–4; cf. Grant, *Miracles and Natural Law*, pp. 238f.

[88] Cf. the proofs in Grant, *Theophilus*, pp. 133–142; J. Daniélou, *Théologie du Judéo-Christianisme* (Paris 1958), pp. 124–127 (ET pp. 110–115).

[89] On this cf. Kretschmar, *Studien zur frühchristlichen Trinitätstheologie*, pp. 27–61.

[90] In the sections of Irenaeus for which F. Loofs, *Theophilus von Antiochien adversus Marcionem und die anderen theologischen Quellen bei Irenaeus* (1930) made the influence of Theophilus seem probable, the idea of *creatio ex nihilo* plays no major role; only haer. IV 38, 3 is to be cited in this connection: the power and goodness of God are shown in that 'he of his own free choice founds and creates what does not yet exist (τὰ μηδέπω ὄντα)', cf. Loofs, pp. 52f. Quispel, *De bronnen*, pp. 47f. prefers to trace back Tertullian, adv. Marc. II 5, 3 (Opera creatoris utrumque testantur, et bonitatem eius, qua bona, sicut ostendimus, et potentiam, qua tanta, et quidem ex nihilo) to the same provenance as the Irenaeus passage,

III. Irenaeus

Irenaeus compiled his epoch-making theological compendium in the course of controversy with gnosticism. It is the great achievement of the Bishop of Lyons that he not only uttered terse criticisms of particular gnostic theorems or general condemnations, but that he opposed to gnosticism a comprehensive biblical theology.[91] Where the gnostics distinguished a plurality of divine beings, relying on quite arbitrary interpretations of the Holy Scriptures and appealing to all sorts of secret traditions, which could not be checked for the truth of their content, Irenaeus points out that the Old and New Testament Scriptures, which agree among themselves and also with the generally similar church tradition, bear witness unanimously to the action in history of the One true God, which runs from the creation to the incarnation of Christ and then on to the eschaton.[92] In this vast theological framework Irenaeus dealt with the question of the creation in what is in many respects a definitive manner with regard to the controversies of the second century.

Irenaeus is a biblical theologian and a churchman. He lacks an independent philosophical interest, and a speculative question which might go beyond the unambiguous statements of Scripture, seemed to him to lead dangerously near to the heresy he was contesting.[93] Concern about the question of the creation of the world arises for Irenaeus out of the necessity of controversy with the gnostic cosmology. Because of the emphasis in his way of thinking on salvation history, his own theological interest is directed almost exclusively to the creation of mankind, which he sees as the

---

but that is not necessarily convincing. The daring statement haer. II 30, 9, that the will of God is the stuff of all things, which Loofs, p. 15, also claims for Theophilus, might well come from Irenaeus himself: see pp. 171ff. below.

[91] On the importance of Irenaeus for the formation of the New Testament canon and on the theological progress reached by him at this point see Campenhausen, *Die Entstehung der christlichen Bibel*, pp. 213–244 (ET pp. 210–240).

[92] On the anti-gnostic character of Irenaeus's theology of salvation history cf. R. A. Markus, 'Pleroma and Fulfilment. The Significance of History in St Irenaeus' Opposition to Gnosticism', *Vig. Chr.* 8 (1954), pp. 193–224; A. Bengsch, *Heilsgeschichte und Heilswissen. Eine Untersuchung zur Struktur und Entfaltung des theologischen Denkens im Werk "Adversus Haereses" des Hl. Irenäus von Lyon* (1957); N. Brox, *Offenbarung, Gnosis und gnosticher Mythos bei Irenäus von Lyon* (1966), pp. 179ff. The achievement of Irenaeus as 'the creator of the Christian view of history' is fully appreciated by Campenhausen, 'Die Enstehung der Heilsgeschichte. Der Aufbau des christlichen Geschichtsbildes in der Theologie des ersten und zweiten Jahrhunderts', *Saeculum* 21 (1970), pp. 189–212, pp. 206f.

[93] Cf. haer. II 27f.

beginning of the divine work of salvation. Man and his salvation are the aim and goal of the creation.[94] The history of salvation opens with the covenant which God makes with Adam at the creation, proceeds to the covenants with Noah and at Sinai and reaches its zenith in the final and conclusive covenant which is made with mankind through the Gospel. This fourth covenant 'renews man and brings everything finally together'.[95]

But Irenaeus is a clear thinker and by no means uneducated.[96] His concept of God is, like that of the Apologists, strongly marked with popular philosophical ideas.[97] God is unoriginate, eternal, needs nothing, is self-sufficient, and confers existence on everything that is.[98] Irenaeus celebrates the perfection of God, who is all light, all Spirit, all substance, and the source of all good.[99] God embraces everything and grants existence to all things.[100] As the Unoriginate he stands over against every originate being.[101] In his second book against the heresies Irenaeus tries to prove from these premises that the gnostic concept of God is inadequate, self-contradictory and mythological. Irenaeus reaches this conclusion from the observation that a series of Valentinian Aeons are hypostasised intellectual and emotional functions. He therefore raises against the Valentinians the reproach that in their doctrine of the Aeons they attribute human affects to God.[102] But in reality God is simple and is everything that man can say of him, wholly, so that one cannot divide his being into a series of affects, which proceed one

---

[94] Cf. G. N. Bonwetsch, *Die Theologie des Irenäus* (1925), pp. 71–75; G. Wingren, *Man and the Incarnation. A Study in the Biblical Theology of Irenaeus* (Edinburgh/London, 1959), pp. 3–38. The creation of the world is, from this point of view, the precondition for God's saving work among men: cf. haer. III 5, 3; 24, 2; IV 5, 1; V 29, 1; epid. 11.

[95] Haer. III 11, 8; cf. I 10, 3; on the text of III 11, 8, cf. *Irénée de Lyon. Contre les hérésies* III, ed. A. Rousseau and L. Doutreleau I (SC 210, Paris, 1974), p. 286.

[96] Cf. Grant, 'Irenaeus and Hellenistic Culture', in *After the New Testament*, pp. 158–169; W. R. Schoedel, 'Philosophy and Rhetoric in the adversus Haereses of Irenaeus', *Vig. Chr.* 13 (1959), pp. 22–32; A. Benoît, *St Irénée. Introduction à l'étude de sa théologie* (Paris, 1960), pp. 55ff.

[97] Cf. J. Kunze, *Die Gotteslehre des Irenäus* (Diss. Leipzig, 1891), pp. 44–47; Bonwetsch, pp. 50ff.; Grant, *The Early Christian Doctrine of God* (Charlottesville, 1966), p. 26.

[98] Haer. III 8, 3.

[99] Haer. IV 11, 2; similarly I 12, 2; II 13, 3.8; 28, 4. Grant, 'Early Christianity and Pre-Socratic Philosophy', in *After the New Testament*, pp. 85–112, pp. 104f. derives this thought of Irenaeus from an oft-quoted saying of Xenophon: 'He (i.e. God) wholly sees, wholly thinks, and wholly hears' (B 24 Diels-Kranz).

[100] Haer. II 1, 2; IV 20, 6; epid. 4.

[101] Haer. II 25, 3; V 5, 2.

[102] Haer. II 13, 3.8.10; 28, 5; I 12, 1f.

from another. The proof can also be put this way: if you speak of the Nous of God as an emanation from him, then you make God a composite being.[103] The same is true of the Logos: one must in no circumstances imagine that the Logos proceeds from God, who is all Spirit and all Word, in the way that a man speaks. Therefore Irenaeus declines all pictorial representations of the emergence of the Logos from God and contents himself with the statement that this is an unimaginable process.[104] In yet another way Irenaeus sees the 'apathy' of God endangered by the gnostic doctrine of emanation: if the Aeons possess the being of the Father who sends them out, then either all Aeons must be like the highest God free of affects, but then the fall of Sophia would be impossible, or the Aeons taken together possess inclusively the affects and passions of the Father, which would be absurd.[105] To be sure, this critique is rationalistic and largely misses the nature and sense of the gnostic imagery, which it takes literally.[106] But the reflections of Irenaeus must be taken seriously as the attempt at a philosophical debate with the gnostic concept of God.[107] They make it quite clear that for Irenaeus there was no antithesis between revelation and reason.[108]

In his discussion of the problems of creation Irenaeus contests not only the gnostic speculations, but he also has in mind the philosophical, and especially the Platonist cosmology, as he starts from the supposition that the gnostics are dependent on philosophy.[109] Through this intellectual connection constructed by Irenaeus his polemic against the gnostic ideas of creation broadens out into a fundamental critique of the philosophical model of world-formation, which is close to that of Theophilus of Antioch, but takes the discussion further and is more profound.

God created the world through the free decision of his will.[110] The point of such statements is directed as much against the Valentinian doctrine that

---

[103] Haer. II 13, 5; 28, 5.

[104] Haer. II 28, 6; cf. II 17, 2–8.

[105] Haer. II 17, 1ff.

[106] On the polemical method of Irenaeus cf. D. B. Reynders, 'La polémique de Saint Irénée: Méthode et principes', *Rech. de Théol. anc. et médiév.* 7 (1935), pp. 5–27.

[107] Cf. on this now E. P. Meijering, 'Some Observations on Irenaeus' Polemics against the Gnostics', in *God Being History* (Collected Papers, Amsterdam, 1975), pp. 31–38.

[108] Cf. the illuminating discussions of Brox, pp. 201–208, on 'Ratio und Regula' in Irenaeus.

[109] Haer. II 14.

[110] Haer. II 1, 1: Bene igitur habet a primo et maximo capitulo inchoare nos, a demiurgo deo, qui fecit coelum et terram et omnia quae in eis sunt, quem ii blasphemantes extremitatis fructum dicunt, et ostendere, quod neque super eum neque post eum est aliquid, neque ab

The Church Doctrine of Creatio Ex Nihilo   167

the demiurge, in dependence on the Saviour and Sophia created the cosmos,[111] as against the common gnostic view that the creation is the work of angels.[112] God creates through his word,[113] and alongside this comes the idea, taken over from Theophilus, that of God creating through his 'hands' – word and wisdom, the latter being equated by Irenaeus with the Spirit.[114] Against the Valentinian view that the process of world-creation was first set in motion by the fall of Sophia, Irenaeus declares emphatically that the world came into being in accordance with the original plan of God.[115]

Irenaeus's concept of will is in its essence unphilosophical.[116] To be sure, it is a philosophical commonplace that for God his will and the realisation of what is willed go together, that his creation is effortless,[117] but in the sphere of the natural order God can only will the best possible, and his will finds its limit in matter.[118] Against this Irenaeus means, when he speaks of

aliquo motus sed sua sententia et libere fecit omnia, cum sit solus deus et solus dominus et solus conditor et solus pater et solus continens omnia et omnibus ut sint ipse praestans; III 8, 3: Ipse omnia fecit libere et quemadmodum voluit; IV 20, 1; 38, 3; cf. II 2, 1.4; 5, 4; 10, 4; 11, 1; 30, 9; V 18, 2. In a concise form Kunze, pp. 15–20, and Bonwetsch, pp. 52–55, 70f. give instruction on the creation-doctrine of Irenaeus.

[111] Haer. II 1, 1 (n. 110 above); 30, 9.

[112] Haer. II 2; 11, 1; 30, 9.

[113] Haer. I 22, 1; II 2, 4f.; 11, 1; 27, 2.

[114] The relevant texts are collected in J. Mambrino, '"Les Deux Mains de Dieu" dans l'oeuvre de saint Irénée', *Nouv. Rev. Théol.* 79 (1957), pp. 355–370.

[115] Haer. II 3, 2f.; cf. epid. 67; Wingren pp. 6f., 19, reads too much out of these texts when he claims to find in them the idea of a pre-existence of the creation.

[116] Still, one can compare the view of Irenaeus that the creative will of God is the expression of his goodness (cf. haer. IV 38, 3; II 25, 3; 29, 2; V 4, 2) with the statements in the Timaeus about the will of the demiurge; Irenaeus himself quotes, with relative agreement, Tim. 29E (haer. III 25, 5); on that Meijering, 'Irenaeus' Relation to Philosophy in the Light of his Concept of Free Will', in *God Being History*, pp. 19–30, pp. 22f. Very informative also is the controversy which Irenaeus maintains with a speculation about will arising from the school of Ptolemaeus (haer. I 12, 1f.): this system, about which we have no other information, assumed two feminine partners of the highest God, Ennoia and Thelema, who can also be described as 'states of mind' (διαθέσεις) of God; from their union originates the pair of aeons Monogenes and Aletheia (haer. I 12, 1; cf. Hippolytus, ref. VI 38, 5–7; Epiphanius, panar. XXXIII 1.2–7; Athanasius, or. c. Arian. III 60). This amounts, as Irenaeus himself remarks, to psychological fragmentation of the divine act of will in connection with the ancient doctrine of will; the reference to Aristotle, eth. Nic. III 5 (1113a 11f.) ought to be sufficient. Irenaeus confronts this separation of will and thought with his own thesis, that both come together in God, since he is all will, spirit, yes, hearing and the source of all good things (haer. I 12, 2; cf. n. 99 above).

[117] Cf. A. J. Festugière, *La révélation d'Hermès Trismégiste III; Les doctrines d l'âme* (Paris, 1953), p. 159 n. 2

[118] The reference here is only to Timaeus 30A: 'God willed that everything should be good and, as far as possible, that nothing should be bad'. Especially instructive again are the already

the will of God as the sole ground of creation, the absolute freedom and omnipotence of the biblical God. He presents that conception of the sovereign power of God in creation which Galen rejected in his controversy with the cosmogony of Moses.[119]

Irenaeus now sets the free, unconditional creative ability of God against the gnostic as well as the Platonist doctrine of the origin of the world. In a passage in the fourth book of the 'Refutation and Repudiation', which introduces the treatment of the Old Testament prophecies, we find his decisive thoughts on the creation of the world brought together; God has 'through himself' created the cosmos and mankind. Neither angels nor other subordinate powers have acted as demiurges, but God created everything through his 'hands', Word and Wisdom, that is, through the Son and the Spirit.[120] God's creation is absolutely free and unconditional. He took from himself the stuff, the pattern and the form for the things he created.[121] It has been suspected that Irenaeus here takes up the cause of the Middle Platonist theory of the Ideas as the thoughts of God against the Valentinian view that the Aeons are the original patterns of things, independent of and superior to the demiurge.[122] But this is not very likely. For Irenaeus asserts that God also took matter from himself, and he certainly did not mean that matter pre-existed in God before the creation. Irenaeus wants to say no more than that God is creator in the absolute sense: if there are patterns for things, they were produced by him just as matter was. Once this is established the doctrine of Ideas seems to have no importance

---

mentioned discussions of Galen, de usu part. XI, 14 (see n. 41 above), who, contrary to 'Moses's opinion', that for God everything he wills is possible, insists that there are things impossible by nature and that God chooses what is best at any time from what is capable of realisation; cf. Walzer, pp. 23–37; Grant, *Miracle and Natural Law*, pp. 127–134; W. Pannenberg, 'Die Aufnahme des philosophischen Gottesbegriff als dogmatisches Problem der frühchristlichen Theologie', in *Grundfrage systematischer Theologie* (Collected Essays, 1967), pp. 296–346, p. 317 n. 79. Also the hermetic writings, in which the will plays a certain role as a hypostatised characteristic of God, do not go beyond the scope of the traditional Greek concept of will: cf. A. Dihle, art. 'Ethik', RAC VI (1966), 753.

[119] C. M. Edsman, 'Schöpferwille und Geburt Jac. 1, 18. Eine Studie zur altchristlichen Kosmologie', ZNW 38 (1939), pp. 11–44, pp. 28ff. rightly declares that the foundations of the Christian doctrine of creation through the will of God are Old Testament–Jewish.

[120] Haer. IV 20, 1.

[121] Ipse a semetipso substantiam creaturarum et exemplum factorum et figuram in mundo ornamentorum accipiens.

[122] Thus Meijering, *Irenaeus' Relation to Philosophy*, p. 20. Wolfson, *The Philosophy of the Church Fathers* I (Cambridge, MA, 1964), pp. 262f. suggests that Irenaeus, in agreement with Philo, saw the Logos as the bearer of the Ideas. Kunze, p. 16, already contests such an interpretation.

The Church Doctrine of Creatio Ex Nihilo   169

for Irenaeus. In a slight modification of these last thoughts, Irenaeus can also explain that the will of God is the substance or *ousia* – and here that must mean the stuff – of all things.[123] God in his creative activity is bound by no ontological conditions; the sole ground for the origin of all being is his sovereign will.

The idea that God in his creative work followed an ideal paradigm is rejected in connection with the controversy with the Platonising Valentinian doctrine that the cosmos was created as a copy of the pleroma.[124] Theophilus of Antioch had declared that one must not imagine the divine creator like a human craftsman who was only capable of working the given material. Irenaeus now turns the craft argument against the Valentinian doctrine of the world as an image: God needed no blueprint for creation.[125] And, as pointedly as in *Adversus Haereses* IV, 20, 1 he can assert that God took from

[123] Haer. II 30, 9: Ipse a semetipso fecit libere et ex sua potestate et disposuit et perfecit omnia et est substantia omnium voluntas eius. Harvey I, p. 368 n. 1, suggests that *substantia* represents an οὐσία in the Greek original, which occurred through an erroneous copying of αἰτία. But the parallel statements haer. II 10, 2 (n. 130 below) and IV 20, 1 (n. 121 above) show that *ousia / substantia* was original. Through them it is also excluded that *substantia* stands for ὑπόστασις in the original text, which would be possible according to the usage of the translation. Here *substantia* means 'matter' not 'substance': see pp. 170–172 below. The saying, directed against the gnostics, in haer. II 30, 9 is wrongly interpreted by E. Benz, *Marius Victorinus und die Entwicklung der abendländischen Willensmetaphysik* (1932), pp. 327–329 in terms of the Neo-Platonist-Augustinian concept of will. The fragment 5 (Harvey, II, p. 477) brought in by Benz, p. 328 and in which θέλησις and ἐνέργεια of God are distinguished, is certainly not genuine, as Irenaeus nowhere else makes differentiations like this. The passage, which purports to be from a letter to Deacon Demetrius of Vienne, is produced by Maximus Confessor in a small florilegium of texts concerned with the will of God: PG 91, 276BC. The easiest assumption is that the text arose from the needs of the monothelite controversy or at least was attributed to Irenaeus – Maximus gives other questionable quotations from the Fathers; cf. O. Bardenhewer, *Geschichte der altchristlichen Literatur* I (1913), p. 418; M. Pohlenz, *Die Stoa* II (1972), p. 201.

[124] Haer. II 7, 16. In II 8 Irenaeus rejects the related idea that the earthly cosmos is a shadow of the 'upper' world; on this Meijering, 'Some Observations', pp. 32f.

[125] Haer. II 7, 5: Adhuc etiam, si secundum similitudinem haec illorum facta sunt, illa rursus ad quorum similitudinem erunt facta? Si enim mundi fabricator non a semetipso fecit haec, sed quemadmodum nullius momenti artifex et quasi primum discens puer de alienis archetypis transtulit, Bythus ipsorum unde habuit speciem eius quam primum emisit dispositionis? Consequens est igitur, illum ab altero quodam, qui super eum est, exemplum accepisse, et illum rursus ab altero. Et nihilominus in immensum excidet de imaginibus sermo: quemadmodum et de diis, si non fixerimus sensum in unum artificem et in unum deum, qui a semetipso fecit ea quae facta sunt. Aut de hominibus quidem aliquis permittit a semetipsis utile aliquid de vitam adinvenisse: ei autem deo, qui mundum consummavit, non permittit a semetipso fecisse speciem eorum quae facta sunt et adinventionem ornatae dispositionis? Cf. Theophilus, Autol. II 4 (see pp. 159–161 above); on the argumentation of Irenaeus, Meijering, 'Some Observations', p. 33.

170   *Creatio Ex Nihilo*

himself the *exemplum* and the *figuratio* of things.[126] As we have seen, this anti-Valentinian assertion is unlikely to proclaim the Middle Platonist doctrine that the Ideas are identical with the thoughts of God. Against such an interpretation the fact tells, that Irenaeus derives the Valentinian theory of image expressly from Plato.[127] Obviously he understands the Platonist Ideas as a principle, independent of God; but that makes it likely that he did not know the doctrine of the Ideas as the thoughts of God. On the other hand it would be conceivable that Irenaeus, with his distinction between 'pattern' and 'form' of things, was linking up with another theorem of the Middle Platonist doctrine of Ideas; the Middle Platonists taught that the Idea was copied through the Eidos – which was imprinted on matter – and made concrete in individual things; that is, they combined the Platonic Idea with the Aristotelian ἔνυλον εἶδος.[128] The concepts used by Irenaeus, *exemplum* and *figura* or *figuratio*, seem to correspond exactly with the Idea and the Eidos of the Middle Platonists.[129] To be sure, it cannot be proved that Irenaeus was going back to the Middle Platonist theory here: he could have shaped his scheme of pattern and form directly from the Valentinian doctrine of image.

To the Valentinian speculations about the origin of matter from the affects of Sophia Irenaeus opposes the doctrine of *creatio ex nihilo*. Pointedly

---

[126] Haer. II 16, 3: Ipse a semetipso exemplum et figurationem eorum quae facta sunt accipiens; cf. II 16, 1.

[127] Haer. II 14, 3: Quod autem dicunt imagines esse haec eorum quae sunt sursum, manifestissime Democriti et Platonis sententiam edisserunt. Democritus enim primus ait multas et varias ab universitate figuras expressas descendisse in hunc mundum. Plato vero rursus materiam dicit et exemplum et deum. Quos isti sequentes figuras illius et exemplum imagines eorum quae sunt sursum vocaverunt per demutationem nominis semetipso inventores et factores huiusmodi imaginariae fictionis gloriantes. Irenaeus expresses himself vaguely here: does he mean to equate the *figurae* of Democritus with the cosmic images, and the *exemplum* of Plato with the aeons, serving as models for the lower world? As the text reads, though, we must refer the *exemplum* as well to the earthly images, which is hard to accept. Is the Latin text not quite in order or is it an inexact translation of the Greek original? On the doxographical material of Irenaeus cf. Grant, *Irenaeus and Hellenistic Culture*, pp. 160ff.

[128] Cf. Seneca, ep. 58, 18–21; Albinus, did. 4 (pp. 155, 34f.); 10 (pp. 166, 2ff.); on this K. Praechter, 'Die Philosophie des Altertums' (F. Uberweg's *Grundriß der Geschichte der Philosophie* I, [12]1926), p. 529; W. Theiler, *Die Vorbereitung des Neuplatinismus* (1962), pp. 10–12; P. Merlan in A. H. Armstrong, *The Cambridge History of Later Greek and Medieval Philosophy* (Cambridge, 1967), pp. 54f. The same scheme is also to be found in Athenagoras: suppl. 10, 2f.; 15, 4; 22, 5; 24, 2; cf. the index of E. Schwartz's edition, pp. 104f.

[129] A. Rousseau in his Greek retranslation of haer, IV 20, 1 renders *figura* by ἰδέα; but Irenaeus might equally well have written εἶδος: cf. I 5, 2; 8, 1 (ἰδέα); I 7, 2; 26, 1 (εἶδος). The expressions used in the Latin translation for archetype and image vary so much that it is difficult to draw retrospective conclusions about the original text: *exemplum – figura* (IV 20, 1); *exemplum – figuratio* (II 16, 1.3); *figura – figuratio* (IV 16, 1); *archetypa / exemplum – species* (II 7, 5).

The Church Doctrine of Creatio Ex Nihilo 171

he explains – we have already come across this idea – that God had used his will and his power as matter.[130] The meaning of this statement is, of course, simply that God created matter himself.[131] Irenaeus appeals to Luke 18:27 – 'What is impossible to men is possible to God' – and sharply declares the difference between human and divine creation: men cannot create out of nothing, but are bound to use the material given them; the superiority of God over men is shown by the fact that he also produces the very stuff of his creation. This had been in essence the argumentation of Theophilus.[132] Just as in the case of the Valentinian pattern image scheme, Irenaeus asserts likewise of their doctrine of matter that is borrowed from the philosophical tradition: Anaxagoras, Empedocles, and Plato taught, long before the Valentinians, that the creator of the world had made it out of pre-existing material.[133] Irenaeus thus refers the complicated Valentinian doctrine of a creation process in several stages, with participation of two, or even three, divine beings, back to the Platonist model of world-formation: the demiurge created the cosmos according to the pattern of the Aeons, which correspond to the Ideas, and out of the pre-existent material. In this way Irenaeus is able to combat the cosmogonic myth of the Valentinians, interpreted thus in terms of Platonism, with the same arguments which were being used in apologetic confrontation with the Middle Platonist doctrine of three principles.

Several of the last quoted passages come from those sections of Irenaeus's main work in which F. Loofs saw the influence of Theophilus of Antioch.[134] To be sure, the peculiar triad God–Word–Wisdom goes back to Theophilus, but beyond that the question remains whether the characteristic statements of Irenaeus about the freedom and unconditionality of the creation stem in

---

[130] Haer. II 10, 2: Ut putenter posse enarrare unde substantia materiae, non credentes quoniam deus ex his quae non erant quemadmodum voluit ea quae facta sunt ut essent omnia fecit, sua voluntate et virtute substantia usus, sermones vanos collegerunt, vere ostendentes suam infidelitatem; cf. II 30, 9 (n. 123 above).

[131] Cf. haer. II 10, 3: Ipsam materiam cum sit potens et dives in omnibus deus creavit.

[132] Haer, II 10, 4: Attribuere enim substantiam eorum quae facta sunt virtuti et voluntati eius qui est omnium deus et credibile et acceptabile et constans et in hoc bene dicetur quoniam 'quae impossibilia sunt apud homines, possibilia sunt apud deum'; quoniam homines quidem de nihilo non possunt aliquid facere sed de materia subiacenti, deus autem quam homines hoc primo melior, eo quod materiam fabricationis suae cum ante non esset ipse adinvenit. Cf. Theophilus, Autol. II 4.

[133] Haer. II 14, 4: Et hoc autem quod ex subiecta materia dicunt fabricatorem fecisse mundum et Anaxagoras et Empedocles et Plato primi ante hos dixerunt.

[134] It concerns the texts which Loofs (pp. 10ff.) assigns to the source IQT: haer. IV 20, 1 = No. 1; IV 7, 4 = No. 6; II 30, 9 = No. 7.

essence from Theophilus. As we have seen, in the books addressed to Autolycus, the sovereign freedom of the divine will to create is expressly declared,[135] but Theophilus neither states that God took from himself the patterns, forms and material of the things created, nor that his will formed the stuff of creation. The absence of such statements from the extant work of Theophilus does not in itself count for much – the text used by Irenaeus could well have set out Theophilus's creation doctrine more richly than the discussions in the books to Autolycus – but there are also factual reasons to suggest that Theophilus did not so express himself. The Irenaean thesis that God takes the paradigm and the forms of things from himself is unambivalently directed against the Valentinian doctrine of image. Yet we know nothing of any writing by Theophilus against the Valentinians. Whether Irenaeus had read his work against Marcion, as Loofs suggests, or the one against Hermogenes, he can have found a polemic against the image doctrine in neither, for Marcion never took account of ideal patterns for the creation, and Hermogenes too, in spite of his dependence on Middle Platonism, seems not to have found the doctrine of Ideas fruitful for his understanding of creation.[136] Even the statement of Irenaeus that God's will served as stuff for the creation, can scarcely be attributed in this form to Theophilus. From Tertullian's writing 'Against Hermogenes' we may conclude that Theophilus set out a related thesis, but formulated it otherwise: against Hermogenes he seems to have argued that God, if he needed a material for the creation, had his wisdom beside him.[137]

We must refer once more to the passage *Adversus Haereses* IV, 20, 1: in the sentence 'Ipse a semetipso substantiam creaturarum et exemplum factorum et figuram in mundo ornamentorum accipiens', Loofs claimed an attribution of *exemplum* to the Logos and *figura* to Wisdom; the link between *figura* and Wisdom in particular would correspond completely to the ordering and shaping function which Wisdom possesses in Theophilus.

---

[135] See pp. 159ff. above.
[136] With a reference to the anti-Valentinian tendency of the text (cf. especially haer. II 30, 9) F. R. M. Hitchcock, 'Loofs' Theory of Theophilus of Antioch as a source of Irenaeus' II, JThS 38 (1937), pp. 255–266, pp. 258f. also disputes its dependence on Theophilus. But in opposition to Hitchcock I hold it to be basically proven through the research of Loofs that Irenaeus used a work of Theophilus that is lost to us. Only Loofs has grossly overestimated the degree of dependence of Irenaeus on this and other sources; cf. Kretschmar, pp. 27ff.; M. Widmann, 'Irenäus und seine theologischen Väter', ZThK 54 (1957), pp. 156–173; Brox, p. 151 n. 113.
[137] See n. 53 above.

The Church Doctrine of Creatio Ex Nihilo   173

So the latter's influence at this point seems to be obvious.[138] But the interpretation Loofs gives of this is untenable: on the one hand we do not find elsewhere in Theophilus the Platonising idea of a pattern, while in Irenaeus it plays an essential role in the controversy with the Valentinians; on the other hand we have met with the juxtaposition of *exemplum* and *figura* in texts which are in no way dependent on Theophilus. There, however, we saw that the concepts *exemplum* and *figura* stand in a close relationship of correspondence which is wholly independent of the idea that God creates through Word and Wisdom. Possibly we are concerned here with a Middle Platonist scheme that has been taken over.[139] Thus we may see the pointed statements about the creation by God of the patterns and forms of things and about the will of God as 'substance' of creation, essentially as the intellectual property of Irenaeus, even if in other respects he agreed with the creation doctrine of Theophilus.

Beyond the demands of the controversy with gnosticism cosmological questions scarcely worried Irenaeus. For him, it was enough to know that God has produced matter; about the 'How' of its creation Scripture gives no information, and therefore it is not permissible to speculate about it as the Valentinians do.[140] Even so the question what God did before he created the world is unanswerable. The teaching of Scripture is enough, that the world had a beginning in time.[141] The problem how the temporal beginning

---

[138] P. 14. On the understanding of the concept *figura* Loofs refers to haer. IV 7, 4 (IQT no. 6): ministrat enim ei (sc. deo) ad omnia sua progenies et figuratio sua, hoc est filius et spiritus, verbum et sapientia. Loofs suggests that μόρφωσις corresponds as Greek equivalent, to the difficult *figuratio* but that should be understood actively as 'formative force' (p. 14 nn. 2 and 3) – a wholly unusual usage. The expression *figuratio sua* probably is not at all original; the Armenian translation has in its place *suae manus* which A. Rousseau prefers to the Latin version: *Irénée de Lyon. Contre les hérésies* IV (SC 100/I, Paris, 1965), pp. 212ff. Thus it is not possible from haer. IV 7, 4 to establish a particular connection of the concepts *figura* and *figuratio* with Wisdom.

[139] See pp. 170f. above.

[140] Haer. II 28, 7: Hoc autem idem et de substantia materiae dicentes non peccabimus, quod deus eam protulit. Didicimus enim ex scripturis principatum tenere super omnia deum. Unde autem vel quemadmodum emisit eam, neque scriptura aliqua exposuit neque nos phantasmari oportet ex opinionibus propriis infinita conicientes de deo sed agnitionem hanc concedendam esse deo. The use of the verbs 'proferre' and 'emittere' does not mean, of course, that Irenaeus thought of matter as an emanation from God (see pp. 149ff. above on Tatian).

[141] Haer. II 28, 3: Si quis interrogat, antequam mundum faceret deus, quid agebat, dicemus quoniam ista responsio subiacet deo. Quoniam autem mundus hic factus est ἀποτελεστικῶς a deo temporale initium accipiens scripturae nos docent. Quid autem ante hoc deus sit operatus nulla scriptura manifestat; cf. on this passage Meijering, 'Some Observations', pp. 34f.

of the world can be reconciled with the immutability of God, which was to find its ripest solution in the early Church in Augustine, scarcely arose for Irenaeus. It is decisive for him that creation was out of nothing[142] and solely through the will of God. Irenaeus does not go beyond this fundamental proposition.[143]

Irenaeus did not discuss the problems of creation on the philosophical level of his time; in this respect many questions remain open, but there is, on the other hand, no doubt that the simple basic ideas of his doctrine of creation, which Irenaeus put forward with such decisive and unambiguous clarity, are developed from a direct understanding of the essential points of the biblical concept of God. The thought, grasped in a lively manner, of the almightiness and freedom of God dominates his whole theological position. The God who created the world by the sovereign decision of his will and who sustains it, is also the God who in ever new historical interventions leads men towards redemption and final fellowship with himself. The majestic handling of the idea of God's free, historical activity is an essential theological achievement of Irenaeus. In connection with these matters he finds astonishingly radical formulations: 'The will of God must rule and dominate in everything, but everything else must give way to it, be subordinated to it and be a servant to it.'[144] H. Langerbeck has rightly brought to light that Irenaeus, and after him Tertullian, 'had worked into the wholly unsophisticated image of God in the Old Testament' – in a thoroughly legitimate way – 'the voluntaristic features', which were afterwards seen as typically Jewish-Christian.[145]

In the exegetical basis of his creation doctrine Irenaeus also followed ways partly different from those of his predecessors. The biblical creation story moved somewhat into the background; nowhere did Irenaeus expound it consecutively.[146] This is connected with his lack of interest in 'scientific'

[142] Haer. II 10, 2.4; IV 20, 2 (quotation from Hermas 26, 1); IV 38, 3; epid. 4.

[143] Fr. 32 (Harvey II, pp. 496f.), in which the view is contested that only the qualities of things were created, matter being on the contrary uncreated, is certainly not genuine. This idea plays no part anywhere else in Irenaeus. It is discussed, however, in later times by Methodius (autex. 7, 2–9; cf. also c. 9–11) and Basil (hexaem. II 3). Origen concludes from the generally conceded createdness of the qualities that matter also was created: comm. Gen. fr. in Eusebius, praep. ev. VII 20, 2; cf. princ. IV 4, 7 (34). The text ascribed to Irenaeus comes at the earliest from the third century.

[144] Haer. II 34, 4: Principari enim debet in omnibus et dominari voluntas dei, reliqua autem omnia huic cedere et subdita esse et in servitium dedita; similarly V 5, 2.

[145] *Die Verbindung aristotelischer und christlicher Elemente in der Philosophie des Ammonius Saccas*, p. 158.

[146] Irenaeus appeals to Gen. 1:1 in haer. II 2, 5; epid. 43 (on this passage cf. Nautin, 'Genèse 1.1–2', pp. 84–86); Gen. 1:3 is cited in haer. IV 32, 1; Gen. 2:1f. in haer. V 28, 3. A description of the work of creation with echoes of Gen. 1 is found in haer. II 30, 3.

The Church Doctrine of Creatio Ex Nihilo 175

cosmology.[147] Only the passages Genesis 1:26 and 2:7 play a decisive role in anthropology.[148] Alongside them Irenaeus readily draws passages from Psalms and prophets which speak of God's creation.[149] But especially, and this is new, he appeals for the justification of the Church's doctrine of creation in large measure to the witness of the New Testament Scriptures.[150] In a specially impressive and extraordinarily clever polemic Irenaeus interprets the Gospel of St John as an anti-gnostic tract and so wrested from the Valentinians their favourite gospel,[151] which Justin had passed over in characteristic silence: John had written his gospel against the errors of Cerinthus and the Nicolaitans and it overthrew almost all known gnostic teachings on the creation of the world. Just as much as the teaching of Marcion, that the Logos neither created the world nor 'came unto his own' so also the idea of world-creation through the angels and the Valentinian demiurge-doctrine were shown through the witness of John to be untenable and false.[152] Likewise Irenaeus now offers Hermas as a witness for *creatio ex nihilo*,[153] and also the First Epistle of Clement, which is older than the false teachers, confirms the Church's proclamation of the one almighty God, who is the creator and the Father of Jesus Christ.[154] Thus the Old and New Testament Scriptures and church tradition agree in teaching this one truth from which the heretics have departed.

---

[147] It is noteworthy that in epid. 11 there is only summary reference to the creation of the world, while the creation of man is given a thorough description.

[148] Gen. 1:26: haer. III 22, 1; IV praef. 4; 20, 1; 38, 3; V 1, 3; 15, 4; epid. 11; Gen. 2:7: haer. II 34, 4; III 21, 10; IV 20, 1; V 7, 1: 15, 3; epid. 11.

[149] Ps. 33:9 (148, 5): haer. II 2, 5; III 8, 3; Ps. 115:3: haer. III 8, 3; Ps. 33:6: haer. I 22, 1; III 8, 3; epid. 5 (cf. Theophilus of Antioch, Autol. I 7); Mal. 2:10: haer. IV 20, 2.

[150] Haer. III 1, 2 (of the evangelists): Et omnes isti unum deum factorem caeli et terrae a lege et prophetis adnuntiatum et unum Christum filium dei tradiderunt nobis; cf. III 5, 3; 6, 1; 10, 4; 11, 7; 7, 1; 12, 9. Basically valid is: Cum enim declaratum sit manifeste quoniam neminem alium deum vocaverunt vel dominum nominaverunt qui veritatis fuerunt praedicatores et apostoli libertatis nisi solum verum deum patrem et verbum eius, qui in omnibus principatum habet, manifeste erit ostensum quod factorem caeli et terrae, qui locutus est cum Moyse et legis dispositionem ei dederit, qui convocaverit patres, dominum deum confiteri eos et alterum neminem nosse (III 15, 3). Irenaeus's scriptural proof from the New Testament is discussed by Campenhausen, *Die Entstehung der christlichen Bibel*, pp. 217ff. (ET pp. 219ff.).

[151] Cf. haer. II 11, 7.

[152] Haer. III 11, 1f. Irenaeus again appeals to Jn. 1:3 in haer. I 22, 1; II 2, 5; III 8, 3; 21, 10; IV 32, 1. Another exposition of John's Prologue is found in haer. V 18, 2f.; Irenaeus contradicts the interpretation of the Valentinian Ptolemaeus (cf. haer. I 8, 5f.) in haer. I 9, 1–3.

[153] Haer. IV 20, 2 (Herm. 26, 1; see p. 27 above).

[154] Haer. III 3, 3 (see p. 30 above).

Irenaeus expressly declares the contingence of the creation. God created the world and mankind as the result of a free decision of his will;[155] he had no need of man, but he wanted to have an opposite number to whom he could show his benevolence.[156] Also the sustaining of his creatures, transitory by nature, is a work of God's grace; in his boundless goodness he protects them in their being and leads them on to perfection.[157] There is a formal parallel here with the Platonist idea that God holds in being through his will the world which is originate and therefore in itself transitory.[158] But for Irenaeus the sustaining of the creation is not a necessary consequence of the goodness of God, as it is for the Platonists, but a free gift. The ground of the creation is God's goodness;[159] this too a Platonist could have said, and Irenaeus is aware of this.[160] But he understands the creator's goodness quite concretely as his will to save. The creation of man introduces the great process of the 'Education of the Human Race' to full fellowship with God.[161] God involves himself in ever new saving acts, until in the incarnation of the Logos, through whom in the beginning he had created the world and man, his plan of salvation comes to fulfilment.[162] The meaning of the incarnation, which is accomplished in exact correspondence with the creation of Adam, is the restoration and perfecting of the fallen creature.[163] In an enumeration of difficult problems arising from salvation history, into which only a few specially equipped theologians have been able to penetrate more deeply, Irenaeus names as the first question 'Why has one and the same God created both temporal and eternal, both heavenly and earthly things?'[164] The meaning and nature of the creation are to be understood only in connection with the universal economy of salvation.

[155] Cf. pp. 166–168 above; on this Pannenberg, pp. 317f.
[156] Haer. IV 14, 1: Igitur initio non quasi indigens deus hominis plasmavit Adam, sed ut haberet in quem collocaret sua beneficia; cf. 13, 4; on this Bengsch, p. 114.
[157] Haer. IV 38, 3; II 34, 2–4.
[158] Tim. 41AB; cf. Justin, dial. 5, 4; on this p. 128 n. 53 above. On the Irenaean concept of will see pp. 166–168 above.
[159] Haer. IV 38, 3.
[160] Cf. haer. III 25, 5 with the quotation from Timaeus 29E; see n. 116 above.
[161] Haer. III 11, 8; IV 11, 14, 38f.; epid. 8, 11ff., cf. L. Scheffczyk, 'Schöpfung und Vorsehung', in M. Schmaus and A. Grillmeier, *Handbuch der Dogmengeschichte* II/2a (1963), pp. 44–47.
[162] Haer. II 30, 9; IV 14, 2; V 12, 6.
[163] Cf. haer. III 21, 9f.; 23, 1; V 14, 2; epid. 32. Vice versa the creation of Adam prefigures the Christ event: III 22, 3. On the doctrine of recapitulation cf. Widmann, pp. 167ff. In his efforts to ensure the correspondence of creation and salvation at all points, Irenaeus seems to have found difficulties even over the Pauline idea of the 'new creation': cf. epid. 33; on that Wingren, pp. 151f.
[164] Haer. I 10, 3; cf. II 28, 1; on this Bonwetsch, p. 49; Bengsch, pp. 51ff.; Widmann, pp. 159f.

In his arguments with the heretics about creation Irenaeus does not confine himself to the exposition of biblical texts. He also argues from the beauty and the meaningful design of the cosmos, which forms in its multiplicity a harmonious whole.[165] Everyone can directly see in the creation the power, the wisdom and the goodness of the creator.[166] Only the heretics would, contrary to reason and Scripture, have the creator God originate in the fall of a higher heavenly being, explain him as ignorant, and make him responsible for all imaginable evil.[167]

The total coherence and impregnability of Irenaeus's theology, which rests on the premise that Christian tradition and reasonable knowledge are in full accord, has something imposing about it. It was, indeed, only attainable because Irenaeus is quite unaware of philosophical problems. When he emphasises that the heathen philosophers knew the true God from the creation, he is making an exclusively anti-heretical point, not an apologetic one: Irenaeus wants to show that the heretics, who belittle the creator God, exceed even the heathen in their godlessness and find themselves, with their bizarre and unbelievable speculations, in complete isolation.[168] Apart from polemic against heretics, Irenaeus did not pose the question of the relation between Christian and philosophical truth. And so the philosophical arguments with which Irenaeus criticises the gnostic mythology do not arise from a general ontological conception, but are merely directed *ad hoc* against the heretical doctrines.[169]

These limitations in the thinking of Irenaeus are naturally also visible in his statements about *creatio ex nihilo*. The Platonising proposition that God produced the pattern, the forms and the substance of things out of himself, is simply formed as an antithesis to the Valentinian views about the demiurge's creation; in itself Irenaeus's statement is of no philosophical use. Nor did he see the philosophical difficulties which arose for Greek thought from the conception of a creation of the world in time; and he did not reflect seriously on the problem of the divine will. Thus Irenaeus did not get any further in the philosophical elucidation of the idea of creation than Theophilus of Antioch before him. All the same, the contribution made by Irenaeus and Theophilus must not be underestimated: they developed the doctrine of *creatio ex nihilo* with such convincing stringency that from the end of the second century it becomes with astonishing speed the self-evident

---

[165] Cf. haer. II 2, 4; 25, 1f.
[166] Haer. II 6, 1; 9, 1; 27, 2; III 25, 1.5.
[167] Haer. II 9, 2.
[168] Cf. Brox, p. 205.
[169] See pp. 164ff. above.

premise of Christian talk of the creation. We have to see in Theophilus and Irenaeus the specific founders of the church doctrine of *creatio ex nihilo*. For Tertullian and Hippolytus it is already the fixed Christian position that God created the world out of absolutely nothing. And Origen, who made the first great attempt to expound systematically the Christian doctrine of creation and to show that it was reasonable and meaningful even from Platonist presuppositions, makes it clear that he cannot understand how so many eminent men had been of the opinion that matter was unoriginate and not created by God.[170] For him *creatio ex nihilo* is a necessary fundamental proposition, without which the idea of providence is impossible.

Only Clement of Alexandria with his understanding of creation stands on the fringe of the general development. His views on the κόσμος νοητός, on matter and on the process of creation broadly coincide with those of Philo.[171] But Clement also is expressly challenging the philosophical tradition that matter is to be counted among the principles of being, and with the emphatically asserted thesis that the will of God is alone the ground of the creation, he comes close to the position of Irenaeus.[172]

---

[170] Princ. II 1, 4; cf. comm. Joh. I 17, 103.
[171] Cf. J. Daniélou, *Message évangélique et culture hellénistique* (Paris, 1961), pp. 112–114; A. Méhat, *Etude sur les 'Stromates' de Clément d'Alexandrie* (Paris, 1966), pp. 442ff.; S. Lilla, *Clement of Alexandria. A Study in Christian Platonism and Gnosticism* (Oxford, 1971), pp. 189–199.
[172] Protr. 63.3; paid. I 7, 3; 27, 2; strom. II 75, 2. J. Bernays, 'Über die unter Philons Werken stehende Schrift über die Unzerstörbarkeit des Weltalls', AAB 1882/3 (1883), p. 16, traces this concept of will back to Pantaenus with reference to Clement of Alexandria, fr. 48. Yet I cannot convince myself of the genuineness of the fragment extant through Maximus Confessor (de var. diff. loc. Dion. et Greg. pp. 60–62 Öhler). Otherwise H. Langerbeck, *Die Verbindung aristotelischer und christlicher Elemente in der Philosophie des Ammonius Saccas*, pp. 157f.

Recapitulation

If one reviews only the orthodox line of the development that leads to the formation of the doctrine of *creatio ex nihilo*, there emerges a picture unambiguous in its main outline. For the primitive Christian thinkers the origin of the world does not yet present a problem. Even in the early second century, after the intensive concern of gnosticism with cosmology had set in, the spokesmen for church Christianity still stand by the traditional statements about the creation of the world and do not allow themselves to get involved in controversy over the new questions. At the same time philosophically educated teachers like Justin interpret the creation as world-formation and establish a relationship between the 'cosmogony of Moses' and the myth of world-creation in the *Timaeus*. In Justin's thinking there is already clearly a tension between the idea of world-formation and the conviction of the unconditioned omnipotence of God, but only in the following generation is an adequate clarification of the idea of creation achieved. Then in the controversy, partly conducted in parallel and partly overlapping with both the gnostic and the philosophical cosmologies, the world-formation model is overcome and the doctrine of *creatio ex nihilo* formulated as a counter-proposition, which as early as the beginning of the third century is regarded as a fundamental tenet of Christian theology.

The origin of the doctrine of *creatio ex nihilo* looks more complicated if the gnostic tradition is drawn in. We have seen that the idea of *creatio ex nihilo* is already found in Basilides a generation before Tatian and Theophilus of Antioch. It is not to be absolutely ruled out that Basilides took the arguments on which he based the doctrine from a still older tradition. But a hypothetical earlier dating of the origin of the doctrine would still not explain why at a time when it plays scarcely any role anywhere else it is found in Basilides. The thesis of *creatio ex nihilo* seems to result for Basilides from a specific feature of his system: unlike the overwhelming majority of gnostic teachers, he firmly holds to the identity of the highest God with the creator God of Genesis – the Archons are sub-demiurges, themselves originate – and he radicalises the idea of creation in a manner characteristic of gnostic thinking. The view that the productive work of the highest God transcends all human analogies and cannot be imagined as the fashioning of a pre-existent material is also to be found in Marcion and the Valentinians. Gnostic thought thus possessed a certain affinity with the idea of *creatio ex nihilo*. But only Basilides, who understands the highest God as the universal creator of all being, could develop it in its full significance. Marcion allows the true God merely to create the invisible heavenly world, while the divine Fore-Father of the Valentinians creates nothing whatsoever but produces the Aeons by emanation. The demiurge, who creates the cosmos, is, for the Marcionites as well as for the Valentinians, a mere shaper of the material provided for him.

Basilides makes prior use as a basis for his *creatio ex nihilo* of convictions which only occur in the church theologians some decades later. But alongside this degree of consensus there is a deep-seated difference of view to be observed: church theology wants through the proposition of *creatio ex nihilo* to express and safeguard the omnipotence and freedom of God acting in history. For Basilides the non-existent God is the ineffable ground of being; his creative activity is limited to one single act, removed from all human imagining and therefore to be described only approximately as *creatio ex nihilo*: the creating of the world-seed. From this all being proceeds as it were automatically. The cosmos is the work of the two Archons and the process of salvation issues from the first of the three sonships. To be sure Basilides has spoken of the providence of the highest God, but in the system, which we know through Hippolytus, a historical activity of God seems unthinkable.

The creation doctrine of Basilides is left without any broad effect. Not even do the later Basilideans appear thoroughly to hold fast to it, and no influence whatever on church theology can be discerned. In point of fact the doctrine of the creation of the world-seed out of nothing represents a parallel to, not a step towards, the church teaching of *creatio ex nihilo*. It is just possible that Basilides and Theophilus of Antioch started from the same older traditions, and perhaps the idea of *creatio ex nihilo* played a somewhat greater part before the middle of the second century in the discussions of Christian teachers than is immediately apparent from the sources. But all that remained an approach without effective result. Only the anti-gnostic theology of the second half of the second century brought the decisive turning-point: it developed the doctrine of *creatio ex nihilo* in the form in which it became historically significant.

Editions of Ancient Texts

(Migne's Patrology and editions given in full in the notes are not included.)

Acta Apostolorum Apocrypha, ed. R. A. Lipsius and M. Bonnet, I, II 1.2 (1891–1903).
Adamantius, W. H. van de Sande Bakhuyzen (GCS 4, 1901).
— *Tyrannii Rufini librorum Adamantii Origenis adversus haereticos interpretatio*, ed. V. Buchheit (1966).
Albinus, *Didaskalikos*, ed. C. F. Hermann, *Platonis Dialogi VI* (1853).
Ambrose, *Exameron*, ed. C. Schenkl (CSEL 32/1, 1891).
E. Kautzsch, *Die Apokryphen und Pseudepigraphen des Alten Testaments*, I, II (1900).
E. Hennecke and W. Schneemelcher, *Neutestamentliche Apokryphen*, I (^{3}1959), II (^{3}1964).

Apologists
J. C. T. Otto, *Corpus apologetarum christianorum saeculi secundi*, I–IX (1851–81).
—*Die ältesten Apologeten*, ed. E. J. Goodspeed (1914 = 1984).
Die apostolischen Väter, ed. F. X. Funk, K. Bihlmeyer and W. Schneemelcher I (^{2}1956).

Apuleius, *De philosophia libri*, ed. P. Thomas (repr. 1970).
Aristeas: *Lettre d'Aristée à Philocrate*, ed. A. Pelletier (1962).
Aristides: J. Rendel Harris and J. Armitage Robinson, *The Apology of Aristides* (Cambridge, ^{2}1893).
Aristotle: *Ethica Nicomachaea*, ed. I. Bywater (1894).
—*Metaphysica*, ed. W. Jaeger (1957).
—*Physica*, ed. D. Ross (1957).
Athenagoras, ed. E. Schwartz (1891).
—ed. W. R. Schoedel (1972).
Chalcidius, ed. J. H. Waszink (1962).
Cicero, *De divinatione*, ed. A. S. Pease (repr. 1973).
—*De natura deorum*, ed. A. S. Pease, I, II (1955/58).
Clement of Alexandria, ed. O. Stählin, I (GCS 12, ^{2}1936), II (GCS 52, ^{3}1960), III (GCS 17, ^{2}1970), IV (Index, 1934/36).
—*Extraits de Théodote*, ed. F. M. M. Sagnard (SC 23, 1948, repr. 1970).

Coptic-gnostic writings
Koptisch-gnostische Schriften I: Die Pistis Sophia. Die beiden Bücher des Jeû. Unbekanntes altgnostisches Werk, ed. C. Schmidt (GCS 45, ³1962 rev. by W. Till).
Die gnostischen Schriften des koptischen Papyrus Berolinensis 8502, ed., tr. and rev. by W. C. Till (²1972 rev. H.-M. Schenke).
The Nag Hammadi Library in English (³1988).
Nag Hammadi Codex I (The Jung Codex), ed. H. W. Attridge (Nag Hammadi Studies 22, 23, 1985).
Nag Hammadi Codex II, 2–7, ed. B. Layton, I.II (Nag Hammadi Studies 20, 21, 1989).
Nag Hammadi Codices III, 3–4 and V, 1, ed. D. M. Parrott (Nag Hammadi Studies 27, 1991).
Nag Hammadi Codices V, 2–5 and VI, ed. D. M. Parrott (Nag Hammadi Studies 11, 1979).
The Apocalypse of Adam, ed. G. W. MacRae, in Nag Hammadi Codices V, 2–5 and VI.
The (First) Apocalypse of James, ed. C. W. Hedrick, in Nag Hammadi Codices V, 2–5 and VI.
The Apocryphon of James, ed. F. E. Williams, in Nag Hammadi Codex I.
Die drei Versionen des Apokryphon des Johannes im koptischen Museum zu Alt-Kairo, ed. M. Krause and P. Labib (1962).
The Gospel according to Philip, ed. W. W. Isenberg and B. Layton, in Nag Hammadi Codices II, 2–7 (I).
Evangelium Veritatis, ed. M. Malinine, H.-C. Puech and G. Quispel (1956); Supplementum (1961).
J. E. Ménard, *L'Évangile de vérité. Retroversion grecque et commentaire* (Paris, 1962).
The Gospel of Truth, ed. H. W. Attridge and G. W. MacRae, in Nag Hammadi Codex I.
The Hypostasis of the Archons, ed. R. A. Bullard and B. Layton, in Nag Hammadi Codex II, 2–7 (I).
On the Origin of the World, ed. H.-G. Bethge and B. Layton, in Nag Hammadi Codex II, 2–7 (II).
M. Krause, *Die Paraphrase des Sêem*, in F. Altheim and R. Stiehl, *Christentum am Roten Meer* II (1973).
De Resurrectione (Epistula ad Rheginum), ed. M. Malinine, H.-C. Puech, G. Quispel and W. Till (1963).
The Treatise on the Resurrection, ed. N. L. Peel, in Nag Hammadi Codex I.
The Sophia of Jesus Christ, ed. D. M. Parrott, in Nag Hammadi Codices III, 3–4 and V, 1.
Tractatus Tripartitus, ed. R. Kasser, M. Malinine, H.-C. Puech, G. Quispel and J. Zandee, with W. Vycichl and R. McL. Wilson, I: *De supernis* (1973), II: *De generatione hominis*, III: *De generibus tribus* (1975).
The Tripartite Tractate, ed. H. W. Attridge and E. H. Pagels, in Nag Hammadi Codex I.

Corinthians, Third Letter to: Papyrus Bodmer X–XII, ed. M. Testuz (1959).
Corpus Hermeticum, ed. A. D. Nock and A. J. Festugière, I–IV (Paris, 1945–54).
Didascalia et Constitutiones Apostolorum, ed. F. X. Funk (1905).
Diogenes Laertius, ed. H. S. Long (1963).
A Diognète, ed. H.-I. Marrou (SC 33, ²1965).
Ephraem, Hymn 'Contra Haereses', ed. and trans. E. Beck (CSCO Scriptores Syri 76, 77, 1957).
Epiphanius, ed. K. Holl, I–II (GCS 25, 31, 37, 1915–33).
Eusebius, Kirchengeschichte, ed. E. Schwartz (⁴1932).
—Gegen Marcell. Über die kirchliche Theologie. Die Fragmente Marcells, ed. E. Klostermann (GCS 14, 1906).
—Praeparatio Evangelica, ed. K. Mras, I, II (GCS 43, 1.2, 1954/56).
Filastrius, ed. F. Heylen, in CChr 9 (1957).
Galenus, De usu partium, ed. G. Helmreich, I, II (1907/09).
Genesis rabba: Bereschit Rabba, ed. J. Theodor and C. Albeck, I–III (²1965).
W. Völker, Quellen zur Geschichte der christlichen Gnosis (1932).
Hegemonius, Acta Archelai, ed. C. H. Beeson (GCS 16, 1906).
Hermas, ed. M. Whittaker (GCS 48, ²1967).
Hippolytus, Contra Noetum, in E. Schwartz, Zwei Predigten Hippolytus (SAM 1936/3).
—Refutatio omnium haeresium, ed. P. Wendland (GCS 26, 1916).
—Refutatio omnium haeresium, ed. M. Marcovich (PTS 25, 1986).
John of Damascus: Die Schriften des Johannes von Damaskos II: Expositio fidei, ed. B. Kotter (1973).
Irenaeus, Adversus haereses, ed. W. W. Harvey, I, II (1857).
—Contre les hérésies I, ed. A. Rousseau and L. Doutreleau, I, II (SC 263, 264, 1979).
—Contre les hérésies II, ed. A. Rousseau and L. Doutreleau, I, II (SC 293, 294, 1982).
—Contre les hérésies III, ed. A. Rousseau and L. Doutreleau, I, II (SC 210, 211, 1974).
—Contre les hérésies IV, ed. A. Rousseau, B. Hemmerdinger, L. Doutreleau and C. Mercier, I, II (SC 100, 1965).
—Contre les hérésies V, ed. A. Rousseau, L. Doutreleau and C. Mercier, I, II (SC 152, 153, 1969).
—Démonstration de la prédication apostollique, ed. L. Froidevaux (SC 62, 1959).
Justin: see Apologists.
—Acta Iustini: H. Musurillo, The Acts of the Christian Martyrs (1972).
Marcus Aurelius, ed. H. Schenkl (1913).
Maximus of Tyre, ed. H. Hobein (1910).
Melito of Sardis, De pascha, ed. O. Perler (SC 123, 1966).
Methodius, ed. G. N. Bonwetsch (GCS 27, 1917).
Numenius, ed. E. des Places (1973).
Ocellus Lucanus (Okkelos), in H. Thesleff, The Pythagorean Texts of the Hellenistic Period (1965).
Oracula Chaldaica, ed. E. des Places (1971).
Oracula Sibyllina, ed. J. Geffcken (GCS 8, 1902).

Origen, *Die Schrift vom Martyrium*. Buch I–IV *gegen Celsus*, ed. P. Koetschau (GCS 2, 1899).
—Buch V–VIII *gegen Celsus*. *Die Schrift vom Gebet*, ed. P. Koetschau (GCS 2, 1899).
Origen, *Johanneskommentar*, ed. E. Preuschen (HCS 10, 1903).
—*De principiis*, ed. P. Koetschau (GCS 22, 1913).
—*Die Matthäuserklärung*, ed. E. Klostermann, I–III.2 (GCS 40, 38, 41.1–2, 1933–68).
—*Opera omnia*, ed. C. H. E. Lommatzsch, I–XXV (1831–48).
Papyri Graecae Magicae, ed. K. Preisendanz I (^{2}1973) II (^{2}1974).
Philo of Alexandria, ed. L. Cohn and P. Wendland, I–VII (1896–1915).
—*Opera*, ed. M. C. E. Richter, I–VIII (1851–53).
—*De providentia*, ed. M. Hadas-Lebel (1973).
Johannes Philoponus, *De aeternitate mundi contra Proclum*, ed. H. Rabe (1899).
—*De opificio mundi*, ed. G. Reichardt (1897).
Photius, *Bibliothèque*, ed. R. Henry, I–VII (1959–1974).
Platonis opera, ed. J. Burnet, I–V (1899–1906).
Plotini opera, ed. P. Henry and H. R. Schwyzer, I–III (OCT, 1964–82).
Plutarch, *Moralia*, ed. C. Hubert, W. Nachstädt, W. R. Paton et al., I–VII (1925ff.).
Porphyry, *Opuscula selecta*, ed. A. Nauck (1886).
—*Ad Marcellam*, ed. W. Pötscher (1969).
—*Vita Plotini*, in *Plotini opera* I.
Proclus, in *Platonis Timaeum commentaria*, ed. E. Diehl, I–III (1903–06).
Pseudo-Aristotle, *De Melisso Xenophane Gorgia*, ed. H. Diels, AAB 1900.
Pseudo-Clementines: *Die Pseudoklementinen I: Homilien*, ed. B. Rehm (GCS 42, ^{2}1969).
—*II: Rekognitionen*, ed. B. Rehm (GCS 51, 1965).
Pseudo-Longinus, *On the Sublime*, ed. D. A. Russell (1964).
Ptolemaeus: *Ptolémée, Lettre à Flora*, ed. G. Quispel (SC 24, ^{2}1966).
Sallustius Philosophus, ed. A. D. Nock (1926).
Seneca, *Epistulae morales*, ed. L. D. Reynolds, I–II (1965).
Simplicius, *In Aristotelis physica commentaria*, ed. H. Diels, I–II (1882/95).
Stoicorum veterum fragmenta, ed. H. v. Arnim, I–IV (1903–05).
Tatian, ed. E. Schwartz (1888).
—, ed. Molly Whittaker (1982).
Tertullian (CChr 1. 2, 1954).
—*De Anima*, ed. J. H. Waszink (Amsterdam, 1947).
—*Adversus Hermogenem*, ed. J. H. Waszink (1956).
—*Contre les Valentiniens*, I–II, ed. J.–C. Fredouille (SC 280, 281, 1980/1981).
Theodoret of Cyrus, *Thérapeutique des maladies helléniques*, ed. P. Canivet (SC 57, 1958).
Timaios Lokros, in H. Thesleff, *The Pythagorean Texts of the Hellenistic Period* (1965).
Theophilus of Antioch, ed. R. M. Grant (1970).
Die Fragmente der Vorsokratiker, ed. H. Diels and W. Kranz, I (^{17}1974), II (^{16}1972), III (Index, ^{14} 1973).

Index of Biblical References

Genesis
1:1ff.   47–50, 60, 155–157, 174
1:1   141, 144, 168, 174
1:1–3   9
1:1–4   49, 105–107
1:1–5   11
1:2   6, 10–11, 23–24, 40, 49, 58, 60, 100, 105–107, 122, 138, 141–142, 144, 162
1:3   78, 106, 152–153, 174
1:4   12, 106
1:9   106
1:26   106, 109, 144, 175
1:26–27   49, 134
1:26–28   127
1:28   48
1:31   11
2:1–2   174
2:3   19, 106
2:7   22, 49, 94, 134, 175
3:1ff.   60–61
3:21   109
18:8   89

Exodus
33:20   88

Deuteronomy
4:24   13

2 Kings
5:14   58

Psalms
33 (32 LXX):6   175
33 (32):9   175
115:3 (113:11)   175
148:4f.   23

Proverbs
8:24   23
8:27ff.   158

Isaiah
34:4   159
40:22   162
42:15   159
45:7   23

Amos
4:13   23

Malachi
2:10   175

Wisdom
7:25   97
11:17   6, 144
15:11   22

2 Maccabees
7:27   6–8, 16, 22, 119

Luke
5:12–14   58
18:27   171

John
1:1ff.   29, 99, 112, 175
1:3   26, 114, 151, 175

185

John (*cont.*)		Galatians	
1:9	78	6:15	28
Acts		Colossians	
14:15ff.	29	1:15–20	29
17:24ff.	29	1:16	26, 112
		2:18	51
Romans			
1:20	87	Hebrews	
2:20	99	11:3	27
4:17	27–28		
5:13–14	79	2 Peter	
7:2–3	153	3:12–13	28
1 Corinthians		Revelation	
1:28	28	1:17	159
8:6	114	6:13	159
15:8	100	12:9	159
		20:3	159
2 Corinthians		20:11	159
4:6	28	21:1	28, 159
5:17	28		

Index of Ancient Authors and Sources

Acta Philippi 37
Actus Petri cum Simone 37
Adamantius 55, 58–59, 111
Aetius 160
Agapius of Hierapolis 156
Agrippa Castor 65, 81, 84
Albinus viii, 4, 10, 98–99, 107, 110, 138–139, 154, 170
Alcinous viii
Alexander of Alexandria 95
Ambrose 142
Amelius 29
Ammonius 36
Anastasius Sinaites 35–36
Anaxagoras 72, 171
Pseudo-Anthimus 55
Apelles 54, 60, 151, 154–155
Apion 60
Apocalypse of Adam 44, 49
Apocalypse of James 116
Apocryphon of John 40, 44, 49, 51, 76, 109
Apostolic Constitutions 22–23, 77, 156–157
Apuleius 107, 126
Arethas 149
Aristeas, Letter of 6, 8
Aristides 52, 118–120
Aristobulus 8–9, 19
Aristotle 3, 10, 17, 69, 72, 100, 121, 167
Pseudo-Aristotle, *De Melisso Xenophane Gorgia* 7, 17
Arnobius 73

Athanasius 55, 74, 167
Athenagoras 60, 74, 106, 125, 137–139, 147, 152, 163, 170
Atticus 4, 16–17, 17, 19, 124, 138
Augustine 20, 29, 74, 127, 147, 174

Bardesanes 146
Baruch, Apocalypse of 22
Basil of Caesarea 58, 60, 74, 94, 174
Basilides vii-ix, 46–47, 52–54, 62–85, 117, 150, 157, 161
Basilidians 65–66, 77–78, 81–83

Cainites 50
Candidus 60
Candidus (Valentinian) 111
Carpocratians 51
Cassianus, Julius 109
Celsus 48, 56, 122, 126, 128–129, 144
Chalcidius 11, 56, 74, 143–144
Chaldean Oracles 73
Chryserus Nomenclator 157
Chrysippus 144
Cicero 4, 20, 71, 160
Clement of Alexandria xiv, 17, 20–21, 35–36, 46, 53, 55–56, 58, 60, 62–64, 66, 69, 70–71, 74, 79–83, 86–89, 94, 98, 109, 112, 115–116, 122, 144–145, 147, 152–153, 178
  Excerpta ex Theodoto 45, 46, 49, 65, 81, 83, 85, 87, 91–92, 94–100, 101–107, 109–110, 112, 115–116, 144, 151

Clement, First Epistle of 30–31, 60, 175
Clement, Second Epistle of 27
Pseudo-Clementines 60, 79
Colossians 31
Corinthians, Letter to Paul 34
Cosmas Indicopleustes 2

De Resurrectione (ad Rheginum) 42, 46, 86, 89–91, 96, 115
Democritus 72, 170
Didymus of Alexandria ix–x, 153
Diogenes Laertius 135
Dionysius of Alexandria 74
Dionysius of Rome 55

Elders, anti-Marcionite 132
Empedocles 171
Ephraem 34, 49, 58–60
Epicurus, Epicureans 2, 57, 71, 73, 135, 160
Epiphanius 41, 51, 53–54, 96, 167
Epistula apostolorum 34–37, 60
Eulogius of Alexandria 89
Eusebius 8, 13–14, 16, 19, 29, 34, 36, 41, 54–55, 60, 65, 74, 81, 84, 121, 130, 138, 140, 144, 151, 153–156, 158–160
Evangelium veritatis 44, 86, 92, 101, 103, 111
Eznib of Kolb 57

Florinus 155–156

Galen 48, 155, 168
Gamaliel II 23
Genesis rabba 23, 144

Hecataius of Abdera 48
Hegemonius 79
Hegesippus 131
Heracleon 79, 88, 91, 95, 98–99, 102–104, 110–113, 115, 151
Hermas 27, 119, 152, 163, 174–175

Hermetica 88, 106, 125, 149
Hermodor 17
Hermogenes x, 74, 140–147
Hierokles of Alexandria 5
Hippolytus xiv, 7, 40, 44–45, 49, 55, 57, 62–73, 76–83, 88, 91–94, 96, 98, 100–101, 103, 107–108, 111–112, 115, 125, 131, 135, 142–143, 153, 156–158, 161, 167, 176, 178
The Hypostasis of the Archons 40, 44, 49

Iamblichius 47
Ignatius 33, 38
Psuedo-Ignatius 34
Irenaeus viii–x, xiii–xiv, 27, 30, 34, 42–46, 50–54, 56, 60, 62–63, 66–68, 74, 84–87, 90–116, 125, 130–133, 135, 151, 153, 155, 163–177
Isidor 46–47, 62, 66, 79

James, Apocryphon of 68, 116
Jerome 59, 95, 111
John, Apocalypse of 158
John of Damascus 74, 133
John, Epistles of 34, 38
John, Gospel of 41, 64–65, 78, 175
John Philoponus 6, 16, 74
Josephus, Flavius 9
Jubilees, Book of 22
Justin viii–ix, xiii, 34, 38, 42–43, 51, 58, 61, 74, 87, 90, 120–138, 144, 148–149, 152–153, 155, 160, 163, 176
Pseudo-Justin
    Cohortatio ad Graecos 74
    De Resurrectione 133–137, 148
Justin (gnostic) 40–41, 49

Kerygma Petri 37

Leiden Kosmopoiia 108

Leucippus 72

Mandeans 49
Marcellus of Ancyra 158
Marcion ix, 33–34, 40–43, 50, 52–61, 113–114, 129–132, 151, 154
Marcionites 55, 56, 60, 130, 154
Marcus Aurelius 17
Maximus Confessor 169, 178
Maximus of Tyre 104, 126
Melito of Sardis 134
Menander (gnostic) 51, 53, 67, 129
Methodius 111, 141, 143, 149, 174
Moderatus of Gades 98

Naassene Psalm 42, 108
Naassenes 41
Nicolaitans 31, 41, 175
Numenius 4, 45, 48, 54, 56, 98, 104, 110, 121–122, 143–144, 151

Ocellus Lucanus 48
Odes of Solomon 36
On the Origin of the World 40, 46, 49, 76
On the Resurrection *see De Resurrectione (ad Rheginum)*
On the Sublime 48
Ophites 40, 50–51
Origen x, 3, 48, 50, 53, 56, 59, 62, 72, 74, 78, 79, 81, 88, 95, 98–99, 102–104, 110–113, 115, 121–122, 126, 128–129, 137, 144, 147, 151–152, 174, 178

Pantaenus 35–36, 178
Papias 35–36
Paraphrase of Shem 41, 64
Pastoral Epistles 31–33
Paul 28, 31–32, 90
Perates 41
Peter, Gospel of *see Kerygma Petri*
Philip, Gospel of 90, 111, 115

Philo of Alexandria viii–ix, xii–xiii, 4, 6, 8–22, 51, 60, 106–107, 109, 125–126, 135, 139, 144, 152, 154, 160, 162, 168, 178
Photius 5, 89, 147, 149
Plato vii, 8–9, 15, 17, 19, 68, 72, 81, 101–102, 104, 112, 120–124, 128, 136, 141, 144, 147, 160, 167, 170–171, 176
Plotinus 5, 7, 17, 40, 47, 68, 142
Plutarch 4, 10–11, 16–17, 19, 45, 56, 104, 124, 141, 144
Polycarp of Smyrna 33–34
Porphyry 5, 17, 47–48, 68, 98, 104, 124, 155
Poseidonius 71, 121, 155
Proclus 16–17, 124
Procopius of Gaza 142
Ptolemaeus (Valentinian) 40, 42–43, 51, 65, 75, 85, 91–116, 125, 151, 175

Ququites 49

Rheginos, Epistle to *see De Resurrectione (ad Rheginum)*
Rhodon 42, 55, 60, 151, 153–156
Rufinus 111

Sallustius 17
Saturninus 51–53, 67
Seneca 71, 170
Sethians 41, 68
Sibyllines 8
Simon Magus, Simonians 51, 131
Simplicius 17, 74, 98
Socrates Scholasticos 94
Sophia Jesu Christi 44, 46, 76, 114
Stoa, Stoics 2–3, 56–57, 71–72, 107, 121, 135, 144, 160

Tatian 42–43, 61, 145, 148–154, 156, 160
Tertullian ix, xiv, 41–42, 55–59, 60,

78, 85, 88, 90, 94, 97, 101, 104, 111, 131, 137, 140–147, 157–159, 162–163, 174, 178
Pseudo-Tertullian
  Adversus omnes haereses 41, 51
  Carmes adv. Marcionem 131
Themistios 127
Theodore bar Konai 49
Theodoret 22, 74, 95
Theodotus 101–103, 115–116
Theophilus of Antioch viii, x, 60, 74, 77, 138, 140, 144, 147, 156–163, 166, 169, 171–173, 175
Timaios Locros 10
Tractatus Tripartitus 47, 75–76, 88, 91–92, 94, 96, 101–102, 116
Truth, Gospel of see *Evangelium veritatis*

Valentinians ix, 91–117
Valentinus 42–43, 47, 52–54, 85–91, 93, 107, 111–112, 115–116
Varro 127

Xenophon 8, 165

Index of Modern Authors

Adam, A. 36–37, 150, 152–153
Aland, B. 54, 56, 59, 146
Altaner, B. 118
Altendorf, H. D. 38, 130
Andresen, C. 3, 16, 121–123, 126–127, 132–133, 138
Armstrong, A. H. 4–5
Armstrong, G. T. 140
Attridge, H. W. 75

Babut, D. 144
Bailey, C. 71
Baltes, M. viii, 4–5, 14–16, 20, 98, 142, 160
Bardenhewer, O. 169
Bardy, G. 151, 155
Barnard, L. W. 123, 148, 153–154
Barth, C. 102, 108
Bauer, W. 30, 32–33, 60, 73, 130, 150, 154
Bäumker, C. 9–11, 15, 17, 56, 135
Baumstark, A. 156
Baur, F. C. 62–63
Becker, C. 158
Behm, J. 100
Beierwaltes, W. 5, 17
Bengsch, A. 164, 176
Benoît, A. 165
Benz, E. 169
Bernays, J. 6, 16, 105, 178
Betz, O. 48
Beutler, R. 5, 45, 143
Beyschlag, K. 34–35, 38, 42, 51, 63–64, 67, 88, 115, 129, 131

Bianchi, U. 55, 59
Billerbeck, P. 23
Blackman, T. E. C. 54
Blass, F. 7, 18
Böhlig, A. 40, 48–49
Bonwetsch, G. N. 165, 167, 176
Bornkamm, G. 1
Boussett, W. 14, 21–22, 128
Boyancé, P. 51
Braun, F. M. 64–65
Bréhier, E. 9, 14
Brox, N. 32–33, 93, 164, 166, 172, 177
Bühler, W. 48
Bultmann, R. 22, 26
Burkitt, F. C. 46
Burney, C. F. 37

Campenhausen, H. von 31–33, 35, 37–38, 42, 46–48, 50, 54, 59, 65, 82, 113, 127–128, 131, 133, 151, 153, 164, 175
Caspar, E. 42
Cerfaux, L. 64
Chadwick, H. 3, 14, 17–18, 21, 27, 31, 36, 107, 120–123, 125–126, 132–133, 154
Clarke, G. W. 148
Colpe, C. 64
Conzelmann, H. 28–29, 32–33, 36
Courcelle, P. 45, 68
Cullmann, O. 27

Daniélou, J. 51, 163, 178

Debrunner, A. 7, 18
Delius, W. 134
Dibelius, M. 27, 29, 32–33, 36–37
Dibelius, O. 96, 102, 104, 107, 112
Dieterich, A. 66, 108
Dihle, A. 68, 168
Dillon, J. viii
Dobschütz, E. von 37
Dodd, C. H. 54
Dodds, E. R. 45, 155
Dörrie, H. viii, 3–4, 18–19, 29, 45, 57, 68, 73, 94–95, 123, 127–128, 143, 149, 160
Doutreleau, L. x
Drijvers, H. J. W. ix, 49, 146
Drummond, J. 9, 11–12
Duhem, P. 2

Edsman, C. M. 168
Ehlers, B. 146
Ehrhardt, A. 7, 22
Eijk, A. H. C. van 90
Elsas, C. 47, 73
Elter, A. 160
Eltester, W. 27
Elze, M. 38, 148–149, 152–153, 161
Erdin, F. 149

Festugière, A. J. 45, 69, 72, 86–88, 139, 167
Foerster, W. 8, 12, 26–27, 46, 62–63, 66–67, 76, 80, 86, 91, 99, 108, 112
Frank, E. 12
Frend, W. H. C. 52, 81–82
Frickel, J. 63–64
Früchtel, U. 11–12, 15
Fuchs, H. 30

Gager, J. G. 48, 57
Gärtner, B. 29
Gebhardt, O. von 27
Geffcken, J. 119, 138
Giusta, M. viii

Giversen, A. 49
Goppelt, L. 33, 51
Gould, J. B. 144
Grant, R. M. 20, 37, 42, 49–52, 59–60, 67, 76, 86, 97, 121, 125, 137–138, 145, 148, 153, 155, 157–160, 163, 165, 168–170

Haacker, K. 27
Haardt, R. 50, 89–90
Hadas-Lebel, M. 14
Hadot, P. 17, 68, 98
Hager, F. P. 57
Hamman, A. 2
Hannick, C. 13
Happ, H. 9, 17
Harder, R. 48
Harl, M. 11, 13, 97
Harnack, A. von 1, 27, 33–34, 36–37, 42–43, 48, 53–60, 62, 84–85, 109, 111–112, 126, 129–131, 134, 138, 140, 150, 154, 157–159
Harrison, P. N. 33
Harvey, W. W. 169
Hasler, V. 59
Hauck, F. 72
Hauschild, W. D. 49, 145
Heffening, W. 3
Hegermann, H. 28, 31
Heintzel, E. 140, 144, 158
Hendrix, P. 66–67
Hengel, M. 48
Hennecke, E. 119
Henry, P. 8
Hilgenfeld, A. 46, 62, 87, 130–131
Hitchcock, F. R. M. 172
Holl, K. 83, 96, 101
Holte, R. 121
Hommel, H. 3
Hornschuh, M. 35
Hyldahl, N. 120–123, 125, 128, 149

Jaeger, W. 48

Index of Modern Authors

Jansma, T. 146
Janssens, Y. 99
Jervell, J. 49
Joly, R. 121, 125, 136
Jonas, H. xvi, 41, 45, 50–51, 56, 107, 112, 114
Jossa, G. 50

Kilpatrick, G. D. 65
Klijn, A. F. J. 154
Knopf, R. 18, 30, 60
Knox, W. L. 29
Kraemer, G. 5
Krämer, H. J. 3–5, 67, 73, 93, 98, 101, 109, 150
Krause, M. 47
Kretschmar, G. 25, 35–36, 48, 62, 76, 86, 89–90, 129–130, 134, 136, 138, 159, 163, 172
Kroll, J. 106
Kübel, P. 47, 86, 91, 98
Kunze, J. 130–131, 165, 167–168
Kusch, H. 141

Langerbeck, H. 43, 47, 63, 82, 95, 130, 150, 153, 155, 174, 178
Layton, B. ix
Le Boulluec, A. ix
Lebreton, J. 125
Leisegang, H. 73
Lesky, E. 100
Lietzmann, H. 35, 54, 146
Lilla, S. 17, 147, 178
Lindeskog, G. 27
Lipsius, R. A. 130
Loewenich, W. von 65
Lohmeyer, E. 68
Lohse, E. 29, 31, 37
Loofs, F. 130, 163, 171–173
Louis, P. ix
Lüdemann, G. 131

Malherbe, A. J. 125, 137–138
Malinine, M. 46, 86

Mambrino, J. 167
Mann, F. viii
Mara, M. G. 37
Maran, P. 127
Markus, R. A. 164
Marrou, H. I. 100, 114
Méhat, A. 80, 178
Meijering, E. P. 17, 20, 55, 166–167, 168–169, 173
Meinhold, P. 33
Mercati, G. 55
Merki, H. 128
Merlan, P. 3, 170
Meyer, R. 22
Michl, J. 51
Minke, H. U. 30
Molland, E. 33
Möller, E. W. 2, 56, 67, 69, 72–73, 76, 125, 139, 163
Moore, G. F. 23
Mühlenberg, E. ix, 79, 81–82, 101
Müller, K. 43, 88, 94–95, 112, 116
Müller, M. 131

Nauck, W. 3, 29–30
Nautin, P. ix–x, 36–37, 48, 82, 130, 141–142, 144, 147, 157, 159, 162, 174
Nock, A. D. 45, 47, 51
Norden, E. 45, 48, 85
Norris, R. A. 2, 123, 125

Opelt, I. 2–3, 144
Orbe, A. x, 41, 49, 67–68, 73, 78, 97, 103, 152–153
Osborn, E. F. 124

Pagels, E. H. 75
Pannenberg, W. 9, 168, 176
Peel, M. L. 46, 86
Pépin, J. 15, 142, 160–161
Peterson, E. 20, 154
Pétrement, S. 51
Pfättisch, I. M. 121

Places, E. de 79
Pohlenz, M. 2–3, 8, 14, 18, 20, 29–30, 57, 71, 143–144, 169
Praechter, K. 3, 5, 170
Preuschen, E. 87
Prigent, P. 130–131, 134
Puech, H. C. 45, 50, 65, 86, 91, 112, 116, 121

Quispel, G. 46, 51, 62, 67, 70, 72, 76, 81, 85–86, 91, 104, 107, 113, 158, 163

Ratzinger, J. 94–95, 97, 110
Reale, G. ix
Rehkopf, F. 7, 18
Reinhardt, K. 21
Reynders, D. B. 166
Richard, M. 55
Robbins, F. E. 2, 36, 60
Rordorf, W. 129
Rousseau, A. 170, 173
Ruben, O. 105
Rudolph, K. 49, 54, 67
Runia, D. T. ix

Saffrey, H. D. 6
Sagnard, F. M. M. 86–87, 91, 94, 96, 98–99, 101–103
Salmon, G. 63
Sanders, J. N. 65
Schaller, J. B. 6, 23
Scheffczyk, K. 2, 176
Schelke, K. H. 27
Schenke, H. M. 44, 46, 48–49, 63, 93
Schenkl, H. 157
Schlatter, A. 9
Schmid, W. 2, 57, 73, 121, 126
Schmidt, C. 35
Schmidt, K. L. 27
Schmuttermayr, G. xi, 6–9, 27
Schneider, G. 28
Schoedel, W. R. 75, 137–138, 165

Schoeps, H. J. 79
Scholem, G. 76
Schottroff, L. 102
Schüle, E. U. 56
Schwabl, H. xiii, 45, 109, 139
Schwantes, H. 27
Schwartz, E. 43, 138
Schwyzer, E. 18
Scott, W. 88
Seeberg, R. 119
Siegert, F. ix
Simon, H. 25
Simonetti, M. 40, 72–73, 83, 87, 90, 158
Sorabji, R. ix
Spanneut, M. 3, 56, 143, 149
Spoerri, W. 106, 139
Staats, R. 36
Staehelin, H. 63–64
Stählin, O. 87
Stead, G. C. vi–ix, 68, 85, 88–89, 98–101, 103, 107
Strack, H. L. 23

Taylor, A. E. 72
Testa, E. 36
Theiler, W. 4–5, 7, 18–19, 51, 54, 71, 74, 138, 155, 170
Thirlby, S. 127
Till, W. 46, 86
Toorhoudt, A. 45
Turner, H. E. W. 154

Uhlhorn, G. 62, 66–67, 72, 76, 142
Unnik, W. C. van 30, 36–37, 42–43, 48–49, 86, 89, 90–92, 107, 116, 159
Usener, H. 83, 89

Verdenius, W. J. 128
Visser, A. J. 96
Vogel, C. J. de ix, 109
Vögtle, A. 27–28
Vona, C. 118–119

Wacht, M. 5, 19–20
Walzer, R. 12, 20, 48, 155, 163, 168
Waszink, J. H. 3, 62, 67, 100, 121–122, 131, 140, 142–145, 149, 152, 157–160, 162
Weiss, H. F. xi, 7–9, 12, 16, 18, 22–25, 27–28
Wendland, P. 14, 20
Westermann, C. 26–27
Whiteley, D. E. 26
Whittaker, J. viii–ix, 67–68
Widengren, G. 47
Widmann, M. 125, 172, 176
Wieland, W. 6
Wifstrand, A. 122
Wilckens, U. 29
Wiles, M. F. 65
Williams, C. S. C. 57
Wilson, R. McL. 46, 67, 86
Winden, J. C. M. van 120–121, 123, 125, 128, 143–144, 155
Windisch, H. 64
Wingren, G. 165, 167, 176
Wolfson, H. A. 8–9, 67, 124, 168
Wolska, W. 2
Woltmann, J. 57

Zahn, T. 27, 46, 64, 145
Zandee, J. 46, 86, 90, 102
Zeller, E. 9, 17

Index of Subjects

Alexandria 53–54, 108
Antioch 52–53, 67, 77, 85, 140, 157
Artist, God as *see* Craftsman

Craftsman, God as 14–15, 17, 74–75, 138–139, 160, 169

Demiurge 4, 8, 40, 51, 54–59, 68–69, 72, 76, 79, 86–87, 92, 97, 99, 104–107, 110–116, 128, 142, 146, 151, 153, 160–161, 167, 175, 177
Diacristic cosmogony 107, 110, 139

Emanation 4, 66–67, 72–73, 75, 78, 92, 94–99, 101, 146, 150–151, 166, 180
Evil 11, 15, 40–41, 56–57, 79–80, 93, 125, 139–144, 146, 155

Forming 80, 98–100, 125, 139, 142

Genesis (exegesis, commentary) 2, 30, 36, 47–49, 60, 105–107, 109, 122, 141–142, 144–145, 147, 156, 162, 174–175
Goodness of God 10, 20, 36, 54, 60, 81, 146, 167, 176

Hexaemeron 36, 60, 155
Homoousion 68, 73, 94

Ideas, doctrine of 4, 9, 12, 18–19, 21, 93, 110, 126–127, 138–139, 168–170

Logos 18, 28–29, 78, 89, 96, 99, 113, 121–122, 126–127, 133, 138, 149, 151, 163, 166, 168, 176
aeon of Valentinians 98–99

Monarchy (of God) 155–156, 160, 162

Non-being 7–8, 16–18, 21–22, 27–28, 67–68, 71, 75–76, 129, 139, 152

Omnipotence (of God) 6–7, 10, 12, 15, 20, 24, 26, 30, 58, 74, 78, 128–129, 132–133, 136–137, 147–148, 150, 152, 161–162, 168, 171, 174, 180

Pronoia *see* Providence
Providence 2–3, 6, 55–56, 69, 71–72, 81–82, 114, 128, 139, 178

Resurrection 7, 28, 34, 90–91, 130, 133–137, 163
Rome 42–43, 53, 129, 150–152, 155–156

Saviour *see* Soter
Six days' creation *see* Hexaemeron
Sophia 28, 36, 69, 85, 87–88, 92–94, 97, 99–105, 107–115, 117, 151, 163, 166–167, 172–173
Soter 100, 102–104, 108, 112–114, 151, 167

Time   19–20, 112, 173, 177

Will of God   16, 20, 70, 73, 76, 123, 128, 132, 155, 161–162, 164, 167–178
Wisdom *see* Sophia
Word, creation through the   22, 70, 73, 76, 78, 127, 167, 173